Daily
Guideposts
2008

D0040564

FROM THE LIBRARY OF

_____

GUIDEPOSTS®
CARMEL, NEW YORK 10512
www.guideposts.org

Acknowledgments

All Scripture quotations, unless otherwise noted, are taken from *The King James Version of the Bible*.

Scripture quotations marked (AMP) are taken from *The Amplified Bible*, © 1965 by Zondervan Publishing House. All rights reserved.

Scripture quotations marked (JB) are taken from *The Jerusalem Bible*, © 1966, 1967 and 1968 by Darton, Longman & Todd Ltd. and Doubleday & Company, Inc. All rights reserved.

Scripture quotations marked (MSG) are taken from *The Message*. Copyright © 1993, 1994, 1995, 1996, 2000, 2001, 2002 by Eugene H. Peterson.

Scripture quotations marked (NAS) are taken from the *New American Standard Bible*, © The Lockman Foundation, 1960, 1962, 1963, 1968, 1971, 1972, 1973, 1975, 1977. Used by permission.

Scripture quotations marked (NEB) are taken from *The New English Bible*. Copyright © The Delegates of the Oxford University Press and the Syndics of the Cambridge University Press 1961, 1970.

Scripture quotations marked (NIV) are taken from *The Holy Bible, New International Version*. Copyright © 1973, 1978, 1984 International Bible Society. Used by permission of Zondervan Bible Publishers.

Scripture quotations marked (NKJV) are taken from *The Holy Bible, New King James Version*. Copyright © 1997, 1990, 1985, 1983 by Thomas Nelson, Inc.

Scripture quotations marked (NLT) are taken from the *Holy Bible*, New Living Translation. Copyright © 1996. Used by permission of Tyndale House Publishers, Inc., Wheaton, Illinois 60189. All rights reserved.

Scripture quotations marked (NRSV) are taken from the *New Revised Standard Version Bible*. Copyright © 1989 by the Division of Christian Education of the National Council of the Churches of Christ in the U.S.A. Used by permission. All rights reserved.

Scripture quotations marked (RSV) are taken from the *Revised Standard Version of the Bible*. Copyright © 1946, 1952, 1971 by Division of Christian Education of the National Council of Churches of Christ in the U.S.A. Used by permission.

Scripture quotations marked (TLB) are taken from *The Living Bible*. Copyright © 1971 by Tyndale House Publishers, Wheaton, IL 60187. All rights reserved.

Brian Doyle's interior photo by Jerry Hart. Julie Garmon's back cover photo copyright © 2002 Jeff Von Hoene. Oscar Greene's back cover photo copyright © 2001 by Olan Mills, Inc. Edward Grinnan's photo by Scott Barrow. Rick Hamlin's photo by Lilly Dong. Roberta Messner's interior photo by Jan D. Witter/Camelot Photography. Roberta Rogers' interior photo by John S. Rogers. Elizabeth Sherrill's and John Sherrill's photos by Gerardo Somoza. Van Varner's photo by Steven Boljonis.

www.guideposts.org
(800) 431-2344
Guideposts Books & Inspirational Media Division
Design by David Matt
Design adaptations by Holly Johnson
Artwork by Jim Haynes
Indexed by Patricia Woodruff
Cover photo by Peter Gerdehag/Briljans/Jupiterimages
Typeset by Planet Patti Inc.
Printed in the United States of America

"LIFE IS FULL OF SURPRISES," the old saying has it, and it's the truth there that has kept it a part of our language. Whether it's in the events that are unfolded on the nightly news, the outcome of a baseball game, the ending of a suspenseful story or the unpredictable happenings of our daily lives, something surprising happens to us almost every day. Surprises can amaze and amuse us with their sheer unlikeliness, delight us with unexpected joy, or jar us with an unforeseen bump or detour on our life's journey. Surprises keep our lives from growing stale and remind us that our workaday assumptions and carefully calculated probabilities can't account for all the wonders of this astonishing world and the even more astonishing God Who created and sustains it.

To help keep that sense of wonder alive and lively, we've made "Surprised by God" our theme for *Daily Guideposts, 2008*. Our sixty-three writers will explore some of the countless ways in which God is with us every day, sometimes surprising us with the unmistakable touch of His hand to comfort, heal and encourage, and sometimes in the gentle whispers and fleeting glimpses that give us a shiver of recognition of His sustaining presence in the smallest details of our lives.

Join us as a frazzled mother discovers strength in a surprising invitation to prayer, a reluctant patient finds the unlooked-for benefits in a long-dreaded operation, a procrastinating crafter turns an unfinished project into unexpected laughter and a widow uncovers a message of hope hidden behind a trash can. We'll take you to mountain trails and great cathedrals, to a ranch out West and a city subway, to college classrooms and church Bible studies, to roomy houses and crowded apartments, to majestic forests and peaceful gardens. You'll find surprises aplenty to remind you that wherever you go and whatever you do, God has better things in store for you than you can ever imagine.

We have some very special surprises, indeed, as we make our way through the year. At the start of each month, Elizabeth Sherrill shares some of the "Unexpected Blessings" that God has put in her life. In the middle of each month, Roberta Messner will tell you about some of the things for which she has experienced the joy of saying "A Second Thank-You." And throughout the year in "Give Us This Day," you'll learn how Carol Kuykendall has dealt with her husband's and her struggle with cancer and the surprising lessons those battles have taught her.

In February, join Roberta Rogers as a series of shocking surprises brings her to a deeper appreciation of friendship, prayer and the mighty hand of God. For Holy Week, Scott Walker will take you along the road that winds through Jerusalem to Calvary and beyond it, to the greatest surprise of all. In June, you'll experience the Providence that leads Pam Kidd to Africa's poorest—and to a new appreciation of God's provision. Marilyn Morgan King recently welcomed a new grandson; in September, she shares her wisdom with him and you in "Letters to Tiny Toes." And during Advent, Penney Schwab uses the symbols on the Chrismon tree to help you focus on the One Whose birth is another of God's astonishing surprises.

As always, many old friends—Marion Bond West, Oscar Greene, Isabel Wolseley, Fred Bauer, Carol Knapp and Van Varner, among others—have rejoined us this year. And we're proud to have five new additions to the *Daily Guideposts* family: Amanda Borozinski, a newspaperwoman from Rindge, New Hampshire, who'll tell you how she learned to see the love behind her husband's reticence; Mary Ann O'Roark, a *Guideposts* magazine roving editor from New York City, who'll take you to Scotland, where an open mind can lead to pleasant surprises; Patricia Pusey, a bed-and-breakfast owner and mother of seven in Halifax, Vermont, who'll show you how some wandering cows taught her a deeper trust in God; Richard Schneider, a *Guideposts* roving editor from Rye, New York, who'll take you on a Memorial Day trip to the Tomb of the Unknown Soldier; and Jon Sweeney of White River Junction, Vermont, an associate publisher and father of two, who'll show why the best vacation can be the one you didn't take.

Sometime this year, we will have put our twenty millionth copy of *Daily Guideposts* in the hands of our readers. Some of those books have gone to people who have been with us since we began in 1977; some are going this year to new readers who are discovering *Daily Guideposts* for the first time. However long you've been with us, you're family, joined together through Scripture, prayer and the amazing adventure of walking together in faith. "Life is full of surprises," they say, and so, we hope, is *Daily Guideposts, 2008*—full of the surprises, large and small, that draw us daily closer to our ever-surprising God.

—ANDREW ATTAWAY
EDITOR, *Daily Guideposts*

January

I will praise thee, O Lord, with my whole heart; I will shew forth all thy marvellous works. —*Psalm 9:1*

TUE   *WE WILL BLESS THE LORD FROM THIS*
I   *TIME FORTH AND FOR EVERMORE. . . .*
                              —Psalm 115:18

AS WINTER CLOSED IN, I felt bored with myself and with my life of late. Even Christmas hadn't cut through the boredom. And now New Year's Day? I hadn't made plans to celebrate—I had no energy to reach out. That morning I read the paper and skimmed old magazines, but the hours dragged. I made a pot of tea and contemplated the weary weeks till spring.

Then early that afternoon, my friend Jane called to extend a last-minute invitation. "If you don't have plans, would you like to join us for dinner? After the game, of course." Her husband Ken kept up with college football.

I didn't hesitate. "Why, thank you, yes." Hours later, before we dug into a feast of roast pork, black-eyed peas and sauerkraut salad, Ken said grace. It was a long prayer, which I've forgotten, except for one striking line toward the end: "And thank You for the gift of time."

Time. A gift to be valued, not a season to be endured. Being twenty years my senior, Ken knows more about time than I do. Maybe that's why I remember his thanksgiving, repeating it often on winter days.

Lord, I thank You for the gift of the past year as I anticipate the days of the new. —EVELYN BENCE

UNEXPECTED BLESSINGS

GOD'S BLESSINGS come to us in the warmth
of friendship, the beauty of music, the
splendor of nature. But they also come in
unexpected ways, through the aggravations,
the humdrum days, the difficult times and
people. At the start of each month this year,
Elizabeth Sherrill shares some of the
unexpected blessings she's found in her
own life. —THE EDITORS

LOOKING FOR THE GIFT

WED
2

*FOR MY THOUGHTS ARE NOT YOUR
THOUGHTS, NEITHER ARE YOUR WAYS MY
WAYS, SAITH THE LORD. —Isaiah 55:8*

IT WAS 8:30 AM. Our flight was at 9:45, and
my husband John was still trying to find a taxi. Our

three children waited in the hotel lobby while I tried to rouse someone and pay our bill. It was New Year's Day 1967, and the whole city of Bogota, Colombia, seemed to be asleep. No wonder, really—the New Year's Eve fireworks had gone on till dawn.

We were ticketed on a flight that morning from Bogota to La Paz, Bolivia, where John and I were to spend a year teaching. At last John tracked down a driver who agreed, for an outrageous fee, to transport these strange *norteamericanos*. At the airport he hauled our bags from the trunk, pocketed the bills John gave him and sped away. In the terminal building, there was no one at the check-in counters, no other passengers.

Around 11:00 a sleepy-looking man appeared, pushing a broom. To our questions, he shook his head: Did we really expect a flight to take off on New Year's Day?

But shortly before noon a plane did touch down on the tarmac. A few passengers got off, followed by a man in an airline cap who informed us that this was the flight to Quito, Ecuador. La Paz? "Maybe tomorrow."

Procure a taxi somehow and return to Bogota? Or go to Quito, which our tickets, the man assured us, would cover as a stopover. And so we flew to that breathtaking Andean city and spent four days in an enchanting place we'd never expected to see. That's when we began to look for the gift in the unexpected—to hold our own plans lightly, open to the blessings that come when we let God surprise us.

Bestower of blessing, throughout the new year, show me Yourself in ways I least expect.
—ELIZABETH SHERRILL

EDITOR'S NOTE: This year, we'd like you to share some of the unexpected blessings in your own life. Write them down in "My Divine Surprises," the journal pages at the end of every month.

GIVE US THIS DAY

LAST YEAR, Carol Kuykendall and her husband Lynn were both diagnosed with cancer. In six compelling devotionals this year, you'll learn how Carol dealt with the shock of their illnesses and the challenges of chemotherapy, was comforted by the kindness of family and friends, and came to learn a profound lesson about what's really important in her life.
—THE EDITORS

BEING OPEN

THU
3

"EVERYTHING IS POSSIBLE FOR HIM WHO BELIEVES." —*Mark 9:23 (NIV)*

I PULL OUT MY CALENDAR, flip it open to January and write two words in one of the empty squares: "Begin chemotherapy."

The reality of those words still surprises and scares me. I wonder what this new year will bring as I face this daunting new challenge.

Cancer came into my life unexpectedly in the middle of the night between a Sunday and Monday in mid-December. I suddenly got very sick, and my husband Lynn rushed me to the emergency room of our local hospital. Soon I was wheeled into surgery. My last conscious thought was *At least the surgery will make me better.* It didn't. Instead, it revealed that I have Stage 4 ovarian cancer. Incredibly, Lynn had been diagnosed with a malignant brain tumor just six weeks earlier.

So here I am, looking at my calendar, knowing that these pages and squares will eventually be filled with doctors' appointments, chemotherapy treatments and lab test dates for both of us. How will we cope?

"Be open to the possibilities," one of our pastors told us when he visited me in the hospital. Among all the encouraging words given to us, those keep coming back to me as I flip through that calendar.

Be open to the possibilities . . . that these circumstances hold more than what I see right now.

Be open to the possibilities . . . of God's promise to grow good things in hard places.

Be open to the possibilities . . . of discovering new hope.

Be open to the possibilities . . . one day at a time.

When I look ahead, I have a choice: to fear the future or to stretch my imagination to embrace God's possibilities each morning.

Lord, I don't know what this new year will bring, but You do. Awaken me to Your possibilities, one day at a time. —CAROL KUYKENDALL

FRI

4

HE ALSO SAW A POOR WIDOW PUT IN TWO VERY SMALL COPPER COINS.
                    —*Luke 21:2 (NIV)*

A FRIEND RECENTLY E-MAILED ME this quiz. One question, multiple choice. Choose the most important act of service from the following list:

a. Donating a million dollars to a local charity or church.
b. Being the main speaker at a Bible conference.
c. Organizing a local effort to build houses for the poor.
d. Writing a note to someone who's lonely.
e. All of the above.

I picked *e,* although I can't say I always live by

what I know and believe. Although I try not to compare myself to others, sometimes it's hard. I'll see a story in the newspaper or hear a conversation at church and think, *Wow! If I could only be like them.*

That same day I received the quiz, I got an e-mail from my friend Don. Turns out he had shared some of my writings with men he works with in prison. One of those prisoners had told Don that what I wrote was not only uplifting, but it came "at just the right time."

At just the right time. Who would have known? And uplifting too. That's when I e-mailed the friend who sent me the quiz. I told him there should be a sixth category:

   f. Acts of service that are measured not by what
      you do, but by what God does with them.

And God can do powerful things with *a*, *b*, *c* and *d*. Happens all the time.

I'm going to do something today in Your name, God. May it be used to Your glory, not to mine.
                                   —JEFF JAPINGA

SAT
5

THE DESIRE ACCOMPLISHED IS SWEET TO THE SOUL. . . . —Proverbs 13:19

WHENEVER I OPEN WHAT I laughingly call my "crafts box," an orange-colored cooler with wheels and a handle, I see unfinished projects.

Here's two inches of ribbing that was supposed to be a sweater but never will be, since I don't remember how to do ribbing anymore. There's a pair of baby booties that have no openings where each foot should go. I was on a roll and forgot to stop knitting when I was supposed to.

"Just once I wish I could finish something," I told my friend Katy.

I held up a two-inch disk of red yarn that was supposed to be a hat—that was before I realized I never should have gotten involved with circular needles. "If I ever meet an elf," I joked, "this would be the perfect size."

Katy didn't laugh. "I think you have something here," she said.

"What? A clown nose?" I responded.

"No, seriously. My mother skis, and so many times I've heard her say that her nose feels colder than any other part of her body. Linda, can you knit two strings?"

"No, but I can crochet them."

"If you just attach one to each side of this disk . . ."

In less than five minutes, I had a disk with two strings that tied around a person's head.

"Linda, what you've got here is a nose warmer!" said Katy triumphantly.

Finally, a project that was just right—and finished! That winter, when Katy showed me a picture of her mom and two brothers wearing the nose warmers I had given them, I felt a warm glow of accomplishment.

Dear God, help me to see the possibilities that are wait-ing in the most unlikely places. —LINDA NEUKRUG

SUN
6

THE GENTILES SHALL COME TO THY
LIGHT, AND KINGS TO THE BRIGHTNESS
OF THY RISING. —*Isaiah 60:3*

WE SOUTHERNERS JOKE about the fact that our seasons are not reflected in changing leaves but rather in the food we eat. We have crawfish season, strawberry season, Creole tomato season, Vidalia onion season and—my favorite—king cake season.

Only available during the Mardi Gras holidays, king cake is made in an oval shape from braided strands of cinnamon dough, topped with icing and sprinkled with purple, green and gold sugar. There's a small plastic baby baked inside, and whoever finds it must bring a king cake to the next gathering.

My daughter loves king cake as much as I. She called from New York City to ask me to send her one. She planned to invite friends over during Mardi Gras.

"Sure!" I replied.

The next day I stopped at the bakery to order one. On the way out I picked up a brochure on the counter entitled, "The History of the King Cake."

"The Mardi Gras season officially begins on the Twelfth Night of Christmas, January 6, also known as

Epiphany," it said. "It marks the day the wise men brought gifts to the Christ Child. By doing so they 'revealed' or 'made known' Jesus to the world as Lord and King.

"The New Orleans custom, begun in the late 1800s, celebrates Epiphany with cakes that are baked to honor the three kings. The oval shape signifies their circular journey to confuse King Herod. The plastic baby represents Jesus. And the search for the baby is represented by the mystery of who will get the slice with the plastic baby in it."

So even if you've never been to Mardi Gras, why not share in a beloved New Orleans custom? Bake a king cake or have one shipped to you, and celebrate one of the biggest *Aha!* moments in history.

Wise Father, on this Epiphany, thank You for revealing Yourself to us in Jesus Christ. —MELODY BONNETTE

MON

7

"THE PEOPLE LIVING IN DARKNESS HAVE SEEN A GREAT LIGHT. . . ."
—*Matthew 4:16 (NIV)*

I WALK THROUGH THE HOUSE, clicking off lights. It is early morning, the day after Epiphany. The three kings have, tradition tells us, found the Christ Child. The twelve days of Christmas are over. I can find no more excuses to keep my Christmas lights burning. So candles that have been glowing since the day after Thanksgiving are unplugged. The windows are strangely empty. The rooms have shadows that feel deep and ominous.

I am feeling empty too. The holiday letdown has arrived right on cue.

Later, as I come in from doing errands, I notice something in the center window upstairs: a candle, still lit. I forgot to go into the storage room when I did my early morning rounds. The light is small, but bright and steady.

Christmas is not over. It's never really over—not as long as one good deed, one kind thought, one grateful remembrance still lives in my heart. Like the wise men, I have found what I was seeking: a love too grand to be contained in a single season, a light that breaks through even January gloom.

Holy Child, You are Lord and Light of my life! Let me shine for You in the coming year.
—MARY LOU CARNEY

TUE
8
A WISE MAN IS STRONG; YEA, A MAN OF KNOWLEDGE INCREASETH STRENGTH.
—*Proverbs 24:5*

IN ELEMENTARY SCHOOL, Jeffrey and I usually got along well, but one day we got into a squabble about a game. Jeffrey lost his temper and said, "After school, I'm going to fight you."

Nothing happened, but for the next several days in the school yard when the teacher wasn't looking, Jeffrey would point at me and say, "I'm going to beat you up after school."

One morning it became apparent to my parents that something was bothering me. "What's wrong?" my mother asked.

"I'm afraid of a kid in my class because he says he's going to beat me up after school."

My father immediately got into the conversation. "What do you mean?"

I explained the problem that I was having with Jeffrey. My father stood up, looked at me and said, "Fighting isn't going to solve your problem. Let's see if we can find a better way."

He took me to school that morning and asked me to point out Jeffrey to him. He asked Jeffrey, "Why do you want to fight with my son?"

Jeffrey didn't know what to say; he just stood there and listened.

Firmly but gently, my father said, "Fighting is not the way. Talking is the way to solve problems with others."

Jeffrey and I realized that there was no real reason for our differences. Then my father challenged us: "Shake hands and be friends."

I stretched out my hand and Jeffrey extended his. "Friends," we said. Forty years after that handshake, we still are.

Lord, thank You for a wise father who taught me that there's more to strength than fighting, and for friendships that last a lifetime. —PABLO DIAZ

WED
9

YOU WERE TAUGHT . . . TO BE MADE NEW IN THE ATTITUDE OF YOUR MINDS.
—*Ephesians 4:22–23 (NIV)*

I WAS SITTING IN A CROWDED New York City restaurant, waiting for my friends to appear. I was early for once, and as I scanned the crowd I saw the hostess approaching with two people who had decidedly grumpy expressions. She seated them at the table right next to me. There was some squirming and napkin unfurling and water glasses were put beside them. But something was wrong. "We're not going to be happy at this table," the woman announced, not revealing why. She summoned the waitress and announced they had to move to a different table.

The couple wriggled out and off, and the hostess approached again, leading an elderly woman with a cane and a smile, accompanied by a gray-haired man who nodded and smiled as they squeezed in. "What a nice table!" they exclaimed. We started to chat. It turned out that the woman was in her nineties, her husband even older. They'd been at the museum and regaled me with observations about the exhibit they'd seen. As they laughed and chattered, I saw the younger couple giving the waitress a hard time.

It made me think of all the times I, too, come into a situation thinking, *I'm not going to like this.* I'm switching to *This is great! It'll be an adventure.* It's a simple lesson, but one I never get tired of. It's all in your attitude, isn't it?

Dear God, when my attitude needs adjusting, make it new through Your Word. —MARY ANN O'ROARK

THU
10

WE WILL SING TO STRINGED INSTRUMENTS ALL THE DAYS OF OUR LIFE, AT THE HOUSE OF THE LORD.
—*Isaiah 38:20 (RSV)*

"DAD, COME LISTEN TO THIS! Come quick!" I heard Andy's voice calling me from the living room, where he had been playing the piano for half an hour. I was in the den and couldn't make out the tunes, although the note of triumph in his voice came through loud and clear. Now eleven, he had been tackling the instrument for nearly three years and had graduated from "Twinkle, Twinkle Little Star" and "Mary Had a Little Lamb" to Beethoven's "Für Elise," Bach's "Minuet in G" and other classical pieces. I guessed that Andy had finally mastered the new baroque work that his teacher had assigned and I strode into the living room, pride swelling in my chest.

The first thing I saw was a pair of feet hovering in

midair. Andy was lying on the piano bench, flat on his stomach, his legs thrust out behind him and his face inches away from the keyboard.

"Look, Dad," he said with delight, "I can play the piano with my nose!"

And so he could. I watched, astonished, as he carefully picked out the notes for "Twinkle, Twinkle Little Star."

I didn't know what to say or do. *This is what our piano lessons and piano practice have come to? This is why we spend all this money?* Then Andy looked up at me with a sweet, goofy grin, and all the love in the world rushed into my heart. I began to laugh, and Andy laughed with me.

Lord, help me remember that while learning requires discipline, it's also pure joy. —PHILIP ZALESKI

FRI
11

TAKE A LESSON FROM THE ANTS, YOU LAZY FELLOW. LEARN FROM THEIR WAYS AND BE WISE! —*Proverbs 6:6* (TLB)

I'VE BEEN OVERWEIGHT much of my life. Not grossly overweight, mind you, but like many middle-aged people, I've somehow let that waistline go. I love the water, and when I moved to Florida I began swimming nearly every day and taking a water aerobics class five days a week. But still I didn't lose weight, and my cholesterol kept going up.

Then our condo clubhouse's exercise room was re-modeled, with state-of-the-art machines, treadmills, elliptical trainers, a recumbent bike and lots of weight-lifting and stretching equipment. It was right across the street and free. No excuses.

I kept putting it off. Then I read some facts about ants. An ant can lift twenty times its weight. That's the same as a man who weighs two hundred pounds lifting two tons. And even though an ant's brain is the largest among insects, the human brain is forty thousand times larger. So why was the ant outsmarting me when it came to exercise?

I walked across the street and learned how to use all the machines. I plopped my more-than-ample bottom on one after another, lifting, pulling, reaching, stretching, groaning. I made new friends in the weight room. I looked out the windows at the Intracoastal Waterway and the boats churning along. On the treadmill I started thanking God for all my blessings.

Before long it was a habit. Sometimes I stay for an hour because there are so many people to chat with while we're all working out. I've never felt better or stronger in my life, though the ant still has me beaten in the lifting department.

Lord, encourage me to get healthy by moving this body You gave me every single day. —PATRICIA LORENZ

SAT
12

ONLY BY PRIDE COMETH
CONTENTION. . . . —Proverbs 13:10

I'M AFRAID I'M GETTING more stubborn with age. I used to be so flexible—or so it seems—but now I'm always so sure of myself. Not long ago at a dinner party with neighbors, I heard myself declare with absolute certainty to the woman next to me that a TV show we both watched was about the Korean War. "I don't think so," she said. "It's set during World War II." I disagreed—strenuously, dogmatically, with no room for argument. Then later we were talking about New York City geography.

"Rikers Island is in Sheepshead Bay," I declared.

"I don't think so," she said. "It's in the East River. You can see it from the Triborough Bridge."

"No, that's another island," I said. I should have admitted to some uncertainty, but I stuck to my guns. "Rikers is across town."

Only when I was home did I consult a map. You can imagine how foolish I felt to discover that my dinner companion was right. *Not much I can do about it now*, I thought. It would have been nice to apologize, but I couldn't even figure out how to bring it up.

Two days later I was on my morning jog through the park when I saw my neighbor, who was taking a brisk walk with a friend. *Now is the time*, I thought. *Just say it.* As we got close, I called out, "You were right about Rikers."

She smiled and waved. "You were right about Korea," she said.

I laughed and quickened my step. Perhaps admitting my mistakes is something else that can come with age. Half the time I might even be half right.

Dear God, let me be the first to admit I'm wrong.
—RICK HAMLIN

READER'S ROOM

A YEAR AGO, I joined an exercise program for women that requires only thirty minutes of one's time per session. I was surprised that I actually liked the exercise. I also enjoyed the camaraderie with other women, and over time discovered that I was developing muscle tone where I didn't even know I had muscles.

But I needed to know exactly how this program fit into God's plan. Did my going there bring Him glory? From my daily journaling I came to see that He was indeed involved, working in two ways: I was becoming a better steward of my own body and I was learning discipline, good qualities that carried over into other areas of my life.
—*Martha Suter, South Bend, Indiana*

SUN

13

O Lord, our Lord, how majestic is your name in all the earth! You have set your glory above the heavens. From the lips of children and infants you have ordained praise. . . .
—*Psalm 8:1–2 (NIV)*

I CALLED HOME ON A SUNDAY AFTERNOON, when my parents are generally enjoying the peace and quiet of the day and the ample sections of the newspaper. I wanted to catch up a bit and see how the weekend had gone. My dad answered and proudly told me that Alex, my nephew, had learned his first Bible verse in Sunday school.

I scolded my dad for being one of those proud grandpas who believe that his twenty-one-month-old grandchild could be capable of memorizing, retaining and reciting anything more complicated than asking for a cookie. Dad laughed and said, "Just listen."

I heard him pass the phone to Alex and pick up on an extension. "Alex," he said, "'Be not—'"

And very loudly from across the room, I heard this little voice pipe up. "'*Fwaid,*'" he said in his singsong tone.

I burst into laughter. *Be not afraid.* What a wonderful first lesson: to trust a loving and caring God. What a great reminder to a jaded aunt who needed to remember that through God, all things are possible, even a toddler's memory verse.

Lord, let me always have Alex's joy in knowing Your Word. —ASHLEY JOHNSON

MON
14
SUFFERING PRODUCES PERSEVERANCE; PERSEVERANCE, CHARACTER; AND CHARACTER, HOPE.
—*Romans 5:3–4 (NIV)*

IT HAD BEEN SIX YEARS since I'd lost my left leg to cancer, and I had finally found a sport I could compete in: ski racing. I'd been skiing for years, but this was my first race. I was nervous. An official wearing a radio headset was counting down: "Five . . . four . . . three . . . two . . . one . . . go, racer!"

I pushed through the starting wand and accelerated out of the gate. On the first turn I almost lost my balance as my ski scraped across the ice. I continued to flail through the course until the third turn, when my ski slid out from under me and I crashed. I looked down to see if my ski was still attached to my boot. It was, so I was allowed to get back up.

Three turns later I fell again. I got back up. Then I fell again. In total, I fell five times before I finally crossed the finish line. At this rate I was sure I'd never make the Paralympics, the quadrennial competition for athletes with physical disabilities. Then I remembered something my coach had said: "It's not the falling that matters for you right now as much as the getting back up."

That's just the path my ski racing career has followed—a lot of falling, a lot of praying, a lot of getting back up. Five years later, when I did make the Paralympics, I managed to fall a lot less, but I never forgot the lesson I learned from that first race: Persistence, not perfection, is what counts.

Father, give me perseverance. Give me the hope I need to get up after I fall down. —JOSHUA SUNDQUIST

TUE
15

AND OF SOME HAVE COMPASSION, MAKING A DIFFERENCE. —*Jude 22*

I BOARDED QUEEN MARY 2 in New York City en route to Rio de Janeiro, Brazil. It was perfect: a new ship to investigate and Commodore Ron Warwick in command. I had sailed many times with him on the *QE2*, but though he and I had shaken hands innumerable times, we didn't really know each other.

At Fort Lauderdale, Florida, we took on more passengers and headed out. I was lunching when it happened. *Bump.* "Did we hit a pothole?" a man said, joking. But the "bump" was more serious. We returned to Fort Lauderdale because the ship had hit a seawall, knocking out one of four external propulsion pods.

The next day we sailed again. Then came the report: Because the ship had been delayed, we would miss two ports in the Caribbean and one in Brazil. Around me passengers were outraged, even mutinous. I attended several of the insurrectionists' meetings and looked on as Commodore Warwick listened while they demanded their passage money back.

Word came from the head office: Half the money would be refunded. "No," they shouted. "All!" A lawsuit was threatened.

Finally, the day before we reached Rio, we were told that full fares for that segment of the cruise would be refunded. I sympathized with those who had counted on the bypassed ports. Their disappointment was real. Mostly, though, I felt admiration for Commodore Warwick, who had stood there as recriminations were hurled, his patience, his compassion solidly confirmed.

Father, grant me the virtue of a gentleman like the commodore. —Van Varner

A SECOND THANK-YOU

ROBERTA MESSNER has long been intrigued with Luke 17:11–19, the account of Jesus healing the ten lepers. "Only one of those ten even said thank you to Him, and that has always made me sad," she says. "And I've wondered . . . why stop with saying thank you just once?"

Join us each month as Roberta revisits some of the things for which she has thanked God and experiences the joy of saying "a second thank-you."

—THE EDITORS

THANK YOU FOR GIFTS UNDISCOVERED

WED
16

THANKS BE TO GOD FOR HIS INDESCRIBABLE GIFT!
—*II Corinthians 9:15 (NIV)*

I SHOULDN'T HAVE BEEN snooping around in Mother's bedroom, but I suspected there were

some things in there that I might be interested in. I'd
noticed Mrs. Melton at church calling Mother aside
to the trunk of her car and saying something about
"clothes for Roberta." Mrs. Melton's daughter Paula
was a few years ahead of me in school and had lovely
clothes. I thought she might have given us something
that I could wear to a concert at my junior high school
that Friday night.

I wasn't disappointed. In a shopping bag were all
sorts of designer clothes, the likes of which I'd only
dreamed about. And just my size too! The outfit that
really stole my heart was a royal blue wool tweed jumper
with a dropped waist and a pleat in the center. A Peter
Pan-collared blouse went with it, complete with kitten
scatter pins. These were no ordinary hand-me-downs.

I confessed my snooping to Mother. "You can't
wear those, honey," Mother said. "I know people
mean well when they give us things, but it's embarrassing. Someday you'll understand."

"No one will know, Mother," I begged. "Paula
doesn't even go to my school. Please."

But Mother was firm in her decision.

I've heard that when we get to heaven, there are
going to be all kinds of unopened gifts with our names
on them—the presents God provided for us while we
were on earth that, for one reason or another, we never
enjoyed. I've decided that in this new year, I don't
want to miss one more of them. As a second thank-
you to Mrs. Melton, I'm going to savor every present
God places in my path this year.

Thank You, Lord Jesus, for all the indescribable gifts You have for me. —ROBERTA MESSNER

THU
17

LOOK UPON MINE AFFLICTION AND MY PAIN; AND FORGIVE ALL MY SINS.
                                    —*Psalm 25:18*

LAST YEAR I HAD A HIP REPLACED, the result of a skiing accident years ago. I learned a lot from the experience, but the most important lesson was about pain.

For five years I had put up with the pain in that joint. Finally, when it became so severe that I wasn't sleeping and I began to have trouble walking, I resigned myself to surgery.

Just six hours after the operation, the doctor and nurses had me sit up on the side of my hospital bed and then stand on the brand-new joint. There was pain from the eight-inch incision, but as I prepared for the deeper pain in my hip, there was nothing. "I can't believe it!" I said. "Why didn't I do this sooner?"

While I was recovering at home, some friends asked me to help with a problem they were having with a member of their work team. I spent long hours on the phone and uncovered tremendous pain that had gone on for years. On one of my laps around the couch and back again, it hit me: *We need surgery here.* The old joint holding these people together was diseased and no amount of ignoring it would help. It needed to be cut out and something new put in its place.

Several people balked at the pain this "surgery" would cause, but slowly and surely my argument persuaded them. Weeks later, the team was well on its way to healing.

Do you have a pain in your life where surgery will help? Why wait around while things only get worse? I promise you'll end up saying, "Why didn't I do this sooner?"

Thank You, Father, for giving us the gift of pain so that we know something is wrong, and for being the Great Physician Who can heal us when we are ready.

—ERIC FELLMAN

FRI
18

I KNOW YOUR THOUGHTS . . . WHICH YE WRONGFULLY IMAGINE. . . . —*Job 21:27*

AS MY HUSBAND GENE and I checked into the hotel, I discreetly checked out the concierge. Sometimes they intimidate me, especially the women. How could they know so much? How did they get so smart? Why do they always have such good hair and elegant shoes? How can they pull out a map and give directions to anywhere? I was sure that she and I would be nothing alike.

The next morning Gene walked confidently to her desk. "The concierge will give us directions," he explained.

"Let's just find our own way," I suggested and slunk quickly behind a huge column to watch.

"May I help you?"

Undoubtedly she'll be able to. Even if we spoke Swahili.

Gene asked his question, and she replied, poised, polished and perfect, by pulling out a map.

The next day we were eating in the hotel restaurant when I discovered I'd lost my billfold in a huge conference center. Gene hopped up, beaming. "I'll go explain to our concierge."

Ridiculous idea.

I sat there alone, feeling foolish, unable even to consider eating.

Gene was back in a flash. "I gave her the information," he said.

I twirled an index finger around sarcastically in a "Let's celebrate" gesture. Then around the corner came the concierge, wearing her beatific smile. She touched me on the shoulder. "Marion," she said warmly, "I've located your wallet. Take this note to the information center at the conference hall. They're holding it for you."

I jumped up and hugged her, and she hugged me right back. At home in Georgia again, I sent her a gift of gratitude. We've become pen pals. Actually, we have a lot in common. But she still has better hair!

Father, I goofed again. Thank You for my new friend.
                          —MARION BOND WEST

SAT
19

SPEAKING THE TRUTH IN LOVE, WE WILL
IN ALL THINGS GROW UP INTO HIM WHO
IS THE HEAD, THAT IS, CHRIST.
                    —*Ephesians 4:15* (NIV)

WE ADOPTED A PUPPY LAST WINTER. A beagle.

Our twelve-year-old daughter Sarah has wanted a dog for years. She'd *awww* and *oohh* while watching dog shows on television and volunteer to take friends' dogs for walks. We knew that she was yearning for a four-legged friend.

My wife Danelle and I have always been cat people; however, it's difficult to take a cat on vacation or even a quick trip to the corner store. You never hear a cat person calling out, "Here, boy!" And a cat will never make you feel like you are the most terrific person on the planet.

We adopted our beagle from the local shelter, filling out paperwork designed to convince strangers that you are completely trustworthy and entirely prepared to make this life-changing decision. Sarah named her Astra.

Danelle had doubts from the beginning about whether we were ready for a puppy. Frankly, I didn't know any better. "I'll help out a lot," I said. "Sarah and I will work together on it."

We spent two frustrating months trying to recast our lives around Astra. She wouldn't be housebroken. She wouldn't stop terrorizing our three cats. And caring for her was beginning to affect the relationships among the humans in the house.

After several weeks of emotional wrangling, Sarah said one morning, "I don't think that ours is the best home for Astra." I agreed. We made phone calls and a few days later found that we could place our beagle with the family that had adopted her brother.

Slowly, our home didn't just return to normal, our understanding and love for each other deepened. We found that sometimes it's right to make a change, even one that feels painful.

Give me the wisdom, Father, to know when to stick out a difficult situation and when to make a change.
                                    —JON SWEENEY

SUN
20
STAND UP AND BLESS THE LORD YOUR GOD FOR EVER AND EVER: AND BLESSED BE THY GLORIOUS NAME, WHICH IS EXALTED ABOVE ALL BLESSING AND PRAISE. —Nehemiah 9:5

OUR MINISTER BROUGHT A LARGE VASE filled with cut roses of various colors and set it on the altar. He asked the members of the congregation to gather in a semi-circle at the front of the church and face the altar.

Because we're a small church, there were maybe thirty people in that circle. The minister then asked each of us to come, one at a time, and select a rose from the vase, face the congregation and name someone who had been a blessing in our life.

Some people named a parent or a friend or a teacher or a co-worker. When my husband Larry went forward, he selected a yellow rose and said, with a catch in his voice, "Thank You, God, for the women in my life."

He walked over and handed the rose to me, but I knew that special tribute included not only me, but his mother and our daughter. Years later, I still have the pressed petals from that rose.

Today I'm thinking again of those who have blessed my life. The list is long, including Larry, our children, our grandchildren, our parents, our friends. Topping the list, of course, is God, ever present, ever loving.

Lord, today I will thank someone who has touched and blessed my life. —MADGE HARRAH

MON
21
"SEE, I AM DOING A NEW THING! NOW IT SPRINGS UP; DO YOU NOT PERCEIVE IT? I AM MAKING A WAY IN THE DESERT. . . ."
—Isaiah 43:19 (NIV)

AS OUR MINISTRY PLANNED for a new year, I proposed what I truly believed was a big, holy and audacious goal: to preach a message of racial healing in twenty Black and twenty white Mississippi churches. We called it our 20/20 Initiative.

I am a native Mississippian, and I remember when groups of white deacons guarded the doors to their churches to prevent people like me from entering. So it seemed daring to hope that twenty predominantly white congregations would now welcome me not only in their pews but to their pulpits. Blacks in the state still struggled with hurt and anger. How many would welcome a message of racial reconciliation, even from an African American preacher?

The response overwhelmed me. Fifty-two churches (thirty white and twenty-two Black) invited me to preach at their worship services. Across the state, I met believers of different races and denominations who desire to embrace a new vision of a reconciled Body of Christ.

Lord, help me never to underestimate Your ability to open doors, eyes and hearts. —DOLPHUS WEARY

TUE **22**   *O JERUSALEM, THAT BRINGEST GOOD TIDINGS, LIFT UP THY VOICE WITH STRENGTH; LIFT IT UP, BE NOT AFRAID; SAY UNTO THE CITIES OF JUDAH, BEHOLD YOUR GOD!* —Isaiah 40:9

MOST MORNINGS I LOG ON to my computer at work, open the e-mail program and just start hitting the delete button. Hot stock tips, instant loans, online degrees, "genuine faux" watches, rapid weight loss programs, cyber casinos—all kinds of junk e-mail clutter up my in-box.

I rarely open up any of this junk. That's because I've gotten pretty good at identifying them by the subject line. Some of them are pure gibberish: "President's Marsupial Plan" or "Bulk Rag Injection." Some are a little more insidious: "Security Notification" or "Order Delivery Status." Some border on the sinister: "Your credit has been accessed!" But I usually see through their tricks and unmercifully delete them.

The other day an e-mail from an unknown source popped up on my screen with the subject line "God Loves You."

"Yeah, right," I muttered. "I wonder what God loves so much that He wants to sell it to me." I hit DELETE with a mixture of annoyance and satisfaction.

A day later it was back. I deleted it again. This time I felt a little uncomfortable; I don't like deleting God. *That's what they're counting on*, I thought. *They probably wanted to refinance my mortgage if I would kindly hand over my Social Security and bank account numbers. I didn't just fall off the turnip truck, you know.*

A couple of days passed and there it was again: "God Loves You." I hesitated, finger poised above the DELETE key. *I'm going to regret this*, I thought, certain I was being suckered. I opened it.

Nothing—just a blank white screen. No pitch. No product.

God loves me.

The Internet is an interesting place, and I'm not sure I could even tell you *where* it exists. But one thing is sure: Certain messages always get through.

Thank You, Lord, for the reminder that Your love is everywhere, even in my in-box.
—EDWARD GRINNAN

WED
23

"THUS SAYS THE LORD, THE GOD OF ISRAEL, 'WRITE ALL THE WORDS WHICH I HAVE SPOKEN TO YOU IN A BOOK.'"
—*Jeremiah* 30:2 (NAS)

THE WARM EMBRACE OF BOOKS wraps itself around you the moment you step into my living room—floor-to-ceiling shelves of books. The somber and bright colors of their spines sport an extraordinary range of titles and reflect the influence they have had in giving texture to our lives. The lower shelves are reserved for children: Dr. Seuss, fairy tales, Rudyard Kipling's *Jungle Book* and all of Winnie-the-Pooh.

Dusting the main surfaces of the living room is done with a few quick flicks. Dusting the bookshelves is a never-ending job because of all the pauses of flipping through pages and sitting on the stepladder to reread cherished passages. It took me hours and several cups of tea to dust Anne Morrow Lindbergh's *Gift from the Sea*!

Several special books have a place of honor on my library table. This morning as I dusted, I peered into *Cornerstones of Christianity*, published in 1914. It's been in the Angus family for generations and came to us when Grandma died. "I remember sitting on Mother's knee while she read its Bible stories to me," my husband said. He turned to page three and ran his fingers along the words:

> *Book of books*
> *Inspired by God*
> *Beautiful in Expression*
> *Light of Life*
> *Enduring Eternally.*

Light of our life, Book of all books . . . the cornerstone that strengthens and sustains us now and forevermore. Hallelujah, Lord! —FAY ANGUS

THU
24

JESUS CALLED THEM UNTO HIM, AND SAID, SUFFER LITTLE CHILDREN TO COME UNTO ME, AND FORBID THEM NOT: FOR OF SUCH IS THE KINGDOM OF GOD.
—*Luke 18:16*

A MAN WHO WAS ONCE the governor of a state told me that the thing that saved him when he was exhausted and filled with despair at the lies and machinations of men was kids.

"Whenever I got really dark and hopeless," he said, "I would go visit a classroom. The kids would just pop with energy and questions and opinions. By the end of my term, I was canceling meetings left and right, scheduling three school visits a day, and stopping at every park and playground we passed.

"The very best times were when kids told me stories right out of their hearts. I'd be sitting in a tiny chair with my knees up, and they would tell me about their puppies or skateboards or grandmas, and it was like someone pouring hope into my head.

"I'll miss that more than anything, being with all those kids. If we say we'll take care of them and don't, then we're just sinning, and there's no worse sin than ignoring or mistreating a child. You know that and I know that. I walked away from being governor more fired up about public service than before, but now I bend all my energies to fixing stuff for kids. Is there anything more crucial than that?"

Dear Lord, suffer the children to come to us too, all day, every day, and suffer us to be kind and open and generous and intent and honest and attentive to them.
— BRIAN DOYLE

FRI
25
GOD SAID, "I COMMAND THE EARTH TO GIVE LIFE TO ALL KINDS OF TAME ANIMALS. . . ." AND THAT'S WHAT HAPPENED. GOD MADE EVERY ONE OF THEM. THEN HE LOOKED AT WHAT HE HAD DONE, AND IT WAS GOOD. —*Genesis 1:24–25 (CEV)*

"DAD, WE NEED TO GET A DOG. Kyle's going to need a buddy when I go away to college," our son Joel urged. "You know how we all struggled to adjust when Ryan went away to school last year."

It was true. And while it had been five years since we had buried our first and only dog Gem, the pain of parting with her was still intense. Joel turned his attention to convincing his mother.

"Mom, let's get a Boston terrier. How can you ever have a bad day when you start each morning looking at a Boston terrier?" She was unmoved.

While we were visiting Ryan at college a few months later, we happened to see a litter of Boston boxer puppies, an adorable blend of Boston terrier and miniature boxer. So Dutch became a member of the Nace household.

Five years later, our veterinarian recommended that we adopt middle-aged Rookie as a playmate for high-energy Dutch. No one wanted Rookie; Dr. Nippert had found a home for him only to have him return with an allergic reaction to fleabites. When we met Rookie, he had been shaved from his curly beige armpits to his plume tail. His middle was covered with angry boils, which made him a good candidate for the sorriest looking dog.

Now handsome Rookie and Dutch are senior citizens and each other's best buddies. Dr. Nippert says we've been good Samaritans. But as any pet-lover will tell you, we're the ones who have been blessed by the gift of unconditional love and friendship.

Lord, thank You for enriching our lives with awesome companions. —TED NACE

SAT
26

AND WHEN HE HAD CONSULTED WITH THE PEOPLE, HE APPOINTED SINGERS UNTO THE LORD. . . .
                            —*II Chronicles 20:21*

ON FRIDAY, MY SON CHASE left North Carolina for Kansas City, to take part in the Metropolitan Opera National Council Auditions for young singers. He left without receiving the letter that told him where, when and in what order he would sing. "Just enjoy yourself," I tried to reassure him before he boarded his flight.

Though he said all the right things, we both knew he was nervous. After all, he'd been studying voice for only four or five years. Most of the other singers at the regional competition would be older and more experienced.

Though Chase had done well in elementary school and junior high, the death of his father years earlier seemed to cast a shadow on him. His struggles in high school had left him uncertain about his abilities. I homeschooled him his senior year, and he took courses at the local community college. In a choral-singing class, the director identified Chase's musical gift.

"This is not an entrance audition. It's just for fun," I said to him when he called, hoping Chase wouldn't hear my heart pounding over the phone.

"Keep looking for the letter," he told me.

Soon after his departure, the letter arrived. He was number eighteen out of forty singers and he was to sing at one o'clock.

On Saturday, I waited patiently to hear. There was no word by two or three o'clock. By five, I was no longer able to pretend that I was patient. I called and, after receiving no response, went to a late lunch. When I returned home, there was a message.

"Mom, I won an award. I was the youngest person to win an award and the only one still an undergraduate. I talked to the judges and they said . . ."

I heard joy and excitement in his voice, but the greatest thing I heard was acceptance and peace.

Thank You, Lord, for gifts of creativity and beauty that triumph over the discouragement and uncertainty of our lives. —SHARON FOSTER

SUN

27

O GIVE THANKS UNTO THE GOD OF HEAVEN: FOR HIS MERCY ENDURETH FOR EVER. —Psalm 136:26

EVERY SUNDAY in the Attaway household, we have pancakes for breakfast. Sometimes we have banana, sometimes buckwheat, and in season, strawberry or blueberry. This morning it was Swedish pancakes, one of the kids' favorites. The children eagerly set the table and sat with forks poised as the serving plate came into range. As I put the first batch of pancakes on the table, Mary asked, "Can we say grace?" I nodded and headed back to the kitchen.

A few moments later a wail arose. Stephen, my normally placid three-year-old, was howling. I popped my head into the dining room to see what was up. He had a pancake on his plate. Someone had even put lingonberry jam on it and rolled it up. What was wrong?

"They didn't wait for me to pray!" Stephen bawled.

"He was right here when we said grace!" Elizabeth said.

"Never mind," I said to Stephen. "Daddy's here now and he can say grace with you."

Andrew yawned and sat down next to Stephen. Soothingly, he said, "I haven't said grace yet either." Together father and son bowed their heads and said a blessing over the food. Then, while the older kids debated the gastronomic advantages of moving to

Sweden, my little guy began to eat. He ate an astonishing amount. And not surprisingly, he was thankful.

*Father, everything tastes better when I stop to say
thank You.* —JULIA ATTAWAY

MON
28

*IS NOT MY WORD LIKE AS A FIRE? SAITH
THE LORD. . . .* —Jeremiah 23:29

ONE BLUSTERY, ICY DAY, unable to escape
the piles of paper on my desk any longer,
I sat down to work—sorting mail, paying bills, catching up on correspondence. Next to me was a warm
crackling fire. Several times I felt like quitting, but as
I stirred the coals, my mind cleared and I tackled the
next pile. Halfway into the afternoon, the fire appeared to be completely out. I added kindling, then
blew till the ash-covered coals flamed again. When I
brought in a couple of logs from outdoors, I was rewarded with a roaring fire for my last batch of letters.
   The next morning I picked up the stack of envelopes to take to the post office. Seeing the empty
fireplace, I fondly remembered the warmth it had provided, as constant and comforting as God's love. *I
wish I could experience God's presence with me today
like that warm fire*, I thought, but I would be in and
out of the car, running errands, going to work.
   An idea came. I sat down, still clutching the pile of

envelopes, and before I headed out I took a little time to read Scripture. My spiritual fire was built. Then in order to have some "fuel" with me, I grabbed an index card and jotted down a few verses from the day's reading: *Rejoice always, pray constantly, give thanks in all circumstances* (I Thessalonians 5:16–18, RSV). I set that card on the dashboard. At the post office a man hobbled by with a cane, and the card inspired me to pray for him and for other people I encountered during the day. As I dealt with the demands of work and family, God's Word kept me aglow.

Dear God, thank You for the comforting fire of Your presence. During my tasks today, rekindle my awareness of You. —MARY BROWN

TUE
29
IN YOU THEY TRUSTED AND WERE NOT DISAPPOINTED. —*Psalm 22:5* (NIV)

SEVERAL YEARS AGO, inspired by a book I'd read, I made a list of thirty people I hoped to meet one day. The list was wide and varied, including writers, motivational speakers and celebrities. Amazingly, over the last several years, I've met eighteen people on that list. Some of them were everything I'd expected and others were major disappointments.

Not long ago, after one such disappointment, I was

complaining to God about how disillusioned I'd been. Then God spoke to me in my heart: *Debbie, you asked to meet these people and I'm happy to send them into your life, but I want you to make another list.*

"Another list?"

This time leave the spaces blank. I'm going to send thirty people into your life whom I want you to meet, and I promise you none of them will be a disappointment.

This prayer-time conversation has had a curious effect on me. Now, whenever I meet someone, I look at him or her with fresh eyes and wonder if this is one of the people God is sending into my life. I find that I'm more open, more receptive, waiting expectantly for those God wants me to meet. Since then, I've been blessed in countless ways. I've still got my original list, but it's not nearly as important to me as the one God asked me to keep.

Father, thank You for the special people You have sent into my life. Not a single one has ever disappointed me.
—DEBBIE MACOMBER

WED
30

"SAY OF YOUR BROTHERS, 'MY PEOPLE,' AND OF YOUR SISTERS, 'MY LOVED ONE.'" —*Hosea 2:1* (NIV)

A PERSON CAN SHED TEARS without shedding strength. I learned that by watching my older sister Sue on a cold winter night in Columbus, Ohio.

My brother was sick and couldn't go out on his newspaper route. He had found someone to deliver the morning papers, but he also needed someone to collect the weekly payment—forty-two cents—from his fifty customers. Sue volunteered; she'd never understood why she couldn't be a paperboy in the first place.

My parents sent me with Sue to help her, although I did nothing but shyly stand behind her, my mittened hands stuffed deep in my pockets. Customer after customer gave her fifty cents, quickly shut their storm doors, waiting for my sister to coax eight cents from the metal coin changer, and opened the door just wide enough to take the change from her bare hands. Once in a while, a generous or impatient customer would say, "Keep the change," and Sue wouldn't have to take off her gloves to work the coin changer.

It was dark by the time we reached the end of the route. Tears trickled and froze on Sue's face as she worked the coins free of the changer, but she was smiling through them. "I knew I could be a paperboy," she said.

Dear God, thank You for the examples of love and courage You've given me. —TIM WILLIAMS

THU
31
HEREIN IS LOVE, NOT THAT WE LOVED GOD, BUT THAT HE LOVED US. . . .
—*I John 4:10*

IN A WESTERN MOVIE, my husband would be the heroic cowboy. You know the type: strong and silent, good looking, slow talking, quick drawing. I can picture the scene: dust swirling through an empty street, the sound of spurs jingling. In a flash, he would vanquish the bad guys, save the damsel and ride off into the sunset.

Jacob is calm, stable and thoughtful—qualities that most of the time I truly appreciate. But sometimes the fact that he doesn't tell me I look nice or say, "I love you" leaves me feeling empty.

The other important man in my life, my grandfather, had been outgoing and affectionate. He always had a compliment, an "I love you," a hug or a friendly joke.

One day I was feeling low, wondering why Jacob hadn't noticed my new haircut or said anything about the way I'd cleaned the kitchen. I decided to call my grandmother and ask her for some advice. After I told her how I was feeling, there was a long pause on the line. Then Grandma excused herself. Three minutes later she returned. "Honey, I should have read this to you a long time ago."

"What is it?"

"After your grandfather died, I was cleaning up his things and I found this note. Let me read you what it says: 'Dear Aliene, I never told you this often enough, you were the love of my life. I should have told you that more. Love forever, Gordon.'"

For a while we were both silent. "You see," she said, "your grandfather had a hard time saying he loved me too. But I always knew he did."

Lord, when my heart is heavy, show me Your "I love you" in Your Word. —AMANDA BOROZINSKI

MY DIVINE SURPRISES

1 _____

2 _____

3 _____

4 _____

5 _____

6 _____

7 _____

8 _____

9 _____

10 _____

11 _____

12 _____

13 _____

14 _____

15 _____

16 _____

17 _____

18 _____

19 _____

20 _____

21 _____

22 _____

23 _____

24 _____

25 _____

26 _____

27 _____

28 _____

29 _____

30 _____

31 _____

February

He discovereth deep things out of darkness. . . . —*Job 12:22*

UNEXPECTED BLESSINGS
HEARING THE WORD

FRI

I

TEACH ME THE WAY I SHOULD GO. . . .
—*Psalm 143:8 (RSV)*

I STEPPED ONTO THE TRAIN wishing I could nap on the way into town. No chance with the loudspeaker booming out every few minutes! Automated station announcements were new on our commuter line: an intrusive recorded voice declaiming, "This station is Chappaqua. The next stop is Pleasantville . . . Hawthorne . . . Valhalla . . . North White Plains." I could recite the route in my sleep.

But sleep was just what I wasn't getting! For the past three months I'd followed a new morning routine supposed to promote health and creativity. Up at 5:00 AM, thirty minutes for meditation, thirty for exercise, shower, high-protein breakfast, at work by 7:00. Actually, this was my husband John's natural rhythm. Always up early, unforgivably cheerful, he thrived on the predawn hours. I did not. I was barely functional before 8:00 AM.

As the train pulled out of the station, I leaned my head on the seat back and closed my eyes. "This station is Dobbs Ferry." It was several seconds before my sleep-deprived brain registered the strange words. We couldn't be arriving in Dobbs Ferry; that station was on a different line altogether! I looked out the window at the familiar Hawthorne platform. Somehow the wrong recording had been installed on the train. "The next stop is Tarrytown . . . Croton-on-Hudson . . ." With each misapplied pronouncement, there was a ripple of laughter.

Mine sprang from deep inside. The station announcements were perfectly valid, just intended for somewhere else. And that early morning discipline, the out-of-place recording told me, was a splendid one where it fit. Tomorrow morning, I promised myself, I'd go back to the schedule that worked for me.

Bestower of blessing, there's so much advice today from so many sources! Open my ears to hear Your clearly spoken "This is for you." —ELIZABETH SHERRILL

SAT
2

SURELY YOU HAVE GRANTED HIM ETERNAL BLESSINGS AND MADE HIM GLAD WITH THE JOY OF YOUR PRESENCE.
—*Psalm 21:6 (NIV)*

MY SATURDAYS HAVE BEEN DIFFERENT this winter. For the past ten years, I've spent them working. But not this year.

This year, John's and Mary's Saturday ballet classes are two hours apart. So my wife Julia and I have to split up ballet duty: Julia and Mary leave at nine for Mary's ten o'clock class and return at noon, so I can take John to his class at one.

There's a lively group of moms and dads at the school, and I enjoy chatting with them as I drop off John. But once the door to his studio closes, I'm off to the café at the nearby bookstore. I reserve one of the tiny tables with my coat and get in line for a cup of coffee. Back at the table, I take out my book, sip my coffee and enjoy an extraordinary luxury for a parent of five: an hour to myself.

I like books that I can chew in small bites: Books of essays on inspirational or biblical themes work best. I take another sip of coffee, turn the page, put down the book and enjoy the chance just to be quiet.

When my hour is up, I go back to the studio, say hello to Luigi, the jazz dancing teacher, and pick up John. Perhaps we'll go to the Museum of Natural History to look at the gold exhibit or head to a Chinese restaurant for dumplings. If the weather's nice, we'll take a walk in Central Park. Today we walked up Broadway and picked up a catalog of John's favorite toys at a shop near the subway station. Even though he's ten, he still likes to hold my hand as we walk.

I'm trying to get to work a little earlier during the week, but I don't think I'll be giving up these Saturdays anytime soon.

*Lord, thank You for the glimpses of Your presence that
You give me in quiet reflection and in my son's smile.*
                                    —ANDREW ATTAWAY

SUN
3

JESUS . . . SAID, "YOU LACK ONE THING;
GO, SELL WHAT YOU OWN, AND GIVE THE
MONEY TO THE POOR, AND YOU WILL
HAVE TREASURE IN HEAVEN; THEN COME,
FOLLOW ME." WHEN HE HEARD THIS, HE WAS
SHOCKED AND WENT AWAY GRIEVING, FOR HE HAD
MANY POSSESSIONS. —*Mark 10:21–22 (NRSV)*

I'VE ALWAYS BEEN DISTRESSED by Jesus' instructions
to the rich young man to give everything to the poor.
Because I think Jesus means it. And I don't know
anyone—including myself—who does it.

I listen closely when preachers talk about this
Gospel passage. Frequently, they suggest that their listeners give to the church, but that's not what Jesus
said. He said "the poor." And He said *everything*,
"what you own."

Recently, the deacon at our church gave a talk on
these verses. It centered on one woman, Dora, who
tried to closely follow Christ. Dora was involved in all
kinds of charitable work, and she had little patience
for people unmindful of the poor. One afternoon she
was in the church basement, picking up clothing that
had been left during the week for her to distribute.

She was delighted to find many fine women's coats; since it was winter, this was a spectacular find. She loaded the coats into her car, unaware that the women's committee was meeting in the community room upstairs.

Then, the committee members discovered that their coats were gone, and the chairwoman called Dora. "You took our own coats for donations!" she cried. "We left our keys in our coat pockets!"

"Well," Dora replied, "I can bring back the keys, but the least you all can do is donate your coats."

Now, like me, you may think that Dora's charitable heart got a bit carried away, but I think you'll agree that she took Jesus' words seriously. Just as I must, for myself.

Jesus, You gave Your life for us "poor." Help me do the same. —MARCI ALBORGHETTI

MON

4

"HE WILL YET FILL YOUR MOUTH WITH LAUGHING, AND YOUR LIPS WITH REJOICING." —*Job 8:21 (NKJV)*

WHEN I WAS A BOY, we lived in the Ohio village of New Richmond, near Cincinnati. One year the river overflowed, turning our town into a little Venice. We kids were thrilled! We sat on the front porch and watched motorboats and canoes putt-putting through our liquid streets. We launched our own toy boats and tracked them for as far as we could see.

When the waters finally receded, we drove around town "admiring" the damage—houses tilted on their foundations and cars buried in mud. We marveled at the big, whiskered catfish flopping in the gutters, and we chased ugly crawdads that were trying to find their way back to the river. We collected slugs in jars, slimy creatures as big as breadsticks. We knew little of the cost of the flood, we were so busy being excited with the adventure of it all.

Now, as a grown-up, I tend to see only the pain of adversity and miss the fun altogether. When a blizzard buried our campus under four feet of snow, I saw shoveling duties, messy streets and being trapped indoors. My students, on the other hand, saw an opportunity to build the world's biggest snowman and an igloo dorm room. They were happy to be free of classes for a while and they enjoyed a long snow-ball war.

There's nothing funny about adversity, but when times are tough, I still need to laugh and play—perhaps more than ever. From laughter comes perspective and the strength to recover.

Lord, help me to laugh, even when nothing seems funny. —DANIEL SCHANTZ

TUE
5
*FOR YE SHALL GO OUT WITH JOY, AND BE
LED FORTH WITH PEACE. . . .*
—*Isaiah 55:12*

I PUT BABY HENRY into his stroller and bundled up four-year-old Solomon for our walk. Solomon donned the bright orange furry top hat he'd found in a second-hand store. Together, we walked down our country road to the town road that has a sidewalk and traffic.

Solomon helped push the stroller, and I kept my hand on his just to make sure he was safe. As a car approached, Solomon tugged his hand away and waved. The driver seemed a little surprised and waved. His wave was all the encouragement Solomon needed.

When the next car came, Solomon giggled. As it got closer, he jumped up and thrust his arms high and wide as if he were shipwrecked on a desert island, hailing a passing ship. The driver, passenger and some children in the backseat waved back. Another car came. This time Solomon waved before they were close enough to see. The car approached: A tiny tap on the horn made Solomon double over in giggles.

In town, we bought the newspaper and some drinks. The man behind me at the register tapped Solomon's orange hat. "You're quite an ambassador, young man," he said. "I see you waving at all the cars, making people's day."

"What's an ambassador?" Solomon asked. "Some-one who makes people happy?"

On the way back home, Solomon started to wave and I joined him. It felt silly at first, but it was fun watching the faces perk up. I looked down at Henry in his stroller, wondering when he'd learn to join us in wishing the world a good day.

Lord, help me to be an ambassador of Your joy to all I meet today. —SABRA CIANCANELLI

WED
6
TO GIVE UNTO THEM BEAUTY FOR ASHES, THE OIL OF JOY FOR MOURNING. . . .
—*Isaiah 61:3*

I WAS TWELVE THE WINTER Mother decided to make soap.

We'd just visited a mountain homestead where the farmer's wife was leaching wood ashes, which she would boil with rendered lard to produce her family's soap. Mother was inspired. Soon, back home, a package arrived at our door: a soap-making kit. Proudly, Mother showed us the hopper that would hold the ashes over which water would be poured and the crock for holding the resulting lye.

And, of course, I was involved. It was my job to collect the fireplace ashes Mother needed for her soap. Week after week, scoop in hand, I shoveled ashes into leaky brown bags and stored them in the basement. Inevitably, I was called back to vacuum the fine ash silt that settled on the living room furniture. When I finally escaped, I'd run upstairs to bathe (with store-bought soap) to get the dust out of my hair and ears.

When spring came, Mother spent an entire day pouring water through the ashes we fed into the hopper. She boiled the resulting foaming liquid with perfumed oil instead of lard, but everything else she did just as the mountain woman had done, adding salt to the mixture and pressing it into molds to create bars of what—much to my surprise—was really and truly a fragrant and effective brown soap.

Ashes—like sins, I thought, remembering that long ago event—are dirty and ugly, coating everything around them in their gray pall. But in the right hands, those dusty, dead ashes could be transformed into something cleansing and health-giving.

Soon today I'll join others while our pastor places ashes on our foreheads, a symbol of penitence. And as he does, I'll be putting my sins in God's hands, asking Him to make of them something He can use.

Father, may this season of Lent be a time of true transformation. —JOHN SHERRILL

THU

7

BE ANGRY, BUT SIN NOT; COMMUNE WITH YOUR OWN HEARTS . . . AND BE SILENT.
—*Psalm 4:4 (RSV)*

THE INAUDIBLE VOICE on the loudspeaker crackled and mumbled something no one understood. We didn't have to. The fifteen-minute wait on the platform was clear enough: Our train was delayed. Fresh mobs of commuters piled into the already packed subway station as we all stretched our necks to look down the dark, empty tunnel. I looked at my watch and screamed silently: *Come on! Let's go!* I wished I could yell at the top of my lungs and relieve the stress that was building up. *You're making me late!*

Five minutes later the train finally roared into the station. As it opened its doors, we pushed and shoved our way in until we were pressed up tight against each other's winter coats. *I hate New York*, I thought as a woman's oversized bag pushed into my back. The train took off, then slowed down and stopped. Another inaudible voice over the loudspeaker attempted to tell us the obvious: We weren't moving.

I managed to retrieve my iPod from my coat pocket and put on a praise album that I had recently downloaded. With each note of the piano, I could feel the tension in my neck relax. A voice filled with such sweet anointing lifted my spirit. I forgot how uncomfortable, annoyed and late I was. In the middle of the madness, I spent a moment with God, and His peace surrounded me with an indescribable calm. My rush-hour quiet time reminded me that I can always go to Him for solace, no matter how hectic my circumstance might be.

I'm glad when I can snatch quiet moments with You, God. Thank You for always meeting me there.
                                                —KAREN VALENTIN

FRI
8

FOR THEY HAVE REFRESHED MY SPIRIT AND YOURS: THEREFORE ACKNOWLEDGE YE THEM THAT ARE SUCH.
                                —*I Corinthians 16:18*

ON A VISIT to an out-of-town department store, I'd appreciated the help of a young sales associate as I shopped. A week later, filing my receipts, I saw her name written on a sales slip. I dialed the local branch of the chain to ask if they could pass on my thanks to Jessica and her supervisor.

Nora, the store executive I spoke with, said my call had made her day. "A call first thing after opening in the morning usually means a complaint," she told me. We enjoyed a pleasant conversation, which ended with Nora's invitation to visit the store and meet her. She would e-mail my thanks to Jessica's manager Ruth.

Afterward I thought of how much had been accomplished by that one brief call: I felt good, the local store manager felt good, the out-of-town manager would soon feel good and Jessica was going to feel good! Sure, it would have been less hassle to file that sales slip and forget about it. Instead, like the offer of loaves and fishes that Jesus multiplied, taking a moment to be encouraging fed a multitude—or at least four women scattered among the crowd.

Jesus, every encouraging word I speak is one more loaf and fish in the basket. By Your provision, may many be nourished. —CAROL KNAPP

SAT
9

DO YE LOOK ON THINGS AFTER THE OUTWARD APPEARANCE? . . .
                    —*II Corinthians 10:7*

WE'RE SITTING AT FAITH'S piano recital, and I realize how my children appear to outsiders: as if they've come from different planets. Fifteen-year-old Faith has a proper and classy outfit, with nary a hair out of place. (Believe me, I know: I was the one waiting for the bathroom.) Hope, fourteen, has perfected the "sophomore slouch"—arms crossed, barely awake, wearing torn jeans and a sweatshirt. Ten-year-old Grace, her hair still wet from swim practice, still wearing her warm-ups, is doodling on the recital program, focused on her own little world.

At first glance, Faith seems aloof, a little standoffish. (She's not.) Hope looks like every other teen, desperate to fit into the adolescent crowd. (Nope.) And Grace appears careless and self-centered. (Wrong again.) Heaven knows they have their faults, and if this devotional were much, much longer I could list them for you. But they're also wonderful, caring and engaging young women, despite their appearance.

I'm roused from my thoughts by the opening chords of George Frideric Handel's "Sarabande." Faith and I had gone through several tête-à-tête conversations the last few weeks as I implored, cajoled and threatened her about practicing more—and here she is, sounding absolutely astounding. And I thought, *Dear God, how often I've made that mistake: so quick to judge, so quick to pigeonhole. Dear God, how easy it is to categorize, how hard it is to understand.* And before Faith has finished the final bars, I say a small, overdue prayer:

Dear God, the only thing I can ask is for forgiveness for my eagerness to cast the first stone.
                                        —MARK COLLINS

SUN *FOR YE ARE ALL ONE IN CHRIST JESUS.*
10   —*Galatians 3:28*

AFTER BEING PART OF ONE parish family in Wyoming for twenty-three years, finding a new church in New Hampshire has been difficult. I raised my four children in that Wyoming parish, and worship, music, baptisms, weddings, funerals, dinners and religious ed classes wove strong connections. Friendships created at church continued to grow in the community; the people at church were also my neighbors.

Not so in New Hampshire, where the town didn't even have a church. A new friend brought me to one she had attended as a child, but the young people there didn't attend my daughter Trina's high school. We drove in a different direction, found a church close to her school, and were welcomed by the familiar faces of students and teachers.

Even after I moved to an apartment ten minutes from work, I continued to drive an hour to that church until soaring gas prices made the trek unreasonable, especially with three churches now within walking distance of my home. A dear friend I'd known for thirty-five years attended one, so I began going to church with her. But I still felt I didn't truly belong.

Then one Sunday after communion, God focused my attention on a prayer I'd been saying: "Thank You for all these people, my church family." Of course! No matter which town or state I worship in, whether the building is nineteenth-century or built last year, whether the parishioners wear formal or casual clothes, when we worship, we are all one family in the Lord. I may feel like a tumbleweed right now but, wow, do I have roots! It will take more than a lifetime to meet all my relatives.

Father of all, keep me mindful of all my brothers and sisters in Christ. —GAIL THORELL SCHILLING

MON
11

*"I WILL GO BEFORE YOU AND MAKE THE
ROUGH PLACES SMOOTH. . . ."*
—*Isaiah 45:2 (NAS)*

"OKAY, EVERYBODY, outta those nice warm beds! You've got square tires this morning!"

It was a jovial disc jockey's way of warning commuters that the weather was extremely cold, traffic would be slow and they had better allow themselves a few extra minutes for defrosting windshields before slowly rumbling along frozen streets on their way to work.

Those of us who live on the Canadian prairie know all about "square tires." At temperatures of twenty-five to thirty degrees below zero, tires become so stiff after a car has been sitting outside overnight that it initially makes for a bumpy ride. After driving a few hundred yards, the rubber becomes flexible again and the ride smoothes out.

I know what it is to get up in the morning and experience a bumpy ride—and not only in a car. This morning was one of those days. I just didn't want to climb out of my warm, cozy bed. Negative thoughts had drifted in that obscured the vision through my spiritual windshield. My tough resistance to a new project made it difficult to shift gears and get going. My rigid insistence of wanting things to go my way made for a square-tire start to my day.

I can tell you what smoothed out the ride though. It was committing my plans and attitude and direction to

God before I ever left the driveway. In reading portions of His Word and remembering His promises, I felt my reluctance thawing out and my spirit warming to whatever He had in store down the road.

Lord, when it comes to Your leading, make me flexible. Amen. —ALMA BARKMAN

 *A SECOND THANK-YOU*
THANK YOU FOR THE
PATIENCE OF PARENTS

TUE
12

LOVE IS PATIENT, LOVE IS KIND. . . .
                        —*I Corinthians 13:4 (NIV)*

EVERY DAY, I SEE HER as I drive by: a woman who follows her young son down Piedmont Road as he delivers the newspapers on his route. He's bundled up in his jacket against the morning cold; she keeps warm inside her car. She's taught her young charge well, I see. He gently places the papers on his customers' porches rather than tossing them on the steps from the street.

I pass them on my way to work the early shift at the Veterans Administration Medical Center in Huntington, West Virginia. I've never met them, yet I feel as if I've known the woman for years. She is my mother, all mothers, all the parents who have lovingly taught their children the beautiful power of work.

I didn't always recognize my mother's gifts, of course. In my young years, when she would drive me to the long-distance customers on my cosmetics route, I sometimes thought she was mean. After all, what decent mother would make her child work when other kids were headed for the swimming pool or the movies? But in the end, I saw that she gave me priceless, lasting gifts: confidence, problem-solving skills, the ability to interact with all kinds of people.

Today, though my mother is in heaven, I thank her once again through my support of children who are learning their way in the world. I joyfully purchase the candy bars, wrapping paper and oranges their schools are selling, hire them to mow my lawn or shovel snow. And as I do, I also say thank you to the patient parents who guide them—sometimes at five o'clock in the morning.

Lord, thank You for parents who show us patience as we learn to work. —ROBERTA MESSNER

WED
13
GIVE EAR, O LORD, UNTO MY PRAYER. . . .
—Psalm 86:6

MY EYES WERE LOCKED on my computer screen, watching a stock that I was preparing to sell for a client. The stock's three-letter symbol was green, indicating that it was up for the day. Three clicks on the keyboard and the stock was sold. *Amazing,* I said to myself. *Technology is truly amazing.*

Thirteen years ago, when I started out as an investment adviser, we didn't rely on e-mail, much less the Internet. When I bought or sold a stock for a client, I had to write out a ticket, walk across the office to stamp it and hand it to our trader, who entered it in a box that was the size of a microwave. Now with my laptop I could access billions of pieces of information and send e-mails to anyone in the world with just a click of a button.

As I sat at my desk, pondering the mysteries of the Internet, my eyes fell on a note I'd made for myself: Pray for Harrison at 1:00 PM. I'd promised my six-year-old son that I'd pray for him while he was taking his spelling test.

I closed my door and hit the COMPOSE button on my e-mail. "Hey, God," I typed, "Harrison's spelling test will start in a few minutes. I hope You can hang close to him and that he'll feel You near." I could imagine my words flying straight to God's ear faster than any e-mail.

Funny thing, technology. As amazing as it is, it doesn't come close to the speed-of-light communication that's been available to humankind since time began.

From my mouth to Your ear, Father, my prayers fly.
—BROCK KIDD

READER'S ROOM

I HAVE BEEN SUFFERING from panic attacks and anxiety for years. I joined a bowling league with a lot of kind, sweet people. It's not easy for me to do this, but I'm stepping out with seeds of faith and letting God do the rest.
—*Denise Pegurri, Holbrook, Massachusetts*

THU
14

Have not I written to thee excellent things . . . ? —*Proverbs 22:20*

I ALWAYS WANTED THE MEN I dated to write me love letters. I'm a writer, after all, and words are important to me. I fantasized about receiving flowery notes expressing the dream of romance I cherished, telling me how much I meant to the man with whom I would spend my life.

Then I met Keith. He was much shorter on words than anyone I'd ever dated; I don't think he'd ever written a letter in his life. But he was good at action.

On our first date, he brought me roses. When I got bronchitis, he brought me soup. He was always concerned about my feelings, and he couldn't do enough for me—except that no matter how much I hinted about his writing me a letter, he just couldn't bring himself to do it. In my heart, I clung to my long-nurtured image of true romance.

After a year, I resigned myself to the inevitable: I'd never get a love letter. Then I had to go out of town on business. I packed my suitcase, and Keith drove me to the airport.

At the conference hotel, I opened the suitcase. On top of my clothes was an index card that read, in Keith's awful handwriting, "I love you." I realized then that he had been giving me love letters all along, only he wrote them with his heart.

Lord, You often know what I need before I do.
—RHODA BLECKER

FRI
15

THEREFORE SHALL YE LAY UP THESE MY WORDS IN YOUR HEART AND IN YOUR SOUL. . . . AND THOU SHALT WRITE THEM UPON THE DOOR POSTS OF THINE HOUSE, AND UPON THY GATES.
—*Deuteronomy 11:18, 20*

SOME YEARS AGO, when my wife and I moved into a new building on Chicago's North Side, I noticed our next-door neighbor touching a small metal object on her doorpost as she left her apartment.

What's that? I wondered.

As weeks passed, we became acquainted, and one

morning over coffee I summoned up the courage to ask about it.

"Oh," she said, putting down her cup, "it's a *mezuzah*. Hebrew for doorpost. Inside is a small scroll of parchment with Scripture from Deuteronomy 6:4–9 and 11:13–21, an affirmation of our faith in God, to keep His words in our minds and hearts, as He commanded."

"*Hmm,*" I said, impressed. "At first I thought it was some kind of security device."

She smiled. "In a way, it is."

Lord, I don't have a mezuzah on my doorway, so remind me, before I step out into the world, to stop a moment to ask You for Your guidance and protection.
— RICHARD SCHNEIDER

SAT
16

"DO NOT FEAR OR BE DISMAYED BECAUSE OF THIS GREAT MULTITUDE, FOR THE BATTLE IS NOT YOURS BUT GOD'S."
—II *Chronicles 20:15* (NAS)

LATELY, I'VE BEEN ASKED to talk to groups of women about my depression. Back in 1994 when my illness began, I promised God that if He'd help me get better, I'd try to help others. I meant one-on-one, not speaking to crowds.

Each time I'm asked to share, I get nervous and clumsy. One Saturday morning at a brunch, I set up my visuals and then, while walking back down the four stage steps, I fell and landed on my bottom. Thank goodness the artificial plants hid me and no one noticed.

See, you can't do this. You can't even walk without falling.

The women at my table made polite conversation and ate their chicken salad. I couldn't eat because my hands were shaking. Someone introduced me, I teetered up those same four shiny wooden steps. *Help me, God. Too many faces are staring at me.*

Then the miracle happened. My hands steadied. I heard my shaky voice become strong. I told my story, and the group laughed and cried with me. Afterward, I asked God, "How could I have felt that I was soaring when earlier I couldn't walk down the steps without stumbling?"

God seemed to say, *You asked me to help, Julie.*

Lord, when I ask You to help, I never have to face any difficulty alone. —JULIE GARMON

SUN
17
NO ONE HAS EVER SEEN GOD; BUT IF WE LOVE ONE ANOTHER, GOD LIVES IN US AND HIS LOVE IS MADE COMPLETE IN US.
—*I John 4:12 (NIV)*

WHEN I WAS A TEENAGER and a new immigrant to Canada, I often felt friendless and unloved. At the time, my family attended a small Sunday school in a community hall in Surrey, British Columbia, conducted by a mailman and his wife.

We older children would arrive early to help Mr. McGladdery shove the benches in place. His wife would deposit her baby on the lap of her oldest daughter and hurry to the dilapidated piano. Then her husband would go to the front of the room, rake his fingers through his hair and announce the first hymn. After we'd sung a few songs, he would give a Bible lesson using simple English words that even we, who struggled with the language, could understand.

"For God so loved the world, that he gave his only begotten Son, that whosoever believeth in him should not perish, but have everlasting life" (John 3:16), he read. Then he said, "Put your name where it says 'the world' and 'whosoever.' God loves each one of you individually, personally."

On Sunday afternoon, my sister and I would often visit the McGladderys. More than once we disturbed their afternoon nap. No matter, they urged us to "come on in." If it was supper time, Mrs. McGladdery would put two more plates on the table and invite us to eat with them. And always, they treated us warmly, as if we were family.

Knowing Mr. and Mrs. McGladdery did more for me than help me find my way in a strange new world. Experiencing their unconditional love on Sunday afternoon made the love of God they proclaimed on Sunday morning all the more real.

Father, I marvel at Your unconditional love, which accepts me as I am. I want to grow in this love and pass it on to others. —HELEN GRACE LESCHEID

MON
18
AND BE NOT CONFORMED TO THIS
WORLD: BUT BE YE TRANSFORMED BY THE
RENEWING OF YOUR MIND, THAT YE MAY
PROVE WHAT IS THAT GOOD, AND
ACCEPTABLE, AND PERFECT, WILL OF GOD.
—Romans 12:2

JESUS' FIRST DISCIPLES, Peter and Andrew, would probably have smiled at the bumper sticker I saw the other day. I'D RATHER BE FISHING, it said. You'll recall what Jesus said to the two when He saw them casting their nets: "Follow me, and I will make you fishers of men" (Matthew 4:19).

Legends that people put on their cars or the imprints on their T-shirts say a lot about what's on their minds. Some things are funny, some gross, some political, some organizational, some religious, like WWJD—What Would Jesus Do? The Gospels give us a good idea about the answer, most of the time. But on some issues, people disagree.

Abraham Lincoln noted that knowing where God is on some issues takes a good deal of cogitating. During the Civil War, an opponent of the president suggested that God was not on Lincoln's side.

Lincoln's answer: "My concern is to be on God's side, for God is always right."

How can we ascertain God's will? I've always been told to discuss issues with others, to study the Bible and to pray for God's guidance. My difficult questions are usually resolved that way.

Direct us, God, when we face a tough decision,
Give us wisdom, give us courage, give us vision.

—FRED BAUER

A WAY THROUGH THE WAVES

TWO YEARS AGO, Roberta Rogers and her family faced a series of events that threatened to overwhelm them. Join Roberta over the next week as she shares the ways in which the bonds of friendship, the power of prayer

and the mighty hand of God brought her
through the floodwaters to dry land.
—THE EDITORS

FLOOD TIDE

TUE
19
*"WHEN CALAMITY OVERTAKES YOU LIKE
A STORM, WHEN DISASTER SWEEPS OVER
YOU LIKE A WHIRLWIND. . . ."*
—*Proverbs 1:27 (NIV)*

IT CAME ON OUR FAMILY like a tsunami, a series of
events that left us gasping for respite.

The first wave began on November 22. In the
morning, our son Peter called to say he had just been
given the "stay behind" slot as his reserve unit left for
Iraq, and a photographer from *Sports Illustrated* came
to my mom's assisted-care facility to photograph the
two of us for an upcoming story on Red Sox fans.
These were grand things. But late that night I sensed
the first rumble: "Mom," our son Tom said when I
answered the phone, "Susan was carjacked at gun-
point this evening."

As it turned out, November 22 was to be Mom's
last day up. On December 10, she died, after thor-
oughly enjoying her "fifteen minutes of fame." On
January 5, Susan, six and a half months pregnant with
our first grandchild, was admitted to the hospital, her
contractions growing. On January 8, our son John's
wife of barely a year moved out, leaving us all devas-

tated. On January 11, Tom called us just before mid-night: "Congratulations, you have a grandson! We've named him William John Rogers and nicknamed him Jack. He weighs three pounds, nine ounces. He cried when he was born, which is a great sign. He's off to a good start." Then, on January 30, Bill and I arrived at his mother's assisted-care facility to be told that she had died just a few minutes before. The last wave had crashed.

But in the losses and worries, we began to find trea-sures—the greatest of them were people, both known and unknown to us, who would pray us all the way through into calmer waters.

Thank You, Lord, for the living strength of prayer and the love that sustains us in times of crisis. I think of _____ who desperately needs Your
(INSERT NAME.)
touch right now. —ROBERTA ROGERS

JACK'S FAN CLUB

WED
20

BROTHERS, PRAY FOR US.
—*I Thessalonians 5:25 (NIV)*

"JACK'S FAN CLUB" WAS A LIST of e-mail addresses I used to keep "replying to all." It was children, cousins, brothers, nieces and a nephew, neighbors, friends as far away as Cambodia and Papua New Guinea—all talking to God about us and about a small boy in the NICU (Neonatal Intensive Care Unit) in Atlanta. I felt every single one of those prayers as we struggled through the days and nights of January, February and March.

While my husband Bill and I in Virginia made plans to memorialize our mothers, our daughter-in-law Susan virtually lived at the NICU. Our son Tom divided his time between his job and the hospital. His employer kindly kept his travel to a minimum and told him to be there for his wife and son first. Every evening as he drove home from the hospital, Tom updated us in his tired voice: "Well, two steps forward, one back . . ." And I would send out the "reply to all" e-mail late that night, knowing that all I could pray was "Help us, Lord." I knew our prayers would rise as sweet incense before God's throne and His answers would be free to waft over us.

How do I know that everyone was praying? Well, through three surgeries plus all the usual problems a premature baby can face, Jack showed all the healthy signs too: He figured out how to pull the oxygen-push canula out of his nose, and his hands had to be mittened; his eyes clearly focused on his mother's face; he was stoic at the pricks of IV and blood needles, and fussed like any baby when they tried to bathe him.

And while all this was going on, I, his grandmother five hundred miles away, slept at night. I, who do not sleep all that well in the best of times, slept.

Thank You, Lord, for the small and great miracles prayers bring. —ROBERTA ROGERS

WELCOME HOME

THU 21

"YOU SHALL LIVE IN THE REGION OF GOSHEN AND BE NEAR ME—YOU, YOUR CHILDREN AND GRANDCHILDREN. . . ."
—*Genesis 45:10 (NIV)*

ON A COLD FEBRUARY DAY, still over a month away from what had been his due date, our grandson Jack endured his third surgery. Now the doctors would wait and see if he could digest food normally. They told Tom and Susan that if all went perfectly and Jack reached five pounds, he might go home by the last day of March. But on March 10, Tom called his dad and me, joy and panic mixing in his voice: "The doctor says we can bring Jack home in two days!"

With his prayer groups behind him, Jack had simply surpassed the best estimates. He ate and ate and gained and gained. He charmed his NICU nurses, smiled at his weary mother and firmly held his father's finger. His blood work and breathing and all the other tests were where they needed to be. The doctors found no reason to keep him any longer.

"We're pushing to have a monitor to bring home," Tom added. We could tell that the monitor, which the doctor said they didn't need to bother with, was really for Tom and Susan, to keep their hearts pumping evenly without worrying if Jack's was.

Bill and I turned to smile at each other. Jack was a baby now, not a "preemie," and he was about to make our son and his wife into a family, just as one January morning thirty-some years before, Bill and I had stood in our kitchen, heavy winter coats still on, and stared down at bundled sleeping Tom and marveled and wondered and worried.

Lord, thank You for grandchildren as they pull us backward and forward in time. —ROBERTA ROGERS

EDITOR'S NOTE: We invite you to join us one month from today, on March 21, as we pray for all the needs of our Guideposts family at the thirty-eighth annual Guideposts Good Friday Day of Prayer. Send your prayer requests to Good Friday Day of Prayer, 66 E. Main St., Pawling, NY 12564.

SURPRISED BY JOY

FRI

22

AND GOD SHALL WIPE AWAY ALL TEARS FROM THEIR EYES. —*Revelation 7:17*

THE YEAR OF OUR FAMILY TSUNAMI, we also had a series of family celebrations. In early February, we all met in Ohio to remember the ninety-year-long life of Bill's mother Marian. Tom left Susan and still-hospitalized Jack in Atlanta. David and Matti drove up from Fort Knox, Tennessee—David on leave from a special assignment. Peter (who was the only one in his reserve unit not in Iraq) flew in from Cape Cod and my brother Nat from New York. We used a cousin's summer house to hang out and be a family, taking a drive around the places lived in first by Bill as a child, then us as newlyweds, then the boys in their younger years, filling in memories together.

In mid-June, we all met again in Connecticut to memorialize my mother Kathryn. This time we rented a suite at a hotel where we could all meet, eat, laugh, cry and remember. We even had a fancy dinner with whatever friends could join us. Susan stayed at home in Atlanta with Jack, still too small to travel. Cousins I hadn't seen in years, but who had reconnected with us as part of Jack's fan club, became instant hits with our sons, who had never known them before.

On a Friday night in late August, our son John took us to an elegant restaurant for our fortieth wedding anniversary. As we sat in the lounge awaiting our table, my cell phone rang. It was Tom's number. "We have arranged a special delivery for you, but it's outside on the porch!"

When we went out, looking for flowers or balloons, there was nothing there. Then, laughing, out from behind the bushes came David . . . Matti . . . Peter . . . my brother Nat . . . Tom . . . Susan . . . and Jack.

Oh, Lord, how kind, how wonderful You are to grant such joy after such sorrow! —ROBERTA ROGERS

SAT
23
FOR EVERYTHING THERE IS A SEASON, AND A TIME FOR EVERY MATTER UNDER HEAVEN . . . A TIME TO KEEP, AND A TIME TO CAST AWAY.
—*Ecclesiastes 3:1, 6* (RSV)

NOT LONG AFTER I TURNED FIFTY and was getting rid of stuff I hadn't used in years, my father told me I was experiencing a new phase in psychological development. "When you hit fifty," he told me, "you seek simplification."

"Is that what I'm doing?" I asked, giving him a sideways glance while debating whether to keep an autographed book from a friend to whom I no longer sent Christmas cards.

In the three years since, I've often experienced this "urge to purge." I've gotten rid of kitchen gadgets, Easter decorations, lawn furniture. When I sold my house, I threw out bookcases, furniture and dishes I once cherished.

Then I began to worry. Was simplification nothing more than the discovery of meaninglessness in everything I once enjoyed?

Last week, my three-year-old grandson Rome squirmed onto his big beanbag, with blue blankie and thumb, excited to watch his new *Dora* show.

Suddenly, out came his thumb. Frowning, he said to his mother, "Mama, I'm not sucking my thumb very well today."

I laughed. Rome was growing up. What used to bring him pleasure and meaning no longer did.

I went home feeling reassured. I'd get over this urge to purge and get on with my own "psychological development" too. I would learn to find pleasure in my new need for simplicity.

Dear God, keep me growing, keep me learning, keep me loving, keep me focused on You, Whom I will never outgrow. —BRENDA WILBEE

SUN
24
TRAIN UP A CHILD IN THE WAY HE SHOULD GO: AND WHEN HE IS OLD, HE WILL NOT DEPART FROM IT.
—Proverbs 22:6

WHEN I TAUGHT FIFTH GRADERS in Sunday school, I was always looking for a way to make a lesson more interesting. For instance, I wanted them to see how dependent they were on the people in their lives— brothers, sisters, parents, friends, teachers, coaches. I wrote those words on some building blocks. Then I instructed my students to build a tower out of the blocks. "Make it as tall as you can," I said. They stacked the blocks so high they had to stand on chairs to finish. "Now," I said, "take one out." Which would it be? Friend? Sister? Brother? Teacher? I didn't have to say anything. The children saw how the building blocks stood together—or they fell.

There were other lessons I tried to pass along, but one of my biggest challenges came the day a boy showed up in clothes that were ragged and very dated. I could tell that the other students were snickering at him. How could I get them to see that we were all children of God, no matter what we looked like?

"Take a piece of paper," I said, "and draw a house on a hill." For fifteen minutes they worked quietly with great focus. When they'd finished, I spread their work out on the table and they studied the drawings. Some houses were big, some small, some stood alone, some were surrounded by trees. "Which one is right?" I asked.

There was a long pause. "Mr. Greene," one lad said, "they're all right. They're just different."

"Yes," I replied. "Aren't we all?"

Show me the way, Lord, to show others the way.
—OSCAR GREENE

MON
25

THOU SHALT LOVE THY NEIGHBOUR AS THYSELF. . . . —Leviticus 19:18

SOMEDAY OUR AGING apartment building might get new plumbing that would allow owners to have their own washing machines, but I can only think of that prospect with a great sense of loss. I would miss our communal laundry room.

We have to walk down two flights of stairs, through the basement, then outside and down another flight of stairs to do our wash. Of course, it's not very convenient. Some days I've found myself dashing through a rainstorm to keep a bag of clean laundry from getting wet. In the summer the room can get steaming hot, and in the winter you need a sweater. And it's not always very tidy.

But it's the one place I know I can run into my neighbors and get a bit of news. I'll find out how Lauren's daughter is doing on her medical mission trip to Africa and how Roger's mother's health has been. Crystal will recommend a good book to read, and Margo will let me know how she's getting on with the book she's writing (only three more chapters to go!). Margaret and I, while folding, will compare notes on our churches and our children (guitar lessons going well, French homework not so good).

In the heart of this big and supposedly cold city of New York, going to the laundry room is like gathering around the old cracker barrel in a general store or seeing folks at the post office. It's what helps me follow the Golden Rule. Without it, I wouldn't know my neighbors so well or know how to love them. Washing, drying, sorting, folding—we get our washday chance to connect.

God bless my neighbors. —RICK HAMLIN

 *GIVE US THIS DAY*
A REASON TO SMILE

TUE
26 *"LET LIGHT SHINE OUT OF
DARKNESS"....*
—II Corinthians 4:6 (NIV)

"OMA, EVERYBODY WILL THINK we look so pretty!" my three-year-old granddaughter Gabi exclaims as we sit together on a bench in front of a big mirror in my bedroom, putting on our wigs—iridescent blue wigs.

Gabi doesn't know it, but our giggly little dress-up session is helping me through an extremely difficult life transition. I've lost most of my hair because of chemotherapy for my ovarian cancer, and I'm trying to get used to wearing a wig. Yet, even around my family, I feel terribly self-conscious.

I don't know why the hair loss was so hard. I suppose it's because my hair was one place where I had a sense of control. Cut it—or not. Wash it—or not. Color it—for sure! And when I lost control over what was going on inside my body, somehow this attack on the outside seemed especially harsh.

"My prayer is that you'll walk this journey in your own unique way," a friend told me. We both knew what she meant. "My way" meant finding something to smile about, some way to lighten up the dark, hard places.

So when I bought a couple of look-just-like-me

wigs, I also purchased an outrageous blue one. Gabi's mother bought her one, too, knowing that this three-year-old might help me find something to smile about as I faced this transition.

Now here we are, sitting in front of the mirror, trying on our wigs and giggling as we imagine making a grand entrance into the kitchen where the rest of the family has gathered.

"Do you think we need some blue eye shadow?" I ask Gabi, who scrunches up her shoulders and nods. Finally, we're ready, and we parade down the hall and into the kitchen. *"Ta-da!"*

"Ohhhhhh . . . pretty!" everyone exclaims in unison.

Gabi doubles over, laughing so hard she can't walk. So I pick her up and together we twirl around the room, feeling very proud and pretty in our sassy blue wigs.

Lord, thank You that laughter helps lighten up the dark places on a difficult journey.

—CAROL KUYKENDALL

WED
27

HUMBLE YOURSELVES BEFORE THE LORD, AND HE WILL LIFT YOU UP.
—*James 4:10 (NIV)*

ONE DAY, AS I PULLED into our garage, I was silently congratulating myself for running a successful church committee meeting. When I pushed the button to automatically close the garage door, it wouldn't work. I got out of the car to pull down the door by hand. *Crash!* It fell heavily to the cement floor.

The next day when my teenage son John and I were leaving for Scouts, I tried to pull up the door. It wouldn't budge. John got out to help, and we both pulled as hard as we could with no luck. Finally, John made a mighty effort and managed to open it. It was time to call a repairman.

The repairman pointed to a huge rusted coil and explained, "You have a broken spring. A double garage door like that weighs 225 pounds. When the spring's working properly, it eases the door open and closed, and it feels like you're only lifting a few pounds. You never realize how much the door weighs because it seems so easy to lift."

That day I learned something about garage doors. And I also learned something about myself: I'm not as good as I think I am at heavy lifting. Usually when I accomplish something like a successful church committee meeting, I assume I did it through my own efforts. But it's really God who does all of the heavy lifting, opening and closing the doors I couldn't possibly manage by myself.

God, thank You that You're always behind the scenes, lifting me up when I don't even realize it.

—KAREN BARBER

THU
28

. . . A guide to the blind, a light to those who are in darkness.
—*Romans 2:19 (NAS)*

GETTING AROUND IN NEW YORK CITY is difficult for me. I don't have to do it often, but when I do I'm always apprehensive. *What if I get lost? What if I miss a connection? What if there's no one to ask for directions? What if everyone moves faster than I do and I get left behind?* But recently I had to confront a new fear: riding the subway.

I was with a small group of people, but still it felt daunting. My MetroCard wouldn't work at the turnstile, and I held up the impatient line. Then the train swooshed to a stop and people rushed on like a human tidal wave. They looked grim and confident. *How do they do this every day?* My apprehension increased.

As the doors shut and I found a seat, I noticed a glorious German shepherd right across from me. It was a guide dog, and its master's hand rested securely on its harness. I studied it, amazed. Its massive head rested on crossed paws as though it were relaxing on a comfortable rug in front of a fireplace.

The train stopped abruptly and more people crowded on, some of them standing within inches of the dog's feet. The dog didn't even glance up. As the train stopped at station after station and the doors opened and shut again and again, the dog yawned, until at one particular stop it stood up. The young

man stood up, too, and as he held on to the dog's harness, they calmly exited the train and disappeared into
the crowd.

*Lord Jesus, show me how to place my hand in Yours, so
You can guide me through my fears.*
                                        —MARION BOND WEST

FRI
29
*CERTAINLY THIS IS THE DAY WE LOOKED
FOR; WE HAVE FOUND, WE HAVE SEEN
IT. —Lamentations 2:16*

TOO OFTEN, WHEN MY "to do" pile
threatens to topple, I excuse my inefficiency with "I
could get caught up on all these tasks if I just had an
extra day!"

Well, today is that day—a whole extra twenty-four
hours to spend as I please! It's one of those every-
four-year days inserted in our calendar to compen-
sate for the quarter-day difference between man-made
years and astronomical ones.

I must confess that as a senior citizen, I've had more
complementary extra days than those who haven't
reached my age. In fact, I've even had a few freebies
that can't be attributed to leap year but instead to
crossing the international date line. On one of those
trips, I even had two birthdays when one February 17
came back-to-back with another. But that gained
day was "lost" on the return a week later when

February 23 jumped to 25, so I can't really count that as an extra.

So what will I do with today's gift of twenty-four hours? I wonder if, by midnight tonight, I'll tell myself, *I got my "to do" list done!* Or will it be, *I can't believe I wasted all that time!*

Thank goodness, Lord, for the time You give me that I can spend just with You. —ISABEL WOLSELEY

MY DIVINE SURPRISES

1 _____

2 _____

3 _____

4 _____

5 _____

6 _____

7 _____

8 _____

9 _____

10 _____

11 _____

12 _____

13 _____

14 _____

15 _____

16 _____

17 _____

18 _____

19 _____

20 _____

21 _____

22 _____

23 _____

24 _____

25 _____

26 _____

27 _____

28 _____

29 _____

March

T he Lord hath made known his salvation:
his righteousness hath he openly shewed. . . .

—Psalm 98:2

SAT   *If I must boast, I will boast of the*

I   *things that show my weakness.*
                        —II Corinthians 11:30 (RSV)

NOELLE, MY EIGHT-YEAR-OLD daughter, is in ballet class. She is learning *relevés*, *pliés* and *ronds de jambe*. The little girls cross arms and join hands and then amble left to right and right to left. Tiptoeing, aware of their posture and position, with their heads held high, they create as much beauty as their little bodies will allow. Truthfully, it's mostly a chaotic swirl of bodies in motion, but it sure is cute.

There is one girl in the class who, even though she's dressed in a leotard that perfectly matches the others, doesn't blend in. Lindsey is in a walker. Her hands clutch the handles tightly. Her legs don't allow her to do even the simplest dance step. She is assisted by a young woman who moves her from place to place, and oftentimes that is simply out of the way of the others.

After class, Noelle sat on the floor with the other girls, chatting, taking off their ballet shoes, putting on sweaters, stuffing dance clothes into their bags. Meanwhile, Lindsey was being tended to by her caregiver.

Today, Lindsey might not have performed a soaring *jeté*. But in a sense, I think she did. She took an art form defined by the long lines of an extended leg, the poetry of a turned wrist and a lighter-than-a-feather gallop across the stage, and said that that definition didn't apply to her. And so, with a piano clanging in the room, her leotard on, mirrors in all directions, girls flowing all around her, Lindsey stood in one place, not moving an inch, and in a way known only to her, danced.

Lord, no matter what my limitations, give me the courage to try. —DAVE FRANCO

SUN
2

EACH OF YOU SHOULD LOOK NOT ONLY TO YOUR OWN INTERESTS, BUT ALSO TO THE INTERESTS OF OTHERS.
—*Philippians 2:4 (NIV)*

"WE NEED VOLUNTEERS to sign up to help build our next Habitat for Humanity home," the minister announced.

Why should I help build a house for someone else when I don't even have my own home yet? I asked myself. I'd been trying to buy a house for a while. I still hadn't found one that I wanted that fit into my price range.

That afternoon I attended a women's prayer circle at church. A young lady shared her story. "I'd been trying to have a child," she said. "After a few years I became quite discouraged. I prayed daily for God to help me deal with my disappointment. A friend suggested I join her in a local project to crochet knit caps for premature babies to wear at the hospital. I balked at the idea. I even stopped volunteering in the church nursery. But she was persistent. Eventually I started crocheting little pink and blue caps." She paused for a moment and looked across the room. "One day while crocheting I found myself praying for the moms and for those tiny babies. I realized that my own disappointment was finally gone."

Eventually the woman did have a baby, born a month early. "Imagine my surprise," she said, "when the nurse brought me my little girl and she was wearing one of the preemie caps I had crocheted!"

After the meeting I walked to the church office. I dug around in my purse for a pen and signed up to help build a house for someone else.

Gracious God, grow within me a generous heart, ever mindful that it is in giving that we receive.
—MELODY BONNETTE

UNEXPECTED BLESSINGS

CHANGING THE FOCUS

MON
3

RETURN, O MY SOUL, TO YOUR REST; FOR THE LORD HAS DEALT BOUNTIFULLY WITH YOU. —*Psalm 116:7 (RSV)*

IT WAS A DARK, end-of-winter day in early March with a cold drizzle falling on the grimy remnants of a snowstorm. Four blocks from the dentist's office, I finally found a parking place—and stepped ankle-deep into the slush. I didn't have quarters for the meter and had to cross the street to a sandwich shop to get change. Hurrying to the medical building—it was now 11:10 and my appointment was for 11:00—I fretted as the elevator crawled to the fourth floor, then I rushed down the hall.

The dentist's office was closed.

I stood in front of that locked door, nursing a string of grievances. Whether the mistake was mine or the appointment secretary's, it had cost me a long drive, a wasted morning and soaked shoes! I took the slow-moving elevator down to the ladies' room on the first floor to get some paper towels.

At the sink, a young woman was crying.

Her clothes were drenched, her body shaking with cold. Between her limited English and my still more limited Spanish, I managed to discover that she'd come in to get warm after waiting at the bus stop for more than an hour.

As I drove her to her rooming house, she told me about going every morning to the immigration office, only to be told, "Come back tomorrow." But mostly she talked about her joy at being reunited with her husband, who'd been here alone for three years, and about their great good fortune in sharing a room with only one other couple.

As I went back to my own husband and our many-roomed home, the only grievance left was my own irritation at trifles.

Bestower of blessing, lift my eyes from the anthills of petty annoyances to the mountain range of Your bounty. —ELIZABETH SHERRILL

TUE
4

THEN SAID JESUS, FATHER, FORGIVE THEM; FOR THEY KNOW NOT WHAT THEY DO. . . . —*Luke 23:34*

I RECENTLY HEARD A WOMAN stand up in court and say this to the man who had murdered her daughter: "I forgive you. I refuse to let you haunt my heart any longer, and I choose to let you go into God's hands.

"You took my daughter. Not a moment will go by for the rest of my life without me yearning to touch my sweet child and hear her voice and her laugh and her thoughts and dreams. Not a second. You stole her from me, from her father and her brother, from the hundreds of people who loved her and the thousands more who would have loved her.

"But I forgive you, because I will not let you steal my life also. I pray that God will forgive you. I pray for your healing. I pray for your wife, for your parents, for your sister. I pray for those who can never forgive you.

"It has taken me four long years to say these words, but I will not have you in my mind or my heart one minute longer. I hand you to God. You are God's child and in Him is forgiveness and peace beyond my understanding. I commend you to Him. My sweet baby girl will stay with me in my heart until I die and see her again, and I *will* see her again, I know that beyond the shadow of a doubt, but I will never see or think of you again, for I give you to God. Amen."

There was not a whisper or a rustle for what seemed like years after she sat down.

O God, O Father, forgive us, help us, hold us in Your hands, soothe and salve that mother, keep that young woman in Your love, heal that twisted man. And please, never ever let me forget the way a woman forgave a man the unforgivable. —BRIAN DOYLE

WED
5
"GO! I AM SENDING YOU OUT LIKE LAMBS AMONG WOLVES. DO NOT TAKE A PURSE OR BAG OR SANDALS; AND DO NOT GREET ANYONE ON THE ROAD."
—*Luke 10:3–4 (NIV)*

DRIVING DOWN Highway 98 in Anne Arundel County, Maryland, on the way to my job at the Defense Information School, panic finally hit me. As the trees and the stripes on the road ticked by, it came to me that I only had one more day as an instructor. The next day I would leave my secure position—the one from which I thought I would retire—to follow a new career.

How will I live? What about my kids? I have no savings. I won't make it a month!

Though an office mate had been teasing me for weeks about my bold decision, I'd been unwavering in my resolve. I felt called—this would be my missionary journey, my opportunity to be an ambassador of reconciliation. But in these last five minutes before I arrived at work, my heart began to pound. Suddenly, I thought about withdrawing my resignation.

Just as suddenly, a man's voice interrupted the children's program I was listening to on the radio. "I have an urgent message," he said.

Great! Not only was he interrupting my personal worry session, he was doing it during a program I loved. If my life were going to crash and burn, I should at least be able to listen to the radio without interference.

"The Lord is concerned about His ministers of reconciliation." I forgot to be irritated. "You are precious in His sight, and as He takes care of the birds in the air, He has promised to care for you."

That was seven years ago. Though there have been some moments since then that have challenged my family and me on this missionary journey, I'm still at it and my children are thriving. We're still here.

God, help me to trust Your provision and Your love.
—SHARON FOSTER

THU
6
EVEN A FOOL, WHEN HE HOLDETH HIS PEACE, IS COUNTED WISE: AND HE THAT SHUTTETH HIS LIPS IS ESTEEMED A MAN OF UNDERSTANDING. —*Proverbs 17:28*

SINCE I HAD MY STROKE several years ago, things have not been quite the same, principally with my speech. At first, no one could understand me. Visitors acted as though they did, nodding their heads and smiling patiently. Gradually my words became clearer and I could join in a limited conversation. Limited it remains.

I can greet you, but remembering your name is touch-and-go. I can get along well with ordinary polite phrases, and the telephone is possible if not too much is asked of me. I can even tell a story when the audience is quiet and sees me through, but forget any elaborate, detailed discussion. It's in a group that I have difficulty. Early in the conversation my friends are careful to listen to me, then they forget and somehow I am left out. But I've learned something nevertheless.

My friend Daniel was taking a graduate course in English and was having trouble with an assignment. He spent an entire evening reading it to me, making comments when he didn't understand certain passages. All I did was sit and look attentive. The next day, he told me, "Thank you for helping me understand the rough spots. Your listening to me was a godsend."

Listening? What else could I have done? But then if my listening was valuable to Daniel, why not to others? Since then, I've let the conversation swirl around me as I've tackled what it takes to be a good listener. Here are some of the points I've had to work at: certainly patience; genuine concern for my talker's problem; and above all, as the Bible says, "Judge not."

Father, I, too, have learned the power of silence.
— VAN VARNER

FRI
7
MAY HE GIVE YOU THE DESIRE OF YOUR HEART AND MAKE ALL YOUR PLANS SUCCEED. —*Psalm 20:4 (NIV)*

LAST WINTER I FOUND MYSELF at a shopping mall in the foothills of the Rocky Mountains, searching for clothes to fit my shoestring budget. As I carried a pair of socks (on sale, two dollars) to the checkout counter, an advertisement for a contest caught my eye.

"Tell us your dream!" it said. *"We'll pay for it!"*

At that time there were several months remaining in the ski racing season, and I was nearly broke. But I did have a dream of going to the Paralympics—that's why I was racing. So I grabbed a brochure for the contest, paid for my socks and headed out to my car for the long trip back up to the mountains where I train. When I got home, I wrote an essay for the contest, committing my dream to paper—and prayer.

Time went by, and when I hadn't heard anything, I assumed I hadn't won the contest. But I did make the Paralympics team, and I managed to travel to Torino, Italy, to compete there. Three days before I was going to fly back to the States, I got a call from the clothing company. I had won the contest, but more importantly, I'd already gotten the chance to follow my dream.

Lord, You are the dream giver. Thank You for putting these desires in my heart. —Joshua Sundquist

SAT
8

To all perfection I see a limit; but
your commands are boundless.
                              —*Psalm 119:96 (NIV)*

As I got older, I realized my thighs weren't what they used to be. Not only had they mysteriously become broader (translation: fatter) and less firm, they were now noticeably mottled with what doctors told me were "spider veins," a purple and red filigree of capillaries close to the surface of my pale skin. The spider veins were medically nonthreatening, probably hereditary, but as I one day surveyed the feathery patterns of magenta on my legs, it occurred to me, *Maybe this doesn't look so great to other people.* Many of my athletic relatives and friends, when in bathing suits and hiking shorts, had legs that were tanned and firm. Not me. Flickers of self-consciousness set in.

One weekend I went for a sleepover with my goddaughter Linnea, who was around five at the time. Still in our nightshirts, we sat on the bed and colored with felt-tipped pens. Our markers squeaked along on the pages of coloring books; we produced original compositions. Then Linnea stopped. "What's that?" she asked. She pointed at the patterns on my legs.

"Some people get them when they're older," I said. "Little veins just beneath your skin." I was about to add, "I know it's not very pretty," but Linnea's attention had turned to choosing different colored markers.

I resumed my squeaky coloring, but Linnea's pens took on a softer sound. I looked over to see her drawing lines on the skin of her own legs. Concentrating and serious, she drew squiggles of purple, burnt orange, brick red. "Linnea, what are you doing?"

"I want marks like you have. I like them."

Dear God, help me to disregard my vanity and see my "imperfections" in a new way.

—MARY ANN O'ROARK

SUN

9

BE OF GOOD COURAGE, AND DO IT.

—Ezra 10:4

THE SUNDAY-SCHOOL LESSON TODAY was about taking risks. In the course of the hour, the class cited examples of Bible characters who took a chance: Abraham, who followed God's command to "leave your country . . . and go to the land I will show you" (Genesis 12:1, NIV); David, who stepped forward to battle the giant Goliath; Moses, who courageously led the Israelites out of Egypt; Daniel, who defied a king and risked death in the lions' den; and Peter, who left his boat when Jesus called him to walk on the water.

The common thread in each of these stories is trust in God. What keeps us from acting when we face challenges? Sometimes we aren't sure that it's God's voice we're hearing and we hesitate. Sometimes we're afraid that we'll fail or look ridiculous, fearful of what others will think. But when it becomes clear that God wants us to go in a certain direction and we don't, that's disobedience. Noah's neighbors probably thought he was nuts when he started building an ark. A flood? Forget about it. Jonah heard God's call, disobeyed and became fish food.

What is God calling you to do today? To make some change in your life that will demand courage? Prayer is always my first port of call when tough decisions are required. Speaking of ports, I'm reminded of the seafarers' axiom that observes, "Man was not made for safe harbors." Or as a friend of mine says upon leaving, instead of "Take care," "Take risks."

Lord, renew us even as we grow old,
Give us a zest for life and make us bold.
—FRED BAUER

MON
10

"HOW CAN YOU SAY TO YOUR BROTHER, 'LET ME TAKE THE SPECK OUT OF YOUR EYE,' WHEN ALL THE TIME THERE IS A PLANK IN YOUR OWN EYE?"
—*Matthew 7:4 (NIV)*

I PICKED UP LAST NIGHT before going to bed. Honestly, I did. The children have only been up for an hour, so I've no idea how the file cabinet got covered in plastic animals or what the biology book is doing in the kitchen or when the fourteen-car pileup occurred on the living room carpet.

I am not a neatnik; my standards aren't stratospheric. I want things tidy enough that we can function and avoid major injury. I dole out chores, we vacuum daily, the kids pick up their rooms almost every night. But our apartment always looks as if it hasn't been cleaned in weeks.

Perhaps this is simply the fate of seven people living in five rooms. Perhaps it's because we race out the door—to ballet, to math group, to choir, to church, to something—every day of the week. I could put some of the blame on homeschooling: science experiments and pattern blocks and phonics workbooks do make a mess. Whatever the excuse, trust me: At the end of the day, it's clear this house is inhabited.

People tell me that there will be a time when I'll be wistful for the tiny blocks that now cripple me when I go into the boys' room at night. That's remotely possible. But one day there will be no one left to blame except my husband and me for the mess that's still here. Then I'll have to come clean and admit that my half-read book is among those on the sofa and my coffee cup is next to the computer. It might just be easier to pick up toys. Facing my own shortcomings is a lot harder than tackling someone else's.

Is that a speck of dust, Lord, that keeps getting in my eye? Or is it something bigger? —JULIA ATTAWAY

TUE
11

NOW HE WHO PLANTS AND HE WHO WATERS ARE ONE. . . .
—*I Corinthians 3:8* (NKJV)

I GREW UP NEAR FORT WAYNE, Indiana, where the fabled John "Johnny Appleseed" Chapman is buried, and I have long admired his life.

Apples were not just snacks in early America. They were vital food for people and cattle. They were also used for making preservatives like vinegar and for a variety of drinks, because water supplies were not always good. Foods like applesauce and apple butter were as common as soda and chips today. Even the dead apple tree was used for making furniture.

Johnny Appleseed didn't just walk around, throwing seeds here and there, the way some children's books picture him. Rather, he carried apple saplings and planted nurseries along the frontier trails, where farmers could find them and start their own orchards. As he traveled, he passed out Bibles and Gospel tracts, plus toys for children. He advised farmers about soil management and horticulture. No wonder the heartland is still alive with orchards and farms, families and churches.

Some people have a knack for starting things. Like Johnny Appleseed, they know how to get people interested in positive projects. I admire that kind of person, the kind who stands up at a City Hall meeting and says, "Let's build a park for our children to keep them off the streets." The kind of person who knocks on my door and says, "I'm taking a collection for the little girl who has cancer. Can you help?"

Our potential for good is incalculable, but it is often wasted because no one wants to be the one to say, "Let's do this!" I want to be that kind of person.

Lord, there is so much to do, but I'm sometimes paralyzed by the size of the task. Help me to begin and to trust You for assistance. —DANIEL SCHANTZ

WED
12
THEREFORE, SINCE WE ARE
SURROUNDED BY SUCH A GREAT CLOUD
OF WITNESSES . . . LET US RUN WITH
PERSEVERANCE THE RACE MARKED OUT
FOR US. —*Hebrews 12:1 (NIV)*

I DO NOT SEW. Not even a little bit. But I lost buttons this week—from my coat, my jeans and my favorite sweater—and I have to try.

I stand on a stool and stretch to reach Grandmother's sewing basket on the top shelf of the guest closet. I pull back the lid and see bright spools of thread lining the bottom in colorful disarray. *"Always keep a good supply of thread laid by, so you can match your cloth."* Grandmother's voice is so clear I want to turn to see if she is peeking over my shoulder.

I settle into my reading chair and begin to thread my needle. I can almost feel Mother's hand on mine, guiding it toward that silver sliver's eye—the way she did the summer I was eight and tried to make clothes for my doll. After a few initial fumblings, my needle slips in and out of the buttons, attaching them securely. Suddenly, my hand becomes my sister's as she sews rows of buttons on the sleeve of my wedding gown—a gown she made for me by cutting up her own wedding dress.

Later, as I tuck the sewing basket back on that remote shelf, I feel connected to the women in my family in a way I haven't in a long time; connected to their resourcefulness, patience, generosity. And if my clumsy attempts with a needle and thread are what prompts this closeness, I'm almost eager for my next loose button!

Thank You, Lord, for the threads that bind me to my past and to those I love. May I learn from them even now. —MARY LOU CARNEY

READER'S ROOM

I'VE ALWAYS FELT joy at the sight and sound of the red-tailed hawk.

I'm going through radiation for breast cancer. I walk in the woods daily to stay strong: mind, body and soul. I decided that the red-tailed hawk would be my sign of hope. One day I was emotionally and physically drained. As I pushed myself to walk, I prayed, "God, I could really use my sign of hope."

Right then a red-tailed hawk swooped down in front of me. A godsend. Since then, a red-tailed hawk has been perching on a post outside my window from time to time—a reminder of hope and a gift from God. —*Joanna Bordner, Cutler, Indiana*

THU
13
"IF YOU GREET ONLY YOUR BROTHERS, WHAT ARE YOU DOING MORE THAN OTHERS? DO NOT EVEN PAGANS DO THAT?" —Matthew 5:47 (NIV)

"HEY, RUG! HEY, RUG!" That's what Lil, an older homeless woman on my block calls my shaggy cocker spaniel Sally. Sally is usually willing to give Lil a friendly sniff and a wag of her stumpy tail as she goes about her morning business. For me, it's a little more complicated. Sometimes Lil asks for money. Since I know she will spend it on drink, I try not to give in, though my wife likes to say she hopes Lil spends her dollar on food. Sometimes I'll buy her a muffin in the store where I get my morning paper. Sometimes I break down and give her the change in my pocket.

Then there are times like the other day, when it was raining and I was running late and Sally was not co-operating, that I simply walked on by, head down, tugging on Sally's leash, not seeing the woman huddled under the dry cleaner's awning.

I never feel good about this. I tell myself I can't always stop, I can't always help. But too often the unsettled feeling stays with me. And then I remember what an aunt of mine used to say. It was important to be smart, Aunt Marion would tell us, to be honest and pious and brave. "But if you can be only one thing," she said, "be kind. God wants that most of all."

That's what unsettles me so much: I'm being unkind. Not by refusing to give Lil anything but by
ignoring her. There's always time for a "Good morning" and a wave, always time to say a prayer for her.
For it's kind, as my Aunt Marion would say, and it's
what God wants me to do the next time I hear, "Hey,
Rug! Hey, Rug!"

*Don't let me off the hook, Lord. I always have time to
be kind, and You should never let me settle for less.*
                                    —EDWARD GRINNAN

A SECOND THANK-YOU
THANK YOU FOR INSPIRED INSTRUCTION

FRI

14

*I WILL INSTRUCT YOU AND TEACH YOU IN
THE WAY YOU SHOULD GO. . . .*
                              —Psalm 32:8 (NIV)

THIS PAST YEAR when I addressed a
women's group, I met a lovely lady named Vivian.
She explained that my mother had been her first-grade
teacher back in the 1940s. "She changed my destination," Vivian said. "Our town was economically chal-

lenged, but your mother told us we could change everything through the power of education. I remember running home from school one afternoon to tell my mother, 'We're not poor! My teacher said the whole world's mine because I'm learning to read!'"

From as far back as I can remember, Mother taught me about the joys and rewards of reading. We didn't have much when I was growing up, but thanks to books, we had everything. A poem I saw embroidered on a pillow recently describes my childhood perfectly: "Richer than I, you will never be. For I had a mother who read to me."

I'm buying some books today to donate to a local literacy program. It's one more way I'm learning to say a second thank-you for a mother who taught me one of the great secrets of the universe.

Best of all, reading reveals Your good news, Lord. The whole world (and heaven) is mine! Thank You.
—ROBERTA MESSNER

TO ABIDE WITH HIM

FOR THE NEXT NINE DAYS, we invite
you to join Scott Walker as he takes a
life-changing look at the generosity, courage,
love and forgiveness that sent Jesus on His
journey to the Cross—and beyond it, to the
most astonishing of all God's surprises.

—THE EDITORS

SATURDAY BEFORE PALM SUNDAY

SAT
15

Then took Mary a pound of ointment of spikenard, very costly, and anointed the feet of Jesus, and wiped his feet with her hair. . . .
—*John 12:3*

HOLY WEEK BEGINS with Jesus' miracle of the raising of the dead body of Lazarus, already four days in the tomb. His sisters, Mary and Martha, are stunned and ecstatic that Lazarus is alive again. He is no longer sick, and his frail body is healthy and restored. Of course, they know that one day he will die again and return to the same tomb. But that is someday, years away, they hope.

Mary is so grateful that several nights later, when Jesus is eating dinner with her family, she does something impulsive and extravagant. Taking a container of expensive perfume, she pours the ointment over Jesus' feet and wipes them with her long unbound hair. This extravagant outpouring of her love is an intimate and stunning act. To some it seems that she has lost her senses.

There is a time and a place for extravagant gifts. On December 28, 1974, Beth Rushton gave her life and her faith to me when she shyly spoke her wedding vows. I still cannot fathom the extravagance of her gift. And nearly two thousand years ago, Jesus Christ gave His life for me, a gift that is beyond my comprehension. These extravagant gifts of love have changed and transformed my life.

As Isaac Watts wrote, "Love so amazing, so divine, demands my soul, my life, my all."

Dear Father, may I give my life, my work, my self in gratitude for what You have done for me.
                              —SCOTT WALKER

PALM SUNDAY

SUN *HE STEDFASTLY SET HIS FACE TO GO TO*
16
JERUSALEM. . . . —Luke 9:51

MOMENTS THAT CHANGE HISTORY often seem insignificant. Such an event was Jesus' entry into Jerusalem.

Leaving the home of Lazarus in Bethany, Jesus knew that entering Jerusalem would cost Him His life. Yet He knew that He must go to the Temple during the coming feast of Passover to teach by word and by action. He must be God's prophet in a politically charged and troubled time.

Luke portrays Jesus' determination in one short and powerful sentence: "He stedfastly set his face to go to Jerusalem." There are moments when I simply have to do what is right and "let the chips fall where they may." I must take the only good option I have and let God take care of the consequences.

I know of a woman who discovered that the large

corporation for which she worked was involved in illegal activity. She was not involved in the crime; she could have remained silent. Instead she spoke up and told the truth. She lost her job, but as a result of her honesty, the company leadership was brought to justice, auditing reforms were made, and all of us are safer today. She did the right thing despite the cost.

Because Jesus did the right thing, He was tortured and killed. He wasn't admired for His actions, but "despised and rejected." There are moments—often quiet moments—when we must "steadfastly set our face toward Jerusalem" and do the right thing, regardless of consequence. When we do, God walks with us.

Dear God, please walk with me today and give me the courage of my convictions. —SCOTT WALKER

MONDAY IN HOLY WEEK

MON
17
"SHE OUT OF HER POVERTY HAS PUT IN EVERYTHING SHE HAD. . . ."
—*Mark 12:44 (RSV)*

WHEN THEY ENTERED Jerusalem, Jesus and His disciples went immediately to the Temple. The disciples were overcome with the grandeur of the imposing structure. King Herod had withheld no expense in the design and construction of this architectural wonder.

Lost in amazement, the disciples followed Jesus

through the teeming crowds until they came to the large trumpet-shaped coffers where offerings were given to support the Temple. Standing in the shadows, Jesus watched as wealthy Passover pilgrims from all over the Mediterranean world deposited gold and silver coins into the Temple treasury.

Suddenly, an impoverished woman pushed her way to the front and let two tiny coins fall from her fingers. Looking into her eyes, Jesus sensed that these copper *lepta* were all that the woman possessed. Her life savings were less than a day's wage, and she gave it all to God.

Moved by her action, Jesus turned to His disciples and said, "Truly I say to you, this poor widow put in more than all the contributors to the treasury; for they all put in out of their surplus, but she, out of her poverty, put in all she owned, all she had to live on" (Mark 12:43–44, NAS).

Much of what I have given to God has been what I can afford to give, what is left over at the end of the day, the tenth that I have budgeted as my tithe. Seldom have I given as this widow, knowing that there is nothing remaining over, no savings account to back me up, no one to bail me out.

When Jesus looked into the widow's eyes, He knew He must give His all. And it would cost more than two copper coins. It would cost Him His life.

Dear Father, may I follow You without fear of cost or consequence. —SCOTT WALKER

TUESDAY IN HOLY WEEK

TUE

18

"A NEW COMMANDMENT I GIVE TO YOU, THAT YOU LOVE ONE ANOTHER, EVEN AS I HAVE LOVED YOU, THAT YOU ALSO LOVE ONE ANOTHER. BY THIS ALL MEN WILL KNOW THAT YOU ARE MY DISCIPLES, IF YOU HAVE LOVE FOR ONE ANOTHER." —John 13:34–35 (NAS)

DURING HIS FINAL HOURS in Jerusalem, Jesus knew that time was running out. He needed to tell His disciples the most important things to remember.

As He looked at the disciples who followed Him, their faces strained with anxiety and apprehension, Jesus was aware that love was being squeezed out of their hearts by fear. Anger and jealousy were surfacing; envy and competition were evident. In that moment Jesus turned to His followers and said, "A new commandment I give to you, that you love one another, even as I have loved you."

Jesus knew His disciples would be remembered by one thing: their ability to love everyone, even in the most difficult of times.

More than a thousand years later, a young man named Francis read the Gospels and gave his life to Christ. He began to love everyone, even animals, and to minister to them. He created a movement called the Lesser Brothers to bring love and compassion to the most desperate and poverty-stricken. In the rule that he made for them, he wrote, "Let all the brothers . . . preach by their deeds."

Jesus said it another way: "By this all men will know that you are My disciples, if you have love for one another."

Dear Father, may I use my actions this day to show others how much I love them. —SCOTT WALKER

WEDNESDAY IN HOLY WEEK

WED
19
"AND I WILL ASK THE FATHER, AND HE WILL GIVE YOU ANOTHER HELPER, THAT HE MAY BE WITH YOU FOREVER. . . . I WILL NOT LEAVE YOU AS ORPHANS; I WILL COME TO YOU." —John 14:16, 18 (NKJV)

LOOKING INTO THE WORRIED EYES of His disciples, Jesus knew they realized that He would soon be killed. They would be left alone without their leader.

It was at that moment that Jesus talked with them about the coming of the Holy Spirit. They would not be left alone like orphans. The very presence of God—Father, Son and Holy Spirit—would be forever with them.

When I was fourteen years old, my father suddenly died of a heart attack. After his death, we moved from the Philippines back to my mother's hometown, Fort Valley, Georgia. I remember the fear of those first weeks of grief and separation and readjustment to a new world and a new life. I was afraid that my mother would also die and that my sister and I would be left alone in a world that we did not know and could not trust. It was a terrible anxiety for a teenager to live with. I didn't want to be an orphan thrust into the care of people I didn't know.

So it was with Jesus' disciples. And so it is when I fear that God isn't with me, doesn't hear me, is far away from me. In these moments I need to hear the reassuring promise of Jesus: "I will not leave you as orphans; I will come to you . . . the Father will give you another Helper, that He may be with you forever . . ."

Dear Lord, reassure me that You are with me. May I witness the presence of the Spirit moving in my life today. —SCOTT WALKER

MAUNDY THURSDAY

THU
20

"ABIDE IN ME, AND I IN YOU. AS THE BRANCH CANNOT BEAR FRUIT OF ITSELF, UNLESS IT ABIDES IN THE VINE, SO NEITHER CAN YOU, UNLESS YOU ABIDE IN ME." —*John 15:4 (NKJV)*

ON THE NIGHT WHEN JESUS SHARED the Passover with His disciples, He told them to *abide*.

When I was in seminary, I studied the Gospel of John with the world-renowned English scholar George Beasley-Murray. I'll never forget the day he taught us the meaning of the word *abide*.

"The root meaning of *abide*," he said, "is to lean back against something with all of your weight. It is like sitting down in a forest, placing your back against a great oak tree, and letting your entire weight rest or *abide* against its stout trunk. To *abide* is like lying down on a bed and letting your full weight sink into its softness until you are enveloped by sleep and rest."

Recently I visited a young woman, the mother of four children, who is enduring the ravages of advanced cancer. After we talked for a while, I asked her if I could pray with her. Holding her hand, I asked God to give her the ability to abide in His care. When I finished praying, she looked up and asked me, "Scott, what does it mean to 'abide' in something?" I told her what Dr. Beasley-Murray had taught me about the word.

Now when I visit her in her hospital room, she grins and throws her arms out across her mattress and says, "I'm abiding as best I can."

Dear Father, as I live this day, please abide in me as I abide in You. —SCOTT WALKER

GOOD FRIDAY

FRI
21
AND JESUS, CRYING OUT WITH A LOUD VOICE, SAID, "FATHER, INTO YOUR HANDS I COMMIT MY SPIRIT." AND HAVING SAID THIS, HE BREATHED HIS LAST.
—*Luke 23:46 (NAS)*

THE INEVITABLE FINALLY HAPPENED: Jesus was arrested on the night of Passover, interrogated, brutally tortured and then condemned to the most shameful of deaths—crucifixion. Hanging on the Cross in shock and pain, He gradually slipped into a coma. On the edge of the chasm between life and death, He felt rejection and despair and, according to Mark's Gospel, shrieked, "My God, My God, Why have You forsaken Me?" (15:34, NAS).

William Barclay wonders if perhaps, in His final moments, as His vision blurred and His lungs could no longer breathe, Jesus gazed at His mother, standing at the foot of the Cross, and remembered the bedtime prayer, echoing Psalm 31:5, that every Jewish mother taught her child to pray: "Into Your hands I commit my spirit."

Sometimes when confronted with the monstrous evil and destruction in our world, it's hard for me to believe that I haven't been abandoned. It's difficult to believe that love will conquer evil and that goodness will prevail. But in these very moments, I must whisper with childlike faith, "Father, into Your hands I commit my Spirit."

Dear Father, please teach me, Your child, to pray in the words Jesus uttered on the Cross. —SCOTT WALKER

EDITOR'S NOTE: We invite you to join us in prayer today as we observe our annual Good Friday Day of Prayer. Guideposts Prayer Ministry prays daily for each of the prayer requests we receive by name and need. Join us at www.dailyguideposts.com and learn how you can request prayer, volunteer to pray for others or support our ministry.

HOLY SATURDAY

SAT
22

IMMEDIATELY, WHILE HE WAS STILL SPEAKING, THE ROOSTER CROWED. AND THE LORD TURNED AND LOOKED AT PETER. THEN PETER REMEMBERED THE WORD OF THE LORD, HOW HE HAD SAID TO HIM, 'BEFORE THE ROOSTER CROWS, YOU WILL DENY ME THREE TIMES.' SO PETER WENT OUTSIDE AND WEPT BITTERLY. —*Luke 22:60–62 (NKJV)*

AS SATURDAY, THE SABBATH, DAWNED, Peter was hiding. We don't know where he was or if he was still weeping. But he must have been racked by guilt. He had denied knowing Jesus by word and action. And in the courtyard of the high priest's house, when he heard the cock crow, he looked into the steady gaze of an imprisoned Jesus, his broken commitments pierced his heart.

I have stood with Peter. I know the guilt of not keeping my promises, my vows, my good intentions. And my weaknesses and mistakes have hurt other people, disappointed loved ones and filled me with remorse.

This year I discovered a poem by Elizabeth Barrett Browning, "The Meaning of the Look," a reflection on what Jesus might have been thinking as He quietly gazed on Peter in the courtyard.

> *The cock crows coldly—Go, and manifest*
> *A late contrition, but no bootless fear!*
> *For when thy final need is dreariest,*
> *Thou shalt not be denied, as I am here;*
> *My voice to God and angels shall attest,*
> *Because I know this man, let him be clear.*

Today, between Good Friday and Easter, I stand with Peter, sorry for my sins. But the good news is that because God is God, He forgives me. And when I die, He'll be standing at the gate of heaven, shouting across the universe, "Because I know this man, let him be clear."

Father, thank You for Your gracious love that never denies that I am Your beloved child.

—SCOTT WALKER

EASTER

SUN
23
*THEN THE SAME DAY AT EVENING,
BEING THE FIRST DAY OF THE WEEK,
WHEN THE DOORS WERE SHUT WHERE
THE DISCIPLES WERE ASSEMBLED . . .
JESUS CAME AND STOOD IN THE MIDST, AND SAID TO
THEM, "PEACE BE WITH YOU." WHEN HE HAD SAID
THIS, HE SHOWED THEM HIS HANDS AND HIS SIDE.
THEN THE DISCIPLES WERE GLAD WHEN THEY SAW
THE LORD. —John 20:19–20 (NKJV)*

ACCORDING TO JOHN'S GOSPEL, at sunrise following
the Sabbath, the women coming to anoint Jesus'
body discovered the empty tomb. Peter and the beloved disciple ran to investigate. They found the grave
clothes on the rock ledge of the tomb wall; only the
face covering had been laid aside by itself. Perplexed,
the disciples returned to their place of hiding.

When night came, the door to their secluded room
was closed and bolted. Suddenly Jesus stood in their
midst. The wounds of His Crucifixion could be clearly
seen. He spoke to them and then disappeared.

The next day, Luke tells us, He appeared to two of
the disciples walking to the city of Emmaus. Though
they talked for hours as they hiked together, the disciples did not recognize Jesus. It was only when they
stopped at an inn for dinner that they identified Him
by the unique way He blessed and broke the bread.
Again, He disappeared.

Holy Week begins with the raising of Lazarus and ends with the Resurrection of Jesus. Lazarus's body was raised just as it was before his death; Jesus' body was completely transformed. Jesus was physically present, and yet not bound by time or space.

The Resurrection of Jesus is shrouded in a mystery I can't possibly understand or imagine. But when I live in Easter faith, I learn that there's a truth beyond my understanding, that there are realities beyond my imagination, and that God is the Lord of life and death and all creation.

Father, thank You for the wonder, the mystery and the miracle of Jesus' Resurrection. —SCOTT WALKER

MON
24
HIS SISTER STOOD AT A DISTANCE TO SEE WHAT WOULD HAPPEN TO HIM.
—Exodus 2:4 (NIV)

I HAVE FIVE SISTERS. Four are younger than I am and had little effect on my long-term plans while I was growing up. Sue, who is one year older, was a constant reminder that I might not be a major-league baseball star. Rocky Colavito and Al Kaline would never welcome me into the Detroit Tigers lineup as long as I was a worse hitter than Sue.

When I was eight years old, I was finally able to

join Little League. Sue came with me to the tryouts. I
brought my dad's Louisville Slugger bat, even though
I had trouble balancing it on my shoulder. Swinging it
was out of the question. One of the coaches handed
me a smaller bat, but I managed to hit only an occasional foul ball.

On the way home, I was sadly rethinking my future with the Tigers when Sue tugged me back to the
present by saying, "I could have hit—"

"I know," I snapped. "You could have hit line drives
past the outfielders. But they don't let girls play Little
League."

"You don't know anything," Sue said. "I could have
hit those pitches because I'm older than you. Next
year you'll be nine. And you'll hit like I do. For now,
just let them walk you. You've got the smallest strike
zone of anyone out there."

She was right. I got on base a lot that year without
lifting my bat. The next year, I hit a winning home
run over the center fielder's head in the opening game.
I wasn't as good as Sue, but the Tigers had traded
Colavito that winter. They would need someone to
replace him.

Dear God, I'm so grateful for a sister who saw the in-
justices in her own life but could still see the need for
kindness in mine. —TIM WILLIAMS

TUE
25

*THAT THEIR HEARTS MIGHT BE
COMFORTED, BEING KNIT TOGETHER IN
LOVE. . . .* —*Colossians 2:2*

TWELVE YEARS AND more than four hundred thousand children's sweaters—this isn't a small miracle, it's a huge and amazing miracle! It all began on March 25, 1996, with a footnote to a devotional I wrote about my very modest efforts at knitting sweaters for needy children.

I was writing full of nostalgia for my childhood in a small English village, where little girls were expected to knit and sew at least competently. I never did make the grade sewing; my stitches were never even and seams never straight. But I did manage knitting—those wonderful soothing repetitive stitches that somehow turned into scarves or, after a year or two, simple sweaters for what were then called "displaced persons." I made mine especially for the displaced (and cold) children of the world who weren't lucky enough to live in cozy Hampshire.

I expected maybe a dozen requests for the pattern that was offered, but letters poured in from *Daily Guideposts* readers, and they've kept coming as the years pass. The project quickly became the Guideposts Sweater Project, now known as Guideposts Knit for Kids. Sweaters of every color and size, all following the very simple pattern we sent out, kept coming in every mail delivery. They soon outgrew my office. And many came with letters, prayers for the children or even incomplete garments with stories of their own. (I took those home to finish and always had a pile to work on.)

So here we are, years later. Guideposts Knit for Kids is stronger than ever. A stamped, self-addressed envelope sent to Guideposts Knit for Kids, 39 Seminary Hill Road, Carmel, NY 10512 or a visit to www.knitforkids.org will bring you the pattern and help us on the way to five hundred thousand warmer children.

Lord, bless the knitters for the prayers knitted into every stitch for the children of the world.
                                          —BRIGITTE WEEKS

WED
26

THE MEMORY OF THE RIGHTEOUS IS A BLESSING. . . . —Proverbs 10:7 (RSV)

THE SUN WAS WARM, but the wind had a sharp edge to it as I lifted the sap bucket off the maple tree. The bucket was full, and I focused my attention on the task of removing it from the small hook that held it securely to the tree.

When the ground thawed, the sap was drawn upward toward the branches to give the tree new life. This was the liquid that we would boil down to make maple syrup.

I lowered my eyes to the gathering pail on the ground and carefully poured the gallons of clear liquid into it. As the last drop fell, my eyes moved from the bucket to the granite marker that sat beneath the maple tree. It had been resting there for more than eleven years. On the stone were engraved the names of four family members who had passed away. Just looking at their names brought a rush of fond memories.

I paused for a moment and retreated from the labor at hand to remember my dad, my aunt, my cousin and my mom, and the impact each had on my life. The memory of their love flowed into my soul just as the sap flowed from the maple tree into the bucket. God felt very close on that warm spring day as I gathered maple sap by the old rock wall.

Thank You, Lord, for allowing me to remember all those who were Your hands and heart here on earth, those who shaped my life and helped to make me who I am today. —PATRICIA PUSEY

THU
27

EVERYONE WAS AMAZED AND GAVE PRAISE TO GOD. THEY WERE FILLED WITH AWE AND SAID, "WE HAVE SEEN REMARKABLE THINGS TODAY."
—*Luke 5:26* (NIV)

I COMMUTE ABOUT THIRTY-FIVE MILES each way to work. For years, it was the same each day. It got to the point where I could tell exactly where I was by the tree or house or turnoff I was passing at the time. I knew every inch of that road.

Maybe that's why I was so startled one morning by a sign that had appeared overnight on the side of the landfill. PREPARE TO BE AMAZED, it said. Nothing else, just that, in white letters on a blue background. A couple of miles down the road, another sign. Then another and another—six identical signs in a stretch of about ten miles. PREPARE TO BE AMAZED.

All day long I couldn't get those mysterious signs out of my head. Their message had me noticing other things too. Did the sun always reflect off that barn? Were the trunks of those trees always such a beautiful shade of brown? Did that colleague always have such a broad smile? Did I always get this excited about my work? When I drove home, the road signs were gone. But they'd already done their work.

Now I commute to work every day along a new highway. When everything starts looking the same, I put a sticky note on the dashboard: PREPARE TO BE AMAZED. On those days I see signs of God's presence that I have either missed or simply not appreciated. And that, I think, is pretty amazing.

Give me eyes to see this day, God, Your work and presence in the people and places of my life, especially those I may have overlooked. —JEFF JAPINGA

 **GIVE US THIS DAY**
REJECTING THE LIE

FRI
28

"Stop doubting and believe."
—*John 20:27 (NIV)*

"MOM, YOU HAVE TO BELIEVE GOD!" my daughter Kendall told me emphatically when she stopped by our house one evening on her way home from work.

I knew she was right. I had just gotten the results from a biopsy, showing my ovarian cancer had spread to my lungs, confirming my Stage 4 status. I felt discouraged, and the lies had started seeping into my soul: *Cancer always wins. You'll never get well. God doesn't hear your prayers. Ha! Your faith isn't even strong enough to get you through this.*

I knew these were lies from the enemy of my faith. But they started growing bigger than God's promises as I allowed them to echo through my mind.

A few days later, Kendall walked into the house and plunked a wrapped package down on the kitchen counter. "This is to help you remember to believe God," she said.

Inside was a wooden block with letters spelling out the word BELIEVE.

I placed it on a windowsill above the sink and was stunned to see, for the first time, that the word LIE is tucked right there in the middle of the word BE-LIE-VE.

Wow! What a powerful reminder that when I feel discouraged, I can focus on the LIE . . . or step back and BELIEVE God's truth, which is so much bigger: the truth that God knows our suffering and walks with us and will meet all our needs. Most of all, that He promises a future filled with hope, regardless of our circumstances.

Now, every time I wash my hands at the sink or rinse a dish or get a drink of water, I see that word BELIEVE . . . and I remember.

Father, help me focus on the truth of Your promises instead of fixating on a lie. —CAROL KUYKENDALL

SAT
29

WHETHER YOU TURN TO THE RIGHT OR TO THE LEFT, YOUR EARS WILL HEAR A VOICE BEHIND YOU, SAYING, "THIS IS THE WAY; WALK IN IT."
—*Isaiah 30:21 (NIV)*

I LIVE WITH MY WIFE DANELLE and two children in a small log house on twenty acres in Vermont. We bought the place eight years ago, thinking that we would walk in the woods every day, summer and winter, exploring the flora. But for the first several years that we lived in our idyllic setting, we spent less time there than we did in our cars.

Two years ago, Danelle and I were working in the garden in early spring. While pulling the old growth of the previous season in preparation for tilling the soil for the new one, we began talking about our next vacation. Should we take the kids to California or to a dude ranch in Colorado? Then we looked around the yard and the woods. The sun was beaming through the birches; the early morning mist was rising in the hills behind our house. Birds were flitting to and fro, already hitting the feeders.

"We're always planning the next place to go. Why don't we just stay put this year?" Danelle said.

So that's what we did. We finally planted the entire garden, went for long walks, relaid a stone walkway, transplanted trees. It was our best summer ever.

Later that year, we tried the same tactic in our marriage. "Let's turn off the television in the evenings and spend more time talking," Danelle said. Evening after evening, we looked at each other and discussed what was important in our lives. We set goals. We dated. A marriage that had been slowly ebbing away became one that was coming back together.

Sometimes the best opportunities are sitting close by, only waiting to be noticed.

Show me what is eternal in my life, Lord, and help me see how to live in it each day. —JON SWEENEY

SUN
30

AND, BEHOLD, THERE AROSE A GREAT TEMPEST IN THE SEA. . . . AND HIS DISCIPLES CAME TO HIM, AND AWOKE HIM, SAYING, LORD, SAVE US: WE PERISH. AND HE SAITH UNTO THEM, WHY ARE YE FEARFUL, O YE OF LITTLE FAITH? THEN HE AROSE, AND REBUKED THE WINDS AND THE SEA; AND THERE WAS A GREAT CALM. —Matthew 8:24–26

THE TWO-HOUR DRIVE to New Jersey in the pouring rain was longer than I expected. "Are we there yet?" my daughter Christine asked.

"No," I replied impatiently. *Why did I accept this preaching invitation so far from home?*

The drive became more stressful when we arrived in town but couldn't find the church. Several turns and a few lights later, we were finally there. The worship was going full blast. The pastor was strumming the guitar and his wife was leading the singing of the mostly Spanish-speaking congregation. Their young son was playing the drums while an older man banged away on the bongos. The joy of the people filled the church and our hearts.

My sermon was on "Weathering the Storms of Life," and my text was the Gospel story about Jesus calming the storm. "Don't forget to preach in Spanish *and* English," the pastor reminded me.

In the car, as we began the drive back home, my wife Elba handed me an envelope. Inside was a note: "I am going through a terrible storm, but like you

said, 'The bigger the trial, the bigger the blessing.'
Thank you for those words, and thank you for speaking them in English—perfect timing."

Lord, help me always to be willing to put up with a little inconvenience to reach someone in time of need.
                                                    —PABLO DIAZ

MON
31
HE WHO TRUSTS IN HIMSELF IS A FOOL, BUT HE WHO WALKS IN WISDOM IS KEPT SAFE. —*Proverbs 28:26 (NIV)*

THERE'S SOMETHING ABOUT ALLIGATORS that intrigues me so much that I'll bike five miles to a park to see the gators that live in the lake there. Once, I saw a seven-foot-long gator sunning itself on the shore. I jumped off my bike, grabbed my camera and quietly moved closer to get a good shot.

Five feet from the massive creature, I took another step. The gator started to move slowly toward the water. I stepped closer. Just as I lifted my camera, I heard a loud, nerve-numbing growl and then *pow!* Its tail slapped the water. The gator had done a 180-degree turn and was telling me to back off. I raced off on my bike without looking back.

I learned later that an alligator can run as fast as a horse and that I'd better keep my distance. That made me think about all the things in my new life in Florida I had to learn to respect. Like the sun. It, too, can be a killer. So I started using sunscreen liberally every time I ventured out.

Another thing I need to respect is my diet. There are so many restaurants and early-bird specials down here that it would be easy to eat out three or four times a week. But I need to avoid the high-fat, high-cholesterol, high-sugar, low-fiber foods that many eateries serve.

Yup. Those gators have taught me a lot.

Lord, remind me daily to respect limits—of others, as well as my own. —PATRICIA LORENZ

MY DIVINE SURPRISES

1 _____

2 _____

3 _____

4 _____

5 _____

6 _____

7 _____

8 _____

9 _____

10 _____

11 _____

12 _____

13 _____

14 _____

15 _____

16 _____

17 _____

18 _____

19 _____

20 _____

21 _____

22 _____

23 _____

24 _____

25 _____

26 _____

27 _____

28 _____

29 _____

30 _____

31 _____

April

God is the Lord, which hath shewed us light. . . . —*Psalm 118:27*

UNEXPECTED BLESSINGS
LETTING GOD'S PLAN UNFOLD

TUE
1

LORD, ALL MY DESIRE IS BEFORE THEE. . . .
—*Psalm 38:9*

I HURRIED TO THE BUS TERMINAL in Christchurch; I had to get a window seat! For two weeks I'd taught a workshop in New Zealand. With the honorarium, I'd booked a five-day, once-in-a-lifetime tour of the South Island.

Alas for my hopes, I arrived to find a line already waiting for the bus door to open. Was this how it would be all five days, I wondered—everyone dashing for the best seats?

I could ruin the trip for myself, I knew, if I got upset over a minor matter like seating. *It isn't minor*, a fretful little voice answered back. *You'd see so much more from a window seat!* I knew that voice very well, the me-centered one insisting on its own way.

The driver arrived, the line began to move. By the time I climbed the steps, cheerily chatting couples seemed to occupy every spot. Then three-quarters of the way back, I spotted a pair of empty seats. At the back of the bus a woman was coming out of the restroom. Sprint down the aisle, slide into the window seat before she does? *No!* I told the greedy voice.

"It looks like you and I are the only ones traveling alone," I said as we reached the row together.

She looked at me anxiously. "I hate to ask you this," she said, "but . . . could I request a tremendous favor? I'm such a nervous traveler! Would you mind terribly if I asked you to take the window seat?"

It was not just a seat and a long-lived friendship I gained that day, it was an answer to that me-first voice. *I know the desires of all My children,* God told me as we settled contentedly into our seats. *I can't put them together while you're racing ahead of Me.*

Bestower of blessing, keep me alert today to the rhyming of Your universe. —ELIZABETH SHERRILL

WED
2
SHE ANSWERED HIM, "YES, LORD; YET EVEN THE DOGS UNDER THE TABLE EAT THE CHILDREN'S CRUMBS."
—*Mark 7:28 (RSV)*

DOGS SCARE ME. I've been a runner or walker for twenty-seven years, and like many pedestrians who've been terrorized by man's best friend, I'm wary of the beasts. There's a street I like to walk near the beach, a pretty lane with lovely old houses and gorgeous gardens. It would be the perfect path except for one house with two large hounds. Across the porch entrance is a rickety barrier that looks as if it wouldn't hold in a toddler. Fortunately for me, there are always people sitting on the porch when I pass, so when the dogs start to bark and growl, the people murmur some magic words and the monsters subside and glare at me with their tiny, bloodshot eyes.

Yesterday I walked early. As I approached the dogs' house, I noticed that the keepers were absent. I was about to go back to the main road when I saw the mailman nearing the house. *Yes!* Letter carriers in our area are allowed to carry pepper spray to protect themselves from vicious pets. Not only were these beasts about to get a comeuppance, I would be a happy witness.

The mailman bounded fearlessly up the porch steps and the dogs went crazy, charging the puny barrier. Then, to my astonishment, he started to talk to them. They stopped, cocked their barrel-sized heads and lifted their ears. He spoke in a low, comforting voice, and after the dogs were completely calm he pulled two dog biscuits out of his bag. They delicately took the treats from his fingers, and as they munched away he delivered the mail.

I walked by slowly, wondering how often I let fear cloud my perspective and how much more I could accomplish with a few kind words and a treat or two.

Lord, help me not to let my fears rule my actions.
                                    —MARCI ALBORGHETTI

THU *DOES HE WHO FORMED THE EYE NOT SEE?*
3   —*Psalm* 94:9 (*NIV*)

A WHILE AGO, a project I had thrown my-self into began to unravel. Nothing my col-leagues and I tried could stop the downward spiral. We lifted up our problem to God in prayer, but it seemed as if He weren't paying attention.

I needed a break, so I took a canoe trip and spent a few days alone, with no cell phone, e-mail or meet-ings. One evening the sky was exceptionally clear, and I sat on the lakeshore and watched the moon rise. As soon as it cleared the treetops, a shaft of light streaked across the calm surface of the lake and pointed straight at me, ending right at my feet.

I got up and walked along the shoreline, and the beam seemed to follow me. No matter how far I moved from where I'd been sitting, the light followed. I turned around and walked in the other direction, and it still followed me. I decided to try a little exper-iment. Since I was on an island, I walked all the way around to the opposite side, where the rise in the mid-dle of the island blocked my view of the moon and the streak of light disappeared from sight.

Thinking I had escaped, I crept up the rise and peeked out over the boulders. There it was, that silver arrow pointing straight at me once again. Just because I was behind an obstacle didn't mean the light wasn't there. All I had to do was look for it.

Lord, help me to avoid the obstacles that obscure my view of Your ever-watchful care. —ERIC FELLMAN

FRI
4

THE RIGHTEOUS GIVES AND DOES NOT HOLD BACK. *—Proverbs 21:26 (RSV)*

WE HAD JUST CROSSED 48th Street when Maggie said, "Elizabeth's good at math, and Mary's good at ballet, and John likes history and is good with little kids. Mom, what do you think my special thing will be?"

I inhaled deeply and sent my brain cells on a mad scramble for ideas. My five-year-old is bursting at the seams with personality, but it's hard to describe her gifts. Frankly, I don't think she needs any special talent. But nattering about how all she needs is to be herself wasn't going to cut it.

"You know, Maggie, one thing that makes you special is that you have a naturally generous heart."

This is true. Maggie gives automatically, without prompting and without regret. She assumes that part of the reason she has things is so she can share them.

"Do you remember the other night when you and I were going out for a 'special time'?" I asked. Maggie nodded. Time spent alone with Mom or Dad is precious when you've got a horde of siblings, even if all you do is slip out to the grocery store together.

"Remember how Stephen started to cry because he wanted to come? Do you remember what you did?"

Maggie grinned. "I said of course he could!"

"Yes, you did. You gave up your time with just me and included him without even a pause. That kind of generosity is unusual. It's also pleasing to God."

Maggie looked surprised but beamed with delight. I hope she understands that sort of gift is more than enough.

Father, help me pay more attention to growing in grace than to trumpeting my abilities. —JULIA ATTAWAY

SAT
5

THE LORD IS MY ROCK, AND MY FORTRESS. . . . —Psalm 18:2

THE ANCIENT BULK of Edinburgh Castle loomed in front of us, a towering pile of battlements and crenellations, palisades and cannon, topped by rows of bright flags flapping in the wind. Countless tourists surged toward the entrance, speaking all the languages of the world. I wanted only to be back home in western Massachusetts.

Carol and I had come to visit our older son John, an exchange student at the University of Edinburgh. The reunion had been perfect, and John had delighted in showing us the attractions of the city. We had enjoyed every minute, but after a while the new sights, sounds and tastes (like haggis, stuffed into scalded sheep stomachs) had begun to wear me down. I needed a chance to re-collect myself. Yet here we were, about to plunge into the most crowded tourist spot in Scotland.

As we trudged up the winding castle lane, I grew more and more disheartened. The tapestries and crown jewels and regal chambers glittered with beauty, but I had had enough.

Then we crested the castle mound and found ourselves before a small stone building, no larger than a glorified tent. I stepped into a whitewashed interior with a stained glass window bejeweling the walls. The building was quiet, empty and filled with light. It was, I read, St. Margaret's Chapel, the highest point in the castle, a twelfth-century structure built to honor the celebrated queen and saint. I sat down and let the silence and beauty wash over me. All of Edinburgh lay below me, as if held in the hand of God. At the top of a castle three thousand miles from Massachusetts, I said a prayer and finally felt at home.

Help me, Lord, to find Your peace in the heights and the depths. —PHILIP ZALESKI

SUN

6

HE READ IN THEIR EARS ALL THE WORDS
OF THE BOOK OF THE COVENANT WHICH
WAS FOUND IN THE HOUSE OF THE LORD.
                            —*II Kings 23:2*

THIS MORNING I TOOK twelve-year-old Elizabeth
downtown to sing with her children's choir at the
11:00 AM service at St. Malachy's. My wife Julia and
the other children stayed home; five-year-old Maggie
is sick—she's droopy and has been sleeping most of
the day.

When Elizabeth and I got home, I decided I'd go
back downtown to get a movie to cheer up Maggie.

"Can I go with you?" asked eight-year-old Mary.

"Of course."

Mary picked up her jacket and a copy of *The Little
Princess* and followed me out the door.

Both Julia and I are ardent readers; when we were
dating, she made me bring a book to her apartment
one evening to see if we could read together without disturbing each other. But Mary—sociable, grace-
ful, life-of-the-playground—was different; she hadn't
seemed to share our enthusiasm until this year.

Suddenly, she can't seem to get enough of books.
She's been through all the *Little House* books, *The
Secret Garden*, E. Nisbet, *Mary Poppins* and Lewis
Carroll. Yesterday afternoon she came home from the
library with four Nancy Drew mysteries; by dinner-
time, she'd made her way through three of them.

When we got on the downtown A train, Mary opened her book. By the time we'd found the DVDs we wanted, had a snack and taken the subway back home, Mary was a third of the way through it. I had to tell her to put down the book, so she could safely get off the train.

Last year we gave Mary her first grown-up Bible; now that she's such an enthusiastic reader, maybe it's time to make sure that book is always on her reading list.

Lord, may the love of words lead Mary and all my children to the love of Your Word.

                                    —ANDREW ATTAWAY

MON

7

BEHOLD, NOW IS THE ACCEPTED TIME; BEHOLD, NOW IS THE DAY OF SALVATION.
                              —*II Corinthians 6:2*

MY WIFE SANDEE'S COUSIN CAROL got the news, the diagnosis. The kind of news no one wants to hear, especially at twenty-three.

Always a practical woman, Carol arranged for a quick marriage to her boyfriend Gary. Despite the urgency of the situation—or maybe because of it—we celebrated. We danced. And then we went home and waited: our turn to get the news, to grip the phone hard, to find the right words of comfort in the face of someone dying so young, so suddenly.

Last week we got the call. Cousin Carol had passed away . . . twenty-five years *after* the original diagnosis, twenty-five years *after* the wedding.

She didn't beat the odds; she crushed the odds, but at a price. Radiation, a bone-marrow transplant (a gift from her brother), more radiation, surgery, endless chemotherapy, endless time in the hospital. And she was not a "patient" patient; she was never too shy to tell you what she thought, even if you hadn't asked. There was, quite literally, no time like the present. She had learned not to wait for the right moment. Every moment was the right moment; every moment was now.

During the eulogy, Gary told us a story: A few days before she died, Carol had arranged for box seats to the sold-out opener of her beloved Washington Nationals' baseball season. But no one made it to the game; we all met for her funeral. "Somehow," Gary said, "she still got the best seat."

It's true. Carol sits in the best seat in your heart— she and the others who have gone before. She's the one telling you not to wait. She's the one telling you that odds are meant to be beaten. She's the one telling you to love hard. She's the one telling you to enjoy the game *now*.

Lord, give Carol Your peace, and may we all meet again in Jerusalem. —MARK COLLINS

TUE
8

*AND I, BEHOLD, I ESTABLISH MY
COVENANT WITH YOU, AND WITH YOUR
SEED AFTER YOU; AND WITH EVERY
LIVING CREATURE THAT IS WITH YOU. . . .*
—*Genesis 9:9*

YESTERDAY AT A BUSY INTERSECTION during the five o'clock rush hour, traffic suddenly came to a four-way standstill. A mother mallard and ten golden-fuzzed ducklings were crossing the street. The scene reminded me of Robert McCloskey's classic children's story *Make Way for Ducklings*.

Once the ducks reached apparent safety, my wife Shirley and I breathed a sigh of relief and went on our way. But then disaster struck. My wife, looking out the back window, reported that Mama had led her brood across a storm-sewer grating and one of the babies had fallen through. At the next corner I turned the car around and returned to the scene of the accident. Mama and company were waddling downhill toward the water, unaware that one of their entourage was missing. On our hands and knees, we peered down and saw the duckling scrambling about, unhurt but clearly frantic. The only way to reach the baby was to lift the iron grate, but it was sealed.

I called 911 and an understanding desk sergeant said he'd send someone out. Half an hour later, an officer arrived. By now, the desperate duckling had disappeared in the ductwork. (Try saying that in a hurry.)

We checked the outlets, but the policeman said it would take the street department to lift the grating and try to make a rescue.

The next morning I called for an update and learned that workmen had indeed made a search, without success. They theorized that the duckling had found a way out by itself. I thanked them for their effort.

"You went to all that trouble for a baby duckling?" someone asked. Yes, and I have infected my four children with the same "reverence for life" disease. Funny how virulent such caring can become.

> *Improve our sight, dear God, until we see*
> *In all things living Your divinity.*
> —FRED BAUER

WED
9

YOU, THEN, WHO TEACH OTHERS, DO YOU NOT TEACH YOURSELF. . . .
—*Romans 2:21 (NIV)*

I'VE JUST POSTED midterm warnings: Three of my fifteen community college students are failing their reading improvement class. They don't do any of the work, yet still they appear in class, listening, taking notes. What gives? Why do they bother?

Why do I? I spend hours trying to make my class

stimulating, relevant and worthwhile. I meet with students and respond to e-mail. Yet sometimes I can't help feeling that I've flopped miserably.

"Let's face it," says one colleague. "We can't reach them all. If we can reach a handful, well, we've made a difference."

Okay, I'll try this again. I revisit my grade book. Yes, three students have Fs. Maybe their midterm grades will jolt them into action. They still have time to catch up and keep up. *Can I find another three who are thriving?*

Aha! A sprinkling of As and B+s: The serious veteran who delved into a military history book, finished it and started another. He admits he enjoys reading now and would never have read a book without being prodded. The reluctant reader who says she loves her outside reading, although it progresses slowly. She's much more confident these past weeks. The self-effacing young man who wrestles with dyslexia but whizzes through logic exercises faster than I can. No one read to him as a child.

With three weeks left in the semester, one of the failing students still comes to class, now laden with make-up assignments. She's trying, really trying to read better. Trying isn't failure. Ever.

Divine Teacher, let me never despair of my students—or of my own ability to teach them.

—GAIL THORELL SCHILLING

THU
10
SO SHALL YE KEEP THE WATCH OF THE
HOUSE, THAT IT BE NOT BROKEN DOWN.
—*II Kings 11:6*

WHEN I MOVED into my apartment on Manhattan's Upper West Side, Andrés, the night porter, had been there for ten years. Thirty-five years later, he's still there, the guardian of the locked front doors after 11:00 PM. During the course of a night, he'll scrub the floors so that the marble retains its luster, buff the windows until they are truly diaphanous, and at dawn he'll stock the elevator with newspapers (*The New York Times* and, for some, *The Wall Street Journal*).

Andrés and I are friends. My pointer Clay was our original bond, and Andrés had a powerful German shepherd that I admired. I visited his home in the city and in the Catskills, where he eventually moved his family. He did me the honor (and the responsibility) of asking me to be godfather to his son Alejandro, which meant that I had to learn enough Spanish to get me through the baptism in the unfamiliar Catholic church. I have gone through Christmases, birthdays, a first communion and a high-school graduation; today Alejandro is married and away in the U.S. Navy.

He's a fine man, Andrés. It was gratifying to know he was there when I took my dog for her late-hour airing. I'd scratch on the door when we came back from Central Park, and Clay or Shep would come in wagging her tail in breathless anticipation of a cookie. Andrés always made a production of it.

That's not the only reason for gratitude, however. I wonder how many people in this city realize that they sleep safely because of a night protector. I do. Though Andrés would say it doesn't become him and shake his head in embarrassment, he's my own guardian angel.

Father, angels appear in various guises, don't they? So why not Andrés? —VAN VARNER

FRI
11

JESUS SAITH UNTO HER . . . I ASCEND TO MY FATHER, AND YOUR FATHER; AND TO MY GOD, AND YOUR GOD. —John 20:17

MY DAUGHTER AND I were talking long-distance. The birth of her second child was imminent, and she had invited her father to be with her, though he would have to wait in the hospital's visitors lounge.

"It was so comforting last time knowing Dad was nearby," she said. "I guess I'm just a daddy's girl."

I felt a twinge. I'd also been at the hospital last time. Now I was in Southern California caring for my aged aunt, and I would miss this birth. Still, I wanted so much to ask, "Aren't you my girl too?"

All day long I couldn't push her "Daddy's girl" remark from my mind. I knew parenting wasn't a competition, but her words hurt. I lay in bed that night feeling lonely and left out. "Father," I prayed, "where do I fit in?"

His answer came quietly to my heart, *You're a daddy's girl too. You're My girl.*

Peace filled me. Here was the essential relationship for me and my family: We were each a child of God. Everyone had a place. Everyone belonged.

I drifted to sleep, thankful for the bond between my daughter and her dad, secure in my place as her mother and safe in the arms of God.

How blessed I am, my God, to reap the richness of the mystery of both father and mother love, held within Your heart for me. —CAROL KNAPP

SAT
12

THE RIGHTEOUS SHALL FLOURISH LIKE A PALM TREE. . . . THEY SHALL STILL BEAR FRUIT IN OLD AGE. . . .
—*Psalm 92:12, 14 (NKJV)*

I FEEL A LITTLE FOOLISH, planting trees at my age. I won't live long enough to see them mature. I planted forty trees on our new property, and it's the hardest work I've ever done. It involves digging out several cubic feet of rock-hard clay, then filling the hole with black dirt, using only a shovel and a wheelbarrow. Only then can I plant the tree and expect it to survive.

White oaks grow very slowly, but they can live four hundred years. Ginkgos may be the slowest growing tree in the world. They are called the "Tree of Hope" because some of them survived the blast at Hiroshima. Their beauty is worth the wait.

Why am I planting trees whose shade I might never enjoy? For one thing, I have learned late in life that things can happen if I just get started. There's a saying that "Old age is ready to tackle those tasks that young people spurned because it would take too long."

Furthermore, even if I don't live to see the trees full grown, my children and grandchildren will enjoy the fruit of my labors. Most of the trees I have enjoyed were planted by people who died before I was born.

I don't think there's any law that says people have to finish everything they begin. Old age is a good time to start things that will outlive me. It's a good time to start writing a book or to build a house. It's a good time to organize a club or a church, something that will be around a century from now.

Lord, help us to begin our tasks with faith and to leave endings to You. —DANIEL SCHANTZ

SUN
13

ACCORDING TO THE KINDNESS THAT I HAVE DONE UNTO THEE, THOU SHALT DO UNTO ME. . . . —*Genesis 21:23*

I'M A SINGLE FATHER, so my time with my six-year-old son Harrison is more limited than I'd like, but I try for the consistency that experts recommend.

For instance, on our weekends together, Harrison and I go to the same restaurant every Saturday morning, where they start cooking our breakfast as soon as we appear. There is baseball or soccer or football, according to season, and visits with family and friends. One Saturday, though, we didn't have time for sports. That night as I tucked him in, I reminded Harrison about church in the morning, lunch with my family and then nap time. "What about throwing the football?" he asked.

"Nap time after lunch," I said. "Those are the rules."

The next morning as we rushed off to church, I glanced at the newspaper sitting on the passenger seat, ready for me to read at nap time. After Sunday school, Harrison joined me for the children's sermon, which was about kindness. "When you do kind things for others," the minister said, "God just might send kindness back to you."

Later in the car, I was lifting Harrison into his booster seat. "Daddy," he asked, "did you see me being kind to Ms. Duncan today?"

"I sure did, buddy. It's great to be kind to one another. God wants us to help others be happy."

"I know," he answered, knowing his father too well. "It'll make me *real* happy if you let me skip my nap today and we throw the football instead!"

Father, help me remember that the ultimate in consistency is kindness and that all man-made rules mean little without it. —BROCK KIDD

A SECOND THANK-YOU
THANK YOU FOR SALVATION

MON
14

RESTORE TO ME THE JOY OF YOUR SALVATION. . . . —Psalm 51:12 (NIV)

I INVITED KENNY, a man without any family nearby, to spend Thanksgiving with my sister and me. That evening, as I drove him home, I told Kenny I was especially thankful that God had brought him into my life. Kenny had been helping me around the cabin with landscaping and odd jobs, and we had come to be good friends.

But an inner Voice wouldn't stop insisting: *Tell Kenny about Me, Roberta.* So I began sputtering about God and salvation, hoping that I was explaining them in a way that would be clear and not offensive. I didn't want Kenny to think I'd invited him to dinner and then pressured him into something. So I closed my little speech with: "If you'd ever like to ask Jesus to live in your heart, just let me know."

Almost immediately Kenny's deep voice answered, "Well, how about right now, Roberta?"

In praying with Kenny, I felt the joy of my own salvation return. Suddenly, I was ten years old again and had just asked Jesus to live in my heart. "Jesus is the best Friend you'll ever know, Kenny," I promised.

"Even better than you?" he challenged.

"Oh yes," I said, "even better."

Precious Savior, remind me that the best way to keep thanking You for the good news is to pass it along to others. —ROBERTA MESSNER

TUE
15

FOR THY SERVANTS TAKE PLEASURE IN HER STONES, AND FAVOUR THE DUST THEREOF. —Psalm 102:14

THE OTHER DAY I RUINED both my hearing aids. (I'd put them in my shirt pocket, then washed the shirt. Not recommended!) Replacing them would take three weeks, and meanwhile it was "What did you say?" and "Can't hear you" and "Say again?" until my wife Tib must have been ready to buy a bullhorn.

But it was an odd thing, she told me later, that distressed her most. "It wasn't having to raise my voice and repeat," she said. "It was that I no longer found myself sharing the little things"—the small, fleeting, inconsequential observations that didn't merit communicating at the top of her lungs. "I realized how much of our relationship is made up of just those shared minor moments."

How many such moments, I wondered, did I stop to share with God? Moments when your heart lifts, when you understand something or notice something new. Yesterday morning I saw an insect laying her eggs on the outside of a window pane in our kitchen; I stood and watched—and thanked God for showing me one of His smaller miracles. Later in the day, in a crowded New York City coffee shop, I noticed a man with an enormous belly slumped in front of his laptop, snoring peacefully, accepted and undisturbed as people passed by smiling. A few moments later, another lovely glimpse: a mother with an infant strapped across her chest hailing a taxi in the rain. Little moments to share with Tib . . . and with God.

Help me, Father, to tell You more of the little things that are at the heart of intimacy. —JOHN SHERRILL

READER'S ROOM

IT IS PRETTY to see nature. The moon. The stars. Flowers in people's gardens. The pretty month of April.

Going to church with my wife. The church where she works.

Spending time with my wife. Going bicycling together.

Seeing good things getting done in and to our home.

My work with flowers in a department store.

Being in touch with my family.
—*David Holmgren, Saginaw, Michigan*

WED
16
IN THY PRESENCE IS FULNESS OF JOY. . . . —Psalm 16:11

"I HAVE TO WORK LATE." I could hear the stress in my daughter's voice. "Can you pick up Drake and let him spend a few hours with you?"

I was always glad to spend time with my grandson. "Of course. I'll go straight from work."

When I pulled into the driveway of the sitter's house, I heard Drake before I saw him. He was giggling, peeking through the railing on the porch steps. "Hey, buddy!" I said. With that, he ran down the sidewalk and threw himself into my arms.

Drake had no idea what I had planned for us to do—whether it was sort laundry or take a trip to the park, whether we would eat at his favorite fast-food restaurant or have grilled cheese at my house. It didn't matter to him. His joy was in being with me, basking in the presence of his nana.

I thought about that later when I began my evening prayers. Did I run to God with a list of "give-me's" and "help-me's," or did I approach Him filled with joy at simply being with Him?

I didn't say much to God that night. I just drew near to Him and waited. Whatever He had planned for our time together was just fine with me.

Joy, joy, joy, Father! I fling myself into Your arms . . . and trust. —MARY LOU CARNEY

THU
17

*YOUR ADVERSARY THE DEVIL, AS A
ROARING LION, WALKETH ABOUT,
SEEKING WHOM HE MAY DEVOUR: WHOM
RESIST STEDFAST IN THE FAITH. . . .*
                                    —*I Peter 5:8–9*

I'D GONE BACK TO WALKING four miles a day after years of telling myself that I didn't have the energy. At first, my imagination was getting as much of a workout as my legs. *What should I do if I meet an unfriendly dog?* I wondered. A variety of scenarios played themselves out in my mind.

Then one April morning I left home when the sun was barely up. Birds greeted each other as I walked quickly down the street. At the bottom of the hill, a strange dog charged out of the woods, headed straight for me. My heart thumped as the big fellow, who weighed about a hundred pounds, continued to charge, snarling, teeth showing, muscles straining.

Lord Jesus, help me!

I sensed His answer: *Rebuke him now.*

Somehow I managed to stomp my foot as though I had power and authority and screamed, "Nooooo!"

He froze, then dropped his head as though he suddenly sniffed something very interesting. With his nose glued to the pavement, he made a quick exit back into the woods and disappeared. I felt the fear again and relief. *Thank You, Lord.*

I sensed a silent message: *You can call on Me this*

*way every time the enemy tries to attack you with trou-
bling thoughts, memories or what ifs.*

Now, I wouldn't necessarily recommend that you
try this method with a threatening dog, but I've found
that where dangerous spiritual critters are concerned,
it works wonders.

*Father God, when the enemy comes like a roaring lion
to attack my thoughts, help me remember to call on
Your name.* —MARION BOND WEST

FRI
18

MY TIMES ARE IN THY HAND. . . .
—*Psalm 31:15*

AS IS TOO OFTEN THE CASE, I was behind
schedule and rushing to a meeting with my
colleague Amy. "Sorry, sorry," I muttered, bursting
into her office.

She turned her wrist toward me and said, "Oh,
you're only a couple of minutes late." I stared at her
watch, mortified. I was nearly twenty minutes late!
Amy saw the look on my face.

"Don't worry," she laughed, "I set my watch fifteen
minutes fast."

Amy is one of the brightest and most honest people
I know, and unfailingly practical. A feeble act of self-
deception like this seemed out of character.

"You mean you trick yourself into thinking it's later
than it is?" I asked, a bit incredulous. "Don't you just

factor in that you know your watch is fifteen minutes ahead? That's what I'd do. It wouldn't make any difference."

Amy thought for a moment. "No," she said, "it's not about fooling myself. It's more of a reminder to think ahead and to think about others."

Sometimes, running late and not thinking ahead, I struggle to fit more things into an hour or a day than I can. Maybe I won't set my watch ahead fifteen minutes like my wise friend, but I will take something from her: that being considerate of time is being considerate of others.

I move through time as surely as I move through space as I travel on my journey with You, Lord.
—EDWARD GRINNAN

SAT
19

"NEVER AGAIN WILL I MAKE YOU AN OBJECT OF SCORN. . . ." —*Joel 2:19 (NIV)*

MY COUSIN BUNNY was born in the 1930s, profoundly deaf. Our family decided that no allowances would be made for that, and Bunny learned to lip-read at a very early age. With training, he learned to speak so well that many people had no idea he couldn't hear, which helped him escape some of the teasing other children directed at him when they learned about his condition. When Bunny began to look for work after high school, I could see that my parents were really worried about his future, even though they didn't say anything in front of me.

At Passover the next year, Bunny came to our seder, bursting with news that he had gotten a job in the office at an oil refinery. We asked him to tell us how it happened. Bunny said, "They tried to tell me that they couldn't hire me because I wouldn't be able to hear the alarm if it went off, but I told them that there was nothing at all wrong with my eyesight. I said, 'If I see everybody running for the doors, I'll run, too, and you can tell me about the alarm later.'"

God had given Bunny all the strength he needed to cope with whatever came his way, and over the years that followed, I've discovered that even if there are areas in which I, too, fall short, God has done the same for me.

Thank You, Lord, for Your gifts to us, despite our flaws. —RHODA BLECKER

SUN
20

WHAT DOTH THE LORD REQUIRE OF THEE, BUT TO DO JUSTLY, AND TO LOVE MERCY, AND TO WALK HUMBLY WITH THY GOD? —Micah 6:8

THE GRAY-HAIRED LADY always sat two pews in front of us on Sunday mornings. Gracious, self-effacing, kind, she shook my hand warmly after every service and asked about my wife Ruby's health. I only knew her as Mrs. Morrissey. She taught English at a nearby high school. For a time we served together on the church vestry. As part of our duties, we put together a history of the church for a banquet. I suppose my head got turned by all the praise we received. Not Mrs. Morrissey. "Oscar," she said, "when honors come, wear them lightly."

Sunday mornings I started driving her to and from church. One morning she said on our way back home, "Goodness, I forgot to get some milk and bread." I pulled into a supermarket parking lot. "No, dear," she said, "that's all right. I can do it tomorrow." In her quiet way Mrs. Morrissey was letting me know she did not shop on Sunday.

The biggest surprise came the Sunday Mrs. Morrissey didn't appear in her usual pew. "I'll be out of town," she'd explained mysteriously. I wondered where she'd gone. Then that morning I looked at the church bulletin. There was an announcement that Mrs. Morrissey had flown to Paris to receive a posthumous award given to her famous sister, the aviator Amelia Earhart.

Amelia Earhart's sister. She never said anything about that. I thought for a moment of Mrs. Morrissey in the limelight, and I decided she much preferred her pew two rows in front of us and the fame that came from being a good teacher, a dedicated church worker and a kind friend—wearing her honors lightly.

Gracious Lord, I thank You for sending Mrs. Morrissey and all the others who have inspired me in my life.
—OSCAR GREENE

MON
21 THE WIFE MUST SEE TO IT THAT SHE RESPECTS HER HUSBAND.
—*Ephesians 5:33 (NAS)*

MY HUSBAND RICK AND I have been married for thirty years. I've spent entirely too much of that time thinking about his irritating behavior. I kept a mental list of what bothered me:

- *We don't have inside doorknobs in the log cabin he built us.*
- *He doesn't pick up after himself.*
- *He stopped going to the barber and began cutting his hair in the bathroom sink.*
- *He jumps to new projects without finishing the ones he's already started.*
- *He procrastinates.*

My list grew. Seems there was no end to Rick's annoying habits—or to my nagging. Then I had lunch with a friend who raved about her husband. He brings her flowers and loves antique shopping.

"Yeah, but doesn't he ever aggravate you?" I asked.

"Sure, but the good outweighs the bad."

All afternoon her words moved in my heart. I began to remember the excellent things about Rick:

- *He's generous; he gave a used car to a single mom.*
- *He attends our children's baseball and softball games.*
- *He teaches the Bible to high school boys.*
- *Every day the man makes me laugh.*

I went through the alphabet and thought up positive descriptions:

A—He's available.
B—He's bold.
C—He cares about the down-and-out.
D—He's determined.

Now when I wipe his hair out of the sink or push open the knobless bedroom doors, I say:
"Wow! You built this home just for us."
"You have the gift of giving."
"Your hair sure is thick."

May I honor You, Lord, by honoring my husband with both my thoughts and words. —JULIE GARMON

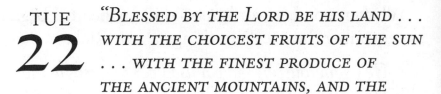

TUE 22

"*Blessed by the Lord be his land . . . with the choicest fruits of the sun . . . with the finest produce of the ancient mountains, and the abundance of the everlasting hills, with the best gifts of the earth and its fullness. . . .*"
—*Deuteronomy 33:13–16* (RSV)

"A forty-minute hike?" my mother gasped. "I didn't know we'd have to hike there!" My family and I were in the Puerto Rican rainforest and had just learned we'd have to trek it to La Mina, the island's tallest waterfall.

"It'll be fine," we convinced her. "You have your asthma pump. We'll just take it slow." It had been more than twenty years since we'd been in Puerto Rico as a family, and we were having a wonderful time rediscovering the island of our roots.

We started the hike with a burst of energy. Even my mother was zipping through and actually leading the way. Our trek was anything but straight and level; the trail twisted and turned and led up and down steep hills. We helped one another cross narrow paths and climb over large slippery rocks as we laughed, talked and encouraged each other to keep going. Streams of light found their way through the tropical palms, there were lush, shiny leaves the size of small umbrellas, and we passed babbling brooks and mini-waterfalls. But the best part of the hike was simply being with my family.

We finally reached the waterfall, and after a moment of admiration we immersed our tired bodies in the cool, refreshing water. "You see," I said to my mother, "wasn't this worth it?"

My mother didn't hear me. She was under the waterfall, letting it spill over her head like blessings from God.

I am awed by Your creation, God. Thank you.
—KAREN VALENTIN

WED
23

PRAISE HIM WITH THE SOUND OF THE TRUMPET: PRAISE HIM WITH THE PSALTERY AND HARP. —*Psalm 150:3*

OUR SON TIM HAS A ROCK BAND. Four sixteen-year-old boys who write their own songs, make recordings to post on their Web site and practice whenever they can. This being New York City, where garages are hard to come by, they have to pool their babysitting money to rehearse in rented studio space. It's a little easier on our ears, but it means we didn't get a chance to hear them until they played their first gig at a club downtown with some other aspiring bands.

"What are we supposed to do?" I asked Carol. "Won't they be embarrassed if we show up?" I couldn't imagine anything less cool than a couple of proud parents in the back taking pictures. How would it look, this gray-haired intrusion?

"I'm not missing this for the world," Carol replied.

I felt pretty conspicuous in my blazer and buttoned-down shirt among the T-shirts and jeans. And I could have used a good pair of earplugs when the other bands played (it was loud, really loud). But when Tim's band performed, Carol and I hooted and hollered and clapped like the wildest of fans.

"You guys were awesome!" I told Tim. Their songs were clever—at least the lyrics I could understand— and their sound was great. And who knew that Tim could dance like Mick Jagger?

"Thanks for coming," he said in between a few high fives.

"Wouldn't have missed it for the world." That's what parents do. They show up . . . even in the most unlikely places.

I praise You, Lord, as I thank You for the gift of parent-hood. Let my enthusiasm show! —RICK HAMLIN

THU
24
"LOOK AT THE BIRDS OF THE AIR; THEY DO NOT SOW OR REAP OR STORE AWAY IN BARNS, AND YET YOUR HEAVENLY FATHER FEEDS THEM. ARE YOU NOT MUCH MORE VALUABLE THAN THEY?"
—*Matthew 6:26* (NIV)

LAST YEAR, I WAS FEELING the weight of our impending move back East. Although we looked forward to being near family again, my wife Carol and I didn't like the idea of giving up the laid-back California lifestyle we'd come to enjoy.

While we prepared our house for the market, our yard became an avian nursery. Nests were everywhere: hummingbirds in the oleander, mourning doves in the giant philodendron, goldfinches in the carrotwood tree and swallows under the eave outside one bedroom. Across the street, a pair of red-tailed hawks returned to their aerie in a eucalyptus tree to raise another brood.

I grabbed my camera and followed a hummingbird in our backyard as she gathered spiderwebs and other materials for a nest in the oleander. I snapped her sitting on her eggs and later as she fed the hatchlings. Sometimes she dive-bombed me, scolding, when she caught me near her young while she was off the nest. But she remained statue-still on the nest when I crept close to photograph her.

Little by little the young birds fledged and flew away. One tiny hummingbird was last to leave. The mother kept calling to it from a tree in the next yard. After a long time the hungry bird hopped to the edge of the nest, then out onto a leaf. Finally, it set its wings in motion, lifted to a higher branch and after a moment's rest, zipped out of sight.

In that moment it was as if God said, *It's time to leave your comfort zone. Don't worry. Your future is in My hands.*

Father, we look to You to take care of us as we move into the unknown. —HAROLD HOSTETLER

FRI
25
"YOU ALONE ARE THE LORD. YOU MADE THE HEAVENS, EVEN THE HIGHEST HEAVENS, AND ALL THEIR STARRY HOST, THE EARTH AND ALL THAT IS ON IT, THE SEAS AND ALL THAT IS IN THEM. . . ."
—Nehemiah 9:6 (NIV)

WHEN MY OLDEST GRANDDAUGHTER Jazmine was about fourteen months old, a circus came to our area. I thought that it would be something she'd enjoy, and so her mother Jody and I drove down to the local fairgrounds where the circus had pitched its tent.

After buying our tickets, we made our way into the grandstand, where Jazmine sat on my lap. At first she clung to me, frightened by all the strange sights and sounds. Then the elephant with his trainer stepped into view. Jazmine's eyes widened with awe as the huge, lumbering beast made its way into the center ring.

"Look at his big ears," I said, pointing. "And his long, long nose."

Jazmine stared at the elephant for a moment and a look of rapture spread over her face. Then she started to applaud, her small hands bouncing against each other in an outburst of joy. She laughed and cheered, and soon I was laughing and cheering too. Jazmine's delight became my own.

Sometime later I paused to watch the sun set in a pink and orange sky. Golden light radiated from the horizon. The view was spectacular. I caught my breath and then, following my granddaughter's example, I looked up to heaven and applauded.

Lord, may I always maintain a childlike wonder as I view the world You made. —DEBBIE MACOMBER

SAT
26

HEARKEN UNTO THE VOICE OF MY CRY, MY KING, AND MY GOD: FOR UNTO THEE WILL I PRAY. —*Psalm 5:2*

"HOW DO YOU LIKE THE THEME 'Ribbons of Prayer' for our spring luncheon?" my friend Sherry asked. I loved it.

She and her committee went to work. Tall maypoles festooned with streamers greeted us as we went through the doors of the auditorium. We were to choose a ribbon from baskets, offer it to the Lord with a promise to pray for a friend, then tie it to one of the maypoles. I chose a gossamer lavender. As I affixed it to the maypole, the friend I committed to pray for was Sherry. Her vibrant, cheerful spirit, the dimple in her cheek that danced with every smile . . . few people knew that she was battling cancer. *Embrace her with Your healing touch,* I prayed. *Extend her time with us, dear Lord.*

On the way home I bought a bouquet of silk flowers, pink peonies and white roses. I made a prayer garland for Sherry and attached it to the tall wrought-iron candelabra standing in our entry hall. The first ribbon I threaded through it matched the one I put on the maypole—lavender. Then deep maroon for her husband and bright colors for the children.

That was more than eight years ago. The Lord extended Sherry's time. She planned many more luncheons. "Ribbons of Promise" . . . "Ribbons of Praise" . . . her maypoles became a symbol of the joy of her faith, her trust and her effervescent love of our Lord.

This week the Lord called Sherry home. I threaded a shimmering golden ribbon through her garland. And today my garland has two new ribbons, green and blue: my commitment to pray for a mother and her troubled son. Sherry's legacy continues.

O Lord of infinite grace, hear our cry. In our weakness be our strength, in our despair our hope. Do for us and those we love, that which we are unable to do for ourselves. —FAY ANGUS

SUN 27 "*FOR WHERE TWO OR THREE COME TOGETHER IN MY NAME, THERE AM I WITH THEM.*" —*Matthew 18:20 (NIV)*

IN ALL THE NEIGHBORHOODS I've ever lived in, I've noticed that when bad things happen, neighbors gather together for support and strength.

When I lived in Wisconsin, a tornado ripped through town a few miles north of us. Afterward the neighbors gathered outside to talk, share stories, and help each other clean up fallen branches and scattered debris.

A few months after 9/11, I visited Ground Zero in New York City with four friends, including my oldest daughter Jeanne. We stood there huddled together, holding hands, trying to understand and calm one another's fears.

When the edges of three hurricanes swept past my new Florida neighborhood, my neighbors and I gathered to share food during the power outage and planned for the next big wind.

A couple of years ago, I visited the Everglades during a drought. I stood on a walkway a few feet above a river that had dried up except for about eighty yards of murky green water. In front of me, thirty or forty alligators had gathered. I guess even gators find comfort and strength in numbers during times of stress.

When I attend church, I always sit in the last pew. It gives me a bird's-eye view of the congregation, and every week as the people file in, I feel peace and security in their presence. It seems as if I'm being sheltered from the problems of life by those around me. There truly is strength in numbers.

Lord, help me to gather with others when times are tough or we just need to feel the warmth of Your love through each other's arms. —PATRICIA LORENZ

MON
28

"WHO GIVES SONGS IN THE NIGHT?"
—*Job 35:10 (NAS)*

AFTER EXPERIENCING an irregularity in my heartbeat, I had been admitted to the emergency room in a big-city hospital for observation.

Hooked up to a heart monitor, I lay awake most of the night, unable to sleep because of the unfamiliar surroundings. Hospital attendants were kind and conscientious, but I longed for morning to come, when the doctor would be in to assess my situation.

Around 2:00 AM a nurse came to make her rounds, pulling back the curtains at the foot of my bed, "Just so we can keep an eye on you." I could now keep an eye on the big round clock that hung across the hall.

2:15 AM. 2:30 AM. Snores were emanating from behind the curtains on either side of my bed, but sleep still eluded me. I could hear the nurses rustling papers, making reports, comparing notes. And then someone at the nursing station began to whistle softly bits and pieces of a song.

"I wish I could do that!" a voice remarked.

"You mean you don't know how to whistle?"

"Nope, never could get the hang of it."

For the next hour or so I was privy to a lesson given by a skilled whistler to a group of novices. Little did they know that the patient in bed four was listening, nor did I want them to know. I just lay there with my eyes closed, listening to the clear, sweet notes of the teacher leading her eager pupils note by squeaky note. In the morning each of the nurses cheerfully began her rounds with "Whistle While You Work."

Remind me often, Lord, that an upbeat attitude encourages everyone's heart. Thank You that my own heart is functioning just fine. —ALMA BARKMAN

TUE
29

FOR YE HAVE NEED OF PATIENCE, THAT, AFTER YE HAVE DONE THE WILL OF GOD, YE MIGHT RECEIVE THE PROMISE.
—*Hebrews 10:36*

THE HELP WANTED ADS leered at me. I'd sent out hordes of résumés to no avail. Still, every morning I prayed: "God, help me find a job that will make me smile."

I saw a job I never would have had the guts to apply for if I hadn't been desperate. "Ordinary people wanted for a two-day fashion show in the shopping mall." *Hmm, I sure fill the bill on that one,* I thought.

By the time I got there, I was quite hopeful. "The manager will see you right away," the receptionist told me.

After that warm welcome, I was astonished when the man gave me a three-second glance and brusquely waved me away. "No," he said, "you won't do." His head was already down reading his magazine.

Feeling sure I'd been led to answer his ad, I boldly asked, "Sir, may I ask why?" At his startled look, I plodded on, "Your ad did say you were looking for ordinary people."

"Oh," he exclaimed, "you got it wrong! We're not looking for ordinary people. We're looking for models who *look* like ordinary people!"

He went back to reading his magazine. And I? Well, I managed to stifle my laughter at the absurdity of the situation until I left his office. And on my way home I passed a bookstore, went in, filled out an application and have been happily employed there ever since!

When I'm down in the dumps, God, remind me that even there You can give me something to smile about.
—LINDA NEUKRUG

WED 30 *WHY DO YOU PASS JUDGMENT ON YOUR BROTHER? . . . —Romans 14:10 (RSV)*

WE FINALLY TOOK A FAMILY sightseeing trip to New York City, a place we'd wanted to share with our children for a long time. Having grown up in a suburb outside of Manhattan, I'd been to the city many times and it was always thrilling—and a little intimidating. So, as tourists from Arizona, we prepared ourselves for everything we'd heard about, from the noise and the traffic to New Yorkers themselves. We knew their reputation— hurried, no-nonsense, even rude. You know, walk fast, especially when crossing the street, and don't talk to anybody unless you have to.

Well, the sights were fantastic: the Statue of Liberty and Ellis Island, the Empire State Building, a Broadway show. But the big surprise was the people. From the talkative cab driver who brought us to the hotel to the helpful ticket agent at Grand Central Station, everyone we met was friendly and truly kind.

My daughter Maria and I were walking down 48th Street near our hotel one afternoon when we saw a couple with a little white dog like ours. Maria insisted on stopping, but I was reluctant. Yet as soon as we approached, the owners were happy to let Maria pet their dog and share stories as only pet lovers do.

One morning we were buying hot chocolate from a street vendor when the woman behind us suggested a small park nearby where we could enjoy our drinks, a beautiful spot we wouldn't have known about otherwise.

The trip convinced me that God is full of surprises. Some of the best ones are His people.

Lord God, I know that You created us in Your image; teach me to expect the best from all You have made.
                              —GINA BRIDGEMAN

MY DIVINE SURPRISES

1 _____

2 _____

3 _____

4 _____

5 _____

6 _____

7 _____

8 _____

9 _____

10 _____

11 _____

12 _____

13 _____

14 _____

15 _____

16 _____

17 _____

18 _____

19 _____

20 _____

21 _____

22 _____

23 _____

24 _____

25 _____

26 _____

27 _____

28 _____

29 _____

30 _____

May

The Spirit searcheth all things, yea, the deep things of God. —*I Corinthians 2:10*

THU
1

*HE WAS PRAYING IN A CERTAIN PLACE,
AND AFTER HE HAD FINISHED, ONE OF
HIS DISCIPLES SAID TO HIM, "LORD,
TEACH US TO PRAY, AS JOHN TAUGHT
HIS DISCIPLES." —Luke 11:1 (NRSV)*

I'VE ALWAYS BELIEVED that you affect people more by what you do than by what you say. I think that's particularly true of prayer.

When I met my husband Charlie ten years ago, I'd venture to say he wasn't praying a lot. But because I prayed, he started to pray with me. Eventually we were praying together daily, though I occasionally suspected that he was praying just to please me. Did he really believe in the power of prayer?

I learned the truth earlier this year when we were flying back to Connecticut from Key West, Florida. We made our Miami connection and were about fifteen minutes into the flight. I was dozing and Charlie was gazing out the window. Suddenly the pilot announced, "Folks, the flight crew has detected a burning odor in the back of the plane, so we are returning to Miami. Please don't panic, and don't be surprised when you see fire and emergency vehicles on the runway."

Amid the fearful chatter of the other passengers, Charlie and I were quiet. He gripped my hand. We were silent for the next twenty minutes until we landed safely.

When we were on the ground, I turned to him and asked, "Why didn't you say anything all that time?"

"Well," he answered slowly, "I thought that under the circumstances, we better concentrate on praying."

I guess he has been getting it all these years, after all.

Listening Lord, thank You for showing me how to pray. —MARCI ALBORGHETTI

UNEXPECTED BLESSINGS
FINDING FORGIVENESS

FRI
2

CONFESS YOUR FAULTS ONE TO ANOTHER . . . THAT YE MAY BE HEALED. . . .
—James 5:16

IT WAS A STREET of new homes and raw brown yards—except for the place next to ours. Most of our neighbors were young parents like ourselves; but this was a retired couple, passionate gardeners whose lawn was a green carpet on our barren street. That spring I'd watch them training rosebushes on the side of the garage or weeding the stately row of red tulips on either side of their front walk.

I was ironing one afternoon, one eye on three-year-old Scotty in the backyard, when a row of brilliant red spots in the bare earth caught my attention. I went to the window, willing them to be Scotty's trucks.

They were tulips. Fourteen of them.

I went out and to Scotty's wails gathered the fragile cups from the little mounds of dirt he'd patted around one-inch stems. For a tempting moment I thought of putting them in the trash—who would know we were the guilty ones? But that older couple, ever after, would believe it was an act of hostility by some unknown neighbor.

And so, Scotty beside me, I carried the poor cropped heads next door, down the walk where fourteen empty stems pointed skyward like accusing fingers, and rang the bell. For a second, when the woman saw the tulips, she grew pale. I don't remember what I said and I doubt she heard it. She took the flowers from me, nodded speechlessly and shut the door.

My husband had come home and put Scotty to bed, with a lecture about flowers you pick and flowers you don't, when about 8:30 PM the doorbell rang. It was our next-door neighbors. She held a pot of geraniums, he carried a tray of begonias.

"These are easy to grow," the man said. "If you like, we'll show your little boy how."

Bestower of blessing, grant me, too, the grace to respond to hurt with the transforming power of forgiveness. —ELIZABETH SHERRILL

EDITOR'S NOTE: Take a few moments to look back at what you've written in the journal pages "My Divine Surprises," and let us know what unexpected blessings God has been surprising you with. Send your letter to Daily Guideposts Reader's Room, Guideposts Books, 16 E. 34th St., New York, NY 10016. We'll share some of what you tell us in a future edition of *Daily Guideposts.*

SAT
3

THE LORD IS CLOSE TO THE BROKENHEARTED; HE RESCUES THOSE WHO ARE CRUSHED IN SPIRIT.
                                —*Psalm 34:18 (NLT)*

DR. ERFLE FLIPPED on the light box and affixed the X-ray of my horse Dancer's hind leg. "I'm afraid I don't have good news."

I gritted my teeth.

Dr. Erfle pointed to the kneelike stifle joint. "It was broken right here. And now her body is stabilizing the joint by fusing into one solid bone. Unfortunately, there isn't anything that can be done. She'll never be sound enough to be ridden."

Tears streamed down my face as I loaded Dancer into the horse trailer and drove home. I had purchased her a year ago as a saddle horse. As soon as I'd brought her home, my twenty-plus-year-old gelding Czar had fallen in love with her. I'd ridden Czar over twenty thousand miles in the mountains; he'd saved my life more than once. He'd never cared for any other horse until she showed up.

The following day, one thought plagued me. *What value is a broken horse? I can't even ride her at a walk.* But as soon as I thought of selling her, I knew I couldn't.

That evening as I pulled open the file drawer to put away the veterinarian's bill, I thumbed through the Ds. Right behind the file labeled "Dancer" was "Divorce."

Again tears streamed down my face. I'd been broken by my divorce. It was almost as if God's still small voice was saying, "It doesn't matter to me if you're broken. I still cherish you."

Dancer had enriched my life by being a companion to Czar. She might be broken, but she was valuable to me—just as I was valuable to God.

Lord, thank You for cherishing me, even though I've been broken. —REBECCA ONDOV

SUN
4

"DO YOU HAVE EYES, AND FAIL TO SEE? DO YOU HAVE EARS, AND FAIL TO HEAR? . . ." —Mark 8:18 (NRSV)

HAVE YOU EVER THOUGHT about how to listen for God's Word in church? I mean, really listen and really hear, no matter what might be keeping you from hearing it. Like your child squirming next to you. Or the person behind you coughing. Or your spouse being the preacher.

Now that might not sound like any big deal to you, but think about this: What does it mean when the person who reminds you to take out the garbage or wash the dishes or not work so hard is suddenly speaking on behalf of God on Sunday morning? The first Sunday of Lynn's four-month substitute-for-our-pastor stint, it was hard for me to hear her sermon. It was *really* hard the second week, and by the third, I was wondering if I needed to find a different church.

I didn't. Not because I figured out a solution or another pastor's spouse gave me good advice. No, it was a second-grader who set me straight. "You're lucky," he said. "You get to go home and ask God what She meant."

The profound lesson in his words hit me square upside the head: We are lucky—blessed—that God chooses unique and remarkable ways to speak to us, including ones we would not choose for ourselves. Sometimes they come in words from a seven-year-old, sometimes they can come in a sermon from a spouse.

Thank You, God, for caring enough to provide me with guidance on a daily basis. Help me to hear and to follow. —JEFF JAPINGA

MON
5
*AND THE LORD GOD PLANTED A GARDEN
EASTWARD IN EDEN; AND THERE HE PUT
THE MAN WHOM HE HAD FORMED.*
                              —*Genesis 2:8*

IT'S LILAC TIME IN PENNSYLVANIA. They're in full and fragrant bloom. Of course, they'll be gone soon, as will our stand of red and white bleeding hearts, multicolored tulips and crimson azalea. But not to fret. I can see iris and peonies pointing toward Memorial Day. I remember that they were always ready by the holiday, in time for decorating graves.

But lilacs have my full attention at the moment. They're particularly striking this year. In the six springs we've been in State College, our two stands have been very sparing with their flowers. And there is a reason. A stately maple, probably eighty years old, used to shade them. Sadly, it was removed by the city last fall because its dead top was threatening the power lines. I say sadly because in my dotage I mourn the passing of all old trees, those sentinels of time. They are such a blessing—shading in summer, shielding the wind in winter and purifying the air year-round.

The lavender lilac bushes are pregnant with grape-like bunches of flowers and the aroma is absolutely breathtaking. Lilacs need full sun to flourish, and now with the maple gone they have no impediment. I lost a much-loved tree and gained some beautiful lilacs.

My mother would probably say, "God never closes a door, but what He opens is a window." And once again, she would be right.

Creator God, we see Your hand in everything,
But perhaps most clearly in verdant spring.
                                    —FRED BAUER

TUE
6

I WILL NOT LEAVE YOU NOR FORSAKE YOU. —Joshua 1:5 (NKJV)

I RING THE BELL to Susanna's apartment, carrying alphabet games and a simple reading textbook. For several months now, I've been tutoring my new friend, a refugee from Liberia, in reading and writing. Susanna is a relaxed and joyful student. When she mispronounces a word, she says, "I know it in my head and in my heart, but my tongue gets too happy!"

But Susanna is not happy today. In fact, her eyes shine with tears. In her rapid, fragmented English, she explains that four of her nieces and nephews have perished in a fire a thousand miles away. She has just returned from a brief visit there and shows me the funeral program, shaking her head in disbelief.

The stories tumble out and old grief resurfaces. In Liberia, her husband and six of her fifteen children were killed by war. Then she was torn from her family by the people in charge. "'You go here! You go there!' they tell us. My daughter and her children, we run away to this country." She had hoped to be safe here. Now this.

A lesson is out of the question. "Shall I go, Susanna, or shall I stay?"

"Stay a little while."

So I simply sit with my friend, whose losses I can't even imagine. For thirty minutes we do not talk, but think our own thoughts, pray our own prayers. Then she raises her head.

"It will be all right," she whispers. "God is here. God is here."

Father, I cling to Your promise never to leave us orphaned. Thank You for people of unbreakable faith like Susanna who draw me closer to You.
— GAIL THORELL SCHILLING

WED
7
HOW HAPPY I AM BECAUSE OF YOUR PROMISES—AS HAPPY AS SOMEONE WHO FINDS GREAT TREASURE.
—*Psalm 119:162* (GNB)

AS A BOY, I loved to discover things for myself. I tramped through the woods like Daniel Boone, looking for some lost civilization or a secret cave.

My grandsons have inherited that love of discovery, and I like to nurture it. Before they come to visit, I buy old toys, tools and crafts at rummage sales, then put them all over the house, garage and shed for them to find. I'll put some old golf clubs in the shed, a radio-controlled jeep in the attic, a toy lathe in the garage. They always find the things I've hidden, and finding them seems to bring the boys special pleasure. "Grandpa, look at this cool jeep I found in the attic. Can I play with it?"

They also find things I didn't plant, like a rope that becomes a lasso, a piece of black plastic that makes a great waterslide and some bricks that can be built into a fort. Children find treasures because they are curious, expectant. Alas, age tends to dull one's sense of curiosity, and that's too bad. I have a feeling I've missed some great treasures because my eyes were distracted by mind-numbing routine and complacency.

Who knows what God has planted for me to find today? A visitor on campus? At the library, might I discover a new author whose books will bring me years of pleasure?

If I slow down a bit, I might be surprised by God, and a childhood feeling of adventure will return.

Lord, give me the eyes of a child and tickle my imagination so that I can see the potential in ordinary things.
—DANIEL SCHANTZ

THU
8

FOR THE WRATH OF MAN WORKETH NOT
THE RIGHTEOUSNESS OF GOD.
—*James 1:20*

AN ADVERTISING AGENCY assigned me to direct a campaign for one of their clients. Over the next few weeks, I managed their staff and wrote the ads. Along the way I showed them the work-in-progress, and they made changes here and there and encouraged me to continue. Before the presentation I laid out the work, and the executives chose the campaigns they thought were best suited to their client's needs. Everybody felt good about the work; we knew the client was going to be very happy.

But during the presentation, the client liked none of it. We were shocked; I went straight home and started feverishly preparing for round two.

The next week I received an e-mail from the agency saying that they were going to relieve me of the assignment. I was angry. I was ready to scream at the top of my lungs, write letters, complain to my wife until she couldn't take it anymore, lose sleep and stop eating. That's certainly how I'd behaved before when I thought I was being the scapegoat.

But then I felt the grace of God like a hand on my shoulder. *Steady now,* He seemed to say. I tried to focus on my anger and hurt, and all I could see in my mind's eye was the love God had poured out in giving me His Son. Suddenly, it seemed that the assignment didn't matter a whit and maybe I'd learned something in the process.

I looked at the e-mail again, shrugged and hit DELETE.

Thank You, Lord, for saving me from anger. May I always remember You are all that matters, and that You alone are my sustenance. —DAVE FRANCO

FRI
9

AND HE TURNED TO THE WOMAN, AND SAID UNTO SIMON . . . I ENTERED INTO THINE HOUSE, THOU GAVEST ME NO WATER FOR MY FEET: BUT SHE HATH WASHED MY FEET WITH TEARS, AND WIPED THEM WITH THE HAIRS OF HER HEAD. —*Luke 7:44*

WHEN I WAS A GIRL and my mother's weary feet needed a massage, I usually found something else to do. Then last year I became caregiver to my hundred-year-old aunt. Rubbing her feet during an illness soothed her so much that I offered this act of comfort to others in her retirement community.

I sit on the floor, in the hair salon or in the lounge, and rub feet while people are getting their hair done or working crossword puzzles or reading the newspaper. I rub the feet of guests while we visit after dinner in the living room or watch a movie. I massage the feet of people bedridden from surgery. And when we're together, I finally—joyfully—rub my mother's feet too.

Perhaps the deepest reason I do what I do is that I feel a kinship with the woman in the Bible who, from vulnerability and gratitude, cast herself at Jesus' feet and washed them with her tears. My foot rubs are as close as I can come to this act of devotion.

Lord, thank You for helping my heart find its way to my hands. —CAROL KNAPP

SAT **10** *"I'M PUTTING MY RAINBOW IN THE CLOUDS. . . ."* —*Genesis 9:13 (THE MESSAGE)*

JULIE'S DAUGHTER KATIE was my first grandchild to marry. We all got caught up in Katie's plans, except for one thing: She had her heart set on an outdoor wedding at sunset. Nothing could dissuade her.

"What about rain?" I asked her gently.

"It's not going to," Katie answered with a smile.

A week before the wedding, Julie told Katie that showers were in the forecast. I added my grim amen.

"It's not going to rain. I've prayed about it, y'all."

Four days before the wedding, I phoned to tell Katie that rain was actually forecast for her wedding day.

"It's not going to rain, Nanny. Thanks though," she said politely.

Then a day before the wedding, when I ran out to

get the mail in between showers and glanced up to scan the sky, I lit up like a Christmas tree. There, hanging in the darkish sky, was a double rainbow! Back inside, I telephoned Julie. "I know," she said, not even bothering to say hello.

Saturday arrived, a bit dreary-looking. As we left the house, I grabbed an umbrella that blended in with my ice-pink dress. At seven o'clock, about two hundred of us sat in white chairs in front of a large gazebo. The wedding music, played by a small ensemble, filled the air. Jamie, the handsome groom, waited with folded hands alongside his brother, the other groomsmen, the bridesmaids and the minister. I checked the sky one more time. The dark clouds behind us seemed to have stopped moving as if on command. Then Katie and her father walked over the lush green grass toward the gazebo and her future.

Father, help me to expect Your rainbow in all life's storms. —MARION BOND WEST

SUN BUT THE FRUIT OF THE SPIRIT IS
11   LOVE, JOY, PEACE, LONGSUFFERING,
     GENTLENESS, GOODNESS, FAITH,
     MEEKNESS, TEMPERANCE: AGAINST SUCH
THERE IS NO LAW. —*Galatians 5:22–23*

IT WAS A MOTHER'S DAY to drive a mother mad. By breakfast, a stiff competition was brewing over which child's feelings could be hurt most easily. A parallel struggle soon emerged for the title of "Most Insensitive to Others." I struggled valiantly to remain calm, trying not to get caught up in the bickering. I took deep breaths, counted to ten, separated the kids. Nothing worked. As a last resort before screaming, I imposed silence on the whole family—no speaking, no grunting, no moaning. Silence.

For a few moments, it was quiet. Then the child who had edged ahead in the crankiness sweepstakes let out an accusatory whine. The peace shattered and I snapped. "You need to pray to the Holy Spirit for help with your tongue today!" I said. The child stared, taken aback. I was taken aback too. My voice had been angry, but the words themselves were anything but. They seemed to come out of nowhere and hang in the air, waiting to be reheard. *You need to pray to the Holy Spirit for help with your tongue today.* The child listened and grew quiet. I listened and sent up a prayer.

I wish I could report that at that moment the sea of contention parted and we all walked through in peace. Unfortunately, that wasn't the case. But the waters did get a little shallower. With heroic effort and a whole lot of prayer, by noon everyone was able to be civil again. It was a minor miracle, perhaps, but a miracle all the same.

Holy Spirit, help me when my tongue is on fire with words that aren't Yours. —JULIA ATTAWAY

READER'S ROOM

FIFTY-ONE YEARS AGO, a grandmother gave me a blooming pink azalea on Mother's Day, one year before I became a mother. Our first son was born in May one year later. That plant has been transplanted as our family has moved from one state to another. This year, the blooms were profusely beautiful to remind us of surviving our own transplanted lives. The azalea has survived the storms, including hurricanes. With God's help, we have come through many physical ailments and emotional turbulence. We hope our lives blossom and endure as the azalea.

—*Allene DeWeese, Florence, South Carolina*

MON
12

"COME WITH ME BY YOURSELVES TO A QUIET PLACE. . . ." —*Mark 6:31 (NIV)*

CLEANING UP THE HOUSE this morning, I came across a snapshot of me sitting quietly on a friend's couch alongside a sleepy black cat and a watchful young dog. I'd started to file away the photo when the big old cat suddenly reminded me of the big old worry I couldn't get out of my mind all week. It's the bane of being self-employed: I have work this week, but what about next month, next year? What if I get dropped from a client's Rolodex? Or erased from someone's Palm Pilot?

A year ago, when this same worry had settled in for a season, I complained to my friend Peggy. "I've prayed and prayed. I ask God to be with me, and yet the worry doesn't leave."

Peggy interrupted. "It sounds as if you're asking Jesus to come and sit with you and your worry."

She was right then and she was right now. I decided not to file away the photo of the three sofa-sitters. It helps me focus on my prayer:

Lord, I want to sit with You alone, not with You and my worries. —EVELYN BENCE

TUE
13
SEEK YE OUT OF THE BOOK OF THE LORD, AND READ. . . . —*Isaiah 34:16*

I LOVE BOOKS. I never miss the Coffee and Books gathering at our public library where new books are reviewed. And I always help out at the library's giant book sales. Boxes and boxes of books come in, and inevitably I come home with more purchases than the donations I made. Books stack up at my bedside, in my study, in my closet, in the cellar. Not to mention the books in the trunk of my car.

"Oscar," I told myself one day, "you need to find something to do with all these books." I couldn't give back the ones I'd bought from the library. And yet, there were so many good books that deserved a reader.

That's when I discovered the book stall that sits in front of our supermarket. I could give away books there. One day I gathered up two boxes of books and put them on the shelf of the book stall. *It'll be weeks before anybody ever takes them*, I thought.

I picked up the things I needed at the supermarket and went through the checkout line. Carrying my groceries to the car, I passed the book stall. To my amazement, half of the books I'd just donated were gone. In fact, the fellow who bagged groceries had dashed out of the store on a break and put some of my offerings in a bag for himself.

Today, I try not to hoard too many books for myself —although if you saw the stack by my bed, you might wonder. There are countless books out there and to my delight, there are just as many readers. Giving them away, I've found, is almost as much fun as reading them.

Thank You for the pleasures, Lord, I get from reading.
                                              —OSCAR GREENE

WED
14

THANK YOU FOR MAKING ME SO WONDERFULLY COMPLEX! IT IS AMAZING TO THINK ABOUT. YOUR WORKMANSHIP IS MARVELOUS. . . . —Psalm 139:14 (TLB)

IF EVER A GROUP OF STUDENTS needed a time to lighten up from the intensity of their studies, they are those at the California Institute of Technology in our neighboring city of Pasadena, where conversation revolves around such things as quasars, quarks and the dynamics of particles in rigid bodies.

On their annual Ditch Day, seniors secure their rooms with complex codes that have to be solved in order to break in, then disappear from the campus. The challenge to the freshmen, sophomores and juniors is to get into the dorms and claim or reject a bribe (generally a feast of some sort) left there to persuade them not to "prank" the room. (One year a senior came back to find all his furniture bolted to the ceiling.)

Professors also get into the fun. The late Richard Feynman, a Nobel Prize winner, offered one thousand dollars to any student who could build an electric motor one-sixty-fourth of an inch on each side. The challenge was successfully met, and the world's tiniest motor, the size of a grain of sand, is still on display at Caltech's Eastbridge Building. To the naked eye it is a black dot, much like the period at the end of this sentence. Through the mirrored magnifier it looks like a small piece of confetti with a line across the top. A notice reads: THIS MOTOR IS WORN OUT AND NO LONGER RUNS.

From mind-boggling intensity, to fun and incredible frivolity, such is the capacity our Creator God has programmed into the human brain. It's all there for us to discover.

Almighty God, enlarge my capacity to see You in all things, great and small. —FAY ANGUS

THU
15
THEN JESUS TOLD HIS DISCIPLES A PARABLE TO SHOW THEM THAT THEY SHOULD ALWAYS PRAY AND NOT GIVE UP.
                                                —*Luke 18:1 (NIV)*

I HAVE A GOOD FRIEND who sometimes can barely get herself to leave her house or even answer the phone. Once, during a particularly bad bout, she let over six hundred unopened e-mails pile up in her in-box. Eventually, a mutual friend went over and helped her go through them. Later our friend told me, "Her hand trembled on the mouse the whole time. Jenny was just terrified of doing anything."

Jenny has a kind of paralysis caused by anxiety. What brings on that anxiety no one can say. She is very smart, usually quite independent, runs her own business and has a solid faith. Why, then, does she allow herself to be made prisoner by her own irrational fears?

I've tried to reason with her. That doesn't work, of course, since Jenny's problems are rooted deep in her psyche. So I resort to prayer, asking God to make Jenny better. Yet every time Jenny has another setback, I find myself more and more dismayed. *Why aren't my prayers helping? Doesn't she want to get better?*

The other day our friend mentioned that Jenny had been making progress, so I e-mailed her just to see. "I'm getting better," she typed right back. How? "I've stopped asking God to fix me. Instead, I ask for help with the small things. 'God, help me get out of bed. God, help me brush my teeth and get dressed. God, help me walk out the door.' I stay focused on the next thing. Little victories."

Sometimes it's the people we pray for who teach us how to pray. Now I pray for the small things too— not just for Jenny, but for myself. When we break down our problems for God, He helps us see them in perspective, which is itself often the most powerful answer to prayer.

Help me, Lord, to see that prayer is a process guided by You, not me, and meant to bring You into every moment of my life. —EDWARD GRINNAN

A SECOND THANK-YOU
THANK YOU FOR FAMILY LOVE

FRI
16

BLESSED BE THOU OF THE LORD, MY DAUGHTER. . . . —Ruth 3:10

WHEN I WAS in my early twenties and newly married, I longed to be a mother. But neurofibromatosis stole that dream. I busied myself with creative pursuits like home decorating and designing a dollhouse complete with working lights, colorful rugs improvised from placemats, and silhouettes crafted from black-and-white cameo earrings.

One weekend there was a home show at our local arena. My five-year-old niece Allison attended with her parents. To her great delight, she won a door prize donated by the local miniatures shop: a gift certificate for anything her heart desired.

A few days later when Allison came to spend the night, she brought along a medium-sized, black-and-white checked box. "This is for you," she explained. I lifted the lid to find a dollhouse-size mom and dad with a little girl and boy. "It's a family for you."

I had never admitted to anyone how I'd longed for a child, yet this dear one had sensed it and tried to heal the hurt in my heart. No, my sadness at being childless didn't vanish at once. But when I put the dolls on display in my dollhouse, for the first time I knew that someone had acknowledged my pain.

Today, that five-year-old girl will soon be the mother of her third child, a little girl. I'm going to find that dollhouse and my "little family." I think I know someone who would enjoy it—and a second thank-you.

Thank You, Lord, for the times when life comes full circle and I get to remember my blessings again.
—ROBERTA MESSNER

SAT
17
A CHEERFUL HEART IS GOOD MEDICINE. . . . —*Proverbs 17:22 (NIV)*

IN THE TOWN where I grew up was a free municipal golf course. "Free" is a really enticing price for a sixteen-year-old, so when it came to selecting an activity for a first date with a girl from geometry class, golf was the obvious choice.

We were having a great time until the fifth hole, when I hit a tee shot that landed right on the green just a few feet from the cup. As I pumped my fist in celebration, my weight shifted in such a way that the knee in my artificial leg gave out and I dropped to the ground.

Falling is always an awkward situation for me because no one knows what to do when the guy with one leg falls down, especially on a date. In this case, my date alternated between grave concern and peals of laughter. I stood up and immediately realized my problem had gone from bad to worse; the foot on my artificial leg had somehow turned around the wrong way, bringing curious glances from the other golfers. I walked over to a tree and started kicking it with my artificial foot, trying to straighten it out. The other golfers must have thought I was having the worst golf game of my life and had anger management issues.

During all of the chaos, I remember thinking I had a choice: I could either feel sorry for myself and let the date be ruined, or we could both laugh about it and get back to golfing.

Lord, don't let me ever take myself too seriously.
                                    —JOSHUA SUNDQUIST

SUN
18

SPEAKING TO YOURSELVES IN PSALMS AND HYMNS AND SPIRITUAL SONGS, SINGING AND MAKING MELODY IN YOUR HEART TO THE LORD. —Ephesians 5:19

I WAS STAYING IN COPENHAGEN, and since the cathedral was on the way to the Tivoli Gardens, I decided to look in. What a surprise! The boys' choir from Sweden's Uppsala Cathedral was just starting to perform.

I slipped into a pew and proceeded to be awed by thirty or so boys, from youngsters to teenagers. For an hour or more they sang a program that ranged from Thomas Tallis (1505–1585) to Benjamin Britten (1913–1976). But when the soloist began to sing, the sweetness and purity of his voice carried me to another place and time.

I thought of my little brother JoJo back in the 1930s. The regularity of his rehearsals annoyed me and, I confess, aroused a certain jealousy. "Why does he have to go sing there? It isn't even our church," I protested.

"Because he has a voice," my mother said, "which you, my unfortunate one, do not."

One Sunday my family attended the church where my brother sang. My irritation continued until the soloist began. I was stunned. The boy with that beautiful voice was my brother. I forgot who he was or where I was while his silken child soprano broke through to everyone in the church. The words were sacred; the tone was angelic.

I never complained about JoJo's rehearsals after that.

I thank You, Father, for Copenhagen. JoJo was alive for me again as I listened to that concert.

—VAN VARNER

MON
19
IN MY FATHER'S HOUSE ARE MANY MANSIONS: IF IT WERE NOT SO, I WOULD HAVE TOLD YOU. I GO TO PREPARE A PLACE FOR YOU. AND IF I GO AND PREPARE A PLACE FOR YOU, I WILL COME AGAIN, AND RECEIVE YOU UNTO MYSELF; THAT WHERE I AM, THERE YE MAY BE ALSO. —John 14:2–3

MY FATHER WAS A CARPENTER, and he built six of our homes. He died two years ago, and my unyielding sorrow has taken on a more practical grief. I have to sell my home and "buy down." In short, I need my dad.

I need him to make repairs on the home I'm selling. I need him to inspect the homes I'm thinking about buying. I need him to brainstorm ideas for transforming cookie-cutter production into character and quality. But I'm on my own. Last week was particularly trying and, in tears, I asked God for perspective.

I was eleven when we lived in the Laurentian Mountains of French Canada. In the isolation of geography and language, my father homeschooled my sisters and me for five months. Part of our education was Bible memory. One of the first passages Dad assigned was John 14: "In my Father's house are many mansions."

How could I forget that Jesus was a carpenter like Dad? My grief and anxiety ebbed, for I knew that whatever I bought, it was not my final home. Too, because I know my dad, I like to think he's lending a hand, and that he and Jesus are making things ready for my final move.

Dear Jesus, truly this world is not our home. The Cross was our down payment for something better, and You're now preparing that final home where we'll forever live with You and our loved ones. —BRENDA WILBEE

TUE
20
ONE THING HAVE I DESIRED . . . TO BEHOLD THE BEAUTY OF THE LORD. . . .
—*Psalm 27:4*

AFTER A LONG DRIVE, I arrived at my sister's house and found her on her knees in a freshly turned flowerbed. "What are you planting?" I asked.

"Roses," Libby said, wiping her forehead with the back of her gloved hand.

I looked at the sturdy stems and green leaves. "What color will they be?"

She laughed. "Any color they want!" Libby proceeded to tell me that she had gotten the flowers at the dump.

"The dump?" I asked, incredulous. "But they look so healthy!"

She told me that the biggest grower in the area tossed out any plant that didn't meet their strict standards. "But these will be lovely. Just wait and see." She patted the dirt affectionately.

That was several years ago, and now whenever I

visit my sister in the summer, large, beautiful roses grace her yard. Pink, yellow, even mottled red and white ones. These flowers, picked from the trash, are thriving, offering their beauty to everyone who sees.

Master Gardener, open my eyes to the potential for beauty in places where I might never look.
                                    —MARY LOU CARNEY

WED
21

NOW THERE STOOD BY THE CROSS OF JESUS HIS MOTHER. . . . —John 19:25

MY FRIEND BARBARA AND I teach together at our local high schools, doing our best to convince young people of the irreversible devastation caused by drinking and driving.

Barbara's grandson Ty was killed by a drunken driver. Barbara shares pictures and stories of her grandson in the classroom. I didn't know Ty before his death, but he has come alive, through Barbara, for thousands of high school students and will continue to do so as long as she shares Ty's life and death with them. I watch their bored, indifferent expressions become focused, delighted and finally tearful when Barbara brings them from Ty's birth to his cross on a desert road in New Mexico.

There is silence, save for an occasional sob, when Barbara finishes talking. It's comforting to see lives changed—and saved—through the story of Ty's life, shared over and over again.

Was Mary cheered at her Son's Cross, knowing that His death was a saving mystery she couldn't fully understand? And after Jesus' ascension, was her grief at the loss of His physical presence lessened as she watched His life and death take on a meaning no one could have foreseen? I hope so. Oh, how I hope so.

Dear God, may Ty's life, and Barbara's courage in sharing it, continue to change hearts and save lives.
—TIM WILLIAMS

THU
22
HE STILLED THE STORM TO A WHISPER; THE WAVES OF THE SEA WERE HUSHED.
—*Psalm 107:29 (NIV)*

I HAVE BEEN ON MANY LAKES in all kinds of weather. It's intensely frightening to be on big water in a canoe when the wind is whipping the water into three-foot waves. It's quite a different—and rare—thing to encounter a complete calm, but it happened to me one summer evening.

Long after sunset, the air became so still that the surface of the whole lake became as smooth as glass. The night was clear and cloudless, and the star-filled sky was perfectly reflected in the mirror of the lake. I felt I could almost touch the moon and the stars spread out before me.

After what seemed hours, a breeze came up, rippling the water and destroying the reflection. As I watched the beautiful tableau melt away, distorted by the moving water, I was disappointed at first, but after a moment's thought I began to laugh. If I wanted to see the stars, all I had to do was look up. Perfect reflections are amazing, but they can never replace the real thing.

Lord, may the many reflections of Your power and beauty I see in this wonderful world always lead me to look to You. —ERIC FELLMAN

FRI

23

"FROM NOW ON I WILL TELL YOU OF NEW THINGS, OF HIDDEN THINGS UNKNOWN TO YOU." —Isaiah 48:6 (NIV)

I WAS EXCITED about my first trip to Scotland last spring. I'd see new vistas, meet new people, try new food. In Edinburgh, I savored cock-a-leekie (a soup of chicken, leeks and prunes). In the fishing village of Plockton, I had cullen skink (pungent chunks of salty haddock simmered with potatoes in cream). There were stick-to-your-ribs tatties (potatoes) and bashed neeps (mashed turnips). And from the bakeries came a celestial concoction of butter and sugar called tablet. Best of all I enjoyed the oatmeal we had for breakfast, grainy and honey-hued and delicious.

But there was one dish I couldn't cozy up to: haggis, the legendary Scottish favorite—the innards of a sheep, chopped fine, mixed with oatmeal and spices, and boiled in a sheep's stomach. *My* stomach recoiled.

One night at dinner I saw haggis on the menu. "I've been intending to try it," I bravely told my traveling companions. "But I'm squeamish about the ingredients."

"I know," the woman across from me said with a shiver. An American from Austin, Texas, she clearly shared my aversion. "*Eeeww,* oatmeal."

"Oatmeal? You're yucked out by the *oatmeal?* What about the other stuff?"

She looked at me as though I were the strange one. "I don't mind organ meats," she said matter-of-factly. "But mixing in oatmeal is too weird."

My whole notion about what was yummy and what was not turned upside down. I ordered the haggis without hesitation. It came steaming and fragrant, and when I dug in, it was spicy and delicious, like sausage or hash or meatloaf with a zing. What had I been afraid of?

It's not just the big new vistas that open up our lives. It's the daily little ones that also surprise.

Dear God, keep my heart open to new experiences—and keep my taste buds open too.
—MARY ANN O'ROARK

SAT
24
THE WORD OF GOD IS QUICK, AND POWERFUL, AND SHARPER THAN ANY TWO-EDGED SWORD. . . . —Hebrews 4:12

MY FRIEND ARTHUR had several books on his hospital bedside table. A couple of contemporary novels, the day's newspaper, a magazine and one small, tattered volume with a worn cover and pages that needed to be held together by a rubber band. Arthur's surgery had been a success and he was feeling better than he had in months. The doctor had only good news and promised that he'd be released soon.

"Do you have enough to keep you busy?" I asked.

"I think so." He gestured to the reading matter on his table.

"What about this?" I held up the slim volume that was falling apart. "Maybe you could afford to get a new copy," I joked.

"I like it just like it is. Take a look."

I slipped the rubber band off and was amazed. Every page had some marking on it. Red pencil underlining, blue ballpoint-pen check marks, words circled, comments in the margin. This book hadn't just been read; it had been a constant companion, a source of comfort and inspiration. I read a starred passage to myself, profound words by a writer who had thought deeply about faith and the human condition.

"I see why you like it," I said.

"I couldn't have gotten through the last twenty-five years without it," Arthur replied.

Leaving his hospital room, I was reminded of a quote I'd once seen on a church bulletin board: "The Bible that's falling apart usually belongs to a person who is not."

Dear God, may Your Word work through me so that I may become who You want me to be.

—RICK HAMLIN

SUN
25

FROM HIS TEMPLE HE HEARD MY VOICE. . . . —Psalm 18:6 (NIV)

WHEN OUR SON JEFF received his MBA from Duke University, I was excited about attending a baccalaureate service in the magnificent chapel that towers over the campus. It would be almost heaven to worship inside the Gothic masterpiece with its beautiful stained glass windows, the pipe organ thundering through the sanctuary. Unfortunately, when we arrived, we found that all of the visitors' seats were already taken.

A woman announced that there was overflow seating in an auditorium next door. As I followed the stragglers into the rather plain auditorium and was handed a program, I felt disappointed. I wanted to be in the chapel, not watching the service on a video screen!

The minister on the screen invited the congregation to stand for the first hymn. Everyone in the auditorium stayed seated. But as the strains of "Joyful, Joyful We Adore Thee" burst through the loudspeakers, I heard an unexpected echo. The people around me were singing as if they were in the chapel. I opened my program and scanned the verses printed inside. Then I sang along with the people in the auditorium and the congregation on the video screen.

As we watched the people on the screen sit down, I realized that I'd forgotten the reason I'd been so eager to attend the service in the first place. I wanted to share in a time of thanksgiving for the part God had played in Jeff's achievement. The architecture and stained glass were simply window dressing.

Dear God, help me to forget about the trappings, so I can truly worship You. —KAREN BARBER

MON
26

THE LORD KNOWETH THEM THAT ARE HIS. . . . —II Timothy 2:19

ONE MEMORIAL DAY, my wife and I visited the Tomb of the Unknown Soldier at Arlington National Cemetery in Virginia. The white marble monolith glowed in the rays of the late-afternoon sun, and the only sound was the click of the lone sentinel's boots as he paced back and forth before it. He would take twenty-one precise steps, then halt for twenty-one seconds, both symbolizing a twenty-one-gun salute, before executing a smart "shoulder arms." Every day of the year, around the clock, in blazing sun or chilly rain, a soldier is on guard.

Before we went home, I picked up a brochure that told the story of the tomb. On March 4, 1921, Congress, following the custom of our allies after World War I, called for the burial of an unknown soldier as a tribute to all the Americans killed in battle. The bodies of four unidentified men who had died in combat were brought to Châlons-sur-Marne, France. Their caskets were placed in a public room off the town square. Then, in a simple ceremony, twice-wounded and highly decorated Sgt. Edward Younger of Chicago set about the lonely task of making the final selection.

While a French military band outside played Frédéric Chopin's "Funeral March," Sergeant Younger, carrying a spray of white roses, entered the dimly lit room with its four plain coffins. He slowly circled the row three times, then gently laid the roses on one. Standing at attention, he saluted and left.

Why did he choose that particular coffin? he was asked later.

"I don't really know," he answered, "but something led me to it."

No one knows who that soldier is, nor who the unknown soldiers of World War II and the Korean War are who rest there with him. But today, it's good to remember that all our fallen, whether they rest beneath weathered tombstones, in unmarked graves or under that marble monolith, are known to God.

Lord, wherever they lie and whenever they died, may all our fallen servicemen and women find eternal life with You. —RICHARD SCHNEIDER

TUE
27

WEEPING MAY ENDURE FOR A NIGHT,
BUT JOY COMETH IN THE MORNING.
—*Psalm 30:5*

OUR NEWBORN SON HENRY was inconsolable. We hummed, sang, rocked, swaddled, played white noise. Henry still cried.

The doctor assured us it was just colic, but I began to worry that something was terribly wrong. Why was Henry so unhappy? Why couldn't I soothe him?

"Don't take it personally," my mom said. But how could I not?

Our family got used to it. When I had to get the shopping done, I took Henry to the store, where he screamed as I held him in one arm and piled groceries into the cart with the other. I learned to live on two consecutive hours of sleep and relied on my nightly bath for twenty minutes of quiet—pure heaven.

The day before Henry's three-month checkup, he woke up, opened his eyes and smiled. He sat contentedly and fell asleep easily in my arms.

"What's wrong with Henry?" Solomon asked.

"I don't know." I felt his forehead.

Henry had a happy day with only a few whimpers and then slept through the night with little fuss.

"Is he okay?" I asked the pediatrician the next day.

"He's fine. Why?"

"He's like a different baby."

"Sometimes they just outgrow colic," the pediatrician said. "Their nervous systems mature and they realize everything is fine."

Henry smiled with an innocence that only a baby who's kept a family up for three months straight can have. His beautiful dark brown eyes studied me with a look of wisdom and pride, as if to say, "See, Mommy, we both passed the test!"

Dear God, when my burden is heavy, remind me that every trial has an end. And thank You for a happy baby and a good night's sleep! —SABRA CIANCANELLI

WED
28

WISDOM IS FAR MORE VALUABLE THAN PRECIOUS JEWELS. —Proverbs 3:14 (TLB)

DURING THE YEARS when I was a single parent raising four children, I often blamed my ex-husband for my financial struggles and down-in-the-dumps feelings. Then one day I ran across a list of five steps to happiness that changed my life forever.

1. *Free your heart from hatred. Forgive.* It wasn't easy, but one day on the shore of Lake Michigan, as I watched the sunrise with my youngest child Andrew, I forgave my ex-husband. After that, even something as simple as taking a deep breath was exhilarating.

2. *Free your mind from worries; most never happen anyway.* I decided to concentrate only on what I had to get done that day and not worry about tomorrow. The worry wrinkles left my forehead and I felt as if I could walk on air.

3. *Live simply and appreciate what you have.* I learned to love it all: the time I had with each of my children; a star-filled night; wildflowers along the bike path; the waves bouncing off the lake.

4. *Give more.* Over a period of ten years, I opened my heart and the empty bedrooms in my home to forty airline pilots. How can you be unhappy when you have so many new friends?

5. *Expect less.* When you do this, every tiny little blessing that comes your way becomes a cause of inner peace and happiness.

Heavenly Father, You have given me all the tools to be happy. Now grant me the grace to become wise.
                                        —PATRICIA LORENZ

THU
29

CHRIST IN YOU, THE HOPE OF GLORY.
                              —*Colossians 1:27*

A FRIEND OF MINE who sells olive oil left
ten bottles in her car one night. During
that time someone stole the oil from her car. She left a
note on the car that day to shame the thief.

The next morning there was a note on her car from
the thief, who apologized. He thought it was wine; he
has a drinking problem, but her note was a wake-up
call to deal with it and he was grateful to her. All ten
bottles of oil were sitting on her fence.

My friend was touched by the whole story, and she
told all her friends. Some of them were also moved,
although some of the grumpy ones, like me, think she
should have called the police. She sold the oil, and the
restaurant to which she sold the last bottle placed such
a huge order for future oil that she bought a bottle of
bubbly cider to celebrate.

She left the cider in the car; the car wasn't locked,
and in the morning the bottle was gone. My impulse
was to snarl at her about locking her car; her impulse
was to write another note to the thief.

As she wrote the note, I thought about St. Paul.
"Christ in you," says the former Saul, "the hope of
glory." When she finished her note, she headed out
to her car, and I watched her go, sprightly and irre-
pressible. With her faith in the least of men, she's
inarguably closer to the Light than I am. That night
when I said grace, I bowed my head and thought,

Please, Lord, help me be just a little less of a bonehead today.

Dear Lord, I'm a mule. But I am trying, really and truly. Can You give me a hand getting these beams out of my eye? —BRIAN DOYLE

FRI
30

THEREFORE CAME I FORTH TO MEET THEE, DILIGENTLY TO SEEK THY FACE, AND I HAVE FOUND THEE.
—*Proverbs 7:15*

"I AM SO PROUD OF YOU!" I tell my longtime friend Portia after she shares her end-of-semester grades with me. She tells me how much work she had to do and how her instructors just don't understand. We giggle. This lament is not unusual for young students, but Portia and I have hit fifty. My children are adults, and Portia's nieces now have school-aged children of their own.

Portia is one of the most intelligent people I know, but she always seemed to retreat when it came to finishing college. She would blow the bugle and turn tail before completing the first semester. In fact, it has been almost thirty years of unfinished first semesters. Now, though she has to struggle to pay for tuition and books, Portia has completed two years at the Apex School of Theology in North Carolina.

Instead of fleeing, Portia looks forward to using her

degree. Her face glows. She is still bubbly, entertaining and youthful. "I'm not sure if I want to preach or be a chaplain or work with youth." She sparkles. "But who knows?"

Lord, help me to persevere in the things that seem impossible. —SHARON FOSTER

SAT
31

SINCE NO MAN KNOWS THE FUTURE, WHO CAN TELL HIM WHAT IS TO COME?
                    —*Ecclesiastes 8:7 (NIV)*

I LOVE BEING AN AUNT. I have three nieces and one nephew to chase, tickle, stuff with sugar and return to my loving siblings. I can easily keep my weekends full of afternoon snacks and playtimes. My nieces are still in newborn onesies, but my nephew Alex is a strong, fearless, independent man at twenty-one months.

Alex is a lucky kid. With two sets of doting grandparents, his afternoons are filled with museum visits, dance parties and swinging beside his playhouse. But if you ask him, his favorite thing to do is to go on the boat. "Nana, DaDe, boat . . . go" is the phone call my parents frequently receive at their lakeside home.

As soon as Alex arrives at my parents' door, he's ready to go, crying, "Boat, boat, boat!" He'll fight his nap all morning, huff and puff through lunch, and then sit perfectly upright in his crib, repeating, "Boat,

boat, boat!" Most Saturdays, my mom gives up after thirty minutes, scoops up Alex and we will head for the lake. Then, the moment the boat is lowered into the water and Alex is zipped up in his life jacket, he lays his head down on the front cushions and falls soundly asleep. He never fails to wake up when the boat is being cranked up into its lift, and he always looks betrayed, as if we've tricked him into thinking he's been on the boat because he has no memory of it.

Sometimes I think I'm a lot like Alex. I get so busy anticipating my next move, next job, next week that I miss out on all the good things that are happening now.

God, these moments only come around once. Help me savor each of them. —ASHLEY JOHNSON

MY DIVINE SURPRISES

1 _____

2 _____

3 _____

4 _____

5 _____

6 _____

7 _____

8 _____

9 _____

10 _____

11 _____

12 _____

13 _____

14 _____

15 _____

16 _____

17 _____

18 _____

19 _____

20 _____

21 _____

22 _____

23 _____

24 _____

25 _____

26 _____

27 _____

28 _____

29 _____

30 _____

31 _____

June

I have called you friends; for all things that I have heard of my Father I have made known unto you. —*John 15:15*

 **GIVE US THIS DAY**
THE MINISTRY OF
PRESENCE

SUN
1

*THE LORD WILL FULFILL HIS PURPOSE
FOR ME. . . . —Psalm 138:8 (NIV)*

"HOW ARE YOU DOING?" my pastor Peter
gently asked my husband Lynn and me as
we sat around our dinner table, savoring the lasagna that
he and his wife had brought us that Sunday evening.

It was the question I hardly knew how to answer
since Lynn and I had both been diagnosed with cancer
in the last few months. After giving a quick update
about our recent chemotherapy treatments, I confessed
something that had been troubling me lately.

"I've let my world grow very small," I said, refer-
ring to the fact that I hadn't been back to church or
work or even out shopping much since my diagnosis.
"I have plenty of good reasons to hide in the safety
and comfort here at home," I rationalized. "I don't feel
so good. My immune system is down. I feel self-
conscious when I wear a wig. And the steroids make
me look all fat and puffy."

Peter paused. "This may not make sense to you,
but people need to see you. For their good. You encourage them when you just show up. It's a . . . ministry of presence."

His words didn't make much sense, but they
seemed to stir something deep inside me, and the next
Sunday Lynn and I went to church. We ducked out

during the last song because I wasn't sure I could answer the "How are you?" questions. During the following week, I got several notes.

"It gave me hope to see you in church on Sunday," said one.

"Your presence blessed my day," said another.

"Seeing you face your battle helps me know that I can face mine."

The ministry of presence is still a mystery to me, but I'm learning that it's not about anything I say or do. It's about showing up, so God can use my presence for His purposes in the lives of others—at church, at a social gathering, maybe even at the grocery store.

Father, stretch me out of my small world for Your purposes. —CAROL KUYKENDALL

UNEXPECTED BLESSINGS
THE LITTLE THINGS

MON
2

LET THE POOR AND NEEDY PRAISE THY NAME. —*Psalm 74:21*

"DON'T THROW ANYTHING OUT!" the voice on the phone instructed. It was 1975 and I was in the melancholy last phase of clearing out my mother's home in Miami Beach. Everything she could use in the nursing home—clothing, furniture, photographs—had already been shipped, other things labeled for sending to various family members. Now only odds and ends remained.

"Nothing of value," I apologized to the lady who'd answered the phone at the thrift shop.

An hour later she pulled into the driveway, followed by two men in a truck. "We'll take everything!" she told me. End tables, dishes, a lamp, old magazines, even a worn bathroom rug went out to the truck. But . . . a handleless cup? A chess set with missing pieces? In growing amazement, I watched the three of them carry away broken clothes hangers, a card table with only three legs.

"You have no idea," the woman told me, "what treasures these will be for someone." They served elderly people living alone in single rooms, poverty invisible on Miami Beach's sunny surface. "With a few repairs and some ingenuity on their part, anything you give us will be used."

Anything? Surely there was *something*, somewhere in the house they wouldn't accept! I found it under the kitchen sink, a dishrag so full of holes we'd been using it to wipe the floor. Even this was carried triumphantly to the truck.

"How—who—" I began.

"We'll wash it," she said, "put a one-cent sticker on it, and someone cooking on a single hot plate will have a way to clean it."

Nothing of value? From that day on I have not called "worthless" anything that need and imagination can turn into treasure.

Bestower of blessing, let me learn from the needy of the world to value each and every provision.
                                        —ELIZABETH SHERRILL

TUE
3

"KNEELING BESIDE HIM THE SAMARITAN SOOTHED HIS WOUNDS WITH MEDICINE AND BANDAGED THEM. . . ."
                                        —*Luke 10:34 (TLB)*

MY FRIEND SCARLETT is as colorful as her name. It had been a while since I'd seen her, but I didn't have any trouble spotting her at our twentieth high school reunion. A few minutes of conversation with Scarlett can bless your whole day.

As we chatted over a cup of coffee, I noticed her deep russet nails. "Scarlett, your nails look beautiful," I said. "What a great polish color!"

"You know," she said, "I had the most amazing day yesterday! I went to my nail salon and the ladies who work there were in the middle of redecorating. They'd painted the walls to match the trim and missed the color just a bit—too purple." Scarlett grabbed my hand and gave it an excited squeeze. "They're Vietnamese and they don't speak much English, so I knew it would be difficult to communicate exactly how to soften the color. I was so blessed to spend the day helping them!"

"You spent the whole day helping them redecorate their nail salon?" I set my coffee down and studied Scarlett's green eyes. They looked alive, just as they had when she was a high school cheerleader.

"I left with wet nails and found the most magnificent color, morning glories, and then I picked out some periwinkle paint to smooth over their original wall color." She twirled her arms above her head. "I found a gorgeous grapevine wreath to go around the ceiling."

"But you don't really know those people," I said.

"That's okay," Scarlett said. "I just loved them—like God loves me."

Father, when I'm tempted to look away from someone's need, give me some of Scarlett's joy in helping.
—JULIE GARMON

WED
4
TO KEEP ME FROM EXALTING MYSELF, THERE WAS GIVEN ME A THORN IN THE FLESH. . . . —II Corinthians 12:7 (NAS)

I HAVE A CONFESSION TO MAKE: I chew on pens. I don't mean nibble. I gnaw. At the end of the day, it looks as if a cocker spaniel has been sitting at my desk. I can't count the number of times I've ended up with ink all over my chin from chomping down too hard on one.

Many helpful people have tried to diagnose my problem. "It's a definite sign of insecurity," one said. "You must be really frustrated or something," concluded another. Still others have claimed that I have a compulsive personality. None of this makes me feel very good.

I've bought expensive pens that are not particularly edible only to revert to the cheap chewy kind (ironically, perhaps, a pen called a Gelly Roll is my favorite). I've made New Year's resolutions and countless promises to myself. Pray, you say? Oh, I've prayed. I've begged to be delivered from this weakness, as I explained to a friend the other day.

"Maybe God doesn't care," my friend responded nonchalantly.

"Of course God cares about me."

"I mean, maybe He just doesn't care whether you chew on your pens. Maybe you should just accept that you are a pen chewer and move on. It sounds like God has."

I wanted to be insulted, but deep down I felt relieved. I'd found the answer: Sometimes no answer to prayer *is* the answer. It wasn't that God had better things to worry about, but that I should. Pen chewing might not be the most seemly behavior, but it's not worth losing sleep over.

God, maybe there are some things about me that I'm just meant to accept. You made me a pen chewer; now help me to move on. —EDWARD GRINNAN

THU **5** *AND TO KNOW THE LOVE OF CHRIST WHICH SURPASSES KNOWLEDGE, THAT YOU MAY BE FILLED WITH ALL THE FULNESS OF GOD.* —*Ephesians 3:19 (RSV)*

WE HAD PLANNED our family vacation time six months in advance when we gathered together to *ooh* and *aah* over our two grandsons Conner, one month, and Austin, six months. A typical Nace family off-road adventure to a remote location like Lake Chelan, Washington, was out of the question. We decided that having three generations together in a mountaintop lodge in Virginia would combine practicality with maximum enjoyment.

We had more than a few moments of hesitation and inner debate before our four-car caravan set out for Virginia, but in the end the WIN principle won out. Several years ago, while attending a seminar, I heard a successful college wrestling coach describe this philosophy of life. Whenever you're facing a decision, keep this question foremost in your mind: *What's Important Now?* Never had it been more applicable to our lives than it was now.

Little Austin suffers from a genetic illness called MPS—Hurler's disease, and his prognosis seemed to vacillate between grim and grave. As we planned our vacation, we were midway between learning to live with Austin's symptoms and the confirmation of his illness. Each of us knew what was important as we made our way to Hensley Hollow Lodge.

When we arrived, the forecast was for torrential rain. We were disappointed by the weather, but one of the family said, "We're here to spend time together. We don't care if it rains all eight days." It did—and truly it didn't matter. By the end of that time we had 750 digital snapshots reflecting love and celebrating life.

No matter what lies ahead for Austin, we have vivid, uplifting memories of health and joy. There's no doubt that that is *What's Important Now.*

Thank You, God, for helping us see what's really important. And please hold Austin in Your healing hand.
— TED NACE

FRI

6

WE HAVE BECOME GIFTS TO GOD THAT HE DELIGHTS IN. . . .
— *Ephesians 1:11 (TLB)*

THE RAIN SPATTERED MUD on my jeans as I trudged through the pasture, leading my mare Dancer. Dark clouds had hidden the blue sky for days and the gloom had drizzled into my soul. To top it off, I'd just weighed myself and I'd already gained ten pounds. I wanted to curl in a recliner by a warm fire and pout until the sun came back. I'd only caught Dancer because she was three months pregnant, and I felt obligated to give her vitamins.

I tied Dancer to the feed trough. I'd studied how

people had taught their babies games in the womb and read about dog breeders who insisted on training puppies before they were born. I'd decided to experiment. Every day I talked to Dancer's baby and sang the same little song.

I leaned my ear into her wet flank. "Hi, Wind Dancer. It's wet and icky out here. What's it like in there? Did you know that today you've got eyelashes? That's pretty cool. I can't wait to see them. And . . ."

Suddenly, as fast as lightning, Wind Dancer kicked at me in the exact spot on her mom's flank where I'd been talking.

I eagerly pressed my face against Dancer's flank again, and it was almost as if I heard God saying, "Rebecca, I delighted in you when I formed you in your mother's womb and I still do."

A tear slid down my cheek. *Who am I not to cherish myself, when the God of the universe loves me just as I am with the extra ten pounds and on a cloudy day?*

I walked back to the house. By the time I got to the top of the hill, my step had lightened.

Lord, help me remember how much You love me, no matter what. —REBECCA ONDOV

SAT
7

BE HOSPITABLE TO ONE ANOTHER WITHOUT COMPLAINT. —*I Peter* 4:9 (NAS)

I ENJOY HAVING PEOPLE OVER, but I'm not a good hostess. I have everything prepared days in advance and I positively don't want any help in the kitchen. Things must go perfectly. Heaven forbid that the salad might not be completely tossed or I'm missing an ingredient for a dish.

Preparations were going smoothly for my dinner party when I tried to open a can of mushrooms. I've always hated the can opener; only my husband Gene knows how to operate it. As he walked in the back door, I was furious. Gene reached over and effortlessly opened the can. My face was a mask of anger.

"Honey, tell me that story about eating at your paralyzed friend's house," Gene said.

It all came rushing back. Some years ago I'd met a boy while working as a hospital volunteer. Coy had been paralyzed from the neck down while diving into a pool. Annie, Coy's mother, cared for him by herself at home. Money was scarce—they didn't have running water.

Annie had invited me and my family of five to their home for supper. There were only four kitchen chairs and four plates, so we took turns. When the dish holding the sweet potato casserole cracked in the oven, Annie threw her head back and laughed. We insisted on tasting the delicious casserole anyway. We laughed a lot, devoured the scrumptious food and belted out Coy's favorite songs. We stayed much longer than we'd planned, and when we left Annie hugged us all good-bye and made us promise to come again. We did.

That story had a lesson I still had to learn. Maybe I could start by asking Gene to open a few more cans.

Father, help me to practice hospitality like dear Annie.
—MARION BOND WEST

SUN
8

"THEREFORE GO AND MAKE DISCIPLES OF ALL NATIONS, BAPTIZING THEM IN THE NAME OF THE FATHER AND OF THE SON AND OF THE HOLY SPIRIT. . . ."
—Matthew 28:19 (NIV)

BAPTISMAL SERVICES in our little Baptist church are happy occasions, celebrated by young and old alike. Friends and relatives of the candidates crowd the pews. Children stand in the aisles to get a better view. Cameras flash. Each new believer is heartily applauded as he or she steps up out of the baptismal tank after being immersed.

At the last baptismal service we attended, a three-year-old girl intently watched her young father wading down into the water. An almost holy hush descended upon the sanctuary as the congregation waited, quietly and expectantly, to hear his vows. Suddenly the stillness was broken by a small voice: "My daddy's gonna get all wet!"

Once the chuckles had subsided, I began reflecting on the more than fifty years that have passed since I was baptized. If my own life is any indication, that young man who vowed to follow God can expect to be showered by His love, cleansed by His Word and refreshed by streams in the desert, for God is faithful to His promise in Malachi 3:10 (NLT): "I will open the windows of heaven for you. I will pour out a blessing so great you won't have enough room to take it in!"

Father, I pray that all new believers will enjoy their experiences with You as much as I have.

—ALMA BARKMAN

MON
9

THEN SAID I, AH, LORD GOD! THEY SAY OF ME, DOTH HE NOT SPEAK PARABLES?
—*Ezekiel 20:49*

I'M WAITING FOR my driver's license photo to develop at the Pennsylvania Department of Transportation. The guy sitting beside me in the waiting room gets a call on his cell phone. "Hello?" he says, then pauses, raising an eyebrow. "Really?" Another pause. "Well, maybe the DNA test is off a little. . . ." He shuts off his phone, grabs his license and leaves.

This little drama gets my mind going. I start to make up a story about him: *He's on the run from the law and the DNA test shows he's guilty. He's here to get a fake ID.*

This is what I do with unstructured time: Spin outrageous tales. *He just discovered that he won't get his inheritance because his dad is not his real father.*

I don't know why I do this. It's a harmless habit, I guess. But sometimes I wonder about the actual stories out there, the real ones that I miss: *A boy in a faraway land chases a soccer ball into the weeds, then steps on a forgotten mine. He wakes up a minute later, and when the pain muscles in, he whispers a desperate prayer to God to make everything right again. . . .*

I'm startled out of my thoughts by a PennDOT worker standing in front of me, handing me my new license. In the photo, I have one eyebrow raised, as if I'm trying to figure out which story is mine, which I have forgotten and which prayer I can whisper to make everything right.

Lord, strengthen my faith that all our stories, somehow, somewhere, may have happy endings.
—MARK COLLINS

TUE
10
OPEN MY EYES THAT I MAY SEE WONDERFUL THINGS. . . .
—Psalm 119:18 (NIV)

WHEN MARY'S END-OF-YEAR ballet assessment came in, I shook my head in disbelief. There at the end of the glowing report was the comment "Mary is very musical."

Admittedly, my eight-year-old has many gifts. She is bright, gregarious, well-coordinated, aware of the needs and feelings of others. She is a natural performer. But she has a hard time singing on pitch. *Musical* is not a term I'd use to describe her. I couldn't figure out what her ballet teacher had in mind.

Around the same time, Mary and Elizabeth both tried out for a children's theater production of *Babes in Toyland*. Elizabeth got the female lead. Mary was cast in a nice role too: She was the dancing doll. The director called with the news, and after conveying his congratulations added, "Oh, and Mary has her own song!"

I was somewhat taken aback. Singing in a group is one thing; a solo is another. Mary was going to stand onstage and sing alone? Yikes! I bit my tongue and focused on being an encouraging mother.

A couple of months of mild trepidation crept by before the show went on. It was a great success. Elizabeth was splendid, and Mary's solo was relatively simple—she even sang mostly on pitch. More to the point, she was a lovely, believable dancing doll. The director knew what he was doing when he cast her.

After the last performance, Mary pranced happily down the sidewalk, all but floating. She may not have the world's greatest singing voice, but her movements are truly lyrical. Perhaps I hadn't understood what her ballet teacher meant because I was only using my ears, not my eyes.

Lord, expand my vision, so I may see beyond my expectations. —JULIA ATTAWAY

WED
11
AND WE KNOW THAT ALL THINGS WORK TOGETHER FOR GOOD TO THEM THAT LOVE GOD, TO THEM WHO ARE THE CALLED ACCORDING TO HIS PURPOSE.
—*Romans 8:28*

THE REDEEMING PART of funeral services for me is the extemporaneous eulogies that come from the congregation. I particularly appreciated the tributes given at a funeral in Ohio that I attended last week. The woman whose life was being celebrated had been a church leader for almost all of her eighty-eight years, and she was saluted for her steadfast faith. Though she herself had experienced many trials, her faith, it was said, never seemed to waver. Romans 8:28 was her faith rock, and she often shared it with those who sought her counsel. That truth gave her strength and courage when questions were long and answers short, she told advice seekers, "and it will do the same for you."

She had taught Sunday school for more than fifty years, and those who had grown in their faith because of her ministry recounted how she had helped them with doubts, illnesses and family problems. Members of Eve's Circle, a monthly interdenominational woman's Bible study, cited her deep caring, her patience, her gift for listening and her powerful intercessory prayers on their behalf.

The woman's children also spoke. Her daughter, now a minister, talked about her mother's unconditional love and encouragement. Her younger son, the woman's principal caregiver when she began to fail, described with some humor her disciplinary hand that had guided him on his faith journey. Her older son marveled at her positive attitude and a passion for living that molded his life. She had hoped he would become a minister, but she expressed pride in his chosen work, the writing of inspirational books and articles.

Why am I telling you all this? Because many longtime readers of *Daily Guideposts* already know her through the things I've written. And most of all, I want to tell you because this very special woman was my mother, Juna Bauer Beard.

We thank You, Lord, for faithful mothers,
Whose love—save Yours—excels all others.
                                    —FRED BAUER

THU
12
THY WORD WAS UNTO ME THE JOY AND
REJOICING OF MINE HEART. . . .
                                    —*Jeremiah 15:16*

IT WAS A WARM SPRING EVENING, and three-year-old Stephen was wearing his summer pajamas, decorated with blue, red, green and yellow dogs, when he crawled out of the collapsible play tunnel that was taking up a third of our living room.

Stephen stood up and glanced over to the sofa where I was sitting. He squared his shoulders, smiled and said, "I look clever in these pajamas."

"What did you say, Stevie?" I asked, sure that I'd misheard him.

"I look clever in these pajamas."

"Do you know what *clever* means?"

"No," Stephen admitted. Then he added, again, "I look clever in these pajamas!"

Well, I may not be an impartial observer, but I think Stephen looks clever in whatever he's wearing. And I wouldn't have been surprised if he'd known what *clever* meant either. Stephen has a love affair with words. When he hears a new one, he'll try it out in sentences over and over until, most of the time, he's figured out how to use it. Sometimes he'll come up with a doozy, like *incinerate*, which he picked up the other day playing knights-and-dragons with his big brother John.

Sometimes I get so caught up in the words that surround me every day—the newspapers, magazines, advertisements, reports, memos and e-mails—that I lose the sense of wonder and delight that words once had for me. But for the next little while, at least, I can get some of that feeling back as I listen to Stephen, looking clever in his pajamas, make the world of words his own.

Dear God, You made this world with Your creating Word, and redeemed it through Your Word-made-flesh. Help me always to use the gift of words to build up my neighbors and glorify You.

—ANDREW ATTAWAY

FRI
13

THEY HIDE THEMSELVES, THEY MARK MY STEPS. . . . —Psalm 56:6

MY TWO ELIZABETHS—my wife Tib and our daughter Liz—traveled to Russia together recently. On the last day of the trip, a very experienced pickpocket opened Liz's purse and stole her digital camera, along with the card holding some two hundred photos of this wonderful shared adventure. The maddening experience has something to tell me about our spiritual enemy.

"I know exactly how the thief worked," Liz said, reconstructing the event. "We'd gone to the Moscow Circus, and during intermission I'd taken the camera out to get some pictures, then put it back in my purse."

The performance over, Liz and Tib joined the jostling, shoving, good-natured crowd working their way up the aisles. When she reached their hotel room that night, the camera was gone.

"Someone must have been watching me the whole time," Liz said. "He knew exactly where I kept the camera, how I carried my purse and what kind of clasp it had. When we stepped into the crowded aisle, he was ready."

Isn't this how the thief who "comes only to steal and kill and destroy" (John 10:10, RSV) does his dirty work? He watches and waits, looking for our vulnerable points.

For me, this vulnerability comes when Tib is

away—I plunge into a self-indulgent, stultifying splurge of salts, sugars and fats. A silly, unimportant sin? Not really, because the experienced old enemy knows my psychology, counting on the fact that later I will feel depressed, estranged from God. And *that* is the enemy's goal.

Father, help me become ever more aware that apart from You I am no match for the enemy of my soul.
                                    —JOHN SHERRILL

SAT   *LIFT YE UP A BANNER. . . . —Isaiah 13:2*

14

ON THE LONG CAR TRIP to Crane Lake on the Canadian border, our family used to pass the time by playing games like Twenty Questions or singing songs. Dad would let loose with "Down by the Old Mill Stream," his voice cracking on the high notes, our station wagon barreling down the highway. Mom had us swaying and snapping our fingers as she crooned "Boogie Woogie Bugle Boy." But the trip wasn't complete until we'd sung Dad's favorite, George M. Cohan's rousing "You're a Grand Old Flag."

Upon arrival at our cabin, the first order of business was to raise the flag. I can still picture Dad on a ladder, leaning precariously against the twelve-foot-tall flagpole, battling gusting winds, struggling to untangle ropes to get "Old Glory" flying. Mom and I watched from the cabin, praying he wouldn't fall down, glad we couldn't hear the language he was using!

Dad was a World War II veteran, and the flag reminded him of the profound relief he felt after a day of horrific combat. Crawling terrified through Pacific island jungles, he returned to base and found "the flag was still there!" That banner of red, white and blue symbolized the freedom he and his fellow soldiers risked their lives to protect. And showing it and singing about it were ways to remember everything it stood for and he believed in.

Dear God, thank You for the symbols that remind us of what we hold dear. —MARY BROWN

A SECOND THANK-YOU
THANK YOU FOR A FATHER'S LOVE

SUN
15

LET THE PEACE OF CHRIST RULE IN YOUR HEARTS, SINCE AS MEMBERS OF ONE BODY YOU WERE CALLED TO PEACE. AND BE THANKFUL. —*Colossians 3:15 (NIV)*

WHEN MY FATHER'S CANCER metastasized to his brain, everything I tried to do for him was met with hostility. One evening after work I dropped by to take him his dinner and he went at it once more: "You expect me to eat this?" he shouted.

The words cut deep; I'd gone to considerable effort to bring him some of his favorite foods—steak, mashed potatoes and gravy, and creamed corn. That night I cried out to God, "Lord, help me remember a time I felt my daddy's love so way down deep that I'll never forget it."

The next day, a co-worker at the hospital brought his new baby girl to the office for everyone to admire. The way he smiled at his little one made the longing for my father's love even more intense.

My memories took me back to an icy January night. I was inconsolable because I'd left my teddy bear at my grandparents' house. Daddy, who didn't own a car at the time, walked two miles on a solid sheet of ice to retrieve my beloved bear. "I finally get it now, Lord," I prayed. "My daddy loves me just as much now as he did back then. When he speaks so angrily, it's the disease talking."

Today, my siblings cleaned out the attic in the home where I grew up, and they had a surprise they couldn't wait for me to see. Among all the odds and ends, they found that long-lost, fuzzy brown bear with the black button eyes. As I hugged it close, I asked God to whisper a second thank-you to my father for all his love.

Help me to keep giving thanks, dear Lord, in all circumstances. —ROBERTA MESSNER

READER'S ROOM

MY HUSBAND AND I went on a land cruise
to Cape Cod and other stops on the East
Coast to celebrate our fiftieth wedding
anniversary. We were especially excited to
go on this trip because we would go out into
the Atlantic Ocean on a whale-watching
expedition.

The day came for the boat trip; it was a
warm, sunny day as we ventured out into the
Atlantic. After a while we were surrounded
by dense fog; a marine biologist told us he
was sorry to report that with such thick fog
we would be unable to find whales. We
were so disappointed!

I began to envision Jesus on the stormy
sea as He stood and rebuked the wind and
rain. I then went out to the deck. Within a
few seconds the fog lifted; we were
surrounded by two hundred pilot whales!
Soon everyone was proclaiming it "a God
thing." What a sighting! What a testament
to His power!

—*Carol Moore, Fort Wayne, Indiana*

MON
16

O TASTE AND SEE THAT THE LORD IS GOOD. . . . —Psalm 34:8

WHEN OUR DAUGHTER JODY graduated from grade school, we decided to celebrate with dinner in a fancy restaurant. As we waited to be led to a table, I noticed the dessert platter filled with a variety of yummy temptations: cheesecake with strawberry topping; a thick, gooey chocolate cake; apple pie and much more. My husband Wayne asked me something, and I turned away from the platter. When I looked back, I noticed that someone had taken a bite out of each of the desserts!

My five-year-old Dale stared at me with a look of pure innocence, his mouth ringed with chocolate cake. I asked him why he would do such a thing, and he told me that he thought the platter was there so guests could sample the desserts before they ordered. Thankfully, the hostess was amused by my son's explanation, and we were all given dessert on the house.

Dale is a junior high school teacher now, and we like to tease him by telling him that he's the reason so many restaurants display plastic food instead of the real thing. But in retrospect, I think Dale might have been on to something: Reach out and taste life, or you might miss out on some of the wonderful experiences God has in store for you!

Father God, Your love overwhelms me. Help me to be open to the opportunities You send my way.

—DEBBIE MACOMBER

TUE **"YOUR SERVANT FOUND COURAGE TO PRAY**
17 **THIS PRAYER TO YOU."**
—II Samuel 7:27 (NAS)

WHEN THE CARDIOLOGIST scheduled me for a stress test because he suspected I had a blockage in one coronary artery, I was more surprised than frightened. I'd been working out on my treadmill for years, and while my family history included heart disease, I always thought I'd been careful enough to avoid it.

After we moved, however, I had spent six hours one day hauling boxes out of the garage, unpacking them and then shelving an entire library of books. I might have, in the doctor's words, "knocked something loose."

The test would consist of two series of pictures of my heart, each taking about twenty minutes. I would have to lie very still, with my hands behind my head, or they'd have to start the test over again.

I hadn't counted on my bursitis. After five minutes into the first series, my left shoulder started to hurt, and soon the pain was so bad that I was afraid my body would begin to shake, ruining the pictures.

I was determined not to have to take the test over, and I tried to find all kinds of things to take my mind off of my painful shoulder. Nothing seemed to have an effect until I started reciting the Twenty-third Psalm: "The Lord is my shepherd; I shall not want."

I could still feel the pain, but it seemed further away, and I was no longer apprehensive that the test would be ruined.

Before they took the second set of pictures, I told the nurse about my problems in the first test, and they were able to pad my shoulder so that there wasn't any pain. So I switched from the Twenty-third Psalm to Psalm 150:6: "Let every thing that hath breath praise the Lord."

Thank You, Lord, for Your wisdom in giving us a psalm for every occasion. —RHODA BLECKER

WED
18

CAST ALL YOUR ANXIETY ON HIM BECAUSE HE CARES FOR YOU.
—*I Peter 5:7 (NIV)*

AS THE TIME DREW NEAR for our friend Mark to be discharged from the Marines, he became anxious about returning home. He had his former job waiting for him, and he could live with his brother while he decided what to do about housing. But while Mark had been away—including two tours of duty in Iraq—most of his peers had moved on with their lives: weddings, mortgages, babies. Mark longed for a relationship and family of his own.

One night, from a computer at Camp Lejeune in Jacksonville, North Carolina, Mark went on the Internet, typed in the ZIP code for our small Indiana town and up came the picture of a lovely, dark-eyed young woman. Mark was smitten! They began to "chat" and that's when Mark realized that Tina did not live in Chesterton, but more than two hundred miles north in Michigan. He had mistakenly typed the wrong ZIP code!

Several months later, Mark was home on leave. He came to dinner one night, holding the hand of his friend from the Internet. As I watched them laugh and pass around pictures of her three children, I knew their meeting had been no mistake. I could tell Mark knew it too.

Oh, Father, how wonderfully kind and clever You are! Let me entrust all my relationships—and worries—to You. And make me bold to seize new ways to connect with others. —MARY LOU CARNEY

THU
19
COME UNTO ME, ALL YE THAT LABOUR AND ARE HEAVY LADEN, AND I WILL GIVE YOU REST. —Matthew 11:28

"WHAT DO YOU WANT, FRED?" I asked our cat. "I wish you'd make up your mind." First he was meowing in the kitchen, then in the bedroom and now at my feet. I was trying to do some work on the computer and there he was, butting against my leg. I reached down to scratch him between his ears. He seemed to enjoy it, purring contentedly, but the minute I stopped he sauntered back to the kitchen. "*Meow, meow,*" I heard him say.

"Okay, I give up. I'm coming," I said. I went into the kitchen. His water bowl was full, his food dish was half full, and my wife Carol had already brushed him once today. "What do you want?" I asked.

He looked up at me with his green eyes and said it again, "*Meow, meow.*"

I guess this is what it's like to be a cat, I thought. *Wanting things that you can't even articulate.* Then I paused. *No, maybe this is what it's like to be a human. Restless, impatient, needy. Sometimes I feel like wandering around the house and whining, wishing somebody would do something.*

I sat down on the floor. Fred nestled his head under the counter the way he often does and rolled over on his back so I could rub his stomach. "Do you know what St. Augustine once said about *his* Master?" I asked, running my hands through Fred's thick fur. "He said, 'Our hearts are restless until they rest in Thee.'"

He purred contentedly. I knew the feeling.

I come to You, Lord, looking for rest.

—RICK HAMLIN

BREAD FOR THE CHILDREN

FOR THE NEXT seven days, Pam Kidd will take you on a journey halfway around the world to help the poorest of the poor—and to experience the ever astonishing  Providence of God. You will discover how a heart to help and an openness to the Lord's leading can replace despair with new hope and worry with peace. —THE EDITORS

DAY 1: THE VIEW FROM THE LADDER

FRI

20

FOR HE LOOKETH TO THE ENDS OF THE EARTH, AND SEETH UNDER THE WHOLE HEAVEN. —Job 28:24

THE VIEW FROM ATOP the ladder in our church's fellowship hall took my breath away. People hustled about, hanging lights, spreading tablecloths, arranging chairs and fussing with flowers.

"Help!" I'd called out to my friends when our daughter Keri announced that she and Ben had decided to get married before graduate school, leaving me no time to save the money that weddings cost these days.

My friends had come through. Our half-finished hall was being transformed into a fairyland. Even with a wonderful caterer and a cake bedecked with hundreds of candied flowers, we were well within my modest budget.

"Oh, God," I whispered, "what can I ever do to pay You back for all of this?"

His answer was immediate: *Answer the letter.*

I swallowed hard. I knew exactly what He was asking.

The letter with a faraway postmark was hidden under a pile of papers on my desk. "I was reading an article you wrote in *Guideposts,*" it said, "and God told me that you're supposed to come to Zimbabwe and write about the street children." Holding the letter, I had laughed out loud. *Africa? No way. Besides, there's Keri's wedding and I'm much too busy.*

I shook my head and began descending the ladder. "Okay, God, I'll go," I said, "but I sure do hope You know what You're doing."

I guess I'm one of those "convenient" listeners, Father, often hearing only what I want to hear. Please keep prodding and don't ever give up on me. —PAM KIDD

DAY 2: HERE I AM

 SAT 21 *Also I heard the voice of the Lord, saying, Whom shall I send, and who will go for us? Then said I, Here am I; send me.* —Isaiah 6:8

I AM STANDING on a dirty street corner as far away from home as I will ever be. The first light of day pushes across Harare's tired buildings and falls in pools on the cracked sidewalk. For days, I have interviewed street children, and I am tired and discouraged. My mission is to attract funding for a church foundation that is struggling to help Zimbabwe's people. Now, more than anything, I just want to go home.

Over and over the children have told me about the lady who brings them tea and bread early each morning. And that's why I'm here. I've come to see their Lady Bountiful. Before leaving this place, where one in five children has been orphaned by AIDS and most end up homeless and begging for food, I need something good to remember.

The children are gathering now. They crawl out of storm drains and emerge from back alleys. They rustle through trash cans looking for empty bottles and cups. Most are barefoot.

"Here she comes!" someone shouts. Some of the children begin to sing. I look up and see a noisy old car turning the corner. It stops and a disheveled woman jumps out. In a flash, she drags a huge soup pot from the trunk, steaming with thick, sweet, milky tea. She pulls loaves of day-old bread from the backseat.

The children form an orderly line, holding their bottles and cups out to receive the tea. Their faces are radiant.

I move away from the crowd. I have never been this angry in my life. *This is it?* I scream silently to God. *You brought me halfway around the world and this is the best You have to offer? Why in heaven's name don't You send someone to help these people?*

His answer comes gently, patiently. *I did,* He says. *I sent you.*

Father, how is it that I so conveniently forget that I am the "someone" You send? —PAM KIDD

DAY 3: THE WIDOW'S MITE

SUN
22

FOR HE THAT IS LEAST AMONG YOU ALL, THE SAME SHALL BE GREAT.
—*Luke 9:48*

BACK IN NASHVILLE, TENNESSEE, my husband David and I were feeling a bit overwhelmed. Before we left Zimbabwe, David had met with Joan, the "Tea and Bread Lady," and discovered that far from being Lady Bountiful, she was nearly destitute herself. She was using every penny she could earn as a bookkeeper to buy food and medicine for the street children.

We had left Joan with a promise to help, but Hillsboro Presbyterian Church, where David is senior minister, was already involved in so many outreach projects that we didn't see how we could take on one more.

But God seemed to be nudging us, so David decided to use a Sunday morning sermon to tell Joan's story. At the end of the service, he invited anyone who wanted to become a part of her ministry to let us know. After the service, a widow on a fixed income quickly made her way to where I was standing.

"I want to help," Tommy Sue said. "I don't have a lot, but I think I can give ten dollars a month."

"Tommy Sue," I said, "ten dollars is a lot of money in Zimbabwe. Your generosity will really help Joan with her work."

By the end of the week, we had three hundred dollars a month in pledges from people in the church. But it was Tommy Sue who became the energizing symbol of our work in Zimbabwe. She was the first to say *yes*.

Tommy Sue became deeply involved in the lives of those faraway people whom she would never see, praying for them and sending them cards and gifts. Today, some years after her death, I still see her as God's messenger, reminding me that God can touch lives, whether in Nashville or Harare, in unexpected ways.

Father, let me remember that You can use whatever I have to give to change the world. —PAM KIDD

DAY 4: FINDING A WAY

MON
23

YEA, I HAVE SPOKEN IT, I WILL ALSO BRING IT TO PASS; I HAVE PURPOSED IT, I WILL ALSO DO IT. —*Isaiah 46:11*

"SO, JOAN," I ASKED the woman whose work in Zimbabwe our church was supporting, "if you could have anything you wanted, what would it be?"

"A building in downtown Harare," she answered, "where mothers could come for sewing and cooking and nutrition classes and where we could cook for the street kids and offer them a place to play. I know it's impossible though. . . ."

Okay, God—I was already bargaining—*if You want it to happen, open the way.*

"So," I asked a friend who was serving the church in southern Africa, "how much do you suppose a building in downtown Harare would cost?"

"I'll check around," he said.

Yikes, God, what am I getting myself into now?

Then a couple from Connecticut who had moved from Nashville, Tennessee, many years before contacted us. "Do you have a project we could help with?" they asked. They offered a large amount of money up front with more to follow.

Our friend in Africa reported that there was a walled compound available near downtown Harare: a lovely house that could serve as Joan's home, plus two more buildings and a garage. "I've talked to a foundation, Pam. They're willing to pay for half the building if you can come up with the rest."

"Buy the building," I answered.

Soon the foundation made another offer: "We'll pay half of Joan's budget if we can use her mission to help with our fund-raising."

With so much of the work taken care of, our next trip to Zimbabwe was to be stress-free. We would visit Joan's new "Home of Hope," then take some time to see the beautiful countryside, where giraffes and elephants and zebras roamed. But God had other ideas.

Father, You say You have purposed it and that You will bring it to pass. I can't wait to see what happens next!
                                      —PAM KIDD

DAY 5: PADDINGTON'S CHILDREN

TUE
24
BEHOLD, I AND THE CHILDREN WHOM THE LORD HATH GIVEN ME ARE FOR SIGNS AND FOR WONDERS. . . .
                                      —*Isaiah 8:18*

BACK IN ZIMBABWE, the countryside had to wait. We found ourselves out at midnight in the dark, cold streets, delivering blankets and food to children sleeping in the back alleys.

For some reason, we kept ending up in the same cab with the same driver. His name was Paddington, and he always just happened to be on hand. And he seemed to share our passion to help the street children.

At the same time something was becoming clear to us: Offering comfort and love to the children was an important calling and Joan was doing her best, but life on the streets is deadly and those who survive become hardened by desperation and hunger. We toyed with the possibility of saving just one child from life on the streets—if we had someone who knew the landscape, someone who could locate a newly orphaned child and find him or her a place to live.

Someone like Paddington?

A native Zimbabwean, Paddington had a special way with people. He found a newly orphaned boy named Thomas and kept him in his rural school by paying his room and board and his school fees. Word spread, and soon Paddington had a second child, then a third. On his own, he rented a house and hired a woman to care for twelve children, all saved from life on the streets.

We were in business!

Father, just when You showed me a need, You showed me a man with a heart to help. All I can say is thank You. —PAM KIDD

DAY 6: SHARING THE DREAM

WED
25

Before they call, I will answer. . . .
—*Isaiah 65:24*

"PADDINGTON," I WROTE to the Harare cabdriver who was now the foster father of twelve, "do you have a dream?"

"Yes," he responded.

"Tell me your dream," I wrote back.

"The children are doing well in school," he wrote, "but they need parents. They need chores to do in the afternoons, animals to take care of and a garden to tend. My wife Alice and I dream of having a farm out in the country where they can be part of our family. We want to teach them responsibility and the importance of education. We want to raise them as our own."

As I read Paddington's letter, I had a strange feeling that this was exactly what God had had in mind all along. Perhaps the future of Zimbabwe was to be raised on that farm. But Paddington's new children were beginning to stretch our budget.

I was leaving for Zimbabwe the next day and was packing when the phone rang. After I hung up, I stood by the phone for five minutes and then started laughing. I laughed and laughed and laughed. "How," I asked God, "am I ever going to get anybody to believe this story?" And then I laughed some more.

The call had been from an old friend. He was going

through a sad time and had just called to talk. "What are you doing?" he asked.

"Packing for Zimbabwe," I answered. And soon I was pouring out the whole story.

"I've got a great idea," he said. "Let me buy the farm."

As it turns out, my friend had become wealthy and he was longing to find ways to use his money to help others.

Father, I stand amazed. What more can I say?
—PAM KIDD

DAY 7: VILLAGE HOPE

THU
26
MERCY AND TRUTH ARE MET TOGETHER; RIGHTEOUSNESS AND PEACE HAVE KISSED EACH OTHER. —*Psalm 85:10*

HERE I AM, sitting in silence on the floor of a hut in rural Zimbabwe, thinking back to my perch on that ladder before my daughter Keri's wedding and the long and improbable journey that has brought me here.

In the center of the hut, Paddington's wife Alice is kneeling over the fire, stirring a pot of thick *sadza* made from maize grown and milled right here on the farm Paddington has named Village Hope.

Alice dishes out the sadza onto tin plates. Two of the girls, members of Village Hope's big family, are making their way around the circle. One holds a bowl while the other pours warm water from a pitcher over the hands of the children—once hungry and home-less—who are gathered around the fire.

Another girl delivers the plates of sadza and greens to each of us. The contentment in the room is palpable. We are safe and warm; there is enough to eat, enough to share. We are a family, brought together through a series of events that have to be called miracles.

Only a God Who delights in surprises could have engineered an outcome like this. Except for saying a few reluctant *yeses* and offering others the opportunity to help, my part in it has been small. But all along God was taking those little *yeses* and using them to make this moment happen.

I'm not suggesting that this is the end of my story—only God will decide that—and there's no use trying to imagine where He might take our Zimbabwe proj-ects next. But I know that I don't have to worry and that tomorrow I can buckle up and hang on for what-ever ride He has in store.

Yet tonight in this smoky hut, sitting on a waxed concrete floor, floating in the silence, I've found at last what I've been searching for all my life.

Peace. Perfect peace.

I have been kissed by peace, Father. There is nothing more I can ask. —PAM KIDD

FRI
27
WAIT ON THE LORD: BE OF GOOD COURAGE, AND HE SHALL STRENGTHEN THINE HEART. . . . —Psalm 27:14

MY HUSBAND HAS BEEN DEAD four years. "It will get easier," I was assured. It didn't. It got harder! When the church phoned, requesting pictures for a new directory, I couldn't stand the thought of mine being put in it without him at my side. "It's okay," the secretary said, "I understand. We'll just list your name."

Later that day I went to take a load of trash to the bins at the edge of the road—formerly my husband's job. Trash had been pulled out of the plastic bags and was scattered down the street. *Bother, that drat raccoon has been at it again!*

As I retrieved a couple of cans that had rolled over to my neighbor's chain-link fence, I was greeted by a sunflower. It had struggled up through a tangle of brush inside the fence, then pushed its bud through one of the links. It bloomed alone, a flower enormously large and bright . . . like a smile from God to brighten up my day. "Thank You, Lord," I whispered.

I took courage from that flower; I, too, could bloom alone. I would phone the church and arrange to have my picture put in the directory.

Lord of eternal light and love, when my heart is lonely, I praise You for the encouragement of sweet surprises.
                                                   —FAY ANGUS

SAT
28
BUT AS FOR ME, I WATCH IN HOPE FOR THE LORD, I WAIT FOR GOD MY SAVIOR. . . . —Micah 7:7 (NIV)

I'M MOVING THROUGH MY FIFTIES, and once in a while I get a nagging feeling that life is passing me by. I know I'll never play defensive end for the Chicago Bears or make it into the Young Presidents Organization (you have to be under forty to join).

So I was having a little pity party about the speeding calendar while canoeing last summer. One morning, while spooning cholesterol-lowering hot oatmeal into my empty stomach, I sat on a rock and watched a pair of loons take off into the rising sunshine.

Loons are known for their hauntingly musical calls. They're larger than ducks, beautifully outfitted in black and white, and can swim underwater for several minutes chasing the small fish that make up their diet. But they have a tough time getting airborne. A loud flapping of wings initiates a frantic acceleration that barely gets them out of the water. Then they run along the surface for a hundred yards or more, webbed feet splashing wildly, in an effort to launch into the sky.

Their cousins on the same lake don't have this difficulty. The much larger blue heron merely stands up, spreads its wings and lifts off like a helicopter. Canvasback and mallard ducks explode into the air in just a few feet. Even the wary eagle seems to glide from treetop perch to soaring heights.

I felt sorry for the loons until I watched them for a while, gliding above the lake, sharp eyes seeking out a tasty brunch. Then I washed out my oatmeal bowl and said to myself, "So what if I'm a loon? Airborne days are still ahead and there's plenty of sky to soar into."

Lord, help me stop worrying about the flight delays in my life and wait patiently on You.

—ERIC FELLMAN

SUN
29
NATHANAEL SAITH UNTO HIM, WHENCE KNOWEST THOU ME? JESUS ANSWERED . . . WHEN THOU WAST UNDER THE FIG TREE, I SAW THEE. —John 1:48

MY COUSIN LIVES up a narrow canyon road on the outskirts of Los Angeles. My favorite spot when I visit her is a rock ledge beneath a spreading live oak overlooking a large grassy field. When I hold very still, the space around me reveals all sorts of activity. The creatures feel safe to show themselves.

One day I sat in the sun and silently began to greet all that I saw. *I see you, coyote, prowling in the grass. I see you, gecko, climbing on the rock. I see you, dragonfly, flitting by. I see you, squirrels, peering at me. I see you, hummingbird, darting among the blossoms. I see you, scampering rabbits. I see you, butterfly, floating on the breeze.*

I spoke aloud and my soliloquy became a dialogue. "Jesus, what do You see?" His answer, calm and sure, filled my heart. *I see you, Carol, sitting under the oak tree, sunning your legs.*

I felt a sudden breathlessness, an acute awareness that Jesus really does see me. He knows every detail—my thoughts and dreams, my battles, my motivations and limitations, the pangs of body and soul, the secret joys and triumphs of my heart. I sensed His deep compassion and caring for me. And like the creatures around me, I knew it was safe to show myself.

Jesus, I love Your eyes that see exactly who I am—and who You intend me to be. —CAROL KNAPP

MON
30

"FOR I KNOW THE PLANS I HAVE FOR YOU. . . ." —*Jeremiah 29:11 (NIV)*

"I HAVE A BUD!" I told my friend Peggy. The night-blooming cereus she had given me years ago was finally about to bloom.

"Give it some shade on your patio, ample water and some fertilizer," she'd instructed. "You'll have an un-forgettable flower to behold—if you can wake up to see it." She smiled knowingly. "It only blooms in the middle of the night."

Now my plant was about to flower. I watched it closely. Its tightly packed bud grew larger and fuller each day. A neighbor walked over to check its progress. "Tonight's the night," she said. "Set your alarm for about two AM. It should be at its peak."

Early the next morning I shuffled sleepily into my backyard and shone my flashlight on the bud. "Oh my goodness!" I exclaimed. It was the most beautiful flower I'd ever seen. The bloom was at least six inches wide. Its large petals revealed hundreds of snowy white filaments inside. And the scent! I'd never smelled such an intense sweetness before. *What a shame that it does this only at night when no one can see it!* I thought.

Then I recalled a conversation I'd had with my friend Johnny. Never one to be the center of attention, he prefers, as he says, "to sit in the last chair." I couldn't understand why he didn't love an audience as I do.

I flipped the flashlight back on, studying my flower. It had bloomed in the quiet of the night and without fanfare, the way God made it—to my unending delight.

Thank You, Lord, for making all of us different—and delightful. —MELODY BONNETTE

MY DIVINE SURPRISES

1 _____

2 _____

3 _____

4 _____

5 _____

6 _____

7 _____

8 _____

9 _____

10 _____

11 _____

12 _____

13 _____

14 _____

15 _____

16 _____

17 _____

18 _____

19 _____

20 _____

21 _____

22 _____

23 _____

24 _____

25 _____

26 _____

27 _____

28 _____

29 _____

30 _____

July

He hath shewed his people the power of his
works. . . . —*Psalm 111:6*

UNEXPECTED BLESSINGS
SEEING IN THE DARK

TUE
1

BELOVED, LET US LOVE ONE ANOTHER. . . .
—I John 4:7

MY HUSBAND JOHN AND I were uneasy as we drove into the manicured country club in Hershey, Pennsylvania. After all, we were coming to interview the notoriously unapproachable Ben Hogan, "the Texas Iceberg," whose machinelike performance on the golf course made him what many still consider the greatest player ever. How would a man famed for stony-faced remoteness respond to our questions?

We'd come to ask him for his secret. How, we wanted to know, had he made his astounding recovery from a near-fatal car crash? Perhaps, we thought, it was the iron self-discipline he'd acquired teaching himself to play golf—swinging a club till his hands bled. Or perhaps it was his legendary concentration, shutting out every thought but getting well, as he'd shut out the distraction of the fans trooping behind him from hole to hole.

When the accident occurred, doctors said he'd never walk again. Incredibly, just three years later, he was back on the links, beginning to reclaim the career that would make him a legend.

We were met in the clubhouse by a short, trim, 130-pound man with a slight limp and, instead of the scowl we were steeled for, a welcoming smile. For an easygoing two hours we chatted about what had made the comeback possible. It did take discipline and focus, he agreed.

"But mostly," he said, "it was the letters."

They'd come by the thousands, from housewives, office workers, students—all with essentially the same message: "We care about you, Ben! We're praying for you."

"Before those letters came," said Hogan, "I told myself I didn't care whether people were for me or against me. To win, I thought I had to shut the spectators out. To find suddenly that you have thousands of people rooting for you . . . why, I just had to get better!"

A terrible accident, surgeries, pain—and a gift bigger and longer lasting than any of them.

Bestower of blessing, help me discern the gifts You wrap in darkness. —ELIZABETH SHERRILL

WED
2

To enjoy your work and to accept your lot in life—that is indeed a gift from God. . . .
—*Ecclesiastes 5:19 (TLB)*

NOT LONG AFTER MY SON ANDREW told me about the hideaway he'd created in his garage, with an old recliner, TV, keyboard and stereo, I saw an article in the *St. Pete Times* titled "The Man Cave." It described all the places men like to hang out, including hunting camps, fraternal lodges, baseball dugouts, barbershops, gyms, men-only Bible studies, barbecues and retreats.

The more I thought about the man cave and how important it is for men to find a place to hang out by themselves or with other men, the more I understood why I enjoy living alone. After all, I've been head of my household. I've had an empty nest since Andrew, the last of my four children, left for college nearly ten years ago. And even though my friend Jack lives just fifty-seven steps from my condo, I still need time alone in my own place—a place to think, dream, organize and decorate just the way I want; a place to pray.

The older I get, the more content I am with my single life. All I have to do to be social is open my front door and step out. Somehow I'm always delighted by the surprises God has to offer out there.

Father, help me appreciate my way of life, but remind me to keep my arms open to all the possibilities around me. —PATRICIA LORENZ

THU *But I say unto you, Love your*
3 *enemies, bless them that curse you,*
      do good to them that hate you, and
      pray for them which despitefully
use you. . . . —*Matthew 5:44*

WHEN I FIND IT DIFFICULT to forgive someone who has wronged me, I remember the man who set out to kill me. At the time, I was soldiering in Europe during World War II. Men on both sides set out to eliminate each other. After the war, I met several former enemy veterans, one of whom had marched on our position. We had some friendly talks; bygones were bygones. The same happened to many Vietnam vets who traveled back to that war-torn country to visit former enemies and to gain closure.

A most remarkable example of this happened long after the Civil War. Veterans of both sides who fought at Gettysburg had a reunion on that historic battlefield. Memories were still fresh; one grizzled vet threatened a former enemy with a kitchen fork during an argument. But someone suggested a reenactment of the memorable Pickett's Charge, in which massed Southern troops advanced on a stone wall defended by Northern men. What resulted back in 1863 was one of history's most bloody and vicious conflicts.

Both Blue and Gray vets agreed to do it. As the aged Confederates crossed the wheat field, many tottering on canes, their former enemies crouched on aching knees behind the stone wall. Suddenly, reunion organizers caught their breaths. Would mayhem result, with cane beatings and pocketknife stabbings?

But as the two groups met, a great moan of emotion arose from the old soldiers as they tearfully rushed forward to embrace each other.

If once mortal enemies can forgive and forget, can't we forgive and forget the slights and offenses of another?

When hearts are hard, Lord, help me to take the first step to forgiveness. —RICHARD SCHNEIDER

FRI
4

DO NOT THINK OF YOURSELF MORE HIGHLY THAN YOU OUGHT, BUT RATHER THINK OF YOURSELF WITH SOBER JUDGMENT. . . . —*Romans 12:3 (NIV)*

WHEN I WAS GROWING UP, I was sure I had a special relationship to the goings-on in Philadelphia on July 4, 1776, because lurking somewhere on my family tree was a genuine Founding Father.

My Great-grandmother Attaway's maiden name was Hall, and she, my father told me, was related to Lyman Hall, one of the three signers of the Declaration of Independence from Georgia. "My brother Lyman," Dad said, "was named after him."

Every year as the Fourth of July approached, I'd casually let my playmates know about my famous ancestor. I'd carefully unfold the facsimile of the Declaration that I'd bought on a family trip to Philadelphia and show them the second signature in the leftmost column. They weren't all that impressed, but I certainly was.

When I was in my teens, I decided to do some research about Lyman Hall. I was dumbfounded to read that his only son had died childless; there were no Halls directly descended from him, let alone any Attaways. Some years later, on a visit to the Georgia State Archives, I learned that many Halls claim a relationship to the founder with no evidence beyond the coincidence of names. And just a few weeks ago, on the Internet, I discovered a family tree of my Hall antecedents, unpretentious farmers like the Attaways, who seem to have been totally unconnected to Lyman Hall.

My pride was taken down a peg, but those youthful hours of poring over the Declaration gave me a love for the words Thomas Jefferson wrote, so very much more important than the names signed under them, no matter whose family trees they grace.

Lord, help me always to remember that my freedom is a gift from You. —ANDREW ATTAWAY

SAT
5
HEAVEN AND EARTH SHALL PASS AWAY,
BUT MY WORDS SHALL NOT PASS AWAY.
BUT OF THAT DAY AND HOUR KNOWETH
NO MAN, NO, NOT THE ANGELS OF HEAVEN,
BUT MY FATHER ONLY. —*Matthew 24:35–36*

DURING A RECENT FAMILY REUNION, our four children got to talking about trips we had made together. When they were young, we did a lot of hiking, including one two-month excursion on the Appalachian Trail. We started at the southern terminus, Springer Mountain in Georgia, and finished on Mt. Katahdin in Maine. That's not to say we walked all of the two-thousand-mile-plus trail, but we sampled parts of it in every state.

"Remember the guy who almost ran his pickup truck off the road, gawking at us?" one of the kids asked.

I certainly did. It was a rainy day, and we had come down off a southern mountain to fill our larder. The "we" included Shirley and me, our four children, a German schnauzer named Heidi and two Sardinian donkeys, Pinocchio and Figaro. I had grown a beard on the trip, was wearing a hooded poncho, carrying a staff and leading one of the donkeys.

Suddenly, a rickety red truck came around the bend behind us and sped past. I waved, but the driver only stared, seemingly shocked at what he saw. Up ahead the road bent sharply to the left, and for a moment I thought he was going over the cliff. But at the last minute he regained control and disappeared. It was just as he drove out of sight that everything became clear: On the pickup's bumper was a sticker that read, REPENT, THE END IS NEAR.

Most of us probably don't need reminders that our earthly life is finite, but an occasional nudge is probably in order, like the Pennsylvania Dutch wisdom I saw in a souvenir store yesterday that read: "We grow old so fast and wise so slow."

Lord, teach us to value each moment, each day,
As well as those folks we meet along the way.
—FRED BAUER

SUN
6
BUT HOPE THAT IS SEEN IS NO HOPE AT ALL. WHO HOPES FOR WHAT HE ALREADY HAS? —Romans 8:24 (NIV)

IT WAS MUCH MORE than the relentless heat and humidity that was dragging me down as I drove to our son Chris's house, where we were helping pack up his household goods before he was deployed to Iraq. I was worried about Chris's immediate future in a war zone and about the unrealized parts of his future. Would he ever get married and have a family of his own? What kind of job would be waiting for him after he got out of the service?

Suddenly, I noticed the name of a church I was passing: Beauty Spot Church. There was a small cinderblock building in back, and in front was a half-finished sanctuary that dwarfed the original building. There were wallboards around the sides sheathing the metal girders, but the front was still open, and I could see through the supports into the unfinished interior.

As I passed, I noticed a man and a woman walking hand in hand up the dirt mound in front of the building. I was past the church before the couple reached the entrance, but something about them moving toward it struck chords of hope deep inside of me. Life is always filled with things that are on hold, unfinished and unknown. Only hope can carry us as God takes our hand and walks with us toward His beautiful future.

Dear Jesus, let hope walk with me on the days I have trouble seeing the dream ahead. —KAREN BARBER

MON
7

I AM COME THAT THEY MIGHT HAVE LIFE, AND THAT THEY MIGHT HAVE IT MORE ABUNDANTLY. —*John 10:10*

ON A SWELTERING SUMMER DAY, I stagger through my New York City apartment door, dripping perspiration and dropping shopping bags. Cans of cat food tumble across the floor, a lemon rolls under a bookcase. My shoulder aches, my knee hurts and I trip over the broom I forgot to put away. Flooded with fatigue and self-pity, I wonder, *Why is life so hard? Why is the weather so hot? And where on earth is the can opener, so I can feed the cats wailing around my ankles?*

The message button blinks on my answering machine. *Now what?* Grumpily, I press the button and hear my sister-in-law's cheerful voice, singing a Mister Rogers song. "It's such a good feeling to know you're alive—"

Jennifer was diagnosed with Parkinson's disease more than ten years ago, when she was in her early fifties. Since then, she's dealt with physical challenges I can barely begin to imagine. Jennifer's gone through long hours of surgery, rigorous therapy, difficult dental work, and has gradually lost a lot of her mobility and independence. It would be understandable if she had become irritable and angry, lashed out in frustration or dissolved into self-pity.

Instead, she's moved to a new house, gone to exercise classes, cultivated friends at church, and supervised and cuddled six grandchildren—and leaves singing messages on my answering machine. Jennifer's not in denial about anything; she's just one of the most commonsense, up-front, positive people I know. No wonder we all adore her.

Once again I press the button on my answering machine. When she sings ". . . when you wake up ready to say, 'I think I'll make a snappy new day. . . .'" I'm up for making one too. I mop my brow, feed the cats and look out my window at the blue of the Hudson River.

It's such a good feeling to know you're alive. Now I'll return Jennifer's call.

Dear God, thanks for the people who remind me "it's such a good feeling to know we're alive."
—MARY ANN O'ROARK

TUE
8

"WE SAW THE NEPHILIM THERE. . . . WE SEEMED LIKE GRASSHOPPERS IN OUR OWN EYES, AND WE LOOKED THE SAME TO THEM." —*Numbers 13:33 (NIV)*

I'M A GIANT . . . at least to the hummingbird and the butterfly.

Last summer, a male Anna's hummingbird laid claim to the feeder in our backyard in Southern California. He perched on a branch a couple of feet above the feeder in a carrotwood tree and chased away all others that got near *his* food supply. He even flew at me a time or two, wings whirring, when I got too close.

There was also a brown and yellow mourning cloak butterfly who claimed our backyard as *his* private domain. Bold as can be, he charged at the hummingbird when the two encountered each other. And twice he determinedly fluttered around my head to warn me that I was in his territory.

Each little creature was bold enough to stand up to someone hundreds and thousands of times his size.

Like the hummingbird and the butterfly, I had to contend with a giant. My wife Carol and I loved Southern California and our friends and church there, but after eight years the longing for family in the Northeast won out. Selling one home and buying another in the midst of a less than favorable real-estate market would be a giant undertaking.

We turned to one of our favorite Bible verses: "Be strong and courageous. Do not be terrified; do not be discouraged, for the Lord your God will be with you wherever you go" (Joshua 1:9, NIV). Holding on to that promise, we faced our giant, sold our house and moved East to begin looking for a new home.

Lord, give us boldness to challenge the giants we face.
—HAROLD HOSTETLER

WED
9

MY HELP COMETH FROM THE LORD, WHICH MADE HEAVEN AND EARTH.
—*Psalm 121:2*

IN ALL THE YEARS I've been at Guideposts (some fifty-two of them), there have been a few special moments when I was certain that God was speaking to me. One of them was at a family dinner table in Sherman Oaks, California.

I was there covering the story of the horrible accident in which Anne Shelly's left arm was severed by a Cessna airplane's propeller. The story won fifteen-year-old Anne a prize in the Guideposts Youth Writing Contest for 1973.

Anne trusted God—completely. From the moment she lay on the tarmac of the airport at Van Nuys, she asked God to give her back her arm. And He did. When I saw her a year later, she could swim, dance, knit, and hug her family and friends.

I ran down in my mind the unusual events, when every passing minute had been crucial: that a young man who heard the accident came running in the dusk, dashed for a telephone; that he called the fire department and explained the trouble so specifically that attendants came prepared to minister to Anne; that the doctor at the hospital's admissions desk, who was there only by chance, should be the very man who knew the surgeons who had performed this type of rare orthopedic surgery; that those surgeons in a peak vacation period should be available and there within the hour.

"What a collection of coincidences," I said at the dining table.

Anne's mother didn't hesitate to speak the words that have stayed with me since. While passing the butter, she said matter-of-factly, "There are no coincidences."

I try to remember those words, Father.

—VAN VARNER

THU **IO** *THIS IS THE ASSURANCE WE HAVE IN APPROACHING GOD: THAT IF WE ASK ANYTHING ACCORDING TO HIS WILL, HE HEARS US.* —I John 5:14 (NIV)

HOW I LOVE this computer/Internet/cell phone age! I know there are abuses, but most of the pluses outweigh them.

For example, here I am in Virginia furiously typing and through the speakers of this same computer I can hear our son Peter, live, directing air traffic from a control tower more than five hundred miles away. If I want, I can "Google Earth" the airport and zoom in until I can see a satellite shot of the control tower where he works. Or I can fly over the skylighted roof of our son Tom and his wife Susan's house in Georgia. Or follow, as I did, our son John on a week's trip in the mountains and by the sea in Croatia. I can find the grass landing strip in our son Dave and his wife Matti's backyard in Kentucky, and fly up Fort Valley inside our own Massanutten Mountain. What fun!

As the mother of four sons, I bless e-mail daily because I know from their college years that receiving "snail mail" letters from them is a pipe dream.

Then there's the Webcam. Bill and I bought two; one perches on a speaker by our computer and the other sits on a desk in Georgia. And our grandsons Jack and Luke look at the grainy square on their computer screen and see us, live, waving, laughing, playing peekaboo with them. And they respond, "Grandpa! Grandma!"

The cell phone—well, that goes without saying. How did I ever survive a trip to the grocery store without one?

All this communication and technology have enhanced my faith in how God can be close to and personal with me; He's had this expertise all along.

Lord, You know where I am. You listen and see and know all about me, live. And You rejoice to hear from me as much as I do when I hear from children and grandchildren. —ROBERTA ROGERS

FRI
11

CONSIDER IT PURE JOY, MY BROTHERS, WHENEVER YOU FACE TRIALS OF MANY KINDS, BECAUSE YOU KNOW THAT THE TESTING OF YOUR FAITH DEVELOPS PERSEVERANCE. —*James 1:2–3 (NIV)*

I WAS LIVID. It was two days before my sister's wedding, and I was stranded at Newark Liberty International Airport, unable to fly because of storms. I argued and pleaded with the gate agent. "It's the weather," she said. "There's nothing I can do."

I spent a sleepless night in a plastic chair and flew out the next morning, bleary-eyed. At the rehearsal dinner I was ready to tell anyone my tale of woe. But it wasn't long before I heard the story of the man in the old-fashioned shirt and too-large khakis seated across the room.

A friend of the groom's, he was currently living on a two-square-mile island in Indonesia. When July rolled around, he decided that he needed to be at this wedding in Florence, Alabama.

He left on a Saturday, swimming off his island and climbing onto a reef so he could flag down a fishing boat. A fisherman took him to a barge, which carried him to a ferry. The ferry got him to Jakarta. From there, he flew to Singapore, then to Hong Kong, London, Minneapolis, and on to Memphis, Tennessee, where he called a bewildered friend who eagerly jumped in his car to go to the airport. He had shown up for each flight without a ticket or any luggage, only buying a change of clothes once he arrived in Florence.

Suddenly, my own travel plight didn't look so bad. More than that, I began to realize what I had in this very room: family and friends who would give anything—do everything—to be together. I couldn't help but think how blessed I was.

Help me, Lord, to be joyful in all the trials I face.
                                        —ASHLEY JOHNSON

SAT 12 *So then, just as you received Christ Jesus as Lord, continue to live in him.* —*Colossians 2:6 (NIV)*

IT'S NOT EASY to bounce back and trust when you have lost a child. After our son Reggie died in an accident a few years ago, Rosie and I wanted to keep our younger son Ryan close, protect him and not let him go.

A couple of summers ago, Ryan participated in an internship program and was required to attend a national conference in Philadelphia. We thought he would be traveling from Mississippi with some of his fellow interns, but it turned out Ryan would be going alone.

We were fearful and stayed near the phone, waiting for him to call. Ryan telephoned from his layover in Atlanta, excited to tell us that a family friend had been on the plane with him, was going to the same conference and would accompany him all the way to the hotel in Philadelphia.

When Ryan called again to let us know he had arrived safely, we praised God for His goodness. We are still learning to walk in Colossians 2:6.

Lord, I know that You are our Lord every day. I ask that You enable me to continue to live in You.
—DOLPHUS WEARY

SUN
13
*AND THIS WAS YET A SMALL THING IN
THY SIGHT, O LORD GOD. . . .*
—*II Samuel 7:19*

SOME FRIENDS LET US USE their cabin in northern Arizona for a long weekend. It gave us a welcome break from the 110-degree Phoenix summer. The cabin sat in a beautiful spot, surrounded by ponderosa pines. The air smelled wonderfully fresh, and all day I heard one of my favorite sounds—the *whoosh* of the wind through trees.

By about the third day, I noticed that a change had come over me. Little things that might have been bothersome at home didn't faze me. Leaning against a tree while on a hike, staring up at the clear blue sky, I got a little sap on my shirt. Back home I would have rushed inside right away, taken it off and thrown it in the wash. But here, I wore the shirt all day. Later, while setting the table, I noticed that hardly any of the dishes matched and some even had a few chips around the edges. *Who cares?* I thought. We were on vacation. The time was so precious, somehow those little details didn't seem to matter.

Why couldn't I do this at home? When the children's shoes were scattered about or their books piled up, a perfectly ordered house seemed like life's most important goal. Sure, sometimes cleanliness is a priority. But the next time I get a little clutter-crazy, I'll ask myself: Would this matter if we were on vacation?

After all, if a vacation is too short to fret over little details, isn't all of life?

Lord, give my heart and mind a vacation spirit every morning, so that I'm able to let go of the small details that matter very little at the end of the day.
—GINA BRIDGEMAN

MON
14

HIS DOMINION SHALL BE FROM SEA EVEN TO SEA, AND FROM THE RIVER EVEN TO THE ENDS OF THE EARTH.
—*Zechariah 9:10*

I WAS TOTALLY WIPED OUT, and not even the nice clean hotel room with its sparkling view of the Rocky Mountains could revive me. The week before I had been to Seoul, South Korea, to celebrate the fortieth anniversary of the Korean edition of *Guideposts* magazine. Then it was back to New York, up to Massachusetts and finally out here to Colorado for a jam-packed conference.

I threw my luggage on the bed and began transferring fistfuls of clothes to the dresser and closet. From the side pocket of my suitcase I tugged a pair of walking shoes I'd brought along in the now unlikely event that I might want to go for a hike, and tossed them into the bottom of the closet. As I did, caked-on dirt went flying all over the newly vacuumed carpet. *Oh no.*

I got down on my knees and swept up the dried

mud with my hands. I was about to toss a handful into the trash can by the desk when I stopped and stared at the dirt in my palm—Korean dirt. I'd last worn these shoes on a tour of a historical Korean village, one of the many tourist spots to which my gracious host Mr. Go took me. Afterward, we'd gone to the border with North Korea and in a drizzling rain stared through the high fence at the forbidding demilitarized zone. We had bowed our heads and said a prayer.

Maybe it was the jet lag, but suddenly I was overwhelmed by astonishment at how small our world really is and what little it takes, even a clump of dirt, to make me feel connected.

Father, cradle this small world of ours in Your hands, and keep us safe and connected to You.
                                    —EDWARD GRINNAN

TUE
15

THEN GOD SAID, "I GIVE YOU EVERY SEED-BEARING PLANT ON THE FACE OF THE WHOLE EARTH AND EVERY TREE THAT HAS FRUIT WITH SEED IN IT. THEY WILL BE YOURS FOR FOOD." —*Genesis 1:29 (NIV)*

"WHAT'S THE FRUIT TODAY?" Laura called, as she wheeled her cart toward the park. I grinned and replied, "Peaches. Fourteen of 'em."

This year we joined a CSA, or Community Supported Agriculture group. We paid a chunk of money in the spring to an organic farmer in upstate

New York, and every Tuesday from June through November, he sends our share of the week's harvest to a city park near us.

At first I worried that the CSA wouldn't be cost-effective. A few weeks' worth of fruits and vegetables later, I didn't care. There's nothing quite like vegetables picked the same day and strawberries still warm from the sun.

I found joy in trailing down the sidewalk with cart and kids in tow, chatting with neighbors en route to the same destination. We made new friends while counting out our beets and selecting our bunches of greens.

But the thing I liked best about the CSA was something I never would have imagined. Each week I had to figure out what to do with our cartful of goodies. How on earth does one cook kohlrabi so that children will eat it? And what should I do with that pile of turnips? Suddenly we had lots of vegetables that I didn't normally buy: exotic Japanese greens, heaps of kale, dozens of radishes.

The effect was invigorating. I looked up recipes, traded ideas with friends and invented new dishes of my own. I loved the adventure. And when I cooked, I could ask, "How can I make the best of what I have?" That seemed even healthier than eating fresh vegetables.

Father, You put everything in my life for a reason. Help me make the most of it. —JULIA ATTAWAY

READER'S ROOM

MY SON is currently serving in the U.S. Army as a Ranger, Special Forces. His unit has deployed four times now because of the conflict. Ever have one of those moments where something just jumps out at you? Becomes alive? The return of my son brought me one of those moments through *Daily Guideposts*.

He called home at about 2:00 AM on July 9. He was in Germany, awaiting his flight to return to the States. Those calls at that time in the morning always catch you off guard and awaken you. Your heart jumpstarts. I got up excitedly and was sure to thank God. I couldn't go back to sleep then, so I got my devotional for the day and read: "As cold waters to a thirsty soul, so is good news from a far country" (Proverbs 25:25). Amazing! How God fits the pieces together, even when we are unaware. He uses us, those who are willing, to carry out His will. Lord, grant us a willing heart.

—*Mary Kay Donaldson, Beaufort, South Carolina*

WED
16

IF GOD IS FOR US, WHO CAN BE AGAINST us? —Romans 8:31 (NKJV)

ONE DAY I WAS WATCHING an old episode of *Gunsmoke*. It was about a safecracker who had just been released from jail and was trying to start a new life. He was determined to win the hand of the woman he had disappointed by his crimes.

Unfortunately, the safecracker's old cronies came around, looking for his secrets to opening safes. The more he resisted them, the more they pressured him, until he once again found himself on the verge of crime. At one point, I found myself saying out loud, "Don't do it, man. Don't listen to them! Do the right thing this time!" I desperately wanted the show to end happily and felt relieved when it did.

I think God feels about me the way I felt about the reformed criminal. He doesn't want to catch me in a crime. Rather, He is cheering me on, hoping I will do the right thing. When I'm tempted, I can almost hear Him saying, "Don't go there! Turn around. I'll help you, if you just turn around." God is on my side. Having Someone Who believes in me is often all I need to find strength.

Thank You, Father, for taking my side when I'm in a precarious situation. —DANIEL SCHANTZ

THU *I DELIGHT GREATLY IN THE LORD. . . .*
17 *FOR HE HAS CLOTHED ME WITH*
     GARMENTS OF SALVATION. . . .
                              —*Isaiah 61:10 (NIV)*

I'VE NEVER GOTTEN A LETTER from an item of clothing—until now.

As I start to snip the large tag on the new skirt I just purchased, I notice this message on the back:

Hello! I am your special garment from Bali. I am unique and often handwoven, hand-beaded, hand-printed and hand-painted. My defects are part of my beauty! Please treat me with special care. Thank you.

I look closely at the skirt: It has huge pink flowers and wonderful lime-green leaves. Beads and sequins are worked randomly into the pattern. A silk pocket on the front rests inches from the hemline. Yes, it is unique. And, perhaps, a tad flawed. But it is lovely nonetheless. I glance at myself in a nearby mirror. Like the skirt, I'm less than perfect. I wish my hair were curly. I wish I were taller. I wish my waist . . . well, I wish I *had* a waist!

My defects are part of my beauty. If I can believe that of a garment, why not of myself?

As I cut the tag with the scissors and it falls into my hand, I see what's on the other side—the name brand on the skirt: FAITH.

Maybe this piece of clothing *is* perfect after all!

You made me in Your image, God. What a humbling and empowering thing! Help me to see that in loving myself—imperfections and all—I'm also loving You.
                                          —MARY LOU CARNEY

FRI
18

BECAUSE YOU KNEW THAT YOU YOURSELVES HAD BETTER AND LASTING POSSESSIONS. —*Hebrews 10:34 (NIV)*

LAST YEAR MY DISEASED HIP JOINT was re-placed with a titanium ball-and-cup lined with ce-ramic. Just twelve weeks after the surgery, I was in Colorado, skiing without pain for the first time in years. Then I started taking stairs two at a time, some-thing impossible just last fall. A few weeks after that, I was chasing my wife Joy around the park on her five-mile daily walk/run and almost keeping up. And finally, just last summer, I went on a six-day solo canoe trip to the Boundary Waters Canoe Area Wilderness in northeastern Minnesota and carried all my own gear, including the canoe, as if I were twenty again.

Then I went for my six-month postsurgery checkup. The doctor told me that everything was looking great, and that if I was careful, my new hip would last a good twenty or twenty-five years.

Now that made me think. *Even with the best results, this great technology is going to wear out; I am going to wear out. Maybe not next year or in the next ten years, but someday I won't be able to take the stairs two steps at a time or carry that canoe over the rocky trails. As good as I feel now, it won't last forever.*

So I asked myself, what does last forever? I decided to make a list and found that it was a pretty short one, with nothing material or physical on it: Faith lasts. Love lasts. Hope is the fuel that keeps them both burning. Character made out of integrity, generosity and kindness lasts too.

Now mind you, I'm still going to exercise this bionic hip and all my other parts to keep them moving as long as possible, but I've decided to exercise the things on my list too. Because, as I understand it, I get to take those with me when I leave the hip behind.

Lord God, thank You for the wisdom You give doctors to heal and help, and for the opportunities You give me to grow and thrive into eternity. —ERIC FELLMAN

A SECOND THANK-YOU
THANK YOU FOR HURTS

SAT
19

[LOVE] KEEPS NO RECORD OF WRONGS.
                —*I Corinthians 13:5* (NIV)

SEVERAL YEARS AGO, I bought a sterling silver charm bracelet, something I'd longed for during my growing-up years. I've since commemorated special "anniversaries of the heart" by purchasing charms to put on it.

One day, I was drawn to a charm that depicted a slice of watermelon. It looked so real that I could see the shiny black seeds and almost feel the pink juice dribbling down my chin. But then I felt as if a belt were tightening around my heart as a long-buried memory surfaced. Suddenly, I was ten years old and had received an invitation to my neighbor Kim's watermelon party. For days, I reveled in the fact that I'd been included, and I planned the navy-blue striped shorts set I would wear to blend in with the other girls.

But when I appeared at the door of Kim's beige brick house and announced to her mother that I was there for the party, I was met with girls' laughter from behind the screen door. It had all been a joke; I was the laughingstock of Madison Avenue. When I went crying to Mother, she told me, "We need to forgive such things, honey, as hard as they are. Want me to help you pray about it?"

As the jeweler interrupted my reverie, I heard the Lord's gentle prompting: *Buy the watermelon charm, Roberta, for this is a most significant anniversary of your heart. That was the day that you learned about hurt, about shame, about the importance of releasing wrongs, about understanding the feelings of others.*

Today, as I finger that watermelon charm, Lord, I say thank You once again. For without life's hurts, we never learn to be helpers. —ROBERTA MESSNER

SUN
20   *THE LORD HATH APPEARED OF OLD*
     UNTO ME, SAYING, YEA, I HAVE LOVED
     THEE WITH AN EVERLASTING LOVE. . . .
                                   —*Jeremiah 31:3*

RECENTLY, I RAN ACROSS a pile of my mother's hankies I'd stashed away after her death nearly ten years ago, and a flood of memories suddenly surfaced.

The nine-inch square of voile with lavender daisies in one corner reminded me I used to tuck it in the pocket of my best dress—with its four points peeking out "just so"—when I had a date. Beneath it was a smaller, mostly blue hankie featuring Peter Rabbit. Mom knotted my nickel in one of its corners so I wouldn't lose it on the way to Sunday school.

The most colorful hankie announced its presence in the pile because red poinsettias and green leaves marched clear around its border. Back then I carried it only at Christmastime. Near the bottom of the stack was one with edging Mom had tatted, along with an embroidered "Isabel" in red in the center.

I recalled, too, how Mom's handkerchiefs always smelled like lily of the valley; how she'd dampen a hankie's corner to clean a spot from my face; how she'd wrap one around a cut finger and the hurt immediately felt better.

Well, I'm preserving Mom's prettiest handkerchiefs—on which the scent magically lingers—by using them on pillow tops, framing them to hang on walls, using them as doilies beneath a pretty dish. This way, they serve as reminders of the days when I took them to church and Mom kept me amused during long sermons by making "twin babies in a cradle": folding the hankie into a triangle, rolling the two opposite ends toward the middle for the "babies," pulling the other two points back against themselves for the "cradle," gently swinging the hankie to make the cradle rock. Can't do that with a tissue, you know.

Thank You, Heavenly Father, for reminders that You still love Your kids—no matter what our ages.
—ISABEL WOLSELEY

MON
21
NATION SHALL NOT LIFT UP A SWORD AGAINST NATION, NEITHER SHALL THEY LEARN WAR ANY MORE. BUT THEY SHALL SIT EVERY MAN UNDER HIS VINE AND UNDER HIS FIG TREE; AND NONE SHALL MAKE THEM AFRAID: FOR THE MOUTH OF THE LORD OF HOSTS HATH SPOKEN IT. —Micah 4:3–4

A YOUNG FRIEND OF MINE is just back from Iraq. He was twenty-three years old when he left, and now he is a thousand times older than I. We sit in the sun and he talks awhile.

"I don't regret my service," he says. "I did a good thing, protecting my friends, trying to help the people there find a peaceful life where they can just work and pray and argue like normal people.

"I prayed, sure. You bet I prayed. I prayed all the time. And I tried to do everything with my fullest attention—that's a kind of prayer too. When I cleaned my weapon, I was intent on cleaning my weapon. When I helped build a shed for a family, I built the best shed there ever was.

"Someday I'll go back. I have to go back. Those poor people, they were just like us. The kids trying to get out of doing their homework, and somebody forgot to let the dog out, and whose turn is it to do the dishes? The prayer of every day. I bet I prayed that prayer more than any other when I was there: 'God, grant us the miracle of a normal day.' I mean, really, what more powerful prayer could you ever pray?"

Dear Lord, on my knees I beg You this: Grant us the miracle of a normal day. I know full well that every day is a miracle, but You know what I mean. And can You shove the world toward being a place where no child has to go to war? —BRIAN DOYLE

TUE
22
THAT THEY MAY SET THEIR HOPE IN GOD, AND NOT FORGET THE WORKS OF GOD. . . . —*Psalm 78:7 (NKJV)*

MY FRIEND JULIA PHONED ME, sounding excited. "I've got something important to share with you. Set aside an hour tonight."

"Sure," I said, intrigued. "What time should I pick you up?"

"Six thirty sharp. Except, I'll drive to your place and then I'll drive us there." I sank into a chair, stunned. Julia had been afraid to drive for at least the five years I'd known her. She wouldn't drive over bridges and she'd never drive after dusk—the list went on and on until her fears stopped her from driving entirely.

"Where are we going?" I asked when she showed up at my door, her eyes bright with excitement.

"I'll show you."

A dozen smooth miles later, we were at a meeting of a self-help organization for people with fear and anxiety, which includes me and just about everyone else in the world. It's called Recovery, Inc., and it got its start in 1953 in Chicago. Abraham A. Low, M.D. wanted to know how what he called "nervous patients"—those of us with fears, worries and even irrational ideas—could be cured. He helped his patients (he called them his "dear ones") to help each other, and as he saw their thinking and actions change, he wrote a book called *Mental Health Through Will-Training*, which is still read today in groups like my friend Julia's.

My jaw dropped as I heard the members talk about how they'd worked to overcome their fears of things like speaking in public or leaving their apartment. And it dropped even further when I heard Julia ask, "Anyone need a lift home?"

God, with Your help, Your "dear ones" have nothing to fear. —LINDA NEUKRUG

WED
23
AND WHATSOEVER YE DO, DO IT HEARTILY.... —*Colossians 3:23*

THE GRANDCHILDREN are coming to visit tonight and I'm in the kitchen cooking dinner. My mind goes back to a warm summer day in childhood. I was itching to get outside when my mother said to me, "Oscar, I want you to help me prepare dinner."

"But, Mother," I gasped. Not many boys my age cooked or even knew how to. Girls helped their mothers in the kitchen, not boys.

"Learning how to cook might come in handy," she said. "You'll be able to help your wife someday."

I muttered something about never getting married, but indeed I did help her that evening and many more evenings. Mother taught me to boil chicken and to use the broth for cooking baby lima beans. I learned from her how to season meat the day before cooking it and how to prepare string beans, cooked cabbage, pork chops and gravy. Other things I picked up on my own, like frying bacon for breakfast while making gelatin for lunch, but seventy-four years after my first lesson I'm still at the stove. Indeed, I'm grateful, and my wife Ruby, who hasn't been well recently, seems to be grateful too.

Tonight, for the grandchildren, I plan to serve chicken wings smothered in gravy, fresh-picked string beans, tossed salad, hot rolls and corn on the cob.

Mother would be pleased.

Jesus, cooking is both creative and a way of serving You each day. —OSCAR GREENE

THU
24

I HAVE LEARNED, IN WHATSOEVER STATE I AM, THEREWITH TO BE CONTENT. —*Philippians 4:11*

MY MOTHER'S FOREBEARS took root in New England in 1627. My dad's parents followed in the late nineteenth century. Their descendants dug in, settled down and lived out their lives close to where they were born. Even my friends have stayed pretty much in the same communities, raising their families and paying off mortgages.

Not me. I went two thousand miles West to Wyoming, where I sold my home of eighteen years to go back to school. Then seven years ago, I put everything in storage and went back East to New Hampshire to be closer to my ailing parents.

Now I continue adjusting to urban life in my apartment near Mom, now widowed and eighty-eight. Meanwhile, my possessions languish in storage. I miss my dishes and flatware and books. I miss having a garden, a washer, a dryer—even a clothesline. I miss knowing all my neighbors. But a remark my daughter Trina's friend Kelly made when she visited for the first time is helping me to refocus my attitude. *"Oooh,"* she squealed, *"a Paris flat!"* I'm trying to see what she sees.

The floor-to-ceiling windows in the kitchen offer a view of Victorian rooftops, half a dozen church steeples, the state capitol dome, treetops and tangled vines. Red geraniums thrive in the light. From here it's easy to forget what century it is. The claw-footed tub in the bathroom has a special charm and the hardwood floors gleam warmly. Even my "Peace Corps décor" of odds and ends blends in nicely: Mom's rocker and futon, Millie's chest, Arthur's bookcase, Doris' quilt, the landlord's wide-pine table and chairs.

I may not be here for long, but I'm home for now. I have everything I truly need and even a few surprises—like a view from a Paris flat.

Lord, how few material things I need to do Your will!
—GAIL THORELL SCHILLING

FRI
25

"BEHOLD, I STAND AT THE DOOR AND KNOCK. IF ANYONE HEARS MY VOICE AND OPENS THE DOOR, I WILL COME IN TO HIM AND DINE WITH HIM. . . ."
—*Revelation 3:20* (NKJV)

LET'S JUST SAY MY HOUSE was untidy the morning I turned the radio dial to a station celebrating

"Christmas in July." By late afternoon they'd played one carol four times: "Joy to the world, the Lord is come." Each time I heard one line as if it were a command: "Let every heart prepare Him room." I was puzzled, *Lord, how do I "prepare You room"?*

That evening I invited friends over for dinner the following night. Next day I emptied waste baskets and discarded clutter. I vacuumed, wiped and washed. I even rubbed a shine onto silver iced-tea spoons I had neglected. Finally I brought in fresh groceries, which I served on a table set with extra plates, surrounded by extra chairs.

When my guests knocked on the door, I was ready with a hearty welcome and some new practices in my spiritual life: Discard the unsightly. Value the good. Clean the dirty. Tend the true. Bring in the fresh. Make room for a guest.

Lord, You are the unseen guest at every meal. Give me grace and strength to prepare myself and my home to welcome You. —EVELYN BENCE

SAT **26** *STUDY TO BE QUIET, AND TO DO YOUR OWN BUSINESS. . . .* —*I Thessalonians 4:11*

IT WAS A SUMMER DAY with temperatures in the upper nineties and no prospect of a cooling storm in sight. Our boys were off at camp, so it was just us two, Carol and me, dealing with the sweltering heat. I called a friend with a pool. "I won't be there," he said, "but feel free to go for a swim."

The sun was a fireball over the Hudson River as we drove out of the city. At seven o'clock that evening, the thermometer on the dashboard said ninety-eight degrees. The pool looked cool and inviting, surrounded by grass and trees. We dove in. Then Carol sat in a lawn chair and read through a stack of magazines while I stood at the water's edge with my book, a little like reading in the bathtub.

The trees trembled in a breeze, shrugging off the heat. The sun slid down the hill until it only illuminated the top branches, then disappeared. The tensions of the day fell from me like the water dripping from my elbows. The only sounds were the wind and the squirrels and the two of us turning our pages, like the companionable silence we shared as newlyweds before the boys were born, the quiet when nothing needs to be spoken because the most important words have been said.

After a while I could barely see the words on the page. "Ready to go?"

"Yes," Carol said, sighing. "That was perfect."

"It was, wasn't it?"

Thank You, Lord, for the moments in my day when silence speaks loudest. —RICK HAMLIN

SUN
27

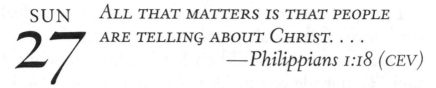

*ALL THAT MATTERS IS THAT PEOPLE
ARE TELLING ABOUT CHRIST. . . .*
—*Philippians 1:18 (CEV)*

THE PINKS OF THE SUNSET flickered across the Montana sky and over the mountains. I felt like a pied piper as I strolled down Lake Upsata Guest Ranch's dirt road toward the pasture by the lake. Several children, guests at the ranch, skipped behind me. Every evening after dinner I'd gather the kids and take them to the pasture where my pregnant mare Dancer lived. I usually loved taking the kids, but tonight I felt empty. It was Sunday and I'd missed church because of work.

Dancer was waiting by the gate for me. I slipped on her halter and gathered the children on both sides of Dancer. I showed them how to put their cheeks against her flank. "Okay, kids, the baby's going to kick when I talk and you'll be able to feel it." The baby always kicked when she heard my voice.

I pressed my face into the mare's flank and said, "Wind Dancer, how was your day?"

Wind Dancer kicked.

The kids squealed and then they all pushed their faces into Dancer's flank and talked to the baby.

Suddenly all the children shrieked. I couldn't believe my eyes: Wind Dancer had pushed out one front hoof on either side of her mom's flank. They stuck out like little doorknobs. Then one of the kids said delightedly, "It's a baby!"

I grasped one of the tiny hooves. "C'mon, kids, feel her hooves. I think she wants you to pet her."

One by one, the children felt her hooves while I said, "God made you inside your mom, just like God's making Wind Dancer. He made each of you special. Isn't that cool?"

I felt in awe of God as I walked up to the lodge, the children running in front of me. I may have missed the message at church, but I'd given the message to the kids and that was all that mattered.

Lord, help me to remember that church happens not only in a building, but in a pasture with children and me. —REBECCA ONDOV

MON
28

GOD IS OUR REFUGE AND STRENGTH, A VERY PRESENT HELP IN TROUBLE.
—*Psalm 46:1*

TROUBLE HAD COME AT ME from all sides, and I wondered how much more I could take. I needed help, so I went to see an elderly friend whose counsel I respected. "My husband's not getting any better," I began. "Every time I see him, he's worse."

My friend nodded. He'd seen my husband in the high-security ward at Riverview, British Columbia's provincial mental hospital. After three years of aggressive treatment, there was still no sign of improvement. Besides, other stresses had bombarded our family of seven: I had totaled our Volvo; a gasoline explosion had sent our thirteen-year-old son to the hospital with severe burns; my daughter, just out of high school, was leaving home for Europe; and illness had made me miss too many days at work, jeopardizing my nursing job.

My friend listened to my outpouring without interruption. Then he asked, "Helen, does God still love you?"

Stunned, I looked at his kind face. I wasn't prepared for this simple question. "Yes," I stammered. "Yes, I think so. The Bible says God's love is everlasting, so it's got to be the same whether my life is good or bad, doesn't it?"

He nodded. "You can stand on this fact: God loves you and will never leave you. Knowing that, you will cope." Then he smiled and said, "Now, before you go home, let's pray."

"Father," he prayed, "I thank You for my sister here. Thank You for Your great love for her. Thank You that You're with her now and always will be. Amen."

During the drive home, I reflected on our visit. My friend hadn't really answered my questions; he hadn't said very much. All he'd done was remind me that I have a refuge. And isn't that what a person lost in a raging storm needs most in life?

Father, thank You for Your welcoming embrace when I come running to You. I feel safe in Your presence.
                    —HELEN GRACE LESCHEID

TUE *AND PRAY IN THE SPIRIT ON ALL*

29 *OCCASIONS WITH ALL KINDS OF PRAYERS*
AND REQUESTS. WITH THIS IN MIND, BE
ALERT AND ALWAYS KEEP ON PRAYING
FOR ALL THE SAINTS. —Ephesians 6:18 (NIV)

REMEMBER THAT FIDGETY FLIER who sat next to you
on your last airplane trip? You know, the guy in the
aisle seat who, while waiting for takeoff, checked his
watch every ninety seconds, folded and refolded and
re-refolded his newspaper, muttering to no one in particular, "Why can't this airline get this plane off the
ground?"

That used to be me, until one gray, drizzly afternoon, as I sat impatiently in seat 16-D on a 757 waiting to take off from LaGuardia Airport. "I don't mean
to interfere," said the fellow in 16-E, "but perhaps
you'd be more comfortable if you focused on something you can control."

That was the beginning of a New York City-to-
Detroit conversation on prayer—and the beginning of
new airline behavior for me. Here's what I do now:
Instead of feeling controlled by what I can't control—
the weather, air traffic controllers, missing connecting
flights—I focus on what I can control. That means
from the moment the plane leaves the gate to the moment its wheels lift off the ground, I pray—for myself,
for others, for the world. During the rest of the flight,
I can do what I want—read, write, sleep, even worry.

But I find I don't worry nearly as much when I focus on God rather than on my wristwatch.

God, when life comes to a standstill, there You are in the midst of it. Help me to look for You.
—JEFF JAPINGA

WED
30
HE SHALL GIVE THEE THE DESIRES OF THINE HEART. —*Psalm 37:4*

MY HUSBAND GENE and I had to have our beloved seventeen-year-old cat Minnie put to sleep. Gene didn't want another cat, but after two catless years I adopted a shelter cat—without talking it over with Gene first. He grew to love Girl Friend, but we made a pact: I wouldn't rescue any more cats. But I kept having a dream: I go out the door and discover an abandoned kitten, and I lovingly gather it up and take it inside.

One hot summer morning, while watering my ferns out back, I heard a squeak. *Oh no, not another baby bird fallen from the nest!*

I checked the bushes and there stood a weary, unbelievably tiny, hungry kitten. *However have you managed to get into our backyard?*

Sitting in the middle of our kitchen floor, I fed the little thing and spoke softly to it. Girl Friend sauntered by and hissed. Gene bellowed, "What's that?"

Joy darted around my heart as though I were a little girl. I had no idea just how much I needed to find
a kitten—and keep it. In time, Girl Friend and Gene
adjusted.

The kitten was a gift from God, so I named the
new addition to our family Grace. Amazing Grace—
she once was lost but now is found. I call her Gracie.
She's a constant reminder of how often God surprises
us with the very desire of our hearts.

*My Father, to think You created this world and still
cared enough to give me an abandoned kitten!*
                              —MARION BOND WEST

THU
31
*THE HUMAN MIND MAY DEVISE MANY
PLANS, BUT IT IS THE PURPOSE OF THE
LORD THAT WILL BE ESTABLISHED.*
                    —*Proverbs 19:21 (NRSV)*

OUR FRIENDS BILL AND DIANA met in high school.
They were sweethearts who planned six years for the
day they would marry, right after college graduation.
The ceremony was gorgeous; the honeymoon paid for.

Then Diana went to law school and Bill to a master's program at the same university. "We'll get our degrees and establish our careers and then we'll buy a
house." That's exactly what they did.

They bought a nineteenth-century two-story on a leafy street, repaired the shutters and cleared the backyard of some junk that the previous owners had accumulated. They were just about ready to have children. Bill said, "First, let's be sure that we have a retirement fund under way." So they saved.

With the retirement fund in good shape, Diana said, "I'd like to give birth in the early spring. Pregnancy during the cool months will be much more comfortable than during the hot summer."

Diana gave birth to a son (she had wanted a daughter) in early April. The baby had colic and kept Bill and Diana up all nightlong for what seemed like months on end. They were constantly tired. And they argued. Both Bill and Diana had trouble adjusting to situations that were unplanned and surprising. Before their son reached preschool, Bill and Diana divorced. The unpredictability of life proved to be the end of their relationship.

But while apart, Bill and Diana began to notice God at work in their lives in unexpected ways. They're back together and their son is now in middle school. They still plan a party better than anyone I know, but they're also able to enjoy the bends in the road.

Heavenly Father, make me grateful for all of Your gifts—those that come as I have planned, as well as those that come in Your own time. —JON SWEENEY

MY DIVINE SURPRISES

1 _____

2 _____

3 _____

4 _____

5 _____

6 _____

7 _____

8 _____

9 _____

10 _____

11 _____

12 _____

13 _____

14 _____

15 _____

16 _____

17 _____

18 _____

19 _____

20 _____

21 _____

22 _____

23 _____

24 _____

25 _____

26 _____

27 _____

28 _____

29 _____

30 _____

31 _____

August

Thou art the God that doest wonders. . . .

—*Psalm 77:14*

UNEXPECTED BLESSINGS
REFLECTING THE LIGHT

FRI
1

FOR THY LOVINGKINDNESS IS BEFORE MINE EYES. . . . —Psalm 26:3

THE LOWER LEVEL of New York City's Grand Central Station at evening rush hour was a strange place to receive an undeserved compliment. I'd missed the 6:58 train by a single minute and faced an hour's wait, seated in a row of plastic armchairs designed without reference to human anatomy. I was hungry and bone tired—too tired certainly to join the line inching forward at the snack counter. I tried to read, but the din in the echoing hall made concentration impossible.

A sixtyish woman pushing a little boy in a stroller, probably a grandchild, stopped in front of my chair. "I'm sorry if I've been staring at you," she said.

I hadn't even noticed her. The crowded terminal with its hurrying commuters was an anonymous swirl.

"I just have to tell you," the woman went on, "that you have a kind face."

I suppose I said something in reply. All I remember was astonishment. Kind? My feelings toward my fellow humans at that point were along the lines of wishing them all on the other side of the earth.

I puzzled over it on the train ride home. Our faces, my reflection in the dark window told me, reveal not a given moment but a whole lifetime's experience. If my face was kind, it must be because I'd been the recipient of kindness throughout the years. Parents, teachers, associates, friends, husband . . . unaware, taking it for granted, I'd received more kindness than animosity and found the world—so cruel to so many—more welcoming than hostile. A lifetime of overdue thank-yous, I thought, called to my attention by a stranger in a train station.

Bestower of blessing, let Your loving-kindness to me shine through each act of mine today.
                                —ELIZABETH SHERRILL

SAT
2

I HAVE BECOME LIKE BROKEN POTTERY.
                        —*Psalm 31:12 (NIV)*

A FEW MONTHS AGO I came down with a sore throat and lost my voice. Since I could speak no louder than a whisper, many of my conversations were relegated to a pad of paper. When I went to a church potluck, I wore a name tag that said, HI, MY NAME IS JOSH. I LOST MY VOICE.

I got so self-conscious after a while that I felt like I'd lost part of my personality. I just wanted to stay home and hide. About a week after I had lost my voice, I was waiting for my clothes to dry at the

Laundromat when a gentleman I didn't know approached me.

"How's it going?" he asked.

I was caught so off-guard that I forgot I could not talk.

"Good," I said. My voice was raspy, but at least I could say something.

We ended up conversing long after our clothes were dry. He told me about a horrific auto accident he'd survived several years before. I told him about how I'd lost my leg to cancer. The next week I brought him lunch at his job, and we talked more about hard times and about God's provision.

My voice had been broken that morning, but I was reminded how God often works through broken vessels—His light just shines through the cracks.

You are the Potter, Lord. Thank You for molding broken vessels to be a part of Your plan.
> —JOSHUA SUNDQUIST

SUN 3 *O SING UNTO THE LORD A NEW SONG; FOR HE HATH DONE MARVELLOUS THINGS. . . . —Psalm 98:1*

I'VE BEEN WRITING SONGS since I was eleven years old. My goal was to write a song that would be recorded. In thirty-five years, it never happened.

Truth be told, I wasn't really sure how to make it happen. You can send your song to a place like Nashville, Tennessee, and hope someone likes it, but after years without a response, you tend to wonder if anybody has listened to it. It's a little like playing Ping-Pong by yourself.

After service one Sunday night, I heard someone playing and singing on the church patio. He was really good, and after his performance I walked up to him and struck up a conversation. I told him that I had heard good things about the kind of guitar he was playing. He said that he wanted to buy another, but didn't know where to buy one. I told him he could get one at a guitar shop here in San Diego.

The next day I took him to the shop. While we were there, I asked him if he ever collaborated with other songwriters, and he suggested that we write a song together. Two days later we met, and after we had made some headway on a nice song, he told me that he was just about to sign with a record label and that the song we had just written could very well be on his first album!

Brandon's album came out a month ago and, yes, I am credited with cowriting a song. I now have a relationship with a publisher who listens to all my songs. People congratulate me and call it an accomplishment. But I know better. It's a miracle.

Lord, thank You that You do not forget about my dreams, even after I do. —DAVE FRANCO

MON
4

WHEREFORE THEY ARE NO MORE TWAIN, BUT ONE FLESH. WHAT THEREFORE GOD HATH JOINED TOGETHER, LET NOT MAN PUT ASUNDER. —*Matthew 19:6*

VERY FEW MARRIED COUPLES escape some friction on the subject of in-laws. Norman and I had our share of it too. Though we were devoted to each other's parents, we both found them trying at times.

From the start, Norman and I agreed to discuss our feelings about each other's parents openly—and in private. We agreed not to get angry or defensive when the subject of in-laws came up, but to treat it as a kind of good-humored verbal pillow fight in which either of us could say anything within reason and not do any damage to the fabric of our own marriage.

I might say, "Why is your mother so full of fears and phobias about things? She's always sure that the worst is going to happen. She sees a disaster around every corner. I don't want this kind of timidity to rub off on my children the way it did on your brothers and you!"

"My mother's not timid!" Norman would counter. "She has a vivid imagination, that's all. At times she thinks you can be pretty callous. She told me that when she was with you in the park the other day and John fell off his tricycle, you didn't even pick him up. You let some stranger passing by do it!"

"That's right," I'd say. "I knew he wasn't hurt. I wanted him to pick himself up. Your mother acted as if he had broken both arms and legs. That's just what I'm talking about!"

I have to admit that the little things Norman and I used to get irritated about do seem to be funny and almost petty. But our frank discussions had a point. In the midst of whatever adverse circumstances we encountered, we always found it helpful to talk it through honestly and openly. Communicating about it helped us keep a positive perspective. And the difficulties became opportunities for us to learn and grow.

Lord, help me to speak honestly but considerately to the loved ones in my life.

—RUTH STAFFORD PEALE

TUE
5

I WILL ALWAYS BE READY TO REMIND YOU OF THESE THINGS, EVEN THOUGH YOU ALREADY KNOW THEM. . . .
—II Peter 1:12 (NAS)

I AM A COMPULSIVE PICTURE-TAKER; each week I go through a roll of film. Four-year-old Solomon has eleven large albums dedicated to him. Henry, our six-month-old, is quickly getting used to the blinding flash that accompanies every one of his milestones: smiles, sitting up, reaching for a toy, a funny face while eating bananas.

Solomon's first sentence, "No cheese, Mama," had nothing to do with food. It was a protest against my incessant camera pointing and my instruction to "Say cheese!"

Our bookcases have been taken over by photo albums. My office desk has stacks of pictures from last year's Easter egg hunt, the Fourth of July parade and our summer vacation on Cape Cod, all waiting for me to find another album to put them in.

"You guys are such proud parents," a friend of mine remarked at the large envelope of photos commemorating Solomon's graduation from preschool.

"It's not that," I said.

"What then?" she asked.

I shrugged.

Later that night as I washed Henry's baby spoon, I realized what my picture taking is really about. Each photo is my attempt to keep them young, so that years from now, when they're grown, I'll still have my little boys.

Lord, it's good to watch them grow, but let me never forget the way they are today.

—SABRA CIANCANELLI

WED 6 IT IS NOT GOOD TO HAVE ZEAL WITHOUT KNOWLEDGE, NOR TO BE HASTY AND MISS THE WAY. —*Proverbs 19:2 (NIV)*

REMEMBER THE CHARACTER Arte Johnson played on *Rowan and Martin's Laugh-In* who shuffled along taking half steps, barely making any progress? Well, that's how my sixteen-year-old cocker spaniel Sally walks these days. Which is hard for me, because I'm usually going a mile a minute, especially first thing in the morning.

"Come on, Sal," I'll say brightly, gently tugging the leash. But underneath my happy voice I'm thinking about all the things I have to do that day, places I have to be, people I have to talk to, e-mails to be sent and answered, deadlines, obligations.

Yet Sally is oblivious, sniffing every object of interest, laboriously greeting friends and strangers alike and sometimes just standing in place, taking it all in.

"Sally!" I'll say a little more emphatically, yet still in that happy voice.

Sally will look right at me, not exactly defiant, but firm, her gaze steady despite the cataracts, her mouth set with determination. I know what she's thinking: *What's the hurry?*

Easy for her to say. What's she got to do? She's retired. When she's not eating, she's either getting ready for a nap or waking up from one. All in all, she's got it pretty easy. *Life is good. So why not take your time?*

Maybe Sally has a point. Life is good, all in all. I'm passionate about my work. I love my friends and they love me, I like to think. My wife Julee's back is still a problem, but she told me the other day it's getting better, slowly but surely.

And then there's Sally, standing there on West 30th Street just staring up at me, not all that much different from when she was a puppy not much bigger than my hand, standing at practically the same spot, looking up at me and challenging me with that same question: *What's the hurry?*

Lord, I'm so blessed by everything and everyone You put in my life. Teach me to slow down and enjoy them.
                                   —EDWARD GRINNAN

THU
7

LET US THEN APPROACH THE THRONE OF GRACE WITH CONFIDENCE. . . .
                                   —*Hebrews 4:16 (NIV)*

MY GRANDSON CAMERON loves to play soldier, so for his ninth birthday his mother, my daughter Jenny, decided to give him a military-themed party. The invitations were draft notices and my son-in-law designed an obstacle course for the ten boys who were to attend. My oldest son Ted, who'd served as an Airborne Ranger, painted camouflage on the boys' faces, and they ate MREs in the field. (For us civilians, that's meals ready to eat.) The party was a huge success.

Later that summer, Cameron spent an entire day outside arranging his toy soldiers. When he'd finished, he insisted his mother take a picture, just in case she happened to meet a general. How or when this was supposed to occur was of little concern to my grandson. He instructed his mother to hand over the picture so that the Army could make use of his battle plan.

I enjoyed telling my husband about Cameron's exploits, and I have to admit that we were both impressed. Even at the age of nine, he felt he had something of value to offer others. *We all do*, I thought later, *whether it's a shared recipe or an unexpected birthday card to a shut-in or even what we're convinced is a brilliant business plan.*

So I've made Cameron's message my own: Believe in yourself and in God's ability to use your talents as He sees fit.

Lord, thank You for the lesson in self-confidence that my grandson has taught me. —DEBBIE MACOMBER

FRI
8

"NOW THEREFORE AMEND YOUR WAYS AND YOUR DEEDS. . . ."
—*Jeremiah 26:13* (NAS)

MY HUSBAND KEITH'S computer died, so he got a new one. One of the handiest features was something called "Restore": If his computer were somehow injured by an Internet download or mail attachment, he could return the system to a previous healthy state. "That's what I need in life," I said, "a restore point!"

Several weeks later I said something to a friend I probably could have couched in gentler language. She reacted strongly and left our lunch before I could figure out what was wrong. When I did figure it out, I called her, but she wasn't home. Then life and other obligations intervened, and I let it slide.

The next time I saw her at a Friday-night service at the synagogue, she turned away before I could greet her. Keith and I sang and participated in the responsive readings, but I was distracted. When we got to the *Amidah* (silent prayer), we rose and stood for the only part of the service called the *Tefilah*, which means "prayer."

I kept thinking about my friend and how much I cared about her. When the Amidah was over and people began to sit down, I left Keith's side and went to where she was. I put my arms around her and said, "I miss you." She hesitated a moment, then hugged me back.

I'd found my "restore point."

Help me, Lord, to guard my words and deeds, because it's not easy to go back. —RHODA BLECKER

SAT
9

I SOUGHT THE LORD, AND HE HEARD ME, AND DELIVERED ME FROM ALL MY FEARS.
—*Psalm 34:4*

ONE MORNING I WOKE UP with thoughts whirling through my head. I had some decisions to make at work and I had no clear vision of what I should do. I decided that a bicycle ride would help.

"Honey, do you want to go with me on the bike trail?" I asked my wife.

"No thanks, I'm going shopping," Elba said.

I was relieved. This outing was less about bike riding and more about being alone with God so that I could get a better perspective on the things that were bothering me. The bike trail, paved in black tar and lined with trees, was ideal for thinking and praying once you got past the challenging hills.

I rode down the path and reached a crossroads I'd never seen before. I tried to follow the signs but couldn't find the bike trail. Stopping on the street corner, I looked around as the cars drove by me, but the path wasn't in sight. I decided to give it one more try and finally spotted the trail. I'd never looked in that direction because I had assumed the path was elsewhere.

Then I heard a still small voice in my heart: *If you seek Me in all directions, you will find your way through the problems of the day.*

I got back on my bicycle, confident that with God's guidance, I would choose the right path.

Lord, when I can't seem to find my way, let me keep my eyes on You. —PABLO DIAZ

SUN
10 *THE LORD SHALL GUIDE THEE*
CONTINUALLY. . . . —Isaiah 58:11

EVERY SUMMER MY WIFE AND I visit a
small Episcopal church in upstate New
York, where over the years we've watched one particular youngster grow up. Eric was still in grade school
when he developed an ambition that neither he nor
his family could understand. He wanted to learn
Russian.

"Where did it come from, this interest in Russian?"
Eric's mother wondered aloud over coffee in the
parish house one morning. They had no Russian
neighbors, no great exposure to movies or books
about Russia.

Each year as we watched Eric growing taller, we'd
ask if he'd found a way to study Russian. "Not yet,"
he'd answer, but always with a smile that said, *I'm not
worried. It will happen.*

On one visit, Eric's mother told us that he'd started
asking for a teacher. "He doesn't want language tapes.
It must be a 'real' teacher!"

Not long afterward a toy store opened in town, op-
erated, to everyone's surprise but Eric's, by a Russian
lady who said that yes, she'd enjoy teaching the boy.
"*If* he has a good ear," she added. She hated to hear
her language pronounced badly.

The boy and the Russian grandmother hit it off instantly. After a few weeks she was asking if Eric was

certain he hadn't been exposed to Russian before; the boy was speaking with almost no accent.

When we saw Eric last he was in college, where he'd gone straight into the advanced class in Russian. He still doesn't know, he admitted, where this strange attraction to a particular language may lead. But he said this with the same smile that's teaching me so much about being open to God's guidance. *I'm not worried. I'll find out in time.*

Remind me, Father, that I don't have to know the end of the story to recognize Your guiding hand.
                                        —JOHN SHERRILL

MON
11

FAITH IS THE SUBSTANCE OF THINGS HOPED FOR, THE EVIDENCE OF THINGS NOT SEEN. —*Hebrews 11:1*

MY FATHER POSITIONED HIMSELF over the golf ball and adjusted his grip on his new driver. "Okay, Karen," he said, "when you swing the club, you have to keep your eyes on the ball at all times." *Swish!* He hit the ball and sent it soaring through the air until it landed with a bounce on the green. *"Así!"* he said victoriously in Spanish. "Just like that." Seeing my father play golf in Clearwater, Florida, was just one of the many unexpected changes in my parents' lives within the last year.

"You're moving to *Florida?*" I'd asked when my

parents first made the announcement. My sisters and brother and I were stunned. The idea was almost laughable. My parents' idea of spontaneity or adventure was going out for Italian instead of cooking the same old dish of chicken with rice and beans. So none of us really believed them. They would never move hundreds of miles away from the family! But three months later, they officially retired, purchased a condo in Florida, and filled their New York City apartment with cardboard boxes, sealed and ready to go.

A year later, it's evident that they were meant to live in Florida. My hard-working parents have learned how to relax and play, and they couldn't be happier. Just like the golf ball that my father took a swing at, their lives landed right where they needed to be.

Why should I be surprised, Lord? Life is just fine when we step out in faith in You! —KAREN VALENTIN

TUE
12

OUT OF THE MOST SEVERE TRIAL, THEIR OVERFLOWING JOY AND THEIR EXTREME POVERTY WELLED UP IN RICH GENEROSITY. —II Corinthians 8:2 (NIV)

THE WILLIAMS FAMILY has been at the Bible Witness Camp in Pembroke, Illinois, for more than fifty years. The camp is located in a rural setting in one of the poorest townships in America. I was invited there by Mary, the youngest daughter in the family. "The women are so excited about you coming!" she tells me.

The Williamses have given their lives to a mission. Though Pembroke is predominantly Black, the Williamses, who are white, have woven themselves into the hearts and lives of the people they love—over their extended family's objections and in a county that separates around issues of race. As she drives, Mary points out homes to me. Pembroke is my last speaking engagement before I leave Illinois. No longer able to afford my Chicago apartment, I have packed all my things. Finances have bruised me. I'm sad and questioning.

As I look at the houses, I'm embarrassed to be fretting over my own needs when people are living without lights, without plumbing and in trailers that barely stand.

"The women are so excited!" Mary repeats and thanks me for coming. I smile, hoping that I can hold back tears enough to encourage the few people she expects to attend. It will be a small gathering—perhaps sixteen, including adults and teenagers.

When I enter the room, it's overflowing with women of all ages and races. They are adding chairs and young girls are crowding the front row. I share what I have learned, we sing, and they share their lives with me. The love in the air is palpable and tangible. It is electrifying. These people who seemingly have so much less than I have shower me with affection. In their abounding arms, I find my way home.

Lord, thank You that You always care for us. Help us to care for one another. —SHARON FOSTER

WED
13

NOW YOU ARE THE BODY OF CHRIST, AND EACH ONE OF YOU IS A PART OF IT.
—*I Corinthians 12:27 (NIV)*

OUR VAN IS WELL-KNOWN in the neighborhood. It's sixteen years old, with two hundred thousand miles on it and enough rust to qualify as two-toned. My children call the van by its given name: "Are You Still Driving That Thing?"

About a month ago, That Thing refused to run. I assumed the worst and spent many evenings either underneath the van with an orange trouble light or venting to family and friends. Finally, I repaired the bad radiator/leaky valve cover/dirty transmission filter/wayward ignition wire, and the van was back on the road.

My wife Sandee was impressed. "You fixed it yourself?" she said.

Yes, yes, I did. But then again, no, I didn't. I did the work, but Sandee had pointed out the original (and subtle) leak. My brother recommended a compression test and told me where to buy a kit. Mr. D suggested the cooling system as the culprit. Megan let me borrow her truck, even though she needed it herself. My children took turns holding flashlights and handing me tools. My next-door neighbor loaned me the perfect snub-nosed wrench. Parents who ordinarily didn't carpool with our children suddenly appeared, ready to help. And when I fixed the van, they all congratulated me.

For what? It takes a village to fix my ancient van. It takes a village to fix all sorts of ancient, intractable problems: broken cars, broken hearts, broken lives. I can't reattach the number four plug myself, but if you hold the light, we can do it together.

Lord, even when it seems impossible, I'll trust You that we can do it together. —MARK COLLINS

READER'S ROOM

MY SEEDS OF FAITH are acknowledging to my Savior my absolute dependence on Him each moment of my life. It is a journey of wonder, delight and thankfulness to walk with Him.

I have time to enjoy the very air I breathe and to see His majesty in His creation each day, whether it be a pretty flower, butterfly, warm sun, starry night, blue sky or raindrop.
                                  —*LouAnn LaFever, Lubbock, Texas*

A SECOND THANK-YOU
THANK YOU FOR FRIENDS

THU 14 *ALWAYS GIVING THANKS TO GOD THE FATHER FOR EVERYTHING. . . .*
—*Ephesians 5:20 (NIV)*

I MISSED A STEP AND FELL recently, and in doing so, I cut my head. When the wound healed and it came time to wash my hair, my thoughts turned to my friend Sue. *But she can't help me,* I realized. *She's visiting family in Oklahoma.*

For thirty years, I'd had surgeries on my head that resulted in a considerable amount of bleeding, and I'd developed a comfortable routine: travel to the Cleveland Clinic for surgery, come home to recover and when I felt better, find someone to drive me to Sue's house to have my hair done.

Always, Sue would have some luscious-smelling concoctions at the ready to make me feel more like a queen and less like the postoperative wreck that I was. What wasn't often part of the routine, I realized, was my hearty thank-you, for I usually felt poorly and couldn't wait to get back home to bed.

So I telephoned Sue in Oklahoma to thank her at long last. *How many other tasks that friends complete without fanfare,* I wondered, *get lost in the routine of friendship?* As a second thank-you to Sue, I'm vowing to take a longer look at what friends do for me—and never to forget to say a big and heartfelt "Thank you!"

Thank You, Lord, for precious friends. May I always give thanks to them, and for them to You.
—ROBERTA MESSNER

FRI
15

ADD TO YOUR FAITH . . . PATIENCE; AND TO PATIENCE GODLINESS; AND TO GODLINESS BROTHERLY KINDNESS. . . .
—*II Peter 1:5–7*

I HAD MY HANDS in the meat loaf when the phone rang. Many cooks use spoons or forks to mix such ingredients, but my hands work better for me. That's why I had to snag a table knife, then a couple of paper towels to scrape off the excess before grabbing the ringing receiver, which, by the way, still feels greasy.

"May I speak to Mrs. Wolseley, please?" the caller asked.

"This is she," I answered, trying to recognize the young woman's voice.

Five seconds later, I said, "Not interested!" and slammed down the phone.

Another telemarketer, this one pitching siding, for goodness sake! I returned to the meat loaf mix, still grumbling in exasperation.

A few days later a letter arrived from my teenage granddaughter. "I finally found a temporary job. But it's a bad one," she wrote. Karen had spent weeks trying to find part-time work to help with her finances while carrying a full school load.

Well, you guessed it. She, too, had turned to selling by phone.

"Grandma," her letter continued, "people scream at me and call me names and slam down the phone. I don't want to bother them. I'm just trying to get through college."

Telemarketers have interrupted our dinner hour—yes, and meat loaf mixing too—several times since Karen's letter arrived. But I no longer yell, "Not interested!" and bang down the receiver. You see, the voice on the other end of the line may belong to somebody's grandchild who's nearly as nice as mine.

Lord, help me to be patient and to speak kindly to everyone—even when I'm exasperated.

—ISABEL WOLSELEY

SAT
16

BE WATCHFUL, STAND FIRM IN YOUR FAITH, BE COURAGEOUS, BE STRONG. LET ALL THAT YOU DO BE DONE IN LOVE.
—*I Corinthians 16:13–14 (RSV)*

WHEN I WAS TWELVE and a camper at Camp Firwood, I could not stand up when trying to water-ski. Getting onto the water wasn't the problem, but standing up was. I bumped along on my bottom, waves pounding my tail. The trauma was so remarkable, I've been afraid to try waterskiing ever since.

My youngest son spent this last summer driving the water-ski boats down at the same Camp Firwood. He begged to take me waterskiing.

"What if I can't stand up?"

"That was forty years ago!"

So one Saturday afternoon, campers gone and the grounds to ourselves, Blake took me out. Patiently he worked my skis on and lowered me into the water. Patiently, and with a million assurances, he wrangled me into a position behind the boat, holding on to the tow rope. I remember how *I* used to be the teacher, patiently teaching him how to swim. Now the tables had turned.

"Ready?" he hollered, hopping behind the wheel.

"Hit it!"

Up came the ski tips. But try as I might, I couldn't stand. After sufficient struggle, I let go. Blake brought the boat around again and we tried a second time. On my third try, Blake said, trying not to laugh, "I see what you mean. You just can't stand up. Well, guess it's the stair-climber for you this winter."

He's not going to let me off the hook. We have a "standing" date for next summer. And so now, when I work up a sweat at the gym, I have two special prayers. One is to stand firm, as the Apostle Paul admonishes, in my faith, courageous and strong. And the second is to stand strong when I try waterskiing again next year!

Thank you, Lord, for both spiritual and physical challenges. And for Your heavenly patience when I try, but still fail. —BRENDA WILBEE

SUN
17

GOD HATH MADE ME TO LAUGH, SO THAT ALL THAT HEAR WILL LAUGH WITH ME.
—Genesis 21:6

I'D BEEN WORKING ON MY SPEECH for weeks, maybe years. It was the final night at home for our two daughters before they headed off to college. I wanted to remind them to do their best and to choose their friends wisely and not to dillydally away their study time. I needed to make sure they knew how important it was to attend class and to take careful notes.

I summoned them into my bedroom. "Girls," I began, "there are some things you should remember when you're away at school."

We stood awkwardly in silence for a few moments. Then Katie, the eighteen-year-old, casually stretched out on the floor to hear my lengthy instructions. She's always been the jokester. Twenty-year-old Jamie plopped down next to her, put her hands behind her head and stared at the ceiling fan.

"Let's just talk, Mom. Like we used to," Katie suggested.

"Yeah, that'd be neat," Jamie agreed.

Skip the speech? But do they know enough? Are they ready? I wondered.

Then we did something we'd never done before: I joined them on the floor and the three of us, our feet touching one another's heads, formed a triangle. We talked and laughed about everything from the funny things that had happened during their childhoods to what color toenail polish looked the best and whose Barbie dolls were dressed the finest.

As we said goodnight, I smiled from way down deep. Laughter would always hold us together. The rest, I'd leave up to God.

Dear God, when I'm way too serious and sometimes even try to do Your job, remind me of Your priceless and powerful gift of laughter. —JULIE GARMON

MON
18
THOU, LORD, ONLY MAKEST ME DWELL IN SAFETY. —*Psalm 4:8*

LIKE ANY FIRST-TIME MOM, I was slightly overprotective. Add to that the fact that I had a very difficult pregnancy, and maybe I was a little more than slightly overprotective.

I wanted to hold my baby all the time. I couldn't help but stare at his tiny feet. I'd spend hours watching his delicate fine fingers wrapped around my index finger. I was in love, and I felt it was up to me to make sure nothing happened to him. Ever!

Life sailed along pretty smoothly at our house. Eventually, my son learned to sit up, roll over, crawl and walk. It was about the time that he was learning to run from coffee table to couch that my husband decided he was old enough to "wrestle."

I watched in horror as Jacob picked up Trace, tossed him in the air, yelled, "Body slam!" and dropped him on the couch. Then, while Trace was lying flat on his back—feet and arms flailing—Jacob rained pillows down on him. Seconds later, he picked him up to repeat the process.

"Wait!" I was ready to put a stop to this. Trace was too young to be tossed in the air. He was fragile. Jacob probably didn't know his own strength. What if Jacob missed the couch? Or didn't support Trace's developing neck properly?

I rushed to the rescue. But moments before I scooped up our precious bundle, he began to laugh. He stared up at his father with such love and complete joy that I froze. "Again, Daddy, again!" Trace said between giggles.

Lord, help me to remember that I can protect those I love best by entrusting them to Your care.

—AMANDA BOROZINSKI

TUE
19

LET THEM PRAISE HIS NAME IN THE
DANCE. . . . FOR THE LORD TAKETH
PLEASURE IN HIS PEOPLE. . . .
—*Psalm 149:3–4*

IT WAS BILLED as a summer hoedown at Monte Vista Grove Homes, the retirement community where I was taking care of my elderly aunt. A barbecue luncheon would be followed by a country-and-western duo singing and strumming guitars.

When the music began, I noticed eighty-nine-year-old Betty, a former military nurse, tapping her fingers in time to it. Leaving my table, I invited her to dance. Without hesitation, she held my hands and bounced to the beat. The years vanished in her broadening grin, and she was that spunky young nurse cadet again.

Then Bonnie shuffled my way. She had once taught midwifery in Africa. "I've never danced," she announced, "and I want to try something new on my eighty-sixth birthday." Her heart condition limited her to gentle swaying, but behind her glasses her eyes shone, and in them I could glimpse the adventuring girl.

I sauntered among the tables, hands outstretched, inviting anyone to share a dance. Bob, wearing western plaid, twirled me in circles. Sherman, partially paralyzed from a stroke, balanced against my shoulder while his knees rocked to the tune.

Sheer joy spread through the room, and others

began to dance. This was more than good food and small talk. God's Spirit was moving among us, drawing us together through our spontaneous gestures of caring and connection.

I floated home, euphoric, thinking that the angels in heaven surely must strum a guitar or two and dance a little country.

Jesus, lead me in the dance that connects us with You. You know the steps so well. —CAROL KNAPP

WED
20

IT IS NO TROUBLE FOR ME TO WRITE THE SAME THINGS TO YOU AGAIN, AND IT IS A SAFEGUARD FOR YOU.
—*Philippians 3:1 (NIV)*

STEPHEN, AGE TWO, WAS VERY BUSY. We were at a playground where the sprinklers shoot up like geysers from the ground. I'd brought some old plastic bowls along, and over and over again Stephen ran into the sprinkler, filled his bowl and ran out to dump it. Fill, run, dump; fill, run, dump. Big kids came and tried to con him out of his bowl; no way. Bicycles sped perilously close to his path; he stared them down. His lips turned blue, his legs shivered, but on he went.

"Isn't it funny how kids need repetition?" commented another mom. We wondered together what it was that my son was learning from his play.

As a mother, I know that few important things get done or said only once. Ever since there was morning on the first day, repetition has been part of God's plan. Children hear us say the same words many times, and eventually they learn to speak. Manners and rules and Bible verses are taught more than once, and each repetition drives the message further into our hearts. Sometimes, when offense has been given, saying "I'm sorry" just once isn't enough.

Someday soon Stephen will move beyond dumping bowls of water out of the sprinkler. He'll grow up and develop his own morning routine (will he eat first or shower?), his own ways to deal with stress (deep breathing or something less productive?), his own patterns of communicating with God. At two or eighty-two, repetition will always be a part of his life. I hope that the rhythm that resounds through his days is one of faithfulness and joy.

Jesus, I can never say it enough: I love You.

—JULIA ATTAWAY

THU
21

"IT PRODUCES MANY SEEDS."
—*John 12:24 (NIV)*

ONE MORNING OUT ON MY daily prayer walk, I told God how I was worried about a project I'd taken on. Had I been crazy to hire a professional to film some of my ideas about prayer when I'd never written a script, never been in front of a camera, never used a teleprompter?

As I walked, I felt a rock in the bottom of my running shoe. When I got home and took off the shoe, I saw a nut about the size of a marble perfectly encased in the heel. I was about to throw it away when I thought, *Since it tagged along on my prayer walk, maybe it's some sort of message from God.*

I carried the nut to the old wooden rocker where I meditate. *Can you see the tree in the nut?* I touched the rich old wood of the rocker. *You may see only one little nut. But what if you chose to see it as a future tree? And can you see beyond the tree to all the nuts it will produce?*

How many future nuts would come from the nut in my hand? Maybe a tree could produce a thousand nuts a year. And if it lived a hundred years, that would be a hundred thousand nuts. That many nuts would fill up the whole living room and then some.

I rolled the nut around in my hand and prayed:

God, I get it now. You're not asking me to gather up everything this project needs right now. You're only asking me to get started with the little things I do have. That's the only way things can grow.

—KAREN BARBER

FRI
22
THE BEASTS OF THE FIELD SHALL BE AT PEACE WITH THEE. —Job 5:23

I COULD HEAR THE DRONE of the bees from across the field at the monastery where my family and I were staying for a week. For the third or fourth time that morning, I wondered what I'd gotten myself into. I'd always been fascinated by bees, by their complex society, their dancing "language," their miraculous production of wax and honey, and, yes, their sting, which added just the right note of danger to the mix. Since I was a child, I had pored over countless books on beekeeping. But books were safe. Did I actually want to work with these living darts? Why had I volunteered so quickly to help in the fields?

"Good morning!" said Father Benedict, the beekeeper. "Let's get you suited up." Five minutes later, armored in overalls, rubber boots, thick leather gloves and a veiled hat, I wandered toward a dozen large hives, each holding up to forty thousand bees. No wonder the sound was so intense!

We opened each hive, checking for any signs of disease. I knew the bees couldn't sting me, but still I was nervous. Then out of the blue Father Benedict said, "Hold this," and shoved a wooden frame crawling with thousands of bees into my hands.

I was terrified. For a moment I thought I would drop the frame and run. And then I heard the sound of Gregorian chanting coming from the monastic chapel. This ancient, profound music blended perfectly with the buzzing of the bees, and everything fell into place: the soaring bees with their gold-and-black bodies, the processing monks with their white habits, the making of honey, and the chanting of prayers, insect and human both glorifying the Lord. I turned back to the hive, resolved to do my part to help them in their appointed tasks.

Give me courage, Lord, to accept Your kingdom—even its unfamiliar or frightening aspects—and sing Your praises. —PHILIP ZALESKI

SAT
23

THIS ONE THING I DO, FORGETTING THOSE THINGS WHICH ARE BEHIND, AND REACHING FORTH UNTO THOSE THINGS WHICH ARE BEFORE. —*Philippians 3:13*

MY GRANDSON DRAKE and I were sitting on the family room floor, looking at books, when suddenly he jumped up and ran to the kitchen. He patted the table and said, "Eat. Yesterday." Then he walked around, touching each chair where a family member sat. "Mama. Baby Brock. Me." I smiled. Yes, we all ate together last Sunday. But to Drake, it was yesterday. The past is a new concept to his two-year-old mind, and everything that's not of-the-moment is "yesterday."

Sometimes I'm a bit too much like Drake. It seems as though every hurt, every slight, every unkind word spoken to me happened yesterday. I keep it fresh—and painful—by revisiting it often. I don't let time do its healing work by putting the past behind me.

Soon Drake will learn the difference between yesterday and the many other layers of the past. I'm going to work hard to learn that too.

You are the God of all my yesterdays and all my tomorrows. Give me grace today to place both those things in Your hands. —MARY LOU CARNEY

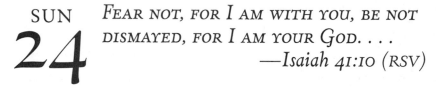

SUN
24

FEAR NOT, FOR I AM WITH YOU, BE NOT DISMAYED, FOR I AM YOUR GOD. . . .
—Isaiah 41:10 (RSV)

WE WERE HAVING SUPPER in our cabin in the mountain village of Platoro, Colorado, when a loud pounding on the door brought us out of our seats. It was Myron Eckberg, our neighbor from up the road. "A cabin at the lodge is on fire!" he cried. "Bring as many buckets as you can find."

My husband Larry and our daughter Meghan grabbed buckets from under the stairs while I collected jackets from the coatrack. The three of us, along with Kayla, Meghan's eight-year-old daughter, jumped into our truck and bounced over the dirt road toward the lodge, a quarter-mile away. When we arrived, we saw a line of people passing buckets of water to each other from the nearby river, their bodies silhouetted against the flames that shot up into the gathering darkness. A friend ran to meet us. "We've called the fire station in the valley," he said, "but the fire truck won't get here for at least another forty-five minutes."

Larry and Meghan rushed off to join the bucket brigade. I kept Kayla with me and gathered other children around me as their parents arrived carrying their own buckets. A cold wind sprang up. I knew the water carriers must be freezing in their soaked clothes, but they kept on going. "Protect them, Lord," I prayed. "Please don't let anyone get hurt."

By the time the fire truck arrived, the first cabin had collapsed, but the water-soaked cabins on either side had been saved. Best of all, no one had gotten hurt. My heart filled with gratitude for the courage and generosity of the people of the town, and I breathed another prayer: "Thank You, Lord, for good neighbors."

Heavenly Father, please help me today to be a good neighbor to everyone I meet. —MADGE HARRAH

MON
25

AND GOD SAID, LET US MAKE MAN IN OUR IMAGE, AFTER OUR LIKENESS. . . .
—*Genesis 1:26*

I'VE ALWAYS HAD TROUBLE seeing family resemblances in the Attaway children. They definitely look related, but none of them look very much like their mother or me. Sure, when they were babies, everyone told me, "He/She looks just like you!" And they did: They were bald, fat and a little bit cranky.

Then last year while I was straightening out my bureau, I found a picture I'd never seen before, a very old picture, postcard size and divided into two frames. In the first was a little girl, about four or five, and two grown men. In the second, the little girl stood by herself, holding a small American flag. I looked intently at the little girl. Hair, nose, mouth, eyes—she looked just like our five-year-old Maggie.

I looked back again at the first frame. As I gazed at it, I realized that the two young men were my uncles. And the little girl, nearly twenty years their junior, was my mother.

A week later, our friend Loretta came over for dinner. As we sipped our coffee, I brought out the picture. She put down her cup, her eyes widened and she opened her mouth. But for a few moments no words came. "How did you do that? Did you do it on the computer? It's Maggie, isn't it? But how did you get it to look so old?"

Someday soon I'm going to get down my wife Julia's and my old family photos and do a little hunting; I'm sure that there are some more family resemblances we'll be able to track down. In the meantime, I'll be thankful if, as they grow up, my children come to resemble their heavenly Father more than they resemble me.

Lord, help me to grow up in Your image and likeness.
—ANDREW ATTAWAY

TUE
26

I WILL INCLINE MINE EAR TO A PARABLE. . . . —Psalm 49:4

IN THE SUMMER of 1943, I was a student in college. Our nation's part in the war was just a year and a half old and I was a half-year away from joining the U.S. Army. That summer, however, I was not thinking of the war; I was having a ball with friends, a full load of fascinating studies and an appetite for new things. One of these was a production of William Shakespeare's *Othello* bound for Broadway. I joined a host of classmates vying for a part as an extra—and got one.

I became Brabantio's lantern-holding servant, and I appeared in various crowd scenes in which I cried out lines that Shakespeare hadn't thought of. The stars were major figures of the stage, and I could hardly believe my luck in mingling with them. Every night I watched Iago (José Ferrer) as he worked his wiles, and I was practically hanging over the bed as Othello (Paul Robeson) snuffed out the life of Desdemona (Uta Hagen). The director, Margaret Webster, the daughter of England's Dame May Witty, was especially kind to me.

Whenever she saw me, she would quote from

Shakespeare, maybe "All the world's a stage" (*As You Like It*) or "Double, double toil and trouble" (*Macbeth*). I would answer with the play, sometimes correctly. I remember "Farewell the tranquil mind." I knew it because Robeson said it every night.

The last time I saw Margaret, she said, "Well done, thou good and faithful servant." I was stumped. "I tricked you," she said, giving me a kiss, "but I mean it just the same." Then she said, "It's not the Bard. It's from Jesus' parable of the talents."

I should have known it then. I do now.

Father, the one quote I'll never forget, just let it be true.
—VAN VARNER

WED
27

DON'T BE MISLED; REMEMBER THAT YOU CAN'T IGNORE GOD AND GET AWAY WITH IT: A MAN WILL ALWAYS REAP JUST THE KIND OF CROP HE SOWS!
—*Galatians 6:7* (TLB)

THE CLOCK RADIO SAID 8:57 AM when the phone jolted me out of a sound sleep. My friend Jack was on the other end. "Are you going to water aerobics?"

Class started at nine at the pool across the street from my condo; I wanted to roll over and sleep for another half hour.

"Isn't it going to rain?" I asked sluggishly. Tropical storm Ernesto was winging its way up the coast of Florida.

"No, it looks okay. Just a little cloudy."

I was the one who convinced Jack that an hour of vigorous water exercises every morning would do us both a world of good, so I didn't have the heart to say no. I pulled on my swimsuit, gulped down a few ounces of orange juice, grabbed my towel and bolted out the door.

At 9:02, I was in the water with a dozen friends, laughing, jumping and stretching to the sounds of an exercise CD. We jogged, skied, did jumping jacks, the pendulum swing, breast stroke pull and the rocking horse. We teased Justina about always being late. Lou brought a big box of sun hats; I chose a dandy orange one with a pelican and the word *Florida*. We planned a Friday night poolside potluck dinner party as we did our leg lifts.

The sky had turned a glorious bright blue, dotted with enormous white cotton ball clouds. The water temperature was in the mideighties, and in between my just-out-of-bed yawns, I had to admit that being outdoors exercising with friends was absolutely the best thing I could be doing.

Lord, sometimes I need a nudge to get up out of my cozy world and do things. Help me to say yes more often. —Patricia Lorenz

THU
28

*"WHY DO YOU SEE THE SPECK IN YOUR
NEIGHBOR'S EYE, BUT DO NOT NOTICE
THE LOG IN YOUR OWN EYE?"*
—*Luke 6:41 (NRSV)*

IN 2006, NEW ENGLAND FACED the first hurricane season after the devastating hurricanes that destroyed New Orleans and parts of Mississippi and Florida in 2005. Forecasters predicted it would be New England's turn. People who barely paid attention to forecasts other than to check if it would be a beach day were riveted to the daily weather and radar reports.

Most of the summer passed with hardly a driving rainstorm. Then the panic started. Hurricane Ernesto was ravaging Haiti and was going to make its way up the East Coast. Forecasters made the most of it, finally vindicated in their yearlong prediction of doom. And when Ernesto lost steam, no one—not forecasters or residents—seemed willing to admit it.

I felt superior to what seemed to me a foolish fear; I'd seen the aftermath of what *real* storms could do in Key West, Florida, and I found the New England worry typical of what I think of as Puritanical pessimism. On the day Ernesto, finally no more than wind and a rainstorm, hit New London, Connecticut, I stubbornly set out for my daily walk. Bundled in rain gear, I imagined my fearful neighbors peering anxiously out their windows, shocked to see me striding along the waterfront streets.

I was the one who got a shock. All along my route, people were playing in the storm. I saw a touch football game. Couples gathered on porches to laugh and drink tea. Neighbors helped remove tree limbs from driveways. People waved merrily as if to draw me into their rejoicing. But now I was the one whose joy was restrained . . . by humility.

Lord, teach me to judge not, lest I be judged.
—MARCI ALBORGHETTI

FRI
29

BECAUSE THE JOURNEY IS TOO GREAT FOR THEE. —*I Kings 19:7*

I WALK VERY EARLY in the morning, when it's still cool and not quite light. One late August morning I came upon a father and his two children, waiting at the end of their driveway for the school bus. The children seemed so little to be going off to school, and their new backpacks made them appear even smaller. The father was kneeling and talking with them as he adjusted the backpack of the smallest one.

As I watched them, I remembered my own apprehension when I started first grade. My school was very close to our house, so I walked. When I arrived at school, I discovered that all the children's mothers had accompanied them—except for mine. She had to go to work. She'd gone onto the front porch with me, knelt down and tied my sash again. Then she turned me around very gently and held my face in her tender hands. She gave me her marvelous "It's going to be okay" smile and said with assurance, "I'm going to ask Jesus to walk along beside you, Mannie. You'll be fine. I promise."

And was I ever fine! My teacher Mrs. Edna Rogers announced that since I was the only one who came to school by myself, I'd be her "special helper."

Maybe, like me, some children won't have their moms or dads with them as they start school this year. This prayer is especially for them:

Father, kneel down by the sides of the children who are going to their first day of school and comfort them with Your tender hands. —MARION BOND WEST

SAT

30

"AND I WILL CAUSE SHOWERS TO COME DOWN IN THEIR SEASON; THERE SHALL BE SHOWERS OF BLESSING."
    —*Ezekiel 34:26 (NKJV)*

"I DON'T WANT TO GO to this picnic," I growl to my wife. "It's hot, I'm tired and I don't want to meet people." I was in my usual start-of-school mood, made worse this year by a hot summer that burned up my garden.

About a hundred of us are crammed into the picnic shelter at Rothwell Park—faculty, staff and their families. The tables are crowded with fragrant foods and sparkling drinks, but the air is heavy and everyone seems tired and grouchy.

Suddenly, thunder—distant at first, but now exploding like cannons on a battlefield. Lightning crackles like enemy gunfire and children run to their mothers. Rain begins to fall so hard that it feels like we've camped out under Niagara Falls. Strong men lift tables of food and carry them to the middle of the pavilion, and we huddle around them. Children are sucking their thumbs and crying, while parents try to comfort them: "The angels are bowling," they say. "The devil is just having a fight with his wife."

At last, the rain slows, and tiny boys and girls race out into the showers, screaming with joy, then scamper back inside when lightning flickers. Soon we are all eating, laughing, rejoicing at the cool air and refreshing rains.

My face is wet, but not with rain. I'm sitting off to the side, reflecting on God's grace. I'm counting my blessings: the cool rain, beautiful children, good food, great co-workers and God's providence. I'm grateful for ears that can hear thunder and for eyes that can see the kindness on the faces of my co-workers. Suddenly I'm no longer afraid of the start of school.

Thank You, God, for knowing just when to send the rains of blessing. —DANIEL SCHANTZ

SUN
31 FOR THE LORD YOUR GOD IS A MERCIFUL
GOD; HE WILL NOT ABANDON OR DESTROY
YOU OR FORGET THE COVENANT WITH
YOUR FOREFATHERS, WHICH HE
CONFIRMED TO THEM BY OATH.

—Deuteronomy 4:31 (NIV)

HOURS AFTER HURRICANE KATRINA, I left the house
to survey the damage. I hadn't evacuated; instead, I'd
driven a few miles from my home to care for my elderly in-laws. Luckily, no trees had hit their home. It
was eerily quiet: There were no barking dogs and no
birds were singing. I carefully made my way across
the property, climbing over fallen trees and debris,
until I reached the highway. The scene before me was
staggering. Hundreds of huge pine trees lay broken
and scattered across the road. Every power line was
down, their cables and transformers twisted and mangled. Once stately homes lay in ruins, their contents
scattered. Cars were crushed beneath the debris. I
stood, shocked at the scene before me.

*What has happened to my town, this place that
I love?* I thought. Panic gripped me. *Lord, where
are You?*

Something on the ground caught my eye; I knelt
down and picked it up. It was a small branch, broken
by the storm into the shape of a cross. Alone on the
highway, surrounded by destruction, I held the cross
up to the sky.

Almighty God, for all the times we need to rebuild—
whether it's our homes, our lives or our relationships—
give us Your strength, Your peace, Your hope.
                                    —MELODY BONNETTE

MY DIVINE SURPRISES

1 _____

2 _____

3 _____

4 _____

5 _____

6 _____

7 _____

8 _____

9 _____

10 _____

11 _____

12 _____

13 _____

14 _____

15 _____

16 _____

17 _____

18 _____

19 _____

20 _____

21 _____

22 _____

23 _____

24 _____

25 _____

26 _____

27 _____

28 _____

29 _____

30 _____

31 _____

September

I thank thee, O Father, Lord of heaven and earth, because thou hast hid these things from the wise and prudent, and hast revealed them unto babes. —*Matthew 11:25*

MON   *My heart rejoiced in all my*
1   *labour. . . .* —*Ecclesiastes 2:10*

MY BROTHER-IN-LAW BEN and I headed down to a cabin in Centre, Alabama, for a get-away-from-it-all weekend. Ben's a dentist and I'm a financial adviser. We both love our work, but sometimes things can get pretty hectic. We were looking forward to a break from our cell phones and back-to-back appointments. Saturday morning, we met with our cabin neighbor Rex, and he drove us to a remote pine-covered forest with trails that were practically empty. Nothing but nature and God.

"I need to check on the drive-in," Rex told us on the way back. He owns a local drive-in theater built by his family.

"No problem," we said.

As it turned out, there was a problem. Two employees had called in sick and before we knew it, Ben and I were standing behind the counter of an old-fashioned concession stand, staring at a line of people. Soon I was filling buckets of popcorn while Ben poured cheese on trays of nachos. We learned to respond to requests for "Extra ice" or "No butter" or "Hold the peppers on the nachos." We laughed and joked and had the time of our lives.

"I sure appreciate you helping me out," Rex said at evening's end.

"Are you kidding?" we responded. "We should be

thanking you. We had a ball! Maybe we found our second careers!"

So the weekend didn't turn out exactly how we expected, but it gave us exactly what we needed: a change from the everyday. Who knew that it would come from behind the counter of a snack bar at an old-fashioned drive-in theater?

Father, help me rejoice in my labor each and every day.
—BROCK KIDD

UNEXPECTED BLESSINGS
HELPING THE HELPERS

TUE
2

AND I WAS WITH YOU IN WEAKNESS. . . .
—*I Corinthians 2:3*

MY DAUGHTER LIZ and I had long looked forward to a trip to Russia. Then, just three days before the departure date, a pain shooting down my right leg sent me to the doctor, who diagnosed sciatica and advised me to stay off my feet. But since the journey from St. Petersburg to Moscow would be by boat, I reasoned, how much walking could there be?

A lot, I quickly discovered. Every day we left the

boat to visit churches, museums, palaces, monasteries —a succession of endless corridors and long staircases that got steeper as the agony in my leg increased.

Enthralled by the glories we were seeing, I took the cane the boat provided and tried to ignore the pain. What I couldn't ignore was the inconvenience to the thirty-three others in the group. "I'm sorry!" became my constant refrain as I slowed everyone down.

Ashamed to be always accepting help and never giving it, I feared I was spoiling the trip for others— especially when I had to resort to the boat's wheel-chair. Now Liz or someone else had to push me, fold and unfold the chair, get it off the boat and back on again. To my repeated apologies, people assured me it was no trouble.

But of course it was trouble, and by the end of the tour I felt that my determination to see everything had been sheer selfishness. As we said our good-byes at the airport, though, came a surprise. One by one, people came up to thank me. To thank *me*! "You've added so much to the trip." And, "Helping you see things made everything I saw mean more."

With treatment at home, the sciatica is gone. What remains is an insight into the times when I'm needy. To need help, to want help, to accept help . . . this can be a form of giving too.

Bestower of blessing, make me an eager giver and a grateful receiver. —ELIZABETH SHERRILL

WED **3** AND JESUS SAID TO HIM, "GO AND DO LIKEWISE." —*Luke 10:37 (RSV)*

"SOMETIMES   HE   CAN   BE   SUCH   A _____."

(FILL IN THE BLANK.)

Have you ever said that, or something like it, about someone? Your spouse, your child, that obstreperous person on your church committee, a neighbor?

Boy, I sure have. One of my biggest challenges was with a colleague. One day after a particularly contentious meeting, I said some harsh words about him and his actions. "I know the Bible says I'm supposed to love this guy," I sputtered to another co-worker. "But I don't and I don't know how I would."

"Maybe you don't have to know," he said, "at least right away. Treat him respectfully and give yourself a break. A lot of the time, love begins with an action, not an emotion. It's something you do, even though you don't feel it."

That advice has stayed with me. I still have days when I can't love certain people in my heart the way Jesus commanded us to love. But I've learned that I can love with my actions and my words—respectful listening, a helpful suggestion, a silent prayer. That has made a huge difference, not only in the way I treat people but often in the way they treat me.

Today, God, show me a person to whom I can show love through my actions. —JEFF JAPINGA

THU

4

MY SHEEP HEAR MY VOICE, AND I KNOW THEM. . . . —John 10:27 (NKJV)

THE EXCITED VOICES of the guests rose above the clatter of the dishes in the Lake Upsata Lodge in Ovando, Montana. I sat at the table, distracted. My job at the ranch would end in October, and although I had some offers, I hadn't a clue what God wanted me to do. I felt as if He were a million miles away.

Suddenly the door swung open and Kathy, one of the guests, announced, "Rebecca, did you know Dancer had her baby?"

I looked at her in shock. My mare wasn't due for another three weeks. I grabbed my camera and all of us thundered down the dirt road to the pasture by the lake. One thought plagued me: *Will the baby know me?*

For the last ten and a half months I'd been talking and singing to Wind Dancer, the baby mule, every day. She'd gotten to know my voice and would kick when she heard me. But all the mule breeders cautioned me, "Rebecca, mules are wild when they're born. Once they get their feet underneath them, you'll never catch them—at least not for the first couple of weeks."

When we reached the pasture the guests climbed onto the fence, peering over at the small sorrel mule baby standing by her mom.

I slipped through the rails. "Hi, Dancer." I scratched

the white blaze on her face. "What a beautiful baby you have." Then I felt a nudge against my side. I looked down just as Wind Dancer slipped between my arm and my body and stood there. *She knows me! She recognized my voice!* Then another thought flashed through my mind: *I couldn't see God and that's why I felt He was a million miles away. He wasn't distant. He was in my heart. He knew me and exactly what I needed.*

Wind Dancer leaned against me. I petted her velvet red coat. *Okay, God, I need to lean on You.*

Lord, thank You for reminding me that You never leave me. —REBECCA ONDOV

FRI
5

THE SOVEREIGN LORD IS MY STRENGTH; HE MAKES MY FEET LIKE THE FEET OF A DEER, HE ENABLES ME TO GO ON THE HEIGHTS. —*Habakkuk 3:19 (NIV)*

NOT LONG AGO I WAS CAMPED near a pond where a bull moose came to feed every evening. He was immense and would have dwarfed one of those Clydesdale horses that sometimes show up in parades. But his antlers, called a "rack," were comparatively small. Every year a bull moose loses his antlers; they grow back larger the next year. A mature bull's rack can be five or six feet wide. This moose's antlers, however, were only about three feet wide, and I wondered why.

My brother later told me that the antlers of older males often grow smaller. Their size and maturity don't have to be advertised so openly to attract mates, and the smaller rack makes it easier for them to move through the forest and is a better weapon against wolves.

When I got home, I decided to live a little more like my wilderness friend. I took a look around my office and began taking down the diplomas and achievement plaques. A couple of ancient dusty trophies went next, along with my collection of autographed pictures. It might be my imagination, but the people who come over to see me seem more at ease, and so do I. It's much easier to move around without all that history clinging to me. And after all, Joy and I have been married for more than thirty years, so why do I need to advertise?

Lord, thank You for the days and years and strength You have given me. Let me grow more comfortable with the person You're molding me to be.

—ERIC FELLMAN

SAT
6
BLESSED ARE THEY THAT PUT THEIR TRUST IN HIM. —*Psalm 2:12*

WE WERE IN MANHATTAN for our youngest son's wedding, and I called our farm in

Vermont to see if we had any messages. The answering machine informed me that my mailbox was full. Since we never have more than one or two voice mails when we are away, I wondered what had prompted so many folks to call.

"Your cows are out!" "I just passed your farm. The cows are in the road!" "I wanted to let you know that your cows are running down the street!" The messages went on and on.

So there we were, two hundred miles away, and the cows were footloose and fancy-free. I hung up and looked at my husband, who was shining his shoes for the wedding, and told him the news. "What can we do, but let God take care of our cows until we get home," Billy replied.

The next day we drove into our dooryard and surveyed the empty pasture. Exhausted from the weekend, we decided we would find the cows in the morning.

And we did. After seven and a half hours of traipsing through the woods in ninety-eight-degree temperatures, we finally corralled them. They were tired and hungry and glad to be home. Dirty, weary and very thirsty ourselves, Billy and I began the task of "walking the fence line." Branches on the electric wire had caused the fence to short out, giving the cows a free pass to misbehave.

I smiled as I prepared dinner later that evening. Lucky for me, we had also walked the fence line while we were away, trusting God that all would be well.

Thank You, Lord, for reminding me that by keeping it simple and trusting in You, I can prevent my spiritual fence from getting short-circuited. —PATRICIA PUSEY

SUN
7

BE DEVOTED TO ONE ANOTHER IN BROTHERLY LOVE. HONOR ONE ANOTHER ABOVE YOURSELVES.
—*Romans 12:10 (NIV)*

MY QUIET GRANDFATHER, though Irish to the bone, dearly loved to make his own salami. He cured them in a tiny shed in the yard, where they hung like lean silent bells. He taught me the musical Italian names of the stages of curing: *gocciolamento,* the dripping stage, when the wet trickled out of the meat one drop an hour; *asciugamento,* the stage of drying, when the salami struggles to maturity, as Grandpa said smiling; and then finally *stagionatura,* the ripening, when the mold on the outside grows like frost or cotton, and the salami rises, as Grandpa said, to its unique flavor from the hand of God.

I spent many hours out there in the shed with him, and all these years later I remember two things in particular: the way he gently and quietly showed me that anything done with the fullest attention was an act of respect and prayer; and the way his face lit up when for once I did not ask for my own favorite salami, but for the one I knew my mother liked best, *finocchiona,* the one with fennel, a green fire on the tongue. He didn't say a word, only smiled wider than ever, but I could tell he was proud of me. I didn't know why then, but I do now: I had stopped being quite so selfish.

Dear Lord, if You have a minute to spare, can You grant me a ton of unselfishness? —BRIAN DOYLE

MON
8

AND HE SHOWED ME A PURE RIVER OF WATER OF LIFE. . . .
—*Revelation 22:1 (NKJV)*

WHEN I WALKED INTO the break room at 8:00 AM and saw that the coffee machine was broken, I gasped. "What am I going to do without my coffee?" My co-workers laughed, pointing to the huge, hand-printed sign tacked to our barren coffeepot: YES, THE COFFEEMAKER IS BROKEN. NO, WE DON'T KNOW WHAT'S WRONG WITH IT. YES, WE'VE ORDERED ANOTHER ONE. NO, WE DON'T KNOW WHEN IT WILL ARRIVE. AND, NO, WE DON'T KNOW WHAT YOU ARE GOING TO DO WITHOUT YOUR COFFEE!

I laughed too. Obviously, I wasn't the first to utter those remarks. My co-workers and I were still huddled in the break room when the next caffeine-deprived soul entered. And when Anna wailed, "What will I do without my coffee? I *need* coffee in the morning!" a co-worker began singing "*Ohhh, I neeeed* coffee in the morning" to the tune of "I Love Paris in the Springtime." The rest of us joined in enthusiastically, if not melodiously.

When our manager walked in and said, "Oh no, the coffee machine's broken!" the whole room roared. And then almost as one, we stood up, ready to begin our workday fueled by laughter . . . almost as good an energy-giver as caffeine!

God, I'm thirsty for laughter. Please show me how to pour some refreshing humor on the minor irritations life may bring my way today. —LINDA NEUKRUG

TUE
9

"MY PRESENCE WILL GO WITH YOU, AND I WILL GIVE YOU REST."
                              —*Exodus 33:14 (RSV)*

EVERYONE SEEMED TO WANT ME at once. I was a bank director and a library trustee. I was teaching Sunday school and working with a team that was pioneering a computer program for technical writers. I loved being needed and hated to say no to anyone who asked. Would I prepare a brochure? Love to. Teach a writing class or two? You bet. Speak at a local university? Certainly.

Soon I was watching the clock at dinner, during lunch and when stopped at traffic. The faster I moved, the better. Then predictably enough, fatigue set in.

My responsibilities weighed heavily on me and I couldn't keep up. *Summer's coming,* I told myself. *You can rest then.*

September came and I was back in harness, although this time the warning signals were more dramatic—chest pains. I rushed to my doctor. After an exam he told me, "Oscar, you need to slow down a little. You're taking on too much work."

"But who will do it if I don't?" I asked.

The answer came in a Bible study. We were studying the book of Exodus and we'd come to the passage where Jethro, Moses' father-in-law, was concerned that Moses was spending all his time, morning to night, counseling others. "What you are doing is not good," Jethro said. "You and the people with you will wear yourselves out, for the thing is too heavy for you; you are not able to perform it alone" (Exodus 18:17–18, RSV). He needed God.

Like Moses, I learned to share my responsibilities with others. All I had to do was ask.

Heavenly Father, teach me to pause and select those things You truly want me to do. —OSCAR GREENE

WED

10

AND THE LORD SAID UNTO MOSES . . .
Go. . . . —*Exodus 4:19*

I'D NEVER USED a Global Positioning System, the satellite hook-up that plots the best route for a car to follow. The rental car agent explained that I simply had to give the GPS two pieces of information—my present location and the address of the conference center where I was headed—and its computer would do the rest. Sounded good, especially since my flight had been late and the meeting was set for twelve o'clock sharp.

"Proceed south on Main Street for one mile," a dulcet female voice instructed. "Now you are heading east on State Route 12." Left turns, right turns, on and on the directions went, until my invisible informant pronounced, "You are approaching your destination."

Great, I thought. My watch read 11:49.

But orange cones blocked the entrance to the building complex! On the driveway beyond, a cement mixer was pouring concrete. I circled the block, looking for another way in, getting entangled instead in a warren of one-way streets. For ten minutes—praying like mad—I poked in and out of various dead ends until on impulse I turned into a narrow alleyway that looked like another false lead but led into the center's service entrance. I arrived just one minute late.

Sometimes God's guidance is like that GPS: His signals are clear and easy to follow. At other times it seems His leading has stopped and we're left on our own. Has He abandoned us? Or is He doing something else when His will seems unclear?

It wasn't, I realized, until my GPS failed me that I'd turned to minute-by-minute prayer. And isn't that the real point of God's guidance? Not just to get us to some goal, but to call us to relationship with Him.

Remind me again today, Father, that relationship is always more important to You than achievement.
                                        —JOHN SHERRILL

THU
11
LET US LAY ASIDE EVERY WEIGHT, AND THE SIN WHICH DOTH SO EASILY BESET US. . . . —Hebrews 12:1

SEPTEMBER 11 ONCE AGAIN, and I was carrying around the troubles of the world. On top of war and rumors of war (I live only three miles from the Pentagon), I piled on personal worries, the car repairs, a friend with cancer, my widowed niece. Hoping to lighten my spirit, I dropped in on a specially scheduled church service.

As the sanctuary filled, a woman shuffled in. She carried several large, stuffed plastic bags and settled them around her in the pew across the aisle from me. I turned my attention to the hymns and sermon, but they did nothing to lift my load. I filed out of the pew and walked forward to receive Communion. At the same time, the woman emerged from her pew, dragging all her stuff with her. *How inappropriate*, I thought, *bringing her baggage to the altar!*

I stepped forward in the aisle, and it hit me. Wasn't

this precisely the right place to bring my fears and
anxiety, my sadness and disappointments, all the baggage of my life? Couldn't I leave all of it with God?
There at the altar, I left the weight of my worries. I
returned to my seat, praying that the bag lady would
also find a safe place to leave her heavy load.

*Lord, help me this day to lay down the burdens I need-
lessly bear.* —EVELYN BENCE

FRI
12

"*THE WIND BLOWS WHERE IT WISHES AND
YOU HEAR THE SOUND OF IT, BUT DO NOT
KNOW WHERE IT COMES FROM AND
WHERE IT IS GOING. . . .*"
—*John 3:8 (NAS)*

OUR FRIEND RITA works as a supervising cashier at
a local superstore. She called us on her cell phone
during a coffee break. "Hey, I've got day shifts all
this week, so I want to come see you and Leo one
evening."

"Great! Come for supper on Friday."

"Okay. I get off work at five, but I have to stay to
make sure everything works out fine. I should be
there shortly before six."

We greeted her with hugs when she arrived. "This
is for you," she said, handing us a card and a package.
"A belated gift for your wedding anniversary."

The card featured a pair of lovebirds (appropriate

even after forty-nine years!) and a touching verse. Inside the package we were delighted to discover a set of wind chimes, slender silver tubes suspended from a blue ring and decorated with a gold sun, blue moon and yellow stars.

At the time of Rita's visit, we were in the midst of making a major decision, and doubts regarding God's will had been plaguing me whenever I tried to rest. *Do this? Do that? Go here? Go there?* The uncertainty was always worst in the wee hours of the night.

We hung the wind chimes Rita gave us over our front steps, and whenever I began to toss and turn, I heard the gentle tinkle of the chimes and, along with it, reassurance as gentle as the evening breeze that God would stay with us "to make sure that everything works out fine."

Dear God, thank You for friends like Rita whose words and gifts You use to bless and comfort me.
—ALMA BARKMAN

SAT
13

BLESSED BE THE LORD, THAT HATH GIVEN REST UNTO HIS PEOPLE ISRAEL, ACCORDING TO ALL THAT HE PROMISED. . . . —*I Kings 8:56*

SATURDAY. WHO DOESN'T love that word? For me it means not just catching up on errands but also catching up on people. There's Arlene at the dry cleaners, who always can't wait to tell me how her son is doing in school (quite well), her voice bursting with maternal pride and gratitude. Hassan at my corner grocery fills me in on his family back in Egypt (some health problems, but they're doing all right now). Maria at the hardware store loves to be helpful ("We got that filter for your air conditioner, Mr. Grinnan"). And Cecil at the natural foods store is a *Guideposts* reader and is full of questions and comments about the most recent issue ("My wife loved that story about the little girl writing to the soldier in Iraq").

If I'm up in the Berkshires, Saturday might mean a climb up Monument Mountain or Mount Everett, or a day hike on the Appalachian Trail. Or maybe I just curl up on the couch with my dog Sally and watch a baseball game (I follow the Yankees, but just about any game will do) while my wife Julee leafs through catalogs.

Of course, Saturdays can also be hectic, and I often never get enough done. Still, after a long week of work, Saturdays are a way to reconnect not just with people but with the blessings of life. I think Saturday comes before Sunday to remind us of all that we have to be thankful for.

Lord, You fill my life with abundance and give me Saturdays to enjoy it so that on Sunday I come to Your house with a full and grateful heart.

—EDWARD GRINNAN

SUN
14

AND THROUGH HIM TO RECONCILE TO HIMSELF ALL THINGS, WHETHER THINGS ON EARTH OR THINGS IN HEAVEN, BY MAKING PEACE THROUGH HIS BLOOD, SHED ON THE CROSS. —*Colossians 1:20 (NIV)*

ON THE DAY BEFORE PALM SUNDAY, a small tornado came through town and bent a cross sideways on its mounting on top of our church steeple. When I drove by several days later, I noticed that the cross had been removed for repair and was sitting on the grass outside the church.

Curiosity got the best of me, and I turned into the parking lot to get a closer look. I'd often marveled at the cross so high and proud against the sky, and felt an impossible wish to touch it.

When I got closer, I was disappointed. The cross was made of plain metal, and the horizontal arms were covered with bird droppings. As I touched the cross, I realized that the thrill I had always felt wasn't about the cross itself but about its position high above everything else.

Several weeks later a crane came and hoisted the cross back onto the steeple. Now whenever I see it, so high and lofty against the sky, I feel no need to go up there and touch it. On it, Jesus Christ touched me.

Jesus, thank You for dying on the Cross, so my sins could be forgiven. —KAREN BARBER

A SECOND THANK-YOU
THANK YOU FOR ENCOURAGERS

MON
15

THEREFORE ENCOURAGE ONE ANOTHER AND BUILD EACH OTHER UP, JUST AS IN FACT YOU ARE DOING.
—*I Thessalonians 5:11 (NIV)*

YESTERDAY, I WENT to an estate sale of an elderly couple who were members of my childhood church. Their cottage was tiny, and a 1940s vintage washer took up most of the room in their little kitchen. I'd never known how simply and frugally they had lived.

As I wandered through the cottage, it occurred to me that the beautiful get-well cards they sent me whenever I had surgery had been a real sacrifice. I remembered one of them especially, a glossy card featuring a birdhouse with robins singing. When the postman delivered it to our house, I had just been discharged from the hospital. That cheerful card made me want to get up off the couch and take a walk around the block. Despite the pain, I wanted to rejoice like that determined bird.

I'd thanked the kind couple all those years ago, but how could I say a second thank-you now that they were gone?

I'll buy something and give it a place of honor in my home, I decided. I discovered a small fisherman planter; it would be perfect for the old fishing cabin I was restoring.

There was no air conditioning in their cottage that day, not even a fan to create a breeze. The heat at 9:00 AM when the sale started was stifling. But uncomfortable as I was, I'd never felt more grateful for the kind and generous people in my past.

Thank You, Lord, for people everywhere who touch the future with their encouraging hearts and words.
— ROBERTA MESSNER

TUE
16

IN YOUR PATIENCE POSSESS YE YOUR SOULS. —Luke 21:19

WE KNEW THAT TEDDY, our thirteen-year-old Welsh terrier, was having trouble seeing, but we weren't aware of how bad his sight was until the veterinarian reported that cataracts were overtaking both eyes. "Can he be helped?" we asked.

"Only with surgery," the doctor replied, and that would cost a small fortune. So we resigned ourselves to soon having a blind dog. That is, until we learned of a more reasonable, though still expensive, animal hospital near Pittsburgh.

So we took Teddy to the surgeon there, and after an examination he concluded that the dog's sight could be saved. Teddy had the cataracts removed, but he still couldn't see. The doctor explained that Teddy's brain was not processing the images sent from his eyes. "He probably had a stroke some time back," the vet reasoned, and so our efforts were for naught. After that, Teddy's health went downhill until he had trouble functioning.

"I think it's time," my wife Shirley concluded one morning. I agreed, and we made an appointment with the vet, a young woman who listened patiently as I stroked and praised Teddy. She had tended the dog before and agreed he was a very special dog. How good it was of her to empathize with me. After I had talked myself out, she asked if I was ready. I answered yes, whispered, "I love you, Teddy" and held him close. Then Shirley and the vet held me.

What I remember most is how the vet silently listened to me as I struggled to let go of Teddy. In Galatians 5:22, we read that patience is one of the gifts of the Spirit. For me, it may be the greatest gift. I'm often short of it, though I admire it enormously in others. I pray for it. Maybe in time, as the shadows lengthen, I'll gain more of this priceless substance.

Teach us, Lord, the subtle art of words withholden,
Until we learn that silence—sometimes—can be golden.
                                    —FRED BAUER

WED
17
*"SHALL WE ACCEPT GOOD FROM GOD,
AND NOT TROUBLE?" —Job 2:10 (NIV)*

FOR A WHILE it wasn't unusual for me to wake up during the night and stay awake, mentally recounting my worries: the bills piled on my desk, finding volunteers for a school project, some small detail of my son Ross's college applications. Naturally this made me feel worse, so one night I thought up a better idea. Instead of worries, I'd itemize my blessings, thanking God for each gift, such as my husband's job, my children's health, our comfortable and happy home.

Then in just a few months, several of these blessings fell away: Paul lost his job after sixteen years when the university closed the theater department; a week later our beloved dog Cookie died; then our daughter Maria was hospitalized for a week with severe digestive problems, right before starting sixth grade. Staying with her in the hospital, I had another of my sleepless nights. Trying to count my blessings, a voice inside fought back, saying, *What do I have to be thankful for? What?*

That's when a new list emerged: Maria was already feeling better than she had in months because the doctors had found the cause of her pain; Paul was busy with several freelance jobs that would hold us over until he found full-time work; all the while friends had showered us with meals, flowers and prayers.

Good times come and so do bad. But even in those bad times, God has blessed me with much more than I deserve.

What do I have to be thankful for, Lord? Gifts to be valued above all else—Your great love and mercy.
                                        —GINA BRIDGEMAN

THU
18

IN THEE SHALL ALL FAMILIES OF THE EARTH BE BLESSED. —*Genesis 12:3*

I MISS MY OLDER SON WILLIAM. I don't know why it should be worse this year than last when he first went off to college. I should have gotten used to it. But I ache at the sight of his empty bunk bed and the unnatural neatness of his desk, the faded posters on his walls and the stuffed animals on his bedspread. When do we start giving them away or getting rid of the Legos? Are we holding on to these things for him or for us?

Of course this is right. He should grow up. I'm proud that he's independent and manages to get good grades without having to be reminded to do his homework and finish his papers or be told that watching TV is not the way to study for a test. All that prodding was exhausting. Didn't I wish for the day when he could do it on his own? Shouldn't I be grateful he's not home?

Then the phone rings. "Hi, Dad," William says, nonchalant. No, nothing urgent to report. Just a few words about an economics class, his on-campus job and the camping trip he might take over the weekend. I hang up, feeling better. There's something about loving your children that makes you worry about them and wonder about them more than they should ever have to know. I let William go—gladly, proudly—but a part of me is always thinking of him, my prayers spanning the distance between us. *Be with him, God. He's Yours.* Never more so than now.

What a blessing children are. Be with all of them, Lord. —RICK HAMLIN

READER'S ROOM

I HAVE HAD generous God sightings. I've learned that I need to let the Lord talk to me. It helps whenever I take a few moments and bow my head in silence with this thought in mind: *Whatever You have to say to me, Lord.* Also, *I am here, Lord. How can I help You?* And, *I'm listening, Lord.* Thank you for *Daily Guideposts.*
—*Milagro Guardiola, New York, New York*

FRI
19
*HE IS GREEN BEFORE THE SUN, AND HIS
BRANCH SHOOTETH FORTH IN HIS
GARDEN. —Job 8:16*

IT'S NICE TO WAIT for the number 5 bus that stops right along Riverside Park in Manhattan. The bus usually comes every ten minutes or so, and on this particular day I went out early so I'd be sure to get to my lunch date on time. But today fifteen minutes passed, then twenty. Now I was fidgety and anxious. "Calm down," I said to myself. "The bus will come. You have time. Take a deep breath. Look around."

I heard a racing and rustling. A squirrel trotted out of the park with a bright green globe in its mouth. "Is that a green Ping-Pong ball?" I wondered aloud just as an elderly man strolled by.

"No, it's a nut," he said. He kept walking, but in a minute came back with another green sphere, which he pressed open. "See, there's a nut inside. The squirrel's getting ready for winter."

A raucous squawking broke out overhead. I squinted up to see a feathery flash of vivid greens— spring green, yellow green, a glimpse of red. A parrot! Then another! I'd always heard about wild parrots in the park but had never seen any. A teenager and some children appeared. *"Pawwots,"* a little boy lisped to me. He wore a moss-green sweater.

By the time the bus pulled up, I'd not only been

entertained during my wait, I'd been educated and delighted, and had fraternized with my neighbors. Plus, now I was alerted to green everywhere: a bit of moss on a bus rider's backpack; the glow of the stoplight saying GO; the lacy leaves of the trees bordering the park.

Instead of fretting, I'd enjoyed the gifts of the day. What a difference!

Dear God, thank You for the wonderful gifts of Your great green world. —MARY ANN O'ROARK

SAT
20

"YOU WILL BE SORROWFUL, BUT YOUR SORROW WILL BE TURNED INTO JOY."
—*John 16:20 (NKJV)*

IT'S FUNNY HOW the same event can make one person laugh and another cry. I often pass through the village of La Plata, Missouri, and I always stop to see the little Santa Fe train station on the north end of town. It's a small white building with a red roof, dating back to the 1880s. With glass-block windows and prairie flowers growing around it, it could be something from a model train set.

More than seventy trains pass through this station every day, and today some Amish folks are waiting, their buggies parked in the shade of oak trees out back. The grown-ups are sitting on gray benches, but the children stand by the train, waiting for the doors to open. The boys are wearing denim trousers and shirts, with black suspenders and straw hats. The girls are draped in Wedgwood-blue dresses, with bonnets covering their hair. Next to the big Amtrak train, they look no bigger than salt-and-pepper shakers.

All at once the doors open and arriving passengers step out, smiling, laughing. Loved ones run to meet them, hugging and kissing. The departing passengers are crying. With hugs they promise to "write every day," and predict that "everything will be fine." The arrivals are smiling because they have weathered the journey safely. The departing passengers are crying because they are facing lonely days. The same event, but opposite reactions.

It helps me understand how, when my wife and I listen to a sermon or a concert, she is upset—and I am thrilled! It explains how a wedding can put a smile on a bride's face while her mother's eyes are filled with tears.

I need to be more understanding about how people see things and allow for different reactions to the same event.

Thank You, Lord, for reminding me that my point of view is not the only point of view.
                                    —DANIEL SCHANTZ

SUN
21

COMFORT YE, COMFORT YE MY PEOPLE,
SAITH YOUR GOD.—*Isaiah 40:1*

LYNNE, MY WIFE'S FRIEND of forty-nine
years, died recently. They met in elementary school and went to college together; Lynne married Keith the same year Dianne and I were married. We live in southwest Colorado, but Dianne teaches in Farmington, New Mexico, where Lynne and Keith lived. For the past ten years, Dianne frequently spent the night at her friend's house after working late in her classroom. She was with her when she drew her last breath.

The Sunday after Lynne's death, Keith asked us to go with him to scatter Lynne's ashes at Purgatory Ski Resort in the San Juan National Forest. On a beautiful morning, we drove to the edge of a spruce hillside and hiked to a nearby meadow. Lynne's favorite mountain, Engineer, dominated the north horizon. Gold and scarlet aspen leaves glimmered on the south-facing slopes of Engineer whenever a slight breeze blew across the meadow.

I knew that Keith didn't believe in God; he preferred stillness to any talk of Him. So as Dianne quietly cried, I silently prayed for some sign of God's comforting presence.

As we were leaving, Dianne wondered which ski run we were near. She found a sign, but I hoped she wouldn't read it. The typical names of ski runs at Purgatory were Lower Hades, Styx and Pandemonium. My wife looked at the sign. "Path to Peace," Dianne said and smiled. So did Keith.

Thank You, Father, for being the God of all comfort to those who know You and to those who don't.
                                    —TIM WILLIAMS

LETTERS TO TINY TOES

NOT LONG AGO, Marilyn Morgan King's youngest son John and his wife Tasha became the parents of a baby boy. When they e-mailed 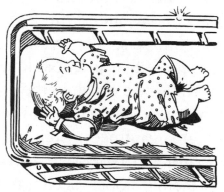 Marilyn a copy of the first sonogram, the only thing she could make out was a little foot, its tiny toes spread out for her to see. So long before he was born, she started calling him Tiny Toes.

While waiting for his birth, Marilyn started writing letters. "Perhaps someday," she says, "he will read them and find something in them to help him know his grandmother. And more important, the letters might be an impetus for him to begin the search to know his true self."

—THE EDITORS

WAGING PEACE

MON
22

HAVE PEACE ONE WITH ANOTHER.
—Mark 9:50

DEAR TINY TOES,

In just a few days you will enter this world. I can hardly wait to hold you in my arms, *ooh* and *ah* over you, and talk with your family about how much you look like your daddy or your Great Uncle Donal or whomever we project onto your little face.

As I wait for you, I've been thinking of some things I'd like you to know about this wild and tender world you're about to join. You'll find it's quite a beautiful place, with its sky-skimming mountains and twisty rivers, furry white rabbits and scary black bears, its shimmering aspens, yolk yellow in autumn, and its starry skies so full of mystery and hope.

It's also a world in which people are trying to love each other and live together in peace. But, my dearest little one, we are failing in that.

Perhaps someday you'll begin the search for peace within. It begins when you start collecting moments. You might set aside your sand bucket briefly to hear the whisper of the wind, or lay down your bat and ball long enough to enjoy a rainbow, or park your bike for a five-minute concert by the birds. Or maybe you'll be in your bed, looking out at the night sky, and everything will stop for an instant and you'll feel a quiet Presence near. Follow that Presence wherever it leads you, for this hurting world desperately needs those who can carry that kind of peace to men and women all over our planet.

As I hold my breath, awaiting your birth, the world holds its breath, awaiting peace.

Love,
Grandma K.

Lord, may Tiny Toes and all of us find inner peace and become strong voices for peace in the world.

—MARILYN MORGAN KING

TRUSTING LIFE'S UNFOLDING

TUE **23**

THE LORD SAID, ". . . SARAH YOUR WIFE SHALL HAVE A SON." . . .

—*Genesis 18:10 (RSV)*

DEAR TINY TOES,

I just received your father's call, telling me that you have arrived! Welcome, welcome, welcome, little one! I've hoped and prayed for you for many years, and loved you since your father first told me you were coming to us.

Here's a true story about your daddy. Auntie Karen was twelve and Uncle Paul, nine, and I thought our family was complete, when I learned I was going to have another baby. Like Abraham and Sarah, I thought I was too old. But the nurse patted my knee and said, "You'll count it a blessing." That's exactly what your daddy has been for me.

He and your mother (Tasha) have also waited long to have a baby, and I often hinted to them not to wait too long. Then one day a voice in my head said, *Quit bugging them!* I reminded myself it was, after all, his and Tasha's life, not mine.

Then one April night John called me and said, "We'll be there for Christmas, Mom. We're flying in . . ." He paused and then added, "Though we've never flown with a baby before." Wild with happiness, I almost dropped the phone.

So you see, dear one, you have helped me learn to trust. It has taken me seventy-five years to discover this most valuable truth: I am not in charge of my life—or anyone else's for that matter. I have come to trust that life unfolds just as it should, when I trust the Spirit and get myself out of the way.

Love,
Grandma K.

Lord, help Tiny Toes to follow his deepest truths, trusting in the Holy Spirit, and wait for the unfolding.
—MARILYN MORGAN KING

THE SOUL'S PICTURE

WED

24

AND THOU SHALT CALL HIS NAME
ISAAC. . . . —Genesis 17:19

DEAR TINY TOES,

Today you have a name! You are Isaac. It seems such a big name for such a tiny baby. Perhaps, like the son of Abraham and Sarah, your name was given by God before you were born. The Scottish author/poet George MacDonald wrote that the true name is one that expresses the "soul's picture" and that we "grow into" the name we are given. So what is the meaning of your name, my little Isaac? It is "laughter," and it is also "kind and gentle one." I trust that you will become your name.

Perhaps you will bring laughter into your family when the world seems dark and disheartening. Could it be that somehow you will help lessen the load of suffering in the world by teaching others to carry their pain lightly? One day when I was a child and crying about something I've since forgotten, Mother sat me down and said, "Always remember this: No matter how bad things may seem, if you look with your heart you will find something to be glad about." I pass this on to you now. May you also offer it to help relieve someone else's suffering.

I seem to be asking so much of you, dear little one, but it's because I sense that you will grow into your name, that you will spread laughter, kindness and gentleness wherever you go. May it be so! The world so desperately needs an Isaac!

Love,
Grandma K.

Lord, may Tiny Toes look into his heart to find the good in all things and then scatter gladness!
—MARILYN MORGAN KING

COPING WITH CHANGE

THU **25** *BECAUSE HE IS AT MY RIGHT HAND, I SHALL NOT BE MOVED.* —*Psalm 16:8*

DEAR TINY TOES,

You don't realize it yet, but you have just begun a long journey, one that will lead you to unknown mountaintops and shaded valleys. The only paths you will see are those made by other feet. You must make your own paths, Isaac dear, with every step you take.

You will walk through thorny weeds and flowering gardens, you will learn to see beauty where others see ugliness, and terror may walk with you part of the way. There will be triumphs and loves and perhaps the great joy of being a parent. You will make mistakes and begin again and make different ones.

Change is essential to life. Just keep going through all the changes, for there is One Who silently walks with you, offering a hand. Take hold of it. Never let go.

You will pass through things that change, but the One Whose hand you hold does not change. Wars will be fought, hurricanes and floods will transform the face of the earth, people you love will die, but the hand that holds you will remain strong and solid through it all.

Love,
Grandma K.

Lord, may Isaac hold tight and never let go of You.
—MARILYN MORGAN KING

FINDING WISDOM

FRI

26

INCLINE THINE EAR UNTO WISDOM,
AND APPLY THINE HEART TO
UNDERSTANDING. —*Proverbs 2:2*

DEAR TINY TOES,

As I hold you and look into your deep blue eyes, I wonder what you see and hear. Mommy's and Daddy's voices are already familiar to you from the womb, and now you know that their faces appear when you cry. You know the feel of their arms and the taste of Mommy's milk. So even now, you are learning by fully living in every moment.

This winding path of discovery will continue for as long as you live. You will find that the knowledge that comes from books and study will greatly enrich your life; always seek for ever deeper answers to the questions that will surely arise out of your own curiosity. May you also discover that some questions can't be answered, no matter how hard you try. Try anyway, and keep on trying.

I hope you will hold on to some questions whose answers elude you. You see, dear Isaac, there's a hidden treasure far greater than pinned-down truths— wisdom. Wisdom won't announce itself. You'll find it in the secrets of trees that whisper in the silence and of clouds that speak in pictures. You'll find it in church when the words you sing swell your heart, as well as on the playground when the teacher calls "Foul!" and you're suddenly full of shame. Wisdom comes from holding on to questions. Just be still and gradually you will come to know deeper questions that will lead you beyond yourself. You will know the territory by the throbbing of your heart.

Love,
Grandma K.

Lord, may Isaac hold on to his questions and recognize wisdom as Your signature.
—MARILYN MORGAN KING

MAPPING ENDINGS

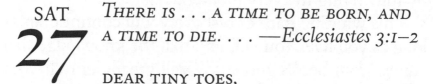

SAT *THERE IS . . . A TIME TO BE BORN, AND*
27 *A TIME TO DIE. . . .* —*Ecclesiastes 3:1–2*

DEAR TINY TOES,

Today I need to write to you about endings. You have experienced the "time to be born," and it seems so soon to bring up that other time, but someday you will need to know. Perhaps, when that time comes, your daddy will get out this letter and read it to you and you will learn to befriend your fear.

I have a deep longing to see you grow up, graduate from high school and college, get married, become a father. How I'd love to be with you and the rest of the family for these marker events! But I am aware, my dear, that someday I will lie down and not get up again. That's okay, Love. It really is. My life has been full, brimming with laughter and tears, attainments and failures, loves and losses, and always companionship with the Beloved One.

Remember what I said about change? It is essential, for there could be no life without it. So when I am gone, look for me in the sunrise and the rainbow, in a baby's smile and your doggie's wagging tail. Look for me in your classroom when something mysterious and wonderful sets you on fire, and in the night sky where no city lights intrude. Thumb through your memories to see what you've filed under "Grandma," for I will live with you in those memories. Then let the past go . . . and live all the loves of your life.

Love unending,
Grandma K.

Dear God, give Isaac the blessing of knowing he is loved in this world and in eternity.
—MARILYN MORGAN KING

LEGACY FOR LIFE

SUN
28

WITH GREAT DELIGHT I SAT IN HIS SHADOW, AND HIS FRUIT WAS SWEET TO MY TASTE. —*Song of Solomon 2:3 (RSV)*

DEAR TINY TOES,

You may wonder why I have written these letters to you, a child so new to this life, still unmarred by the world's troubles. It's because I'm old now and my life will not be complete until I have communicated to you the things this precious life has taught me. In some cultures, the elders make a point of doing this and the youth respect their insights gained by years of living. For the most part, this happens only incidentally in our culture, and I think we have lost something of value because of that.

So I leave you these letters as my gift to the boy and to the man you will become. Perhaps someday you will read them and form your own opinions about what is written here. Do that! Perhaps more valuable than any other advice I've written in these few pages is this: Listen to the Spirit Who dwells in your heart. Make your life count in the smallest ways and in whatever larger ways are given to you. But make it count. Spread your priceless laughter, gentleness and kindness wherever you go, my dear little Isaac. And perhaps someday you will feel the need to write what you have learned on your own journey through life. Let it be a gift to your grandchildren.

Love always,
Grandma K.

Dear God, may inner peace, trust in You and kindly laughter be Isaac's—and our—companions on the way. —MARILYN MORGAN KING

MON
29

GOD WILL COMMAND HIS ANGELS TO PROTECT YOU WHEREVER YOU GO. THEY WILL CARRY YOU IN THEIR ARMS, AND YOU WON'T HURT YOUR FEET ON THE STONES. —Psalm 91:11–12 (CEV)

LOOKING AT COLLEGES has always been a Nace family adventure. For each of the boys, we'd map out a route connecting each of the colleges we were considering and then include a couple of major-league baseball games between the dots.

While we were researching our son Joel's choices

in the Midwest, his older brother Ryan had to head back to New York a few days early. He had our itinerary, complete with phone numbers, so that he could call us in case of an emergency. So the remaining four of us settled into the final thousand miles of driving, soaking up the beauty of our country and cheering for whatever team made a fine play.

My wife Kathy was able to finish reading the book on angels she had started before we left. Sure enough, one of her ideas about guardian angels was strongly affirmed by the author. Ever since the boys began driving, Kathy has pictured a guardian angel as a hood ornament on the car. The book used the very same image.

That night a call was waiting for us when we arrived at our motel. Ryan's car had hydroplaned, rolling over 360 degrees before coming to rest against a sheer rock wall. An off-duty policeman happened to be behind Ryan and helped him squeeze out of his demolished car. Save for a bump on his head, he was unhurt. Kathy had been reading the guardian angel-hood ornament chapter at the very moment Ryan had had his accident.

When we drove back to the accident scene, we gasped. The car was crumpled beyond recognition, save for the cocoon of God-protection that had surrounded Ryan in the driver's seat.

There are no words to fully express our gratitude, Lord. Please hear our hearts. —TED NACE

TUE

30

*"YOU . . . HAVE NEGLECTED THE
WEIGHTIER MATTERS OF THE LAW:
JUSTICE AND MERCY AND FAITH. . . .
YOU BLIND GUIDES! YOU STRAIN OUT A
GNAT BUT SWALLOW A CAMEL!"*

—Matthew 23:23–24 (NRSV)

MY ATTITUDE TOWARD THE INSECT WORLD is live and let live. If a bug doesn't bother me, I won't bother it. But early every fall, my equanimity disappears. At that time of year, when I walk on warm afternoons, I'm besieged by tiny flying insects that hang like fog in the sunlit air. They drive me crazy as I hurry along, unable to avoid getting them in my mouth, nose, eyes and hair.

The other day I was walking with a friend who seemed unaffected by the hovering winged plague. Finally, tired of my groans and batting of the air, he said, "They're not doing it on purpose."

"What's that supposed to mean?" I growled.

"It means that they're minding their own business, sunning themselves, doing what they do. They're not trying to annoy you. You're the one plowing through their routine."

Always ready with a retort, I sucked in a deep breath—and then closed my mouth. He was right. For all I knew, their nature impelled them to enjoy the last vestiges of summer in the same way my nature impelled me. His words made me consider my tendency to think that when someone irritated me, it was because they meant to.

That night a telemarketer called when I was in the middle of an important project. I immediately thought, *She should know better. It's too late to disturb people—to disturb me!* Then I caught myself. She was just doing her job. And I could either make it harder or easier for her.

Patient Lord, thank You for the lessons You send me through nature and friends.
—MARCI ALBORGHETTI

MY DIVINE SURPRISES

1 _____

2 _____

3 _____

4 _____

5 _____

6 _____

7 _____

8 _____

9 _____

10 _____

11 _____

12 _____

13 _____

14 _____

15 _____

16 _____

17 _____

18 _____

19 _____

20 _____

21 _____

22 _____

23 _____

24 _____

25 _____

26 _____

27 _____

28 _____

29 _____

30 _____

October

I f . . . thou shalt seek the Lord thy God, thou shalt find him, if thou seek him with all thy heart and with all thy soul.

—*Deuteronomy 4:29*

UNEXPECTED BLESSINGS
LIVING GRATEFULLY

WED
I

*IN EVERY THING GIVE THANKS, FOR THIS
IS THE WILL OF GOD. . . .*
—*I Thessalonians 5:18*

"IN EVERYTHING GIVE THANKS" was the lectionary reading that morning. Could I do this? I wondered, thank God for *everything* for an entire day? I decided to try . . . and promptly forgot the lofty experiment in the thousand things to do for an up-coming trip.

It was one o'clock before I remembered the morning's resolve. Well, I'd make a fresh start in the car on the way to the post office. Surely on this glorious fall afternoon, there'd be no end of things to thank God for. In this elevated mood, I pulled out onto the street . . . where the first thing I saw was a dead squirrel.

What kind of miserable irony was this! Was there any possible thing to thank God for in this all-too-common small tragedy?

I tried being thankful that the poor little animal must have died instantly. But the joy was gone from the day. The pumpkins on the doorsteps, the red of the maple trees—every sight was overlaid with the image of the dead squirrel. And because I could not forget it, God used it to speak to me.

I did not will the death of My creature, He said, *but you can learn from it.*

The squirrel, God told me, had been very busy. Climbing trees, dashing across streets, digging holes, tucking away acorns, so intent on preparing for the future that it was blind to the present. Animals, of course, can't alter behavior programmed over millions of years. *But you have a choice,* God said. *All morning you've reminded Me of a squirrel, so busy getting ready for tomorrow you forgot that the present moment is the only time you can be with Me.*

Busy? Of course I was busy. Remember God in the midst of my busyness? Of course I could. "In everything give thanks"—isn't this God's way of saying, *Whatever is happening right now, that is where I am.*

Bestower of blessing, thank You for this moment.

—ELIZABETH SHERRILL

THU
2

HE THAT LOVETH NOT KNOWETH NOT GOD; FOR GOD IS LOVE. *—I John 4:8*

I'M ALWAYS IMPRESSED BY PEOPLE who seem to know, right off the top of their head, the perfect Scripture for the moment. I've always had a hard time memorizing Bible verses. Okay, maybe it has something to do with the fact that I don't spend enough time trying. Memorization usually means saying a verse to myself a few times. Sometimes I remember to practice by repeating it the next day, but by day three I've usually forgotten it. So instead of a polished verse that comforts someone, I'm left with a vague idea. I end up mumbling, "You know it says somewhere in the Bible . . . I could probably find it for you . . . Well, basically the idea is . . ."

In October, my son Trace started preschool. After the first day, he came home with a note. "Our memory verse is I John 4:8. Please practice."

I stared at the card. *Are they serious? How can I expect Trace to memorize verses when I can't?*

But I wasn't going to let him be the only child who didn't know his verse, so we got to work. I asked Trace his verse in the car, at home, before bed and in the bath. I asked him to share it with Daddy and Grandma and with anyone who would listen. I cheered every time he remembered just one word.

Trace didn't memorize his verse by his next preschool class or by the next week. But we didn't give up, and in two weeks he had it down. Amazingly, so did I!

God, please help me to remember that although perseverance doesn't come easy, it's worth the struggle.

—AMANDA BOROZINSKI

FRI

3

TURN FROM THY FIERCE WRATH, AND REPENT. . . . —Exodus 32:12

CIVIL DISCOURSE in the Internet newsgroup in which I posted seemed to have vanished. People were calling one another names, and the asterisks in words couldn't disguise the rancor behind some of the vitriolic posts. I usually loved being a part of this online community, but sometimes things blew up, and this seemed like one of those times when I really should have gone somewhere else.

But it was during the Days of Awe, the time between Rosh Hashanah and Yom Kippur, when a Jew is supposed to be making amends to people in preparation for the Day of Atonement. So in the middle of the flame war, I posted an apology: "If, during the past year, I have said or done anything that hurt or offended you, either deliberately or through inadvertence, I'm very sorry and I ask you to forgive me." I figured it was likely just to get lost in all the noise.

A couple of minutes later, someone else posted: "I'm really secular and I don't usually do this, but I'm sorry if I've offended anyone."

Over the next hour or so, two more people posted apologies, and those who didn't, stopped posting from anger. The flame war died out and the group moved on to other things.

I've never been reminded so strongly of the power of a single apology.

Lord, please help me always to be an instrument of Your peace. —RHODA BLECKER

SAT 4

AND OUT OF THE GROUND THE LORD GOD FORMED EVERY BEAST OF THE FIELD, AND EVERY FOWL OF THE AIR; AND BROUGHT THEM UNTO ADAM TO SEE WHAT HE WOULD CALL THEM: AND WHATSOEVER ADAM CALLED EVERY LIVING CREATURE, THAT WAS THE NAME THEREOF. —*Genesis 2:19*

ON A CRUISE DOWN UNDER, I purchased six stuffed toy animals, each of them representing animals indigenous to Australia or New Zealand. In Melbourne, I bought a platypus, wombat and echidna; in Hobart, a Tasmanian devil and a Tasmanian tiger; and in Auckland a kiwi. I had planned to give them to my little great-grandnieces, but I changed my mind. Today they sit in a chair in my living room.

I was all set to wrap them up for the mail when I stopped. I was holding the Tasmanian tiger (sometimes called the Tasmanian wolf—the real thing was wolf-size, but the stripes around its back proclaimed it a tiger). Now it seemed to be staring at me. I thought back to the Melbourne Museum, where I had seen a movie filmed in the 1930s. It showed two Tasmanian tigers, the last in captivity. They are gone, extinct.

I sat down and began to think about all the creatures that are endangered everywhere. My mail is stuffed with appeals for African elephants, polar bears, Wyoming wolves. Did not God in the beginning create "great whales, and every living creature that moveth" (Genesis 1:21)? Did He not give them His blessing and say, "Be fruitful, and multiply" (Genesis 1:22) before He turned to the making of man?

"All right, Tasmanian tiger," I said out loud, "I don't know what caused your end, disease or man's hostility, but I'm going to find out how to send a donation to the endangered Tasmanian devil."

Father, the world's creatures need my help.
—VAN VARNER

SUN
5

JESUS SAID UNTO THEM, I AM THE BREAD OF LIFE: HE THAT COMETH TO ME SHALL NEVER HUNGER; AND HE THAT BELIEVETH ON ME SHALL NEVER THIRST.
—*John 6:35*

IT WAS THE SECOND SERVICE that morning, and I was sitting in the pew feeling positively famished. I hadn't eaten since an early dinner the night before. So, sixteen hours later, all I could think about was food.

Just then the deacons started passing the communion loaf around. My eyes opened up like half dollars. It looked so good. Why, it even looked like it was still warm.

Stop it! I told myself. *How dare you think about the Lord's body for anything other than the spiritual nourishment for which it was intended.*

I tried to settle down and prepare myself for communion. At that moment my stomach growled. I opened my eyes, and the bread was being passed in the row in front of me. *Shame on you!* I chided myself. *Remember, this is spiritual food.*

That's when it occurred to me that this Bread of Life was given to us not solely for our souls but for our bodies. It was important to Jesus to feed the five thousand people. Would it be any less important to feed me today?

The loaf of bread was handed to me. I was right. It was delicious—the bread, the moment and the holy meaning.

Thank You, Lord, for the gift of Yourself that satisfies every hunger of body and soul. —DAVE FRANCO

MON
6

"HE DELIVERS AND RESCUES AND PERFORMS SIGNS AND WONDERS IN HEAVEN AND ON EARTH. . . ."
—*Daniel* 6:27 (NAS)

I'D AGREED TO WRITE A BOOK that I had no idea how to write. When the editors made the final critique, my heart sank. Many chapters had to be omitted, but the story had to stay connected and flow smoothly.

Wearily, I lined up all fifty chapters on the floor like a long train, snaking from the front door through the living room and into the kitchen. I flopped down near the front door by chapter one, my head in my hands. "Lord Jesus, You've been my helper so far, but if You don't come through now, I just can't finish this." I added a desperate, ridiculous-sounding request. "Lord, would You lend me about thirty IQ points for, say, four hours?"

Slowly I lifted my head. I felt a new energy, and clear thoughts marched into my mind. Ideas and solutions filed into neat rows. I scooted around on the floor, mumbling, rearranging, pulling out chapters, scribbling in pencil for hours. Finally, I crawled back to the front door and sat there with my heart overflowing with gratitude, my back and head resting against the wall. Even with my eyes closed, I sensed an intense golden light, sweet and encouraging, surrounding me and some of the chapters.

Some people might say that it was just the setting sun hitting a sliver of beveled glass in our front door. But to me, it was a sign from the One Who had rescued me—the job was done.

Lord Jesus, You are the same today, yesterday and forever. —MARION BOND WEST

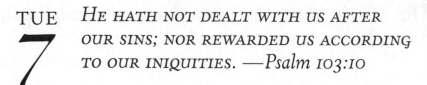

TUE

7

HE HATH NOT DEALT WITH US AFTER OUR SINS; NOR REWARDED US ACCORDING TO OUR INIQUITIES. —Psalm 103:10

I WALK WITH MY EYES downward. I might look deep in thought, but I'm usually considering whether my car is due for an oil change.

My downcast eyes recently discovered an abandoned apple covered with ants. It was a fascinating lesson in nature—how a slew of insects can act like a well-trained army to wrangle some sustenance for the civilians back home.

It occurred to me, from my vantage point up high, that our little blue planet could resemble this apple—four and a half billion of us skittering around the surface, working for our daily bread. I wonder if we appear as disciplined and diligent, or if it looks as chaotic as it sometimes feels.

I also wondered if there were ants down there looking up at me—wondering, perhaps, what kind of being now controlled their fate. I could casually kick the apple into the street, assuring a quick end to their labors, or I could leave the apple where it was, allowing its temporary inhabitants to continue their important work.

I left the apple. In my heart, I'm praying that the One Who holds our little blue apple is more merciful than just. We have a bad history of, for instance, eat-

ing the wrong apple, yet we have been forgiven—
again and again and again.

Lord, have mercy now and forever.
—MARK COLLINS

WED
8

HE WILL BEAUTIFY THE HUMBLE WITH
SALVATION. —*Psalm 149:4 (NKJV)*

LORD, I KNOW I COMPLAIN A LOT, but
today I just want to thank You. Not just for
the things that are right, but also for the things that
are wrong.

Thank You for my limited energy. When I see
the mistakes my high-energy friends make—
overextension, ill temper, neglect of family—I'm glad
You measure out my strength with an eyedropper. I
have enough and not too much.

Thank You for my anxieties, which stalk me like
mosquitoes. Like the check-engine light on my dashboard, they warn me that something needs attention.
When I listen to them, it leads me to prepare, and
preparation brings success.

Thank You for my poor memory. My wife has a
great memory, but I see how she struggles to forget
hurts and failures, how the past crowds into the pres-

ent and ruins her day. I'm glad that things fade quickly for me.

Thank You for my quietness. I envy people who can carry the conversational ball, but that's not me. Hey, all these talkers need someone to listen to them, and that's where I come in. I like to listen, to ask questions, to be supportive.

Thank You for the freedom to make my own mistakes. When I look back on my life, I'm appalled at my stupidity and I'm ashamed of some of my choices. Yet, without the freedom to make those choices, I would never have become who I am today.

Thank You for the aches and pains of aging. Like an early-warning system, they serve to remind me not to overextend myself. They urge me to stop and rest, or to ask for help when I need it, lessons I wish I had learned long ago.

It's good to know, God, that even my afflictions can reflect Your glory. —DANIEL SCHANTZ

THU
9
O JERUSALEM, JERUSALEM . . . HOW OFTEN WOULD I HAVE GATHERED THY CHILDREN TOGETHER, AS A HEN DOTH GATHER HER BROOD UNDER HER WINGS, AND YE WOULD NOT! —*Luke 13:34*

I'VE BEEN THINKING LATELY that there must be some deep inner need to hold on to things when you're age two. Every time we're about to go out the door, Stephen insists on bringing something. It doesn't much matter what he totes along: a cooking pot, a stick, a winter hat in the middle of July. He has to have something with him, no matter where he goes.

Last night Stephen took a pretty heavy tumble. He came running to me, howling. In his arms were a large picture book, two stuffed animals, a fire helmet, several blocks and a large wicker basket.

"Ooh," I said, "that hurts! Do you want me to hold you?" Stephen wailed and nodded. I quickly assessed my options. "I think you're going to have to put some of that down, buddy, before I can pick you up. There isn't room for everything on my lap."

Stephen screeched. He didn't want to let go of his precious things. I knew that something would fall out of his arms if I picked him up and then we'd have hysteria.

The bump on my little guy's forehead was purple, and he clearly wanted comfort. Yet even the promise of snuggling in Mommy's arms wasn't enough to overcome his desire to hold on. He stood there and cried and cried. I stroked his hair as he clung to his possessions—things he hadn't cared about an hour before—and thought how curious it was that he would forsake comfort for these.

Lord, You hold out Your arms to comfort me. Help me set aside the things that prevent me from entering Your joy. —JULIA ATTAWAY

FRI
10

BE JOYFUL IN HOPE, PATIENT IN AFFLICTION, FAITHFUL IN PRAYER.
—*Romans 12:12 (NIV)*

VAST. THE WORD HUNG in my mind, quietly reverberating. Why?

I had been pouring out my disappointment to God over our fruitless search for a house. For months Carol and I had been living with our daughter Kristal in New York State, hoping to buy a home nearby. We looked at more than seventy houses, but none fit what we were looking for.

When we decided to make an offer on one, Kristal and her sister Laurel joined us in a prayer circle, asking God to confirm it by letting our offer be accepted. But next day we learned there had been a higher offer. Disappointed, we continued house hunting.

Yet I couldn't forget that house, a well-maintained four-bedroom Cape Cod that would let Laurel and our granddaughter Kaila have the upstairs to themselves. "Father," I prayed, "if that house is really for us, let it come back on the market." For weeks afterward I kept checking the listings. But it wasn't there.

That's when that surprising word popped into my mind: *vast.*

Yes, God, I thought, *You are vast. Your creation is vast. Your riches are vast. Vast beyond all human comprehension.*

I kept checking the listings. Then *bingo!* The Cape Cod was back on the market; the first sale had fallen through. Excited, we made our offer and within days agreed with the sellers on a price. It is now our new home.

God had supplied what we needed, once again demonstrating that His riches are vast, and they are always available to those who seek Him.

Father, I wish I had a heart of thanks as vast as Your riches. —HAROLD HOSTETLER

SAT
11

THE DESERT AND THE PARCHED LAND WILL BE GLAD; THE WILDERNESS WILL REJOICE AND BLOSSOM. . . .
                                        —*Isaiah 35:1 (NIV)*

UNDERNEATH ONE END of our deck, hidden in toward the back wall of the house, is a hosta plant. Once a year that plant, now almost the size of a bush, puts out glorious white blooms. In the perennial dusk, its flower petals glow white and pure, stark against the gray. But to see it you have to be standing in the backyard, facing at just the right angle. Otherwise, it blooms magnificently with no one but God to see.

I know at least two other hidden "blooms," people providing service seen mostly by God and one or two others. As I write, my cousin's daughter-in-law Dana is in New Orleans, helping Habitat for Humanity build a house. My husband Bill is near Gulfport, Mississippi, hanging sheetrock in a doublewide trailer

with a church team from our town. I don't know
where Dana sleeps, but Bill and the team, working in
unseasonable heat and humidity, are camped out on
the floor of a Sunday school room.

How I admire them and all who go and help, time
after time, task after task, until the broken is repaired
and hope restored.

*Lord, bless those who bloom like my hidden hosta,
perhaps seen clearly only by You.*
                                    —ROBERTA ROGERS

SUN
12
BE SILENT, O ALL FLESH, BEFORE THE
LORD. . . . —*Zechariah 2:13*

AFTER CHURCH ONE October Sunday, I
decided to head for the mountains to savor
the beauty of New Hampshire's brilliant fall foliage
and recapture some of the solitude I had known in
Wyoming.

I forgot to do my math. My Wyoming county had
only forty thousand residents; New Hampshire,
roughly the same size, has 1.3 million—not counting
the thousands of "leaf peepers" who visit. I had barely
entered White Mountain National Forest when I
spotted the miles-long line of vehicles. A wreck? No,
just traffic waiting to exit onto the Kancamagus
Highway scenic drive. On I drove, past endless lines
of cars, trucks and motorcycles parked along the

Interstate, past the two-thousand-foot vertical drop of Canon Mountain. Leaves flamed scarlet, topaz and tangerine, but there was no parking, let alone solitude. I drove on.

Less than an hour later, I exited the Interstate to try some back roads. Sunshine peeking through golden leaves dappled this riverside byway. For at least five miles, I met no other cars. *Peace, at last.*

Refreshed, I arrived in the picturesque town of Littleton and strolled along its charming Main Street. Less than a block away, a covered bridge spanned the Ammonoosuc River. I crossed the bridge, found a patch of grass, sat, and listened to copper leaves rustling overhead and the gurgling river. Passersby smiled, but allowed me my solitude, suffused with the serenity of natural things.

Lord of Creation, season by season Your handiwork restores my soul. —GAIL THORELL SCHILLING

MON
13

AND YOU HAVE BEEN GIVEN FULLNESS IN CHRIST, WHO IS THE HEAD OVER EVERY POWER AND AUTHORITY.
—*Colossians 2:10 (NIV)*

"CONGRATULATIONS!" a co-worker called out when I arrived. It was my first day in my new position as director of broadcasting.

"Thanks!" I replied with a smile.

I walked down the hall to my office, turning to stare at the large production calendar on the wall. Every day was packed with meetings, interviews and tapings. My smile faded a bit. During the job interview, I was sure I could do it. But now, with a staff to lead, a budget to manage and shows to produce, I was nervous.

It reminded me of cheerleading tryouts in junior high school. "Number eight!" the lady had called out. I jumped up and ran to the middle of the gym. I was being called back to perform one more cheer.

We'd practiced the routine all week in our groups, with each group leader beginning the cheer. But this time there was no appointed leader. We stood there, looking down the line, waiting for someone to start. Then I took a deep breath and stepped forward. "Ready? Okay!" I shouted. "Go for it, Tigers, hear us roar . . ."

The next day I jumped off the school bus and ran all the way to the gym. The names of the new cheerleaders were posted on the door. I scanned the list quickly. I'd made it! "That last cheer you did was a tiebreaker," the cheerleading sponsor said. "You won because you took the lead."

Now years later, it was time to take the lead again. I walked over to the production calendar and wrote across the top in big red letters: "Go for it!"

Jesus, help me to remember that the most important thing I can do as a leader is to follow You.
—MELODY BONNETTE

GIVE US THIS DAY
THE PROMISE OF SPRING

TUE
14

BUT IF WE HOPE FOR WHAT WE DO NOT YET HAVE, WE WAIT FOR IT PATIENTLY.
—*Romans 8:25 (NIV)*

"WE WANT TO COME PLANT some tulip and daffodil bulbs around your house so you'll have blossoms in springtime," a friend told me over the phone one cool autumn morning. I had been standing in front of the mirror, drawing eyebrows on my face. Since losing my hair because of chemotherapy for my Stage 4 ovarian cancer, this was a daily task.

I stammered into the phone, stunned by the generosity of this beautiful gesture.

"You just name the day in the next couple of weeks," she continued. "We'll be there, and we're bringing lunch."

This friend knew how I feared the next season in my cancer journey. Soon I would go off chemotherapy and enter the unpredictable season of "wait-and-see-whether-the-cancer-returns."

So we named a date for bulb planting. And they came, on a beautiful blue-sky day: three friends, looking like a trio of Johnny Appleseeds, wearing blue jeans, with hoes in hand and several bags of bulbs and mulch and bone meal tucked under their arms. They placed more than two hundred bulbs into the ground around my house. Then they spread out a lunch of tortilla soup, bread, cheese and fruit on the patio table, and we all sat down.

"I'm not nearly nice enough to deserve all this," I said, overwhelmed by their sacrifice of time and effort.

"Hush, shush," they said. "Let's pray." And so we did.

Thank You, God, for the gift of this glorious day to be together, digging in Your dirt, to ensure that there will be blossoms in springtime. —CAROL KUYKENDALL

WED
15

YEA, THE SPARROW HATH FOUND A HOUSE, AND THE SWALLOW A NEST FOR HERSELF, WHERE SHE MAY LAY HER YOUNG. . . . —*Psalm 84:3*

WEEK BY WEEK I FLY around the living room, hurriedly flicking a duster, eager to get a bothersome job done. Not today. Today I have the house to myself, and I have decided to play some of my favorite records and turn my dusting into a leisurely act of loving remembrance.

I start with our ebony grand piano, purchased from an estate sale a few years after John and I were married. I slowly dust the keys and thank God for the music that has been the very soul of all our celebrations. Familiar faces dance before me, and I smile and ask the Lord to bless them.

I have to stand on a chair to reach the shelves cluttered with books. "When are you going to weed them out and put them into categories?" my husband growls from time to time. I raise my eyebrows and shrug my shoulders, and my heart whispers, *Never!* The clutter of my books is a familiar part of me; I run my fingers over them as a loving touch of friend to friend.

Afternoon shadows flicker dancing leaves on the carpet; I sit in the big armchair, hug my knees and revel in the moment. The shelves of art and bric-a-brac are next. Vases brought from China, with floral designs and figures and golden dragon handles. They are stuck down with earthquake-safe gum. Suddenly I chuckle. On the shelf is a yellow Hot Wheels car. My five-year-old grandson has left his mark. I dust the car and leave it there.

The best is saved for last. I go to the mantle on the center of which is a Hummel Madonna and Child. At a time when money was tight, my mother and I splurged on her as the "every occasion" gift we'd share through that year.

The music has stopped; my dusting is done.

Thank You, Lord, for the comfort of the little things that make my house my home. —FAY ANGUS

READER'S ROOM

IT ABSOLUTELY amazes me how many
people only pray about large subjects. I love
that I can thank God:

    a. for saving me from an accident.
    b. that I didn't drop mustard on my
       blouse.
    c. that I made it in time to a meeting.
    d. that I didn't spill the Eucharistic cup
       this time as lay assistant.
    e. that I didn't fall when I stumbled.
    f. that I kept my mouth shut about

    ——————————————.
    (FILL IN THE BLANK.)

    g. that the stain came out.
            —*Linda Hunter, Louisville, Kentucky*

THU
16

THE LORD WILL SUSTAIN HIM ON HIS
SICKBED AND RESTORE HIM FROM HIS BED
OF ILLNESS. —*Psalm 41:3 (NIV)*

QUEASY STOMACH. Headache. Chills. I'm
sick.

Why today, Lord? I felt like a million bucks when
I went to bed. I've been taking vitamins by the hand-
fuls and eating right. I have a million things to do and

getting sick wasn't on my list. The best thing is just to pretend like it's not happening. *Sick? I'm not sick.*

Uh-oh. It's worse when I stand. Let me just take a minute. I need to pull myself together. I'm sure I'll feel better after I take a shower and grab something to eat.

Ugh. The thought of food . . . maybe I can get some liquid into me. I might be able to handle that. But just a couple of sips. I feel . . . awful.

How am I going to get through this day? Meetings. Deadlines. E-mails. Maybe I can work from home, do it all online. But the thought of even logging on makes me want to crawl back under the covers.

Now my head is really pounding. My stomach is doing cartwheels. My wife Julee takes a look at me. "Not good," she says and points me back toward the bed, which appears to be my one and only destination today. I collapse facedown on the sheets.

Lord, this is not fair. The last thing I need is to be sick. Surely You know that. Why today? What will people think?

They'll think you're sick, the answer comes to me. *And that's okay.*

Is it? I think about this and suddenly feel the nearness of God. I sense I will be praying a lot today. I will not be separated from Him by PowerPoint presentations or strategy sessions or budget meetings. I will give myself up to His care, hard as that is for me to do sometimes.

Funny, getting closer to God wasn't on my list today.

Teach me, Lord, to find every opportunity, even in sickness, to draw nearer to You.
                                —EDWARD GRINNAN

A SECOND THANK-YOU
THANK YOU FOR THE GIFT OF WORDS

FRI
17

IN THE BEGINNING WAS THE WORD, AND THE WORD WAS WITH GOD, AND THE WORD WAS GOD. —*John 1:1 (NIV)*

MY SISTER REBEKKAH and I had attended three funerals in less than a week. Each was a wonderful celebration of a life, but it bothered us that all the accolades were given *after* the person had died. "Let's tell each other what we admire about each other *now*," Rebekkah suggested.

She started. "You're the most generous person I know." A tear streamed down her cheek. "You're a great bargain hunter and, oh, what a dog lover!"

It was my turn. "You're honest, Rebekkah. And such a hard worker." I remembered the time she'd hurled herself in front of a moving truck to keep it from hitting me. "And, of course, loyal to the very end."

I was on a roll. *Why stop with my sister?* I decided.

So that week, whenever I had a few minutes with a friend, I talked about my recent funeral experiences. And before I knew it, we were sharing feelings that might otherwise have gone unexpressed.

Those thank-yous felt so good that I followed them up with notes on old-fashioned stationery. I like to think of those second thank-yous being unfolded again and again on down days when a friend's heart needs the lift that, even in these days of e-mail, only handwritten correspondence can bring. They're the best buy ever for forty-one cents. I should know; my sister said that I'm a great bargain hunter.

Lord Jesus, thank You for the gift of a letter from a friend. And thank You again for Your Word, Your love letter to each of us. —ROBERTA MESSNER

SAT
18

IN ALL THY WAYS ACKNOWLEDGE HIM, AND HE SHALL DIRECT THY PATHS.
—Proverbs 3:6

IT WAS ONE OF THOSE perfect fall days when the sky is so blue it seems painted. My husband and I decided to go for a walk on the Appalachian Trail. We'd never actually been to the trailhead, but it looked easy enough to find on the brochure. Unfortunately, an unmarked road had us driving in circles for half an hour until we stumbled upon the parking area.

"Well, we're here," Tony said.

I nodded. The tips of the trees were just beginning to turn hues of crimson. We parked our car in the empty lot and marveled at our luck. We'd have the trail to ourselves on what was probably the last warm day of the season.

We started on the winding path that led us over hills and deep into the woods. A little while into our walk, confronted with a big hill and another trail, we veered to the left. As we walked and talked, I noticed a white trail marker fixed to a huge maple tree.

"I thought we were on the yellow trail," I said.

"No, we were on the white," Tony insisted.

We walked for an hour or so on the white trail. I was starting to get hungry. "We should have brought something to eat."

We walked awhile in silence.

"What if this trail doesn't loop back to our car?" I asked.

"Relax," Tony said.

We stayed on the trail, our pace quickening. Soon we reached a clearing, and there, right in front of us, was our car. Exhausted, we got in.

On the drive home, I couldn't help feeling disappointed. Instead of enjoying the crunch of the leaves, the smell of approaching winter and the quiet talks we only seem to have on walks in the woods, I was focused on my fear that we'd lost our way. *Next time*, I told myself, *I'll trust the path.*

Lord, give me faith in the path You've marked out for me and let me enjoy every moment of my walk with You. —SABRA CIANCANELLI

SUN
19

LOVE NEVER ENDS. . . .
—*I Corinthians 13:8* (RSV)

EVERY YEAR MY MOM OPENS UP *Daily Guideposts* with anticipation—and dread. She enjoys reading the entries of all the contributors, but she makes a point of finding my devotionals first and telling me how much she likes them.

But dread, you ask? She's afraid I'm going to write about an incident when I was a kid and she got upset—a momentary lapse, let's say, in her parenting skills. So let me see if I can banish the dread once and for all.

Mom, I can't even begin to thank you for all the things you did right as a parent. You were patient, enthusiastic, fun and full of praise. Thanks for teaching us how to play tennis, write thank-you notes, listen to music and be a supportive friend. If we all have such good friends today, it's because we grew up watching you be such a good friend. If we all have good marriages, it's because we grew up seeing how you and Dad talked through your differences. You were a great Sunday school teacher, homeroom volunteer, art museum docent and general organizer of a house with four children going in a thousand different directions.

I've asked Andrew, our editor, to slot this on your birthday, and when you see it I hope you'll know I mean every word. Happy birthday, Mom. You're the best!

Dear God, let me never grow tired of telling the people I love how much they're loved. —RICK HAMLIN

MON
20

"*I WILL ALSO GIVE HIM A WHITE STONE WITH A NEW NAME WRITTEN ON IT, KNOWN ONLY TO HIM WHO RECEIVES IT.*" —*Revelation 2:17 (NIV)*

MY FRIEND SHEILA INVITED ME to lunch to discuss what wasn't happening in her career. She needed to increase her income, but nothing she tried had worked out. She felt a sense of panic because her son had headed off to college and she'd promised to cover his expenses. With nothing more profitable on the horizon, she took on a teaching assignment while continuing to look around. I encouraged her as best I could.

The next time we met, Sheila was beaming and I was certain she had good news to tell me. She announced that she had changed her name. She noticed in the Bible that every time God was ready to do a mighty work in someone's life, He changed the person's name: Abram became Abraham, Sarai became Sarah, Simon became Peter, Saul became Paul. Sheila announced that her new name was Sheila the Faithful.

Amazingly, although her career didn't progress until after her son graduated from college, she was able to meet every single tuition payment.

Sheila inspired me so much that I decided to change my name too. I thought about becoming Debbie, God's Patient Daughter, but that just seemed to be asking for trouble. Debbie the Generous had a nice sound to it; I was sure a generous heart would be pleasing to God. Then, as I was praying for my son Dale, burdened by some of his recent decisions, it came to me: God was asking me to trust Him. So I released Dale into God's hands and became Debbie the Trusting.

Thank You, Jesus, for special friends whose examples of walking in faith inspire me to walk along with them.
—DEBBIE MACOMBER

TUE
21

TEST ME IN THIS AND SEE IF I DON'T OPEN UP HEAVEN ITSELF TO YOU AND POUR OUT BLESSINGS BEYOND YOUR WILDEST DREAMS.
—*Malachi 3:10 (THE MESSAGE)*

BEING THE NEWEST MEMBER of the staff of a large magazine was tough. Despite the kindness of my new co-workers, I felt the need to prove myself. I worked hard to make sure every word in my articles rolled smoothly into the next. I struggled to compile detailed lists of shots that I wanted our photographers to capture. I hustled through clerical duties, always making sure my expense reports were in on time. I wanted to be perfect.

Six months into the job, I traveled with the photographer for a story about fall color in the Smoky Mountains. Each spot was ready for him—models waiting, blankets arranged over back porches and vegetables prediced for the kitchen shots. Our first two days were a breeze, but on the third, the skies opened and rain poured, trapping the models, two cabin consultants and one unhappy photographer in two vans for the duration of the shoot. *Fall color is so fleeting,* I thought. *Oh God, why would You let all my careful planning go to waste?*

One of the cabin owners seemed to sense my frustration. "You know," she said, "this rain will rehydrate the trees, making for an extra splash of color. Come back next week, you'll see." We did, and she was right. The reds were richer and the yellows bolder— perfect for the photographer.

God, help me to trade my vocabulary for Yours, and redefine misfortunes as blessings that are just waiting to bloom. —ASHLEY JOHNSON

WED
22
SHARE EACH OTHER'S TROUBLES AND PROBLEMS, AND SO OBEY OUR LORD'S COMMAND. —*Galatians 6:2 (TLB)*

YEARS AGO WHEN I WAS a single parent of four, I had a number of unhappy, stressed-out, over-worked days and weeks. But luckily I learned a wonderful truth from a friend. "Take time for yourself," she encouraged. "Go to a movie, have your nails done, take a class, go to the library and read magazines. Be good to yourself and then you'll be able to be good to your family, your boss and all the people who depend on you."

So I learned that we humans were not created to spend every waking moment in the service of others. We are not meant to just be someone's servant, husband, mother, caretaker, or employee twenty-four hours a day, seven days a week. We are meant to belong to ourselves and God and then become absolutely the best person God intended when He breathed life into us. Only then can we be good for others.

Say, isn't it time for a break? How about a cup of tea and a good book? Your family will love the new you. Mine did.

Father, help me remember that my number one responsibility is to be happy and fulfilled in my own body, mind and soul, so I can also be the best I can possibly be for the others in my life.

—PATRICIA LORENZ

THU
23
LET NOT YOUR HEART BE TROUBLED. . . .
—John 14:1

AFTER MY CARDIOLOGIST recommended that I take a heart test, I learned it would take days, maybe a week, to get his report. In the meantime, the possibilities kept turning in my mind. *Another angioplasty? Open-heart surgery?*

It began to get the best of me until I remembered my days as a young man with Walgreen Drugstores. Back then, when they had soda fountains, I worked in one as a waiter. I learned to make milkshakes, hot fudge sundaes and tuna-salad sandwiches. After the first few days, I felt at home—except when carrying cups of coffee to the diners. Protocol was to serve it in a dry saucer; spills were poor form.

Try as I might, I couldn't walk across the room without spilling some. It was embarrassing. I would carefully watch the coffee as I walked, only to see it dribble over. The more I tried, the more my hands shook.

A co-worker helped me out. "Don't look at the coffee," she advised. "Focus on where you're going. The cup will take care of itself."

Her advice didn't make sense to me, but in desperation I gave it a try. It took all my willpower to look straight ahead. But to my relief, when I set down the cup, the saucer was dry.

By thinking so much about my heart test, I was letting the "What ifs?" spill into my mind. So instead of dwelling on them, I concentrated on my work and the tasks of the day and trusted in God. And like that cup of coffee, the test results came out okay.

Lord, my life is never free of worries. Remind me that focusing on the positive cuts them down to size.
— RICHARD SCHNEIDER

FRI
24

BLESSED ARE THE PEACEMAKERS: FOR THEY SHALL BE CALLED THE CHILDREN OF GOD. —Matthew 5:9

LAST YEAR THE CHILDREN at my church decided to erect a "peace pole." I had never heard of a peace pole, but I soon found out that there are more than 250,000 of them worldwide. And while they differ in size and material, all the poles display the same prayer, written in a different language on each of its four sides: MAY PEACE PREVAIL ON EARTH.

The kids saved pennies for months to pay for the wood. A talented craftsman in our congregation did the actual work. And on a sunny Sunday, the peace pole was placed near the entrance to our church. The children chose stones from a pile at the end of the sidewalk. One by one, they wrote their names on the stones and lovingly placed them at the base of the peace pole.

World peace is a lofty goal, one that seems to be

undermined daily by conflicts in every part of the globe. But I believe that the power of one dedicated individual—joined with another and then another—is a force to be reckoned with. And I know for certain that two dozen children are going forward to work and pray for peace. It's written in stone.

I pray for peace, God. And I pray for the courage and wisdom to work toward making that prayer a reality.
—MARY LOU CARNEY

EDITOR'S NOTE: A month from today, Monday, November 24, is Guideposts' fourteenth annual Thanksgiving Day of Prayer. Please plan to join all the members of our Guideposts family in prayer on this very special day. Send your prayer requests (and a picture, if you can) to Guideposts Prayer Fellowship, PO Box 8001, Pawling, NY 12564.

SAT
25

LORD, THOU PRESERVEST MAN AND BEAST. —Psalm 36:6

IT WAS A GLORIOUS DAY, and my family was gathered at my parents' house for a visit with my grandparents. My six-year-old son Harrison and my three-year-old niece Abby were playing in a pile of leaves in the front yard. I watched Harrison frolicking, and a dark cloud of worry fell over me. *How can I possibly give him everything he needs? Will he survive being shuffled from my house to his mom's? Is he doing all right?*

"Big Dad," Harrison asked my father, "why are the leaves still sticking to that tree?" All the other trees, except one, had lost their leaves.

"That's a red oak," my grandfather interjected. "We used to say that God made red oaks for the squirrels."

"Why?" Harrison shot back.

"In the autumn the squirrels make their nests from leaves, but when the cold winds come, sometimes parts of their nests blow away. If you watch, you'll see squirrels coming to the red oak to gather new leaves throughout the winter when all the other leaves have disappeared."

"Hey, Abby," Harrison yelled as he ran toward the red oak, "come over here and look at this tree! God made it specially 'cause He loves squirrels so much!"

I looked up at the blue sky and thanked God for this great note of reassurance. If He had planned ahead for the squirrels, then I was confident His plans were laid for Harrison and me and each one of His children. With a great "Whoopee!" I grabbed Harrison and made a dash for the leaf pile.

Father, let me live in the reality of Your love, which reaches out far beyond my knowing. —BROCK KIDD

SUN
26

SHARE WITH GOD'S PEOPLE WHO ARE IN NEED. PRACTICE HOSPITALITY.
—*Romans 12:13 (NIV)*

FOR MORE YEARS than I can count, my wife Shirley and I have taken part in the Church World Service-sponsored CROP (Communities Responding to Overcome Poverty) Hunger Walk to raise money to help stop hunger in our community and around the world.

My mother conducted her own version of CROP when I was growing up. We lived a couple of blocks from the Wabash railroad tracks and hosted people passing through town regularly. The hobos who rode boxcars in those days always seemed to find their way to our house. Someone once told me that migrants would leave a mark on trees or sidewalks identifying a place where hungry people would be fed, but I could never find any such mark.

Mama never turned anyone away. It was the same when friends would show up unexpectedly around dinnertime. "Put an extra leaf in the table," she would whisper to my brother, my sister or me, and then she would stretch whatever she was fixing—stew or tuna fish casserole or pot roast—to accommodate the number of plates. She didn't have to coach us to pass up the potatoes if they were in short supply or go easy on the gravy. We knew the routine, even to the point of fibbing that we weren't hungry.

The Bible often commands us to practice hospitality, suggesting in one place that by doing so we might have "entertained angels unawares" (Hebrews 13:2). Whenever I'm inclined to be less than generous with the bounty God has provided, I remind myself of something my mother told me as a child, maybe when she was feeding strangers on the back porch: "No kindness, no matter how small, goes unnoticed by God."

> *Lord, school us in the doing of kindly acts,*
> *Regardless of station or side of the tracks.*
> —FRED BAUER

MON
27

AND I WILL BRING THE BLIND BY A WAY THAT THEY KNEW NOT; I WILL LEAD THEM IN PATHS THAT THEY HAVE NOT KNOWN: I WILL MAKE DARKNESS LIGHT BEFORE THEM, AND CROOKED THINGS STRAIGHT. THESE THINGS WILL I DO UNTO THEM, AND NOT FORSAKE THEM. —Isaiah 42:16

MY DAUGHTER LANEA is taking an improvisation class. It is the first time that she has been onstage in more than ten years. Lanea is poised, quick-witted, funny and enjoys speaking to crowds—just not onstage.

Being onstage, unable to control or predict how things will go, is terrifying for her. While performing in high school, she fell off a platform, injured her back and severely bruised her feelings. "I feel uncomfortable," she now moans about the workshop she's taking.

"But you signed up to be uncomfortable. No one made you do it," I tell her.

"I know, but I don't feel safe."

That's what growth is, isn't it? I think to myself as I watch her agonize. It's risking that first dive off the diving board; it's registering for classes and checking into that first dorm room; it's boarding the plane for an unknown destination, choosing to travel a way that we don't know.

Then Lanea's frown rolls away and she smiles, talking about a skit she was in. She is taller than I am now. I reach up to touch her face. "I'm so proud of you," I say.

Lord, help me to open my eyes and see and try things that are new and frightening to me.

—SHARON FOSTER

TUE
28

A MERRY HEART MAKETH A CHEERFUL COUNTENANCE. . . . —Proverbs 15:13

OUR DAUGHTER ELIZABETH joined a children's choir that rehearses twice a week in Manhattan's Theater District. So every Tuesday and Thursday evening I pick her up and we share the subway ride home. At twelve, she's exhibiting all the signs of a teenager-in-training, and getting her into a conversation can be a challenge.

"Elizabeth, how was choir practice?"

"Fine."

"How was math group?"

"Fine."

"How was school?"

Silence.

"Is something bothering you?"

Silence.

"Would you like to play Scary Pirate?"

"Sure!"

Elizabeth invented Scary Pirate a few years ago. The scary pirate asks questions, and the prisoner tries to answer enough of them to avoid walking the Planck length (an incredibly tiny length that's approximately 1.6×10^{-35} meters in physics-speak).

"Har, har, har, ye matey!" Elizabeth says. "What's the quadratic formula?"

It's been a very long time since I was in high school, and math was far from my best subject. "I don't know," I say.

"But, Dad, I told you yesterday."

She's right; she did tell me yesterday. And for all of fifteen minutes I remembered it, but not today.

"Okay, Dad, you have one wrong. Har, har, har, ye matey! What's the cosine of forty-five degrees?"

So it goes, one algebra or trigonometry or geometry question after another. If I'm very lucky, I'll remember an answer from a question she's asked before, but most of the time she stumps me. It's lucky the Planck length is so small, or else I'd have worn out a couple of pairs of shoes walking it on all those Tuesday and Thursday nights.

By the time we get home, Elizabeth is smiling. She may still be a keeps-her-feelings-close-to-the-vest pre-teen, but she's a happy one. And even though I'm acutely aware of my educational deficiencies, I'm a happy dad.

Lord, thank You for giving even the intensest preteen a sense of fun. And please help me to remember the quadratic formula. —ANDREW ATTAWAY

WED
29
FOR BY HIM WERE ALL THINGS CREATED, THAT ARE IN HEAVEN, AND THAT ARE IN EARTH . . . ALL THINGS WERE CREATED BY HIM, AND FOR HIM. —*Colossians 1:16*

WHEN I MOVED FROM ALASKA to Minnesota, I was often asked, "Don't you miss the mountains?"

I always answered, "No, I can pull them from my memory anytime. Minnesota wasn't created to have mountains, so I don't look for them. Instead, I enjoy what's here: the fields, the oak trees, the herons and egrets on the lakes and ponds, the changing sky, the magnificent thunderstorms. Embracing how each place was made to be is my secret for living anywhere."

After several years of this standard Q & A, I've started asking myself, *What if I could extend this attitude to people?* It seems so simple. Don't look for what's not there; instead, enjoy what is. Find the richness that already belongs to them.

With some people, it's easy to see and appreciate who they were created to be. With others, it seems an impossible task. But then God beckons me: *Come on, keep looking for things to like in this person. I've put them there.*

Each person and place has a unique topography. From Alaska to Minnesota, from family to neighbors to teammates or co-workers to "me, myself and I," the key to getting along is in accepting the lay of the land.

Lord Jesus, how is it my eyes strain after what isn't there in places and people, and overlook the good that is? Help me to see them as You do. —CAROL KNAPP

THU
30

SO TEACH US TO NUMBER OUR DAYS THAT WE MAY GET A HEART OF WISDOM.
—Psalm 90:12 (RSV)

MY FATHER QUITE LITERALLY counted his days—27,834—and died with a heart of wisdom. "He had no regrets," said a family friend at the memorial service, unintentionally giving me a magnifying glass through which I could see all too clearly my own.

One regret eclipses them all: I gave my children the wrong father. And over the years, while counselors, doctors and ministers tried to help me analyze why, the fact remains that I did, and there are days when I find myself paralyzed by regret.

But then last month Evelyn Rose, my first granddaughter after four grandsons, arrived. I looked into her face and beheld a soul untouched by regret, with a whole life stretching before her. She was an empty book, a clean slate upon which she could write anything. *Dear God, don't let her reach middle age burdened by regret.* An odd sort of optical illusion occurred, for I began to see my face in hers—seeing myself as God does. I, too, have a whole calendar of days stretching before me, a clean slate upon which I can write anything.

Evelyn Rose was born on September 28. In a way, so was her grandmother. In the days that followed, I turned a corner. I joined a new church, made new friends, had my first party in my new home with a group of writers living within ten minutes of me and took under my wing a single mother whose struggles eclipse my own.

It won't be said at my funeral that I had no regrets, but it can be said God let me begin again.

Dear Lord, teach me to count my days—19,878 so far—making each one wisely count for You.
—BRENDA WILBEE

FRI
31

How mighty are his wonders! . . .
—*Daniel 4:3*

MY STOMACH GROWLED. It would be hours before I could go home and eat. I had mistakenly spent my last bit of money before getting a bite after school. *Maybe I should just go home now,* I thought as I rubbed my belly. But my high school gymnastics team was having a meeting to discuss new uniforms and upcoming competitions, and there was no way I could miss it. Coach made it very clear that we were all to attend.

I strolled down Columbus Avenue, passing street vendors selling sandwiches and fresh bagels. "I'm hungry!" I whined to God.

Seconds later, a vendor caught my eye and smiled. I smiled back. "Here," he said, extending a bagel with cream cheese wrapped in cellophane.

"No," I said, waving my hand, "I'm okay."

He extended his hand even further. "Here . . . for you . . . take it."

I took the bagel and looked at him with utter disbelief and gratitude. "Thanks," I said, walking away as if I were in a strange dream. It was a little miracle just for me, manna from heaven. With each bite, I was awed by God's power, touched by His love and grateful for His wonderful gifts: my family, my home, the kind street vendor and my delicious New York City bagel with cream cheese.

Thank You, God. Thank You. —KAREN VALENTIN

MY DIVINE SURPRISES

1 _____

2 _____

3 _____

4 _____

5 _____

6 _____

7 _____

8 _____

9 _____

10 _____

11 _____

12 _____

13 _____

14 _____

15 _____

16 _____

17 _____

18 _____

19 _____

20 _____

21 _____

22 _____

23 _____

24 _____

25 _____

26 _____

27 _____

28 _____

29 _____

30 _____

31 _____

November

Give thanks unto the Lord, call upon his name, make known his deeds among the people. —*I Chronicles 16:8*

SAT *ALL THE SAINTS SALUTE YOU.*
1   —*II Corinthians 13:13*

Oh, when the saints go marching in
Oh, when the saints go marching in.

THOSE WERE SOME OF THE LINES of a song that drove me crazy. Not really crazy, maybe, but at least I was irritated. Back in the 1950s, after our Monday-night *Guideposts* editorial meetings, we would repair to an all-night coffee shop where Len LeSourd, our editor, would unwind by urging the staff to join him in a songfest. Each night you can bet "When the Saints" was sung. I thought that Len was making a fool of himself when he roused us all to sing the song loudly, passionately and, as far as I was concerned, unendingly.

It took Hurricane Katrina to change my mind. When the winds and waters rose against New Orleans, I felt an aching sympathy for that classic old city. I recalled it as a place nurtured on saints, where churches, schools, streets are named for St. Jerome or St. Anne or St. Ignatius Loyola. There is a Bayou St. John, and even the football team is called the Saints. Take your pick, saints are everywhere there, but it was a New Orleans-born friend who set me straight on one thing when I caught her mumbling "Oh, when the saints. . . ."

"Stop," I said. I explained my loathing. Colleen took immediate, fervent umbrage.

"Have you no feeling for New Orleans?" she said.

"That's our song. It's a gospel tune that goes back for eons. You can play it as a somber hymn or jazzed up as a victory march." She was getting wound up. "I learned it as a school kid. We all did. For that matter, I'll sing it now"—which she did, loudly and passionately.

Okay, Colleen, you win. And Len too. Listen to me as I sing. . .

> Lord, I want to be in that number
> When the saints go marching in.
>   —VAN VARNER

SUN 2

"HAVE YOU EATEN FRUIT FROM THE TREE I WARNED YOU ABOUT?" "YES," ADAM admitted, "BUT IT WAS THE WOMAN YOU GAVE ME WHO BROUGHT ME SOME, AND I ATE IT." —*Genesis 3:11–12 (TLB)*

HUSBANDS AND WIVES make terrific scapegoats because they are so handy. My wife and I were enjoying Sunday dinner with old friends from college days. Our hostess Carolyn was filling water glasses from a glass pitcher, when suddenly she bumped her glass and it fell over. A river of water raced across the table, and her husband Larry leaped up to dodge the flow. Carolyn blurted out, "Larry, this is your fault. You filled this pitcher too full." Larry calmly replied, "Carolyn, the moment I saw that water coming toward me, I said to myself, *Larry, this is your fault.*"

We had a good laugh and a good conversation about blaming spouses. Later, I thought how easy it is to blame a mate or even a marriage itself for problems that have nothing to do with either.

When my wife is upset with something her principal said, guess who takes the heat? (Hint: It's not the principal.)

When my credit card is way over the limit, it leads to marital stress because Sharon figures our finances. She needs to know what to expect from me.

Fix the real problem and you fix the marriage, it seems to me. Does it really matter who spilled the water? Or is it more important to get a towel and clean it up?

Help me, Lord, to take more responsibility for my own actions and not to blame the fine woman You gave me to bless my life. —DANIEL SCHANTZ

UNEXPECTED BLESSINGS
ACCEPTING AUTUMN

MON
3

CAST ME NOT OFF IN THE TIME OF OLD AGE. . . . —*Psalm 71:9*

FOR YEARS MY FRIEND MARCIA had raved about the splendid grounds at the palace of

La Granja de San Ildefonso in the mountains near Segovia: patterned flowerbeds, elaborate fountains, tree-lined avenues, a spectacular rose garden. "Be sure to go in summer!" she would insist.

So it was a disappointment when my husband John and I didn't get to this part of Spain till mid-November. "No point in visiting a garden when nothing's growing," I moped to John. But with a couple of hours to wait while he had our rental car serviced, I decided to take a walk there anyway.

There wasn't a soul around as I set out, the only sound my footsteps on the gravel path. The lilac hedge on either side (*This must have been beautiful!*) held only brown seed husks. In a dry fountain, bronze nymphs frolicked above a waterless basin carpeted with dead leaves.

I stopped and looked again. The fallen leaves were scarlet, like flaming stars against the white marble! Ahead, twin rows of elms soared heavenward, the architecture of bare trunks and branches stunning against the sky. Through the leafless woods, I traced the silhouette of a mountain range. Against a stone outcrop, a cluster of red berries was like a shout of joy.

Not the right season for a visit? True, there were no flowers, no green leaves. Here was a sterner, vaster beauty, a beauty of essences. What if I were to embrace November days, I thought, not only in outer nature, but in myself? What if, as I entered my eighties, I learned not just to accept the wrinkles and the slower steps, but to glory in them!

Bestower of blessing, grant me the grace of gratitude for all Your seasons. —ELIZABETH SHERRILL

TUE

4

THE AUTHORITIES THAT EXIST HAVE BEEN ESTABLISHED BY GOD.
—*Romans 13:1 (NIV)*

THE COST OF A PROSTHETIC LIMB is nearly equal to that of a luxury sedan, so when I was growing up my parents relied on health insurance to help pay the cost. But during my junior year of high school, my dad's work-sponsored insurance program changed their coverage so that my family would be responsible for nearly all of my prosthetics expenses.

This was far beyond what we could afford, so I did some research about the level of insurance contribution required by state law. After learning that my type of prosthetic did not have to be covered, I contacted our delegate from the state house of representatives and asked if he would help me. He agreed, and together we proposed legislation to require adequate insurance coverage for amputees.

I was asked to testify on behalf of our bill at the state capitol. I stood behind a podium and explained that there was simply no way my family could afford to pay for my artificial leg if the law didn't change. The vote was unanimous—against the bill. I left the capitol, disappointed in the whole process. It seemed like such a waste of time after all the work we had done—all for nothing.

But when it came time for me to get a new prosthetic a few months later, my dad called our insurance agent to see if anything had changed. It had. In fact, they offered to pay almost all of it!

"Why did the coverage increase?" asked my dad.

"We heard there was pending legislation to increase the state minimum," replied the agent. "So we decided to just go ahead and change our coverage."

Lord, You are above all earthly authorities. Thank You for Your Providence. —JOSHUA SUNDQUIST

WED

5

How beautiful are thy feet with shoes. . . . —Song of Solomon 7:1

FOR THE FIRST TIME, I wished I really *did* have two left feet.

It was one of those glorious, this-weather-can't-last autumn days: sunshine, unseasonably warm temperatures. As I left for work this morning, I grabbed a pair of tennis shoes from the old shoes I keep in the garage, so I could go for a walk at the lake during my lunch hour. I announced my intention to my co-workers on arriving. I watched the clock. Finally, at noon sharp, I said, "I'll be back in one glorious hour!"

I hurried to the car and pulled my tennis shoes out

of the backseat. I slid on the left one and then . . . realized I had another left one in my hand. *What?* I remembered—I had *two* pairs of old tennis shoes in the garage, and I'd only picked up the left ones! I sat in the front seat, feeling the sun on my face and on my shoeless right foot.

Disappointed, I trudged back into the office. "Don't ask!" I said as my co-workers looked up. But as I thought about it, it was just too funny to keep to myself. Soon we were all laughing at my "sole" problem, at how walking that day was a "feet" I wouldn't achieve.

The puns got worse, but I felt better. There is more than one kind of sunshine, and being able to laugh with friends (even at yourself!) can brighten any afternoon.

Help me, Lord, to find humor in frustration. And always to put my left—I mean, best—foot forward for You. —MARY LOU CARNEY

THU
6

REMEMBER THE FORMER THINGS OF OLD. . . . —*Isaiah 46:9*

LAURA, MY WIFE'S MOTHER, passed away last fall. She died peacefully at eighty-six, after a full life, married happily for more than fifty years, so her passing seemed right and proper. Which isn't to say that her death was easy for us. What I found most difficult—apart from the grief—were the many times that my wife had to be absent from home, visiting Laura in the hospice and then settling the estate. Carol did her best to make these prolonged absences as smooth as possible, but inevitably they threw the family off balance. More than once I found myself staring at the walls late at night, wondering when everything would come right again.

Then, at last, the funeral was over, the estate settled, and Carol returned home for good. She brought with her three albums bulging with old photographs, retrieved from her mother's possessions. These photos were a revelation. Here was *Babushka*, Carol's great-grandmother, who guided the family business through the Depression; here was great-grandfather Moses, who collected violins and dreamed of his Russian homeland; here were dozens of other relatives introduced to us for the first time. What joy it was, seeing our family's heritage unfold before our eyes!

The best discovery, however, were the photos of my wife as a baby in her crib, a young girl with a hula hoop, a teenager with Peter Pan collar, a college student with piles of books—my wife before I knew her. To anyone outside the family, these photos would seem ordinary. But to our children and me, they were astonishing, the triumph of love over time, a glimpse into a vanished world, a wonderful last gift from Laura, who had kept them safe all these years.

"That's Mom," I said to our younger son, "when she was your age."

"Wow," said Andy, "I didn't know she was ever that young!"

Young forever, I thought. *Love makes us young forever.*

Thank you, Laura, and Godspeed.

Lord, teach me to love past, present and future in equal measure, for all spring from Your love.
                    —PHILIP ZALESKI

FRI

7

THE LAST ENEMY THAT SHALL BE DESTROYED IS DEATH.
                    —*I Corinthians 15:26*

I KNOW A MAN who has two jobs, policeman and soldier. In both capacities he knocks on doors to tell mothers and fathers and wives and husbands that their son or daughter or husband or wife is dead.

He has to knock on a door five or six times a year, and he tells me that people want to know every last fact about how their loved ones died. Some people just refuse to believe him. Men faint as much as women do, and pretty much everyone to whom he delivers the news ends up telling him stories about the person who died.

"I tell them I will keep the deceased in my prayers,"

he says. "I say this as a private citizen. Generally I stop at church on the way back and pray awhile.

"After a year or so, I don't remember the adults, but I do remember the children. I remember all the children. I wish I could forget their names, but I can't. I could tell you every one. It would take quite a while. Sometimes I think that maybe remembering them is the most powerful prayer I can say."

Dear Lord, all those children, all those innocent children wrenched suddenly from the wild green world into Your heart again. Cover them with our prayers, tell them we love them and always will.

—BRIAN DOYLE

SAT
8

THEY SHALL REVIVE AS THE CORN. . . .
—*Hosea 14:7*

GOD MUST HAVE KNOWN I needed a push that drab November Saturday morning. By my second cup of coffee, I still had no plan for the day. Maybe it was the weather, but I felt sluggish, isolated and old.

Then out of the blue, the phone rang. "Gail!" a man's voice bellowed. "Where are you? I'm reading *Daily Guideposts* and it says you moved! You still in Concord?" It was Uncle Pug, my childhood friend Lynda's dad. Excitedly we exchanged updates, and I learned that he and his wife lived only an hour away in Maine.

"I'm pushing eighty, Gail!" he said.

"*Whoa!* Then I'd just better come see you quick!" I loved to joke with Uncle Pug. We planned to meet for Sunday lunch. In the meantime, his phone call energized me enough to tackle some chores that had been languishing for weeks.

As I drove to Maine the next day, I remembered the night Uncle Pug brought Lynda and me to our first social and showed us how to dance with boys; the day he taught us canoeing; the times he teased me about my boyfriends and challenged me to try the "not too hot" peppers he ate with gusto. Uncle Pug had always made me feel like a million dollars.

Now "pushing eighty," he still did. I found him—as fit, trim and as animated as ever—in his favorite restaurant. Sunlight glittered on the ocean outside as he and his wife Wanda told story after story of their active life: traveling, skiing, fishing excursions, listening to jazz. Life with a capital *L*.

After lunch, we explored unfamiliar lanes along the coast. "Let's see where this goes," mused Uncle Pug, and we'd soon wind up in a secluded ocean cove or someone's driveway.

The energy I felt that afternoon lingers still. Thanks, Uncle Pug!

Lord, thank You for the "spark plugs" You send to revive me. —GAIL THORELL SCHILLING

SUN *"HE TOLD ME, '. . . GO AND SPEAK. . . .'"*
9   *—Ezekiel 3:1 (THE MESSAGE)*

JERRY AND HER SON JEREMY were survivors of Hurricane Katrina, and they had somehow found their way to our church in Athens, Georgia. Jerry became friends with everyone; her son Jeremy, however, was another story. Every week he sat across the aisle from his mom, alone, bent over with his head in his arms. It was impossible not to notice him: At fourteen, he was six feet seven inches tall. His aloneness bothered me. *Someone should go over and speak to him, Lord.*

You go and speak to him.

Huh? It should be a man or a young person, Lord.

I kept getting the same assignment from God, Sunday after Sunday. Finally, during greeting time, I made my way over to Jeremy. He sat very still, head in his arms. He didn't look up as I sat down and rattled my bulletin. "Hi," I managed to say. "Would you like to come sit with us?"

He shook his head slightly.

I spoke to him on two more Sundays. On the next trip I plopped down hard by him, frustrated, my voice no longer gentle. "Jeremy, I know what you're thinking. 'Here comes that white lady again, trying to get me to sit with her.'"

I heard a muffled laugh.

"Well, will you?"

He looked at me for the first time. "You really want me to?"

Suddenly, it seemed I'd never wanted anything so much in my life.

"I do."

He stood up—and up and up. Smiling slightly, he followed me back to my seat.

The next Sunday he sat with me and showed me some of the rap songs he'd written. ("I love You, sweet Jesus," one said.) We sort of hang out at church now, an unlikely but happy pair of friends.

Oh, Father, I love it when You give me assignments that turn out to be amazing fun.
                                    —MARION BOND WEST

MON
10
THE LORD IS YOUR KEEPER. . . . THE LORD WILL GUARD YOUR GOING OUT AND YOUR COMING IN. . . .
                        —*Psalm 121:5, 8 (NAS)*

MOOSE ON THE LOOSE! NIGHT DANGER!

Motorists driving through northern Ontario, Canada, forests are warned by numerous signs that moose are both plentiful and unpredictable, especially in late fall. Any misconception I had about their size was quickly swept away when we saw one, its head the size of a draft horse's, with a rack of antlers almost reaching across a lane of the highway. Thereafter, the signs showing a silhouette of a charging moose were reason enough for Leo and me to find a motel before sunset!

The next morning, while Leo drove, I kept my camera ever on the ready in eager anticipation of getting a photo of one of these magnificent animals feeding near the edge of a swamp at dawn. When it was my turn to drive, however, anticipation turned to anxiety, and I kept my foot poised for the brake pedal, just in case a moose meandered onto the highway.

Life is about as unpredictable as a "moose on the loose," and hoping for the best or dreading the worst often depends on whether I feel that everything's up to me. In reality, yielding the "driver's seat" to God means I'm much more inclined to picture the positives than to dread possible disasters over which I have no real control.

Lord, when I'm feeling particularly vulnerable, remind me again that You are the sovereign one.
—ALMA BARKMAN

TUE
11

THE RIGHTEOUS SHALL BE IN EVERLASTING REMEMBRANCE.
—*Psalm 112:6*

I WAS ON A WALK through the Yorkshire dales in England with two good friends. We'd come through a glorious countryside of rolling hills, stone walls, wildflowers and enough sheep to film a biblical epic. We stopped for a water break beside a small stone farmhouse and admired the garden an older man was tending. He had roses, hydrangeas, vines of sweet peas and, most spectacularly, dozens of red poppies. They reminded me of the crepe-paper ones my grandfather, a World War I vet, used to give us on Veterans Day.

"What a beautiful garden," I said to the farmer.

He nodded his head and muttered something incomprehensible—the local Yorkshire dialect could be pretty hard to decipher.

"I love the poppies," I added.

He said something else I didn't understand.

"Yes, yes," I nodded my head and walked on, trying to decipher his words. "Thanks for showing us your garden." Only a hundred yards later did I put it together, prompted by the memory of my grandfather's red crepe-paper poppies.

"Today is the ninetieth anniversary of the Battle of the Somme," the man had said in his thick Yorkshire accent. Red poppies had grown over too many soldiers' graves in Flanders fields. Red poppies commemorated one of the worst days of carnage in the history of warfare. Red poppies cared for by this farmer, probably because like millions of English families he had lost a relative in World War I.

He would never forget, and he didn't want others to forget, including three Americans hiking by his home on a beautiful summer's day.

Dear God, I pray for peace and an end to all wars.
                              —RICK HAMLIN

WED
12
"I DESIRE TO DO YOUR WILL, O MY GOD;
YOUR LAW IS WITHIN MY HEART."
                              —*Psalm 40:8 (NIV)*

"MOM, MAKE MY HAIR extra neat today. François is teaching, and he doesn't like messy buns."

I dutifully sprayed on a little more water and twisted Mary's hair a bit tighter. I find it funny that Mary is aware of the preferences of her various ballet teachers. Then again, it's funny that I know anything at all about putting up hair.

Before I had a daughter in ballet I knew nothing about buns. Hair wasn't on my radar; I would have happily gone through life clueless about the subtle distinctions in using bobby pins and elastics. But life with children takes funny turns, and I find myself at middle age with a remarkable amount of knowledge about things I never imagined I'd know.

I know about learning disabilities and cleaning snake cages and organizing reenactments of the Revolutionary War. I can test for a broken bone and distract a nap-deprived toddler during rush hour. I know (sort of) what a vector is, and I've learned an astonishing and heartbreaking amount about anxiety disorders. None of these things were on my list of hoped-for accomplishments in life.

Yet somehow this pile of oddities has a lot to do with who I am today. I've grown more from doing what's been plopped in my path than I have from pursuing my own interests. In a way, that's as it should be. I see what I want, but God sees beyond that to what I need. There's a lot that goes into learning how to twist a bun into place.

Lord, whatever I want for myself, help me want what You want for me more. —JULIA ATTAWAY

THU
13

ONE GENERATION SHALL PRAISE THY WORKS TO ANOTHER. . . . —*Psalm 145:4*

IT WAS FIFTY-SEVEN years ago this month when I first met Norman Vincent Peale. The meeting took place in a taxicab, driving to CBS, where Dr. Peale was to speak about his upcoming book *The Power of Positive Thinking*. The comment he made as he stepped out of the cab has stayed with me ever since. "I always try," he said, "to share an attitude of gratitude."

What stood out for me was the word *share*. Gratitude is catching. When I surround myself with people who not only feel grateful but express it, my own capacity for gratitude grows. Ever since that taxi ride I've sought out such people—most recently my friend Steve.

When Steve was twenty, a fall left him with permanent brain damage. After months in a coma and more months relearning to walk and speak, he came to live in our town, where I met him when he joined our church. Today, Steve lives in a group home and works collecting carts at a local superstore.

"I love my job!" Steve told me one rainy morning when I'd offered to drive him to work. "I like people. I stop traffic for them in the crosswalks, help them unload their carts. That's neat. I have everything I need! I have my own room, food, clothes, a church I like and a chance to meet someone new every day."

"Too bad though," I said, looking out at the downpour as we approached the employee entrance, "that you have to be outside on a day like this."

"Oh no," Steve corrected me, "they give you stuff to wear when it's bad outside. You ought to hear the sound of rain on my poncho!"

Father, help me be grateful for the "rain" in my life and help me share this gratitude with those around me.
—JOHN SHERRILL

FRI
14
THEY SHALL DWELL IN THEIR PLACE, AND SHALL BE MOVED NO MORE. . . .
—*I Chronicles 17:9*

LOS ANGELES never had real seasons, so when my husband Keith and I experienced our first autumn in Bellingham, Washington, it came as a welcome surprise.

"We should have moved here before," Keith said.

"We couldn't move until you retired," I reminded him. After all, the swimming-pool business wasn't something that would have translated well to northern Washington State.

Then I had to have minor heart surgery and Keith knee surgery, and it began to feel like we had moved up north just in time to fall apart! "We're having troubles here," I said. "Maybe we should've just stayed in LA."

Keith laughed. "We're getting older," he said. "These things would've happened there, too, and at least here the scenery is great."

Some time later I was looking at the woods next to our house, really seeing the beauty of the fall colors as the breeze wafted red, gold, orange and russet leaves past the window. How beautiful autumn could be! It occurred to me that God was showing me that the beauty is there whether it's Bellingham's autumn or our own. All I had to do was recognize it and respect it and, perhaps, like Keith, even laugh.

"You know," I said to him, "I think we're in the right place after all."

I am so grateful, Lord, for the timely lessons You give.
—RHODA BLECKER

READER'S ROOM

MY SEED OF FAITH this year has been
seeing my youngest daughter and having a
good relationship with my girlfriend. I'm
happy to say I think my faith is getting
stronger and stronger every day! Thank you!
—*Michael Hazel, Dayton, Ohio*

SAT
15

*FOR EVERYONE BORN OF GOD OVERCOMES
THE WORLD. . . . —I John 5:4 (NIV)*

IN 1965, WHEN I WAS just nine, my dad's
cousin Don was cocaptain of the Michigan
State football team. I was a big fan. The Spartans beat
UCLA, 13–3, in the opener, and week after week just
kept winning. They ended the regular season unde-
feated and number one in the nation. There was just
one more game: a New Year's Day rematch with
UCLA in the Rose Bowl. That day, my hero Don
fumbled a punt inside the ten-yard line—that's the
football equivalent of an accountant misplacing a dec-
imal point or a trucker forgetting to check the gas
tank. UCLA recovered, scored a touchdown and
eventually won the game, 14–12.

What do you do when you fumble the ball in the
biggest game of your life? I know what Don did. He

picked himself up, played well the rest of the game and in the forty-plus years since, has become a successful businessman.

I think the most important play of a game isn't the one spectacular or terrible moment, but the one after that. And the one after that. Success or failure is a moment; how you respond to it is the rest of your life.

You know I'm not perfect, God. I'll make mistakes. But with Your help, those mistakes will make me a better person tomorrow than I was today.

—JEFF JAPINGA

SUN
16

REMEMBER THE DAYS OF OLD. . . .
—*Deuteronomy* 32:7

PEOPLE I'VE GONE TO CHURCH with over the years stay in my mind even after they've moved away, and Betty hadn't been gone for long. One morning I'd just returned from the eight o'clock service when Betty called. She'd been a member of our church for forty years and had moved to New Hampshire only a couple weeks earlier. She had hated leaving Medford, but it was time to downsize, let go and move on.

"How are you?" I asked, worried that she was still having trouble readjusting.

"I called because there's someone up here who wants to speak to you."

Soon another voice got on the phone. "Hello, Mr. Greene, this is Joan. I don't know if you'll remember me, but you were my Sunday school teacher in fifth grade. I'll never forget the day you had us sign our names on slips of paper and drop them in the basket for a drawing. I won two books and still have them!"

"My goodness," I said, "that must have been years ago." I hadn't taught Sunday school in more than twenty-five years.

"I'm an ordained minister now and my husband's a minister, and we have three children. I just want to say thank you for being my teacher."

We talked a bit more before I hung up, reassured that Betty would do just fine. Yes, people do come and go in our church, but I think we all stay connected somehow. A part of me never forgets the people I've prayed for and worshiped with—and taught—over the years. No matter the changes, a church goes on forever.

God, be with the people who have been part and are part of my church. —OSCAR GREENE

MON 17 *BELOVED, SINCE GOD LOVED US SO MUCH, WE ALSO OUGHT TO LOVE ONE ANOTHER.* —I John 4:11 (NRSV)

MY HUSBAND CHARLIE AND I spend Novembers in Sausalito, California, just over the

Golden Gate Bridge from San Francisco. A dour café waiter there always remembers us, at least enough to give us a half smile. But last year when we walked in, he smiled broadly and hurried to greet us with a kiss for me and a handshake for Charlie. The bushy mustache that had hidden his perpetually downturned lips had vanished.

At first I thought it might have been the absent mustache that accounted for the change. Perhaps he'd been smiling all those years under all that hair. But, no, he couldn't stop talking and seemed happier to see us than in all the previous years put together.

Eventually a waitress clued us in: He was in love. He'd met a woman who not only loved him, but refused to accept his glum disposition. She'd encouraged him to take up hiking, so he'd lost a few pounds.

Later, back in our rented cottage, we marveled at the change. "Look what love can do!" Charlie said.

That made me wonder: *Why aren't we all smiling like that waiter, rejuvenated and full of joy?* After all, God loves us in a way that human love can only shadow. Yet how often do I feel so utterly loved that I'm ready to change my life to reflect it? How often do I let the world know through my demeanor that I'm loved by the One Whose love redeems the world?

Not often enough. Still, tomorrow's only a few hours away.

Loving Lord, help me to feel and mirror the transforming power of Your love. —MARCI ALBORGHETTI

A SECOND THANK-YOU
THANK YOU FOR UNSELFISHNESS

TUE

18

"FREELY YOU HAVE RECEIVED, FREELY GIVE." —Matthew 10:8 (NIV)

MY FRIEND BARBARA stopped by today to finish up some pillows we've been designing. As I walked her to her van, I stopped by the mailbox under the arbor. Inside was the newest issue of Mary Engelbreit's *Home Companion*. One look at the red and green cover promising EASY WAYS TO MAKE A HOME FOR THE HOLIDAYS and TASTY TREATS TO MAKE AND GIVE, and I was secretly planning my escape. There's nothing I look forward to more than sitting down with a cup of coffee and the latest issue of *Home Companion*.

"Is this the magazine by that greeting-card artist?" Barbara asked. "I went to the grocery store to get the Christmas issue and they were out. The bookstore too."

My mind traveled back forty years. My grandmother had just retrieved the holiday issue of *Good Housekeeping* from her mailbox. I grabbed it from her ottoman as soon as I spotted the cover announcing an article on making gingerbread houses. A few minutes later when Mother came to pick me up, Mamaw handed me the magazine. "You take it, honey. I can look at it later," she said. I murmured a brief thank-you and slid it under my arm, even though I could see the yearning in Mamaw's eyes and remembered the cup of coffee waiting for her on the kitchen table.

All afternoon, I kept thinking about that look in Mamaw's eyes. She ran a little alterations shop from her dining room, and there wasn't much money for extras. Her favorite magazine was her only extravagance, but she had let me enjoy it first.

I handed my new *Home Companion* to Barbara. Sometimes the best way to say a second thank-you for a long-ago deed is simply to repeat it.

Heavenly Father, thank You for Mamaw and all the models of unselfishness who've taught me the importance of giving. —ROBERTA MESSNER

WED
19
"IN THIS WORLD YOU WILL HAVE TROUBLE. BUT TAKE HEART! I HAVE OVERCOME THE WORLD."
—*John 16:33 (NIV)*

WHEN I'M ON THE MOUNTAINTOP, it's easy to give advice to those who are in the valley. Bible verses work well when things in life are on the up and up. But when the valley experience comes to me, how can I best handle it?

In May 1995, a charitable foundation we had been depending on for our ministry in Mendenhall, Mississippi, was accused of fraud. We had participated in its matching grant program, believing that there were anonymous donors who would match any funds we invested with the foundation dollar for dollar. When the truth finally surfaced, I went into a two-week depression. I didn't want to talk to people because I felt I had let down so many who had trusted in our integrity.

Then several things happened that turned me around. One was a devotional time centered on John 16:33. Peace grew in my heart from knowing that God was in control and that He provided all that we had and all that we would need. Then I thought about all the ways God had guided us down through the years. The words *I won't complain* quickly came to mind. I continued to repeat those words over and over again.

The members of our board of directors called to assure me that they were standing with me. And then I wrote to all our donors to let them know what had happened. We received only four negative responses. We still have not gotten all our money back, but I do know more than ever that God cares about our ministry. And if I trust in Him and stay close to Him in prayer, I need not be afraid to move forward.

Lord, help me to know that You are concerned about all that happens to me. —DOLPHUS WEARY

THU
20
I WILL BOAST ALL THE MORE GLADLY OF MY WEAKNESSES, SO THAT THE POWER OF CHRIST MAY DWELL IN ME.
—II Corinthians 12:9 (NRSV)

MY DAUGHTER SARAH communicates clearly. She's smart, determined, eager to learn. She's a budding musician and writer and generally has more interests than she can pursue in a day. But she can also be bold, sometimes brash, and has very little patience.

We had a rule in the house that each of the children must try playing an instrument in the fifth grade, which is when kids in our local public school are first given the opportunity. When it was Sarah's turn, she chose the violin.

Sarah wasn't made for the violin, however. For a year, she screeched and scratched at that instrument, making a valiant effort to match her personality with it. Before the end of the year, she was begging to escape or, at least, for some alternative. "The trumpet," she suggested.

Sarah seems to have been made for the trumpet. Not only does she play it beautifully, but it matches her spirit perfectly. She is bold, she is loud, she is aggressive, she is strong. All of it comes through in her trumpet playing. What a delight it has been to see music and life meet in ways that they never would have had she stuck with the violin.

Take my whole self, God, and use me for Your work in the world. —JON SWEENEY

FRI
21

No HAMMER, CHISEL OR ANY OTHER IRON TOOL WAS HEARD AT THE TEMPLE SITE WHILE IT WAS BEING BUILT.
—I Kings 6:7 (NIV)

I DIDN'T KNOW THAT I LIVE in the middle of constant noise until the day a film crew started shooting my prayer video series in our house. Before the camera started rolling, we turned off the refrigerator, the heat and the computer and unplugged all of the phones. I was sitting in an old platform rocker and—*grrng!*—the old springs let out a loud creak whenever I moved. Then in the middle of filming—*ow, ow, owwwww*—the beagle across the street treed a squirrel. My husband Gordon rushed over and knocked on the neighbor's door. The dog stopped, and we resumed filming. *Bam!* Gordon had come back in, slamming the door.

The next morning when I sat down for my prayer time, a thousand plans and worries about finishing up the video started running through my mind. *My mind is so noisy, I can't hear God.* The Bible says that Solomon was intent on keeping the temple site free of noisy, warlike iron tools and ordered all of the stones to be shaped in the quarry before being brought to the construction site.

Clang, clang. Are your thoughts about your daily business disturbing your prayer time? There's plenty of time back at the quarry for getting things squared away. Sit back and enjoy the quiet. That's where God speaks best.

Dear God, quiet down my busy thoughts so I can enter Your temple of prayer. —KAREN BARBER

SAT
22
MAY THE GOD WHO GIVES ENDURANCE AND ENCOURAGEMENT GIVE YOU A SPIRIT OF UNITY AMONG YOURSELVES AS YOU FOLLOW CHRIST JESUS.
—*Romans 15:5 (NIV)*

ON NOVEMBER 22, 1963, I was nine and in fourth grade at Meadow Lake School in Birmingham, Michigan. It was a raw, overcast Friday, but we were sweaty under our bulky jackets and flushed from playing at recess. We clattered back to our desks eager to hear Mr. Schaeffer read another chapter from *Champion Dog Prince Tom*, about a wayward cocker spaniel who triumphs as a show dog.

Mr. Schaeffer stood by the intercom, his forehead resting against the speaker, as we all came in. Then he turned to us, his eyes red. Mr. Schaeffer, the brush-cut ex-Marine, had been crying.

"Your parents will explain," he said softly. "Classes are canceled. We all need to be with our families now."

Out our classroom window, I saw the yellow line of school buses filing slowly into the parking lot, early by a couple hours. By the time we had all piled onto them, there were whispers that something had happened to President Kennedy. Billy Costello said he was dead; he'd heard it on his transistor radio. No one wanted to believe him.

My dad was already home from work when I got there. He and Mom were glued to the TV, pale and shaken, and I heard Walter Cronkite say that the president had been assassinated.

The skies opened up and the rain came in torrents that night against my bedroom window. My mom sat silently on the edge of the bed in the dark for a long time while I pretended to sleep.

Mr. Schaeffer was right. We needed to be with our families, and, in a way, the country itself became a family that long gray weekend, watching the funeral procession on TV, united by grief yet sharing a strength that helps us endure even the greatest trials together.

Father, our country faces great challenges. Help us to remember that, like a family, we are strongest when we are united. —EDWARD GRINNAN

SUN
23   *From infancy you have known the holy Scriptures, which are able to make you wise for salvation through faith in Christ Jesus.*
                        —*II Timothy 3:15 (NIV)*

I CAN'T THINK ABOUT THE BIBLE for very long without remembering Grandma Fellman. She lived to be ninety-eight and kept her Bible beside her always.

A couple of years ago her now elderly daughter, my aunt, sent me that Bible. Its leather cover is worn and tattered, and some of the pages have come loose from the binding and are threatening to fall out. Several people have suggested that I have it restored, but I like it the way it is. Holding it with the spine in my palm, I can feel the impression of Grandma's hand. She held it that way with me on her lap and her arms around me as we read chapter after chapter.

For some people the Bible is just a complicated collection of sixty-six books by thirty-nine authors spanning thousands of years, a historical document needing criticism and correction. Not so for Grandma Fellman. She often told me, "Honey, this book, from beginning to end, is about one thing: the Savior Jesus. The old part is about how we lost touch with God and He made a plan to send Jesus to bring us back. The new part tells Jesus' life story and how He wants us to live. Follow His way and you will never go wrong."

I hope that the next time Grandma sees Jesus, she'll tell Him that lots of us down here are trying to follow

His way and she'll ask Him to keep being patient with us.

Lord Jesus, thank You for the Scriptures that tell us Your story. Help us to live together in Your way.
—ERIC FELLMAN

MON
24

AND THE CHILDREN OF ISRAEL SAID TO SAMUEL, CEASE NOT TO CRY UNTO THE LORD OUR GOD FOR US. . . .
—I Samuel 7:8

WHEN I SAW THE NAME in the "From" line in my e-mailbox, I couldn't wait to open the message. Freddie and I had met in seminary and developed a friendship. After we graduated, we worked closely together at a church in Boston. People called us Batman and Robin—we were the dynamic duo of ministry. Just two months earlier, we'd reconnected while I was in Boston on business. "You look great," I told him. He was doing well and felt that he was at the top of his game.

I opened Freddie's e-mail and started to read, but I couldn't get past the first line: "The doctors discovered that I have cancer, and I've had surgery."

It was too late to call, so I prayed for him. The next

day I called him at home. I could barely hear him as he began sharing his ordeal. "It was touch and go, because the cancer was near the brain," he explained. "It takes faith to get through cancer. And I have a great family and caring friends." His voice got stronger as he talked about his support system.

"Freddie, I have a strong prayer network of friends," I said. "I'll ask them to pray for you."

"Thank you, Pablo. I really need their prayers."

I hung up the phone and called Efrain and Gisela in Connecticut, Maria and Pedro in Florida, Angela at the Peale Center, and Felix in Cleveland. I sent a prayer request to Guideposts Prayer Fellowship and put a few more on the Internet.

Freddie is right. It takes faith and friends to get through cancer . . . and a whole lot of prayer.

Lord, on this Guideposts Thanksgiving Day of Prayer, bless all the members of our family. And please keep Freddie in Your special care. —PABLO DIAZ

EDITOR'S NOTE: Join us today for our annual Thanksgiving Day of Prayer. On every working day, Guideposts Prayer Ministry prays for your prayer requests by name and need. Visit us at www.dailyguideposts.com, where you can request prayer, volunteer to pray for others or help support our prayer ministry.

**TUE
25** *THERE BEFORE ME LIES THE MIGHTY
OCEAN TEEMING WITH LIFE OF EVERY
KIND, BOTH GREAT AND SMALL.*
—Psalm 104:25 (TLB)

SOMETIMES, WHEN IT'S BEEN A WHILE since I've had a trip up North or out West to visit my children or other family members, I feel lonely. Oh, I've made many new friends since I moved to Florida, but with no family down here, the months in between visits seem long indeed.

But I've discovered that my happiness quotient soars whenever I see blue herons, white egrets, osprey, pelicans, seagulls and sandpipers hover around my home. I love it when the pelicans swoop down into the Gulf of Mexico to scoop up a large fish and then swallow it whole.

My mood lifts when I bike over to the "turtle deck" at the nearby park. In the pond below the deck live hundreds of turtles: Florida cooters that like to stand on top of each other; red-eared and yellow-bellied sliders; chicken turtles; Florida snapping turtles; Florida softshells with shells that resemble pancakes; and the mighty alligator snapping turtle that can grow to 250 pounds and live more than a hundred years. If I remember to bring crackers, the turtles swarm to the deck and brighten my day even more.

The longer I live in Florida, the more I find comfort in sharing this warm climate with so many amazing creatures. Now when I'm lonely, I go pet a stingray at the Clearwater sea animal hospital, visit Snooty, a 1,300-pound manatee at the South Florida Museum Aquarium, or watch an osprey build a nest on top of a huge palm tree. Suddenly, all's right with the world and with me.

Lord, thank You for all the creatures of the air, land and sea and for helping me step out of myself and into their world. —PATRICIA LORENZ

WED
26
"THE KING WILL REPLY, 'I TELL YOU THE TRUTH, WHATEVER YOU DID FOR ONE OF THE LEAST OF THESE BROTHERS OF MINE, YOU DID FOR ME.'"
—*Matthew 25:40 (NIV)*

IT WAS MY THIRD TRIP down the steep stairs in our two-hundred-year-old farmhouse. It was late and I was very tired. The youngest of our seven children, eighteen-year-old Brittany, was fussing and needed attention—once again.

Brittany has cerebral palsy and can neither walk nor talk. She had undergone surgery to correct her severe scoliosis just six months earlier, and she was recovering very slowly. It seemed that nights were particularly difficult.

That evening, her inability to turn herself over to ease the strain on her still-healing spine muscles was causing her yet another uncomfortable sleep. She sighed her thanks as I gently turned her over and adjusted her covers, and before I left her room she was fast asleep.

I paused to observe Brittany in the dim light, and in that moment I forgot about how tired I was after months of interrupted sleep. The peaceful expression on her face caused me to feel blessed to have one of God's special children in my care.

Brittany's calls in the night allow me to hear the quieter voice of God, reminding me that I can be His hands to care for one of His angels.

Thank You, Lord, for using me where Your work needs to be done. Let me always strive to share the comfort of Your love with those around me. —PATRICIA PUSEY

THU 27 "MARTHA, MARTHA, YOU ARE WORRIED AND BOTHERED ABOUT SO MANY THINGS." —*Luke 10:41 (NAS)*

OUR CHURCH HAD BEGUN sponsoring a women's shelter. Carol, who managed it, told the congregation that she wanted someone to invite her gang over for Thanksgiving dinner. Immediately, my mind began working: *Do we have space? Do we have enough china? I've only cooked a turkey once. What if it's no good? I'd better practice ahead of time.*

Despite my concerns, a tiny brave part of me wanted to volunteer. And, nervously, I did.

I got up at four o'clock on Thanksgiving morning to begin working through my list: Start the turkey, recheck the place cards, put pecans on the sweet potato soufflé and so on. I rearranged the refrigerator and cleaned the shelves in case one of the women took a peek.

At around eleven, I realized I couldn't find my husband Rick or our thirteen-year-old son Thomas. I trudged down to the basement and then circled outside the house, calling for them. *How, when there's so much to do, can they manage to avoid helping?*

Thirty minutes later, I heard them stomping their feet on the front doormat. They came in, bundled up and grinning.

"Mom, you've got to come see what Dad and I did!"

"Didn't you hear me calling you?" I asked.

"Just come look," Thomas begged.

We walked halfway down our winding driveway, where they had constructed a fourteen-foot wooden cross at the edge of our woods.

"I figured this might make the women feel welcome," Rick said.

I stood there with Rick and Thomas, gazing upward in humility and silence, giving thanks.

Father, forgive me. Often, I've forgotten about You, to Whom we give thanks today. —JULIE GARMON

FRI
28

AND OUR DAUGHTERS WILL BE LIKE PILLARS. . . . —*Psalm 144:12 (NIV)*

MY DAD WAS AN IMPULSIVE MAN. When I was twelve years old, he asked if I wanted to go to work with him one holiday morning. This would be the first time I had gotten to go with him by myself.

Dad was an engineer at the Nationwide Insurance building in downtown Columbus, Ohio. He took one of us with him only on holidays when no one else was in the building. We got to explore basements, huge boiler systems, executive offices and the rooftop. All of us returned home and bragged to our brothers and sisters about how far we had leaned over the edge, shouting to the pedestrians on the sidewalks far below.

I finished my morning newspaper route in time to leave the house with Dad while everyone else was asleep. When my mother woke up, she didn't know where I was. She sent the rest of the family out to look for me, and to check all the porches for newspapers to see if I'd finished my route. Finally, she called my dad to let him know I was missing.

"You can stop crying. He's with me," my dad said. He didn't say anything for the rest of the lengthy call except "You're right" and "I'm so sorry."

I watched Dad hang up the phone and knew there would be no fun, no exploring and no rooftop. Then the phone rang again. The call was brief, but the transformation in my dad's mood was so miraculous I wondered if the call was from God.

It wasn't, but the message was. My sister Patti had phoned—without permission, I'm sure. "Mom still loves you, Daddy," she said.

Dear God, thank You for sisters—and daughters—whose love can work miracles. —TIM WILLIAMS

SAT
29

THEY ONLY ASKED US TO REMEMBER THE POOR—THE VERY THING I ALSO WAS EAGER TO DO. —*Galatians 2:10 (NAS)*

TODAY I BEGIN BELL RINGING for the Salvation Army. This marks the seventh year that I've manned the red kettle, and if I do as scheduled, I'll be at my station one afternoon every week between now and Christmas. This year my wife Shirley is going to help, giving me relief when my arm goes numb from ringing (just kidding). In truth, she likes the idea of helping the Salvation Army too. We both subscribe to its unofficial slogan, "More bang for the buck," because this organization is one of the most efficient of all when it comes to helping the needy.

People are always telling me of things the Salvation Army did for them or for someone who was down on his or her luck. "When I was a kid, probably seven or eight," one senior citizen related last year, "my widowed mother was trying to raise a family of four, and things were bleak. It was all she could do to keep us fed. There certainly wasn't going to be anything left for Christmas presents," he recalled. "Then on December twenty-fourth, a big red Salvation Army truck pulled up in front of our house, and the driver delivered a basket of food and gifts for everyone. I'll never forget the joy I felt or the words of the worker as he breezed out the door: 'God bless you all.'"

As he deposited some dollar bills in my kettle and turned to go on his way, I saw tears welling up in his eyes. And there were some in mine when I called after him, "Merry Christmas! And God bless you for remembering."

Teach us, Lord,
A life well-lived is not the kind we ration,
And not how long it lasts, but its donation.
                                    —FRED BAUER

A SIGN UNTO YOU

AS WE MAKE OUR
annual Advent journey
to Christmas, Penney
Schwab introduces
us to the Chrismon
tree, decorated
with symbols
instead of the
usual ornaments.
Join Penney as
she shows us
how these
symbols can
help us keep
the message of
Christ at the heart of Christmas.

—THE EDITORS

FIRST SUNDAY IN ADVENT:
THE CROSSLET

SUN
30

*OUT OF ZION, THE PERFECTION OF
BEAUTY, GOD WILL SHINE FORTH.*
—*Psalm 50:2 (NKJV)*

IN THE EARLY 1970S, Bea Alexander told
our churchwomen's group about the most beautiful

tree she'd ever seen—a "Chrismon tree." The pictures of exquisitely crafted white-and-gold ornaments on a stately balsam tree were breathtaking. Bea said that Frances Kipps Spencer of Danville, Virginia, had created the ornaments, which were all symbols of the Christian faith, to remind people of the true meaning of Christmas.

We voted unanimously to replicate the tree in our small church, and immediately ordered the pattern book and kits. Despite the fact that I'm all thumbs, I agreed to make three ornaments. Reality hit two weeks later when I received a bag of wire, pearls, foam and gold trim to make a "Latin crosslet," the symbol for perfection.

I tried, but my ornament bore only a vague resemblance to the picture. "What a joke!" I lamented to the pastor's wife. "My crosslet is about as far from perfect as possible."

She examined the crosslet, then said, "It's a bit lopsided, and the beads aren't spaced right. But that's beside the point. The Chrismon tree isn't about perfect craftsmanship. It's about Jesus."

My crosslet was among the ornaments on our tree the first Sunday of Advent, along with my two less-than-perfect stars placed on the back of the tree. The flaws would hardly be noticeable to the people sitting in the pews. In fact, they made the tree more special. Our congregation of imperfect people entered the season of preparation with an imperfect but beautiful tree inviting us to a deeper faith in our perfect Savior.

Beautiful Savior, may every symbol of Your birth draw us closer to You. —PENNEY SCHWAB

MY DIVINE SURPRISES

1 _____

2 _____

3 _____

4 _____

5 _____

6 _____

7 _____

8 _____

9 _____

10 _____

11 _____

12 _____

13 _____

14 _____

15 _____

16 _____

17 _____

18 _____

19 _____

20 _____

21 _____

22 _____

23 _____

24 _____

25 _____

26 _____

27 _____

28 _____

29 _____

30 _____

December

And the glory of the Lord shall be revealed,
and all flesh shall see it together. . . .

—*Isaiah 40:5*

UNEXPECTED BLESSINGS
SPEAKING OF LOVE

MON
1

For God so loved the world that he gave his only Son. . . .
　　　　　　　　　—*John 3:16 (RSV)*

I KNEW IT HAD BEEN a mistake to go to Wal-Mart on a Saturday two weeks before Christmas! Carts choked the aisles, the picture frames were at the opposite end of the vast floor from men's sweaters, and the tree lights, when I finally tracked them down, were incompatible with our old set.

At the checkout, the shortest line had ten people. As the overloaded carts inched forward, the weary young cashier swiped the bar codes and bagged the purchases without ever glancing at the customer.

I pushed my cart out to the lot and tried to remember where I'd parked the car. I found it, what seemed to my aching feet like a mile away.

As I lifted bags into the trunk, a woman was loading her own car nearby. A little farther off, a man was doing the same, apparently her husband because he called to ask if she had the Santa lawn ornament. I glanced at them both; an improbably blonde woman in a Rudolph the Reindeer jacket, a bald unshaven man. The woman got into her car.

"Love you!" she called as she shut the door.

Two words ringing out in a crowded parking lot. But they transformed the day. *I love you.* That's what the jammed aisles, the laden carts, the lines were all about. All of us had come that day on our personal errands of love. And love is always costly. Love demands time, resources, energy. It requires a lifetime of giving.

Bestower of blessing, let my little Christmas offerings take their place in the great outpouring of love that is the birth of Jesus. —ELIZABETH SHERRILL

TUE 2

"A LITTLE ONE SHALL BECOME A THOUSAND, AND A SMALL ONE A STRONG NATION. . . ." —*Isaiah* 60:22 (NKJV)

MY LITERATURE STUDENTS were in a pessimistic mood. "Can we really do much about the problems in the world today?" they wondered. So I told them about a woman named Harriet, who lived in far more difficult times in the 1850s.

A poor preacher's daughter, Harriet grew up to marry another preacher, who made even less money, not enough to care for their seven children.

One day Harriet sat down at the kitchen table with a tablet and pen, and began to write: children's stories, travel guides, recipes, short stories, whatever. She sent them out to publishers and, to her amazement, she sold many of them. Encouraged, she began to write a novel, a longer work about the evils of slavery, which she had witnessed while visiting a friend's plantation in Kentucky.

That novel became the first to sell a million copies in America. It was translated into thirty-seven languages, and it was the first book to be marketed by modern advertising methods, such as toys and board games and by dramas performed all over the country. Harriet was whisked around the world to meet such people as Charles Dickens, Queen Victoria and Leo Tolstoy. Finally, she met President Abraham Lincoln, who expressed his joy at meeting "the little woman who started this great big war." *Uncle Tom's Cabin* was the tipping factor, the beginning of the end of slavery.

"So," I said to my class, "who knows what you can do? Maybe you can start a new business or invent a new machine or find a better energy source or a cure for a disease."

Lord, revive my faith in the power of one person to change the world. —DANIEL SCHANTZ

WED *WHAT WILT THOU GIVE? . . .* —Hosea 9:14

3 I TRIED TO THINK of something special to make my husband's face light up at

Christmas. Gene had once shared a childhood memory about the boy who lived down the hill from him back in Indiana. His friend had received a new bicycle for Christmas and Gene had even ridden it a few times. But Gene had never been able to have one of his own.

We happened by a store, and I pointed out a spiffy bicycle in the window. "I just might get you one," I said teasingly.

"I do *not* need a bicycle. *Do not* get me one," Gene said emphatically. Deflated, I said nothing.

Later that week we were reading our mail in the living room, Gene with his pile, me with mine. "Here's the bicycle I want, honey," he announced loudly. *Was he teasing me?*

I moved over next to him and looked at the catalog he was holding. It showed a bike surrounded by an overjoyed father, a smiling mother and seven skinny, happy children. They lived in an underdeveloped country, and the bike would provide transportation so the father could get a job. The catalog explained that anyone could give a bicycle, garden seeds or even an ox.

Gene got his bicycle for Christmas—and halfway around the world, lives would be changed forever.

Father, I have so much to learn about true giving. Teach me. —MARION BOND WEST

THU 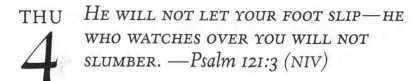 *He will not let your foot slip—he*
who watches over you will not
slumber. —Psalm 121:3 *(NIV)*

4

I'D NOTICED THAT PROBLEMS that didn't bother me during daylight suddenly loomed larger between midnight and 5:00 AM. Things like *Who'll I find to teach my Sunday school class when we go on vacation? What if Social Security benefits run out? Where is that "safe place" I hid the key so I'd be sure not to lose it?*

Finally, I confided these concerns to Sarah, one of my friends. "All these who-what-when-where-whys keep me awake. I don't recall losing sleep over such matters when I was a child."

Sarah chuckled. "When we were children, we simply expected our parents to take care of everything. That's why we didn't worry back then."

"But you seem so calm, so serene. And you don't have parents anymore, either."

"Oh, but I do," she answered. "I have a heavenly Father Who's promised to watch over me. He says He doesn't slumber or sleep. So at bedtime I simply turn my troubles over to Him. You see, He's going to stay up all night anyway, so why should I?"

Heavenly Father, I try to carry loads You never intended for me to pack around. I give them to You now in prayer. —ISABEL WOLSELEY

FRI
5
THE LORD YOUR GOD HAS CHOSEN YOU OUT OF ALL THE PEOPLES ON THE FACE OF THE EARTH TO BE HIS PEOPLE, HIS TREASURED POSSESSION.
—*Deuteronomy 7:6 (NIV)*

"LOOK AT THIS!" I exclaimed, reading the morning paper. Dr. Rhodes, a former professor of mine, was being honored at a local university.

I peered closer at his photo. I hadn't seen him in twenty years, but he looked just the same, maybe a little grayer. His lectures in college had held us spellbound. He taught history not just with facts, but with stories that made it come alive. *How I would love to see him again!* I thought. *Just to tell him what an influence he's had on me as a teacher.* I checked my calendar at work. To my disappointment, I simply couldn't make the event.

A week later I was at the airport, waiting to board a flight. There was only one empty seat by the crowded gate. "Is this taken?" I asked the man next to it.

He looked up. "No, it isn't."

"Dr. Rhodes?" I shook his hand. "I'm Melody Bonnette, a former student of yours."

After catching up with careers and families, I said, "I want you to know how much I learned from you—not just history, but how to teach history. My students always said it was the stories I told that made the most difference. I owe that to you, Dr. Rhodes. So thanks."

I had to catch my flight, but not before I offered a silent prayer to God for giving me the chance to pass on some long overdue thanks.

Thank You, Father, for letting me give thanks for the wisdom I have received. —MELODY BONNETTE

SAT
6

I HAVE SHEWED YOU KINDNESS, THAT YE WILL ALSO SHEW KINDNESS. . . .
—*Joshua 2:12*

I DO STORY TIME at the bookstore where I work, one of my favorite things about my job. I get to pick the stories and read them to a group of children. I've learned that using funny voices and reading with great enthusiasm help to keep the attention of my junior-size audience.

One book I especially like is *Don't Laugh at Me* by Steve Seskin and Allen Shamblin. I like stories with a moral, and this book, which is based on a song, is particularly moving. It's told from the point of view of kids who are teased for being different. Whether they wear braces or glasses or use a wheelchair, they all make the plea: "Don't call me names, please see my pain. . . ."

As I began reading the refrain in front of a group of about fifteen children, I felt a tear plop onto my cheek and then another and another. I tried to compose myself, but the song stirred up feelings of times I'd been chosen last for a team. I was horrified to discover that I couldn't choke back my tears. Finally, I took a big gulp of air and said, "I'm so sorry. Can somebody finish reading this for me?"

I expected a parent to take the book and continue, but I heard a child pipe up, "I can read!" Surprised, I motioned the boy to finish the book.

After a rousing round of applause, four different children offered me tissues, and one of them announced, "This is the best story time I've ever been to."

"And we won't tease you for crying!" another child said.

Dear God, let me be "real" with everyone I meet. My feelings are all from You, so let me not be ashamed to share them with others. —LINDA NEUKRUG

A SIGN UNTO YOU
SECOND SUNDAY IN ADVENT: CHI RHO, ALPHA AND OMEGA

SUN
7

"I AM THE ALPHA AND THE OMEGA, THE FIRST AND LAST, THE BEGINNING AND THE END." —*Revelation 22:13 (NAS)*

OUR FIRST MARRIED YEAR, Don and I were far from family and struggling to make ends meet. That Christmas we made do with a tiny, scraggly tree and a box of gaudy ornaments. We topped the tree with a gold spire from the dime store.

Nearly every year since, we've argued over the tree. I hold out for an artificial tree that doesn't require relocating furniture or picking up needles. Don thinks Christmas isn't Christmas without an eight-footer, preferably one with ten thousand needles and able to hold two hundred ornaments.

Most years he wins. One year the tree had to be hauled home in the truck. Don worked all Saturday evening lading its branches. He plugged in the lights and we were both overwhelmed by memories. Our oldest son Patrick had painted the clay lamb as a first-grader. Michael and Rebecca made the jar lid sparklers in Sunday school. The silver filigree ornaments once decorated my mother-in-law's tree. And we'd put the same gold spire on top of our tree for forty years.

We were leaving for church the next day when I heard a creak followed immediately by a tremendous thud. The tree had snapped the wires anchoring it to the wall, crashed into the piano, then rolled onto the floor. Everything breakable was shattered—ornaments, lights, even the old spire.

My heart sank. Those decorations were part of our lives! I started picking up glass, but Don stopped me. "It's only stuff," he said. "We need to leave for worship."

As the service began, my attention focused on the *chi* and *rho* with the *alpha* and *omega* on the

Chrismon tree. *Chi* and *rho* . . . the first two Greek
letters in *Christ* . . . Jesus. *Alpha* and *omega* . . . the
first and last letters in the Greek alphabet . . . the beginning, end and continuation of all things. Don was
right. We'd only lost stuff.

*Thank You, Lord Jesus, for the Christmas treasures we
keep in our hearts.* —PENNEY SCHWAB

MON
8

"YOU ARE MY LAMP, O LORD; THE LORD
TURNS MY DARKNESS INTO LIGHT."
—II Samuel 22:29 (NIV)

HOW I DREAD THE ONSET of winter. The
shorter days and increasing darkness trigger depression, and I often wake in the morning with a heavy
heart, dreading the day. Lately I've felt on the verge of
tears, stumbling at the edge of despair. When my
emotions are like this, it tests my faith. I struggle to
believe in God's love when I feel so awful.

But I discovered last week that one reward for dark
winter mornings can be watching the sun rise. The
murky sky was filled with heavy dark clouds, and I
began enumerating my troubles: how I missed the
long talks I used to have with my friend Barb who
moved across country, and how I struggled with the
challenges of parenting my two teenage children.

Suddenly the clouds began to reflect the sun's lu-
minous shades of orange, yellow and pink. Soon they

sent out radiant streamers of red and peach and purple and aqua.

Somehow, I thought, my dark emotions or troubles can serve to reflect God's light in a way I wouldn't otherwise see. Through my sadness and discouragement, perhaps because of them, the truth of God's faithfulness has a precious beauty. Maybe I don't feel any different, but the knowledge that He is with me and loves me becomes even more wondrous when I see His light on the dark clouds of life.

Oh, Lord, You are with me in my loneliness. Help me keep my eyes on You. Shine Your light into the dark corners of my life. —MARY BROWN

 *GIVE US THIS DAY*
FAITHFUL FRIEND

TUE
9

AND THE GOD OF ALL GRACE . . . AFTER YOU HAVE SUFFERED A LITTLE WHILE, WILL HIMSELF RESTORE YOU. . . .
—*I Peter 5:10* (NIV)

MY FAMILY PLANNED A DINNER to celebrate the end of my year of chemotherapy treatments. But my two daughters were a bit mysterious about their part of the celebration.

"We'll pick you up at five o'clock and meet the rest of the group later," they told me. So off we drove into the winter's early darkness. Soon we pulled into a long driveway with a sign out front that said KENNEL and entered a home with a pen full of golden retriever puppies in the living room.

"You've always said you want another golden retriever, so you get to pick one!" my daughters told me.

I cried and laughed as I got down on the floor and began playing with the roly-poly, face-licking, tail-wagging puppies.

A half hour later, a bit of my sanity returned. "I have to talk to Dad about all this," I said, knowing that my husband needed to be part of this decision. So we reluctantly said good-bye and went off to meet the others for dinner, where we talked about the pros (and no cons) of getting a new puppy right now.

"A puppy is the perfect way to celebrate this new post-chemo season in your life."

"You're home more now, so you could train him."

"We'll all help!"

"What are you going to call him?" This last question came from my husband Lynn, which told me he was already on board.

At once I knew the answer. "I'll call him Kemo," because in the beginning of this journey, I had to understand that chemotherapy was my friend. Besides, *Kemosabe* means "faithful friend."

A couple of weeks later, we brought Kemo home, and I have a new dream in my heart. Maybe we could go to chemo centers together and let other people know that "Kemo is your friend."

Thank You, Father, for new dreams in new seasons of life. —CAROL KUYKENDALL

WED
10

OUT OF MY DISTRESS I CALLED ON THE LORD; THE LORD ANSWERED ME AND SET ME FREE. —Psalm 118:5 (RSV)

I SLUMPED AT THE BREAKFAST TABLE, in my robe, still bleary-eyed and fuzzy-headed from waking up, when I suddenly remembered that I was supposed to be at the doctor's office for an appointment in forty-five minutes. I quickly got dressed, drove across town and arrived there ten minutes late.

That was the beginning of a day during which everything went wrong. I stopped to shop for groceries and didn't have my checkbook. When I got back home, I took off my glasses and then couldn't find them. I burned the lunch. I spilled ketchup on my slacks. By the time the piano tuner arrived (I'd forgotten he was coming), my nerves were a wreck.

I got the tuner settled at the piano and then I sank into a chair. The tuner ran his fingers up and down the keys, producing jangled sounds. I hadn't realized until then how badly out of tune my piano had become. *Just like my day,* I thought.

The tuner began working on the strings, tapping the keys and testing the tone as he adjusted the pins. One by one the strings slid into place, producing warm, rich tones that resonated through the house.

"I need to retune my day," I said.

Usually I spend a little quiet time each morning, focusing on God and asking for His help through the coming hours. *Well, it's never too late,* I told myself. Relaxing, I closed my eyes, centered down and prayed . . .

Dear Lord, I feel out of tune with You today. Please touch me with Your peace. Amen.

—MADGE HARRAH

THU
11

LET YOUR LIGHT SO SHINE BEFORE MEN, THAT THEY MAY SEE YOUR GOOD WORKS, AND GLORIFY YOUR FATHER WHICH IS IN HEAVEN. —Matthew 5:16

I NOTICED THEM as I drove home that dark evening. Someone had wrapped strings of lights around all the tree trunks in his front yard. Round and round the twinkling colors went, but only about six feet up. After that, the trees ascended heavenward in darkness. *Odd,* I thought. But the next night, as I approached the lights, they didn't seem so odd. They seemed, well, pragmatic.

I had no idea why the lights stopped so abruptly.

Perhaps the homeowner didn't have a ladder or wasn't permitted to climb for some reason. Perhaps he had a limited number of lights and a limited budget to spend on them. Perhaps he didn't have much time to give to decorating but wanted to make the effort. Whatever his reason for this unusual display, it inspired me. He had done what he could with what he had.

Kind of like Mary and Joseph that night in the stable, with a manger for a crib and beds made of fresh straw. Perhaps that's all God ever requires of us: to do the best we can with what we have. It was a comforting thought to ponder while driving through December darkness.

In this season of hustle and bustle, Lord, let me set aside the need to do things perfectly. Help me focus, instead, on letting my light shine . . . perhaps in odd and pragmatic ways. —MARY LOU CARNEY

FRI
12

THE LORD IS ABLE TO GIVE THEE MUCH MORE THAN THIS. —*II Chronicles* 25:9

WE LIVE A FOUR-HOUR PLANE RIDE from most of our family. But neither distance nor time can stop two grandmothers' love. You should see the Christmas gifts waiting for my three-year-old son. Piles of brightly wrapped boxes of every imaginable shape and size tower above him.

One morning another package arrived at our door. I started to complain to my husband. "Don't you think this is a little much?"

Jacob just looked at me and smiled. "What did you say you were thinking of making for breakfast?"

"Hotcakes," I replied, pulling a glow-in-the-dark frog and a toy car from the box with a sigh.

"*Mmm . . .*" Jacob said pouring coffee.

As I got out the big metal mixing bowl, the flour, eggs, sifter and buttermilk, my mind began to drift. My mom was a single parent for a while when I was growing up, and I ended up spending a lot of time with my grandparents. I played all sorts of wonderful games with my grandfather. He possessed a mind and a heart full of stories. He taught me to embrace my imagination. My grandmother had wonderful recipes. She shared with me the basics of cooking that I relied on when I was married. To this day, whenever I make hotcakes, I think of my grandmother lovingly guiding and instructing me. I remember feeling so proud the day she asked if I would make the hotcakes while she set the table.

Jacob's simple question reminded me that glow-in-the-dark frogs, stories, toy cars, piles of presents and hotcakes are all ways for grandparents to say the same thing: "I love you."

Lord, help me to remember that love is a gift.
—AMANDA BOROZINSKI

SAT
13
*BE CONTENT WITH WHAT YOU HAVE,
because GOD HAS SAID, "NEVER WILL I
LEAVE YOU; NEVER WILL I FORSAKE
YOU." —Hebrews 13:5 (NIV)*

I HAVE A KEEN INTEREST in unusual street names. In fact, I'm on the lookout for street signs whenever my husband Wayne and I get in the car.

One of my favorites is Baby Doll Road, which isn't far from where we live. There's a road called Noisy Hole in Mashpee, Massachusetts, and another named Succabone in Bedford Hills, New York. One that made me sit up and take notice was Hell for Certain Road in Hyden, Kentucky. I can't say what kind of people live there, but the name obviously got my attention.

Just recently in our own hometown of Port Orchard, Washington, Wayne and I drove past a street sign that I'd never noticed before. It was on a road I normally travel two or three times a week, yet not once had this sign caught my attention: EASY STREET.

"Quick," I told Wayne, pointing to the sign, "take a right."

He cast me a befuddled look. "Whatever for?"

"I want to see the houses of the people who live on Easy Street." I wasn't sure what to expect, but it wouldn't hurt to take a look. I wasn't really surprised to find that the homes looked very much like those in other neighborhoods close by. But as we wound our way down Easy Street, Wayne and I made a startling discovery: It was a dead end.

Lord, sometimes I'm guilty of wanting to live on Easy Street. Thank You for leading me down the path that leads to You. —DEBBIE MACOMBER

A SIGN UNTO YOU
THIRD SUNDAY IN ADVENT: THE FISH

SUN
14

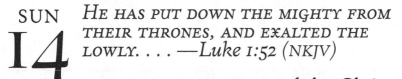

HE HAS PUT DOWN THE MIGHTY FROM THEIR THRONES, AND EXALTED THE LOWLY. . . . —Luke 1:52 (NKJV)

ON AN UPPER BRANCH of the Chrismon tree is a fish. Within the fish are the letters used to spell *icthus,* the Greek word for fish. They are also the first letters of the Greek words for "Jesus Christ, God's Son, Savior." In the early church, when believers faced persecution and even death for proclaiming Christ, the fish became a secret sign of the Christian community.

My mother believed in community. Her first project after we moved to a small town in Oklahoma was organizing a Christmas pageant that brought together Catholics, Protestants and people who didn't publicly profess any faith.

The pageant became an annual event, and the role of Mary became a popularity contest. Then Mother was elected to head the casting committee. She didn't ask for a list of cheerleaders or class officers; instead, she asked the committee to reflect on the character of Mary and choose accordingly. They did. Judy, a sweet-faced country girl with a radiant smile and flowing hair, got the role.

Was there a fuss? You bet. Mother held her tongue until the day she was cornered by the irate mother of an angel. The woman listed several reasons why the committee's choice was wrong: Judy wasn't one of the "in" crowd, her family had too many children and they didn't attend church regularly. She ended her tirade by saying scornfully, "Judy is *poor!*"

"So was Mary," mother said.

I believe in community. I believe especially in Christian community, in the fellowship of believers. But I wonder: *Does my community include the lonely? The rejected? The poor?*

Lord of all, this Advent season and throughout the year, help me widen my circle to include all Your children. Amen. —PENNEY SCHWAB

MON
15   *THAT WAS THE TRUE LIGHT, WHICH LIGHTETH EVERY MAN THAT COMETH INTO THE WORLD.* —*John 1:9*

SOON AFTER I ARRIVED in Pasadena from Minnesota to care for my centenarian aunt, I experienced my first Southern California Christmas. Nothing felt familiar. Roses bloomed where there should have been snowdrifts. People glided along in sandals instead of tromping around in boots. Leafy palms replaced stark bare branches. There were heated outdoor pools rather than icy ponds. The whole scene seemed surreal.

Then there was indoors: We had no Christmas decorations. At home I had always decorated early, so I could light up the tree each night and think about how Jesus came as Light of the world. I tried to bolster my spirit by reminding myself that God had a purpose for me in California.

One evening in the kitchen, I happened to plug in a green glass bottle, stuffed with electric lights, that I'd brought with me. *Hey, it's green,* I suddenly realized. *It's got lights. I just found my Christmas tree!*

Every night I switched off the kitchen lights, plugged in my bottle, turned on some Christmas music, sat in my chair and smiled. God had helped me find a simple means to bring the brightness of Bethlehem's Christ Child to my California kitchen.

Lord of Light, I look for Your bright presence in every new situation and setting in my life.

—CAROL KNAPP

READER'S ROOM

TYPICALLY, when I near the end of a book I
am enjoying reading, I slow my reading
down because I just don't want it to end! I
feel that way about *Daily Guideposts*.
Together, with God's help, all of you helped
light my path this year. Those of you
pictured and who knows how many more
have had something to do with the very
copy that has been mine from which to
learn. Thank you for this year.
                —*Kay Ostrom, Muskegon, Michigan*

TUE
16

*YE ARE ALL THE CHILDREN OF LIGHT,
AND THE CHILDREN OF THE DAY. . . .*
                —*I Thessalonians 5:5*

WHY IS IT that at the busiest time of year
choir directors and congregations expect ten times
more singing than any other month? For us choris-
ters, it means that on top of shopping and card writing
and wrapping, there are extra rehearsals and services.
I tell myself this is pleasurable. The music is beautiful,
and the people who hear it will be inspired, calmed,
transported. But there's a point in the rehearsals when
I grumble, "Never again."

I was close to that point recently when our choir director said in exasperation after we sang the same thing
for about the tenth time, "Softer. More intense. Make

it really musical." We went over the passage again, and from the look on his face, we weren't any better.

That's when Willis, a soft-spoken tenor, raised his hand and said, "I always remember something my music professor once said to me: 'Don't wake the baby.'"

We laughed. After all, Willis' wife was due to have a baby any moment. The image seemed just right. It helped us nail that passage of music. And it gave me what I was looking for as I went through the rest of the holiday season. *The Baby. It's all about the Baby!*

Lord, You came to the world as a child so that we might greet You with childlike wonder.

—RICK HAMLIN

A SECOND THANK-YOU
THANK YOU FOR THE GIVER OF ALL GIFTS

WED 17 *AND WHATEVER YOU DO, WHETHER IN WORD OR DEED, DO IT ALL IN THE NAME OF THE LORD JESUS, GIVING THANKS TO GOD THE FATHER THROUGH HIM.*
—*Colossians 3:17 (NIV)*

IT'S THE FINAL MONTH of my "Second Thank-You" journey, and my heart turns to the Giver of all gifts.

I've gathered up my favorite pens and a basket of beautiful note cards. One box depicts romantic scenes in the south of France; another features a stack of cozy cabin quilts that remind me of the Lord's tender comforts. Each day of this month, I'm writing a thank-you note to God to express my gratitude once again for a special blessing.

I've already completed my note for today and dropped it inside a pink-and-white flowered box for safekeeping. It's what I call "joy jottings," gratitude for the simple gifts that make any ordinary day special, like pecan waffles with hot maple syrup, a pot of paperwhites blooming on a windowsill in the dead of winter, a wreath on the front door that celebrates the changing of the seasons.

Today my heart is full to overflowing, but there will be those inevitable times when life takes a downward turn. I'll go to that box, a journal of sorts, and my heart will remember.

Your gifts get me through each day, dear Lord. Thank You. —ROBERTA MESSNER

THU
18

HE . . . FILLETH THE HUNGRY SOUL WITH GOODNESS. —*Psalm 107:9*

A NEAR-FREEZING RAIN chilled my bones as I pulled up in front of the art center where my company's yearly holiday party was being held. The man who came to park my car was at least my father's age. *He must be miserable working in rain like this*, I thought. I wondered if I could do anything to help . . . but what? I gave him my keys, pulled my coat collar up and ran toward the building.

Inside, the room glowed with lights, music, the smell of good food and friendly faces wherever I looked. I talked to a few colleagues and scanned the room to find my boss. I wanted to let Rob know that I'd just landed a big account, one that he had referred to me.

Finally, I saw him across the room, waiting in front of a chef carving a great slab of roast beef. I made my way through the crowd, but when I reached the serving table, Rob had disappeared.

"Hey," I said to the man with the carving knife, "can you tell me where that gentleman went?"

"Probably to the parking lot. He's made at least four trips back and forth with food and hot punch for the guys parking cars tonight. He keeps telling me how cold it is out there."

"Thanks," I said, grateful for the reminder of what real leadership was. "Maybe you could fill a plate or two for me to take outside too."

Father, don't let me ever forget that real success means grabbing every opportunity to do good.
—BROCK KIDD

FRI
19
AND THE LEAVES OF THE TREE ARE FOR THE HEALING OF THE NATIONS.
—Revelation 22:2 (NIV)

"I DON'T WANT TO GO get a Christmas tree!"

John's angry shout filled the family with tension. It wasn't clear—it's rarely clear—what had brought on his blast of anger. John's mood swings are sometimes sudden. In the past week he'd been feeling down, and I was girding myself for a rough Christmas.

Ten minutes and many deep breaths later, the family tumbled out into the night. There was no way of knowing whether it would be a peaceful evening or not. At least the cool air felt good.

The place that sells Christmas trees was eight blocks from our apartment. Two-year-old Stephen chattered happily as he rode in our collapsible laundry/grocery cart. Eight-year-old Mary spied the shadow of the moon grinning faintly behind its glowing crescent. My husband Andrew pointed out the spire of the Empire State Building lit up in red and green, seven miles to the south. John was reserved.

The Christmas tree vendor, in town from Vermont for the month, still had an ample selection. The fresh pine scent was invigorating. We decided on a tree, and it was straight-jacketed in plastic netting so it would fit into our cart. Stephen gladly gave up his place there and walked, talking, the whole way home.

John read a book while we trimmed the tree and set up the crèche. Five-year-old Maggie asked if she could sleep on the little sofa. Stephen wanted to sleep near the tree too. So did Mary. They trotted off to retrieve pillows and blankets.

"Can I sleep on the big sofa?" John sheepishly asked.

I looked searchingly at my ten-year-old, my constant challenge, and nodded. That's when I knew that however his feelings might shift, whatever the ups and downs, whatever tomorrow would bring, this was still a season of hope.

Jesus, sometimes I wish You'd just fix what is wrong. Help me, instead, to trust in what is eternally right.
—JULIA ATTAWAY

SAT
20

O MY GOD, I TRUST IN THEE: LET ME NOT BE ASHAMED. . . . —Psalm 25:2

I RECEIVED A CHRISTMAS E-MAIL update from a friend of mine living in Boston. It has not been a good year for her. Her father died from cancer, she broke up with her boyfriend and now she has found out she's pregnant.

This is ironic, because she is deeply religious. But

she didn't use the word *ironic*; she used the word *shame*.

During the difficult visit to the obstetrician, she had many questions, but she couldn't stop crying long enough to ask them. Finally she confessed that she had always viewed pregnant single girls as either "incredibly stupid or incredibly selfish."

The obstetrician was quiet for a moment, then said, "Or they're incredibly human."

It was exactly the right thing to say—for her, for me and now for you. My friend is carrying a child; you and I are carrying all sorts of things, too, but our baggage is less obvious. Some of what we carry is stupid and selfish, but what she carries is incredibly human. You would think we'd see the irony of that, but we do not. We march on doggedly, blind to our own faults and only too eager to shame others for their sins.

Maybe my friend should name her child after the obstetrician, but I've already thought of other names. I think the baby should be called Wonderful. Or Counselor.

Sorry, I'm getting my Advent stories of young girls in difficult circumstances mixed up.

Lord, no matter how faithful I may think I am, I'm human too. Keep my friend and her baby and all of us close to You. —MARK COLLINS

A SIGN UNTO YOU
FOURTH SUNDAY IN ADVENT: THE MANGER

SUN
21

AND SHE BROUGHT FORTH HER FIRSTBORN SON, AND WRAPPED HIM IN SWADDLING CLOTHES AND LAID HIM IN A MANGER. . . . —Luke 2:7

SOMETIMES I GO TO SEE MOVIES solely on the recommendation of my teenage grandsons. My friends say my sanity is open to question, but I go because sometimes these movies lead me to examine my faith, to enlarge my understanding of God.

A spoof on drag racing was one such movie. Mixed in with improbable action and racy language was a scene where a family asks a mealtime blessing. The father prays loudly to little Baby Jesus. Halfway through the prayer, his wife stops him. "Jesus grew up, you know," she reminds him. The dad replies that he's more comfortable with little Baby Jesus, then begins a new prayer with the words "Dear little, eight-pound, four-ounce Baby Jesus."

A favorite ornament on our Chrismon tree is the manger, representing the story of the birth of Jesus. It is right and good that we rejoice over Christ's entry into the world as a helpless babe. But even as we sing a lullaby with Mary, God calls us to look ahead. Jesus the child taught in the temple with the authority of God. Jesus the man was tempted as I am but did not sin. Jesus the Savior had the strength, compassion and love to die on the Cross for the sake of the world. As I mature in Christ, I strive to keep the innocent heart of the Infant, yet grow in the wisdom, love and holiness of my Savior.

Forgive me, Lord, when I seek a comfortable Savior, when I strive to keep You wrapped in swaddling clothes, helpless in the crib. —PENNEY SCHWAB

MON **22** MINE EYES HAVE SEEN THY SALVATION, WHICH THOU HAST PREPARED BEFORE THE FACE OF ALL PEOPLE; A LIGHT TO LIGHTEN THE GENTILES, AND THE GLORY OF THY PEOPLE ISRAEL. —*Luke 2:30–32*

I RETIRED after thirty-eight years with Guideposts, and Medicare hadn't processed my records. I was on the phone for hours trying to clear it up. After hanging up in frustration for the umpteenth time, I glanced out of the window to see our Christmas tree leaning forlornly against the garage and I winced. I'd meant to put it up days ago.

As I lugged a box of decorations across the living

room floor, I kicked the morning newspaper aside and my eye caught the headline INTENSIFIED FIGHTING IN IRAQ. I thought of our soldiers there, put down the box and prayed for them. *When does the world ever make time for Christmas?*

It hadn't that first time either, I thought. A poor carpenter and his about-to-deliver wife struggled hopelessly to find a room in a town teeming with visitors; a jealous king ordered a senseless massacre; a people trembled under the oppression of occupying troops. Yet through it all there radiated a hope and joy that would inspire a hundred generations.

I took a deep breath, put on my jacket and went out to get the tree. The world will always have its troubles, but this birthday will always be a celebration.

Lord, when things seem their darkest, let me always see the light from Your manger.
                                        —RICHARD SCHNEIDER

TUE
23

HONOUR THY FATHER AND MOTHER; WHICH IS THE FIRST COMMANDMENT WITH PROMISE. —*Ephesians 6:2*

THE DAY BEFORE CHRISTMAS in 1944, I was a private in a platoon on the drill field of Georgia's Daniel Field. I suddenly spied my dad. He was standing there smiling, though how he got on the base I don't know. It didn't matter. He had come from Kentucky and I was ecstatic. Later in the day, with a one-day pass safe in my uniform, we went to the Augusta train station to meet Mother and JoJo, my younger brother. Despite the trials of train travel then, they had made it from New York. We lacked only my older brother Hamill, far away in the Pacific.

We walked down Broadway, which was a solid mass of khaki, mostly from a huge infantry installation nearby. The four of us had dinner and talked and talked. We talked about Hamill, while we worried for his safety. Mom and Dad sat comfortably together, Mom laughing until tears came to her eyes at Dad's crazy sense of humor. It was hard to believe that they had been divorced for sixteen years.

But it was so. And Mom had made a bad second marriage, from which she never could get free. Recently I came across some letters from Dad to Mom that revealed his everlasting love for her. And when he died, Mom revealed her love for him to me.

Now, both of them are gone, and Hamill and JoJo as well. I shall never forget how, before we ate that succulent turkey and ham dinner, the four of us held hands. Then Dad said, "Thank You, Father. We are a family. Amen."

Father, I know You know why it was my favorite Christmas. —VAN VARNER

A SIGN UNTO YOU
CHRISTMAS EVE: THE ANGEL

WED
24

BEHOLD, I BRING YOU GOOD TIDINGS OF GREAT JOY WHICH WILL BE TO ALL PEOPLE. FOR UNTO YOU IS BORN THIS DAY . . . A SAVIOR, WHICH IS CHRIST THE LORD. —Luke 2:10–11

CHRISTMAS EVE in my little church is my favorite service. The piano-organ preludes always include "Ave Maria" and "O Holy Night." We hear the Christmas story from Luke and sing our favorite carols: "O Little Town of Bethlehem," "Hark the Herald Angels Sing," "Joy to the World."

We dip bits of home-baked bread into the chalice, receiving forgiveness and hope from the familiar words: *The body of Christ, broken for you. . . . The blood of Christ, shed for you for the redemption of your sins.* After Communion the lights go off and we circle the sanctuary. The faces of friends and neighbors, visitors and strangers, all in their holiday best, are reflected in the flickering glow of our small candles as we sing "Silent Night."

Christmas Eve service was part of our schedule two years ago when we spent the holidays with our son Michael and his family. They attend an ultramodern church and the family service was at 4:00 PM. A rock band played carols in an upbeat tempo. The Christmas story was from Luke, but it wasn't in King James English. We had Communion crackers, not bread, and we took them in silence. We all wore jeans.

For a moment I longed for my little church with its candlelight and comfort. Then I spotted a tiny white angel with gold-threaded wings on their tree, almost like the shimmering gold angel on the Chrismon tree. The angel, I remembered, symbolized God's Word coming to each of us. The shining faces throughout the auditorium and the rejoicing spirit all around bore testimony that the Gospel in modern dress was more than okay. It was good news!

Word made Flesh, thank You for the timeless, unchanging message that speaks anew to each generation.
— PENNEY SCHWAB

A SIGN UNTO YOU
CHRISTMAS: THE CROSS ABOVE THE WORLD

THU
25

"YOU ARE TO GO INTO ALL THE WORLD AND PREACH THE GOOD NEWS TO EVERYONE, EVERYWHERE."
—*Mark 16:15* (TLB)

CHRISTMAS MORNING with my son Michael's family began like most family Christmases. Two-year-old

Caden was thrilled with a toy train and tracks. His older cousins were delighted with gift cards for food, clothes and movies.

But after breakfast, the day took a different turn. We tuned up our singing voices and headed to join our "team" at a nearby care facility. All over town, members of Michael's church were doing the same thing. On Christmas morning, pastors and laypeople visit every nursing and long-term care home in the city as part of their mission to share Christ's love.

About thirty residents were waiting. We sang "O Little Town of Bethlehem," "Joy to the World" and all five verses of "We Three Kings." Someone read the Christmas story. We gave candy and gifts—lovingly chosen and paid for by church members—to every resident. Then it was time for tea, cookies and sharing.

One man had rows of military ribbons and medals pinned to his bathrobe. "I'll be rejoining my unit in England tomorrow," he told me. "The war's not won, you know." A woman in her seventies was worried about her ninety-plus-year-old mother: "I don't think she can cope if I go first." A young man receiving wound care was effusive in thanks for his gift of socks. Later, I learned it was the only package he would open and our group would be his only visitors.

As I closed my eyes for the prayer before we left, I pictured one particular ornament from the Chrismon tree at my church: the Cross of Christ on top of the world. I opened my eyes and looked at the residents, and I knew that on this Christmas, we were where we were supposed to be, doing what the Lord of all called us to do.

Lord and lover of the world, let this day be the beginning of my own loving outreach.
—PENNEY SCHWAB

FRI
26
SUDDENLY MANY OTHER ANGELS CAME DOWN FROM HEAVEN AND JOINED IN PRAISING GOD. THEY SAID: "PRAISE GOD IN HEAVEN! PEACE ON EARTH TO EVERYONE WHO PLEASES GOD."
—*Luke 2:13–14 (CEV)*

CHRISTMAS HAS ALWAYS BEEN a particularly poignant time for my wife Kathy and me. Our first child Ryan was born the week before Christmas with a rare disorder that caused massive internal bleeding.

The neonatal intensive care staff encouraged us to baptize our perfectly formed, yet incredibly ill baby, and we did, with a cross of iron nails on the shelf above his bassinet as our visual claim of God's promises. Then, on Christmas Eve, the nurse in charge pulled two rocking chairs close to Ryan's bed. She stretched out all of his tubing and monitor wires so that Kathy and I could hold him for the first time since his birth. It was the most wonderful Christmas gift we had ever been given.

Now fast-forward thirty-one years: This miracle baby is now our pastor. Kathy and I are snuggled together in a pew at St. John's Church in Red Hook, New York, surrounded by Alicia, our son Kyle's fiancée, and our son Joel and his wife Alyssa, their newborn son Conner cradled in their arms. Tonight, Kyle is playing Joseph. He walks slowly down the center aisle, tenderly holding the elbow of Mary, portrayed by Ryan's wife Jennifer. In her arms, wrapped in white bunting, is their baby Austin as the Christ Child. The church is bathed in candlelight as Ryan's expressive voice retells the story of Christmas. When Ryan sees this Holy Family—his family—approaching him, tears spill down his face—and mine.

Lord, may we always be filled with the wonder and joy of Christmas. —TED NACE

SAT
27

AS THE APPEARANCE OF THE BOW THAT IS IN THE CLOUD IN THE DAY OF RAIN, SO WAS THE APPEARANCE OF THE BRIGHTNESS ROUND ABOUT. THIS WAS THE APPEARANCE OF THE LIKENESS OF THE GLORY OF THE LORD.... —Ezekiel 1:28

I'D BEEN VISITING MY SISTER in Seattle. Now I was on my way home to New York City. It had been a wonderful visit—walks to the colorful Pike Place

Market, rides on the Bainbridge Island ferry and, best of all, long talks in the cozy window seat of her cabin in the woods of the Olympic Peninsula. But now as she dropped me off at the airport, we merely mouthed a quick good-bye. After years of tearful and emotional farewells, we've both learned to say, "See you soon" and run for it.

I checked in, wended my way through security and finally took my window seat on the plane. But now true to form, I experienced feelings of separation, sadness and anxiety. Over the years I'd always felt this when parting from loved ones. *What would the future hold? How could we help each other if we were so far apart?*

It had been raining when we said good-bye. Now as the plane took off, I looked out my window, watching the ground fall away below and straining to see if I could locate the area where my sister lived. As I looked down through the mist, the sun came out behind us. To my astonishment, I saw a glistening rainbow below—not an arc, but a dazzling complete circle! No beginning, no end, instead a perfect circle of beautiful pastel colors glowing below me, circling the area, I was sure, where my sister lived.

Stunned and comforted, I now had no doubt. When we leave our loved ones, they are surrounded by a circle of everlasting love.

Dear Lord, bless all the people, near and far, who shine Your love into my life. —MARY ANN O'ROARK

SUN
28

In him was life, and that life was the light of men. The light shines in the darkness, but the darkness has not overcome it.

—John 1:4–5 (ESV)

IT WAS DECEMBER 1944, the height of World War II. My mother and we four children were refugees in Poland, having barely escaped from Ukraine. The front was once more dangerously close. Because of frequent bombing, villages were draped in darkness. Nobody ventured out at night.

Two refugee women had invited us to a Christmas Eve party in a neighboring village. To get there, we'd have to walk over frozen fields in the darkness. My mother decided that her children, ages two to eight, would not miss out. She carried my little sister piggyback while the rest of us followed close behind.

When we arrived, we squeezed in among the women and children sitting on the floor, and joined in singing carols that spoke of joy and peace and the Light of the world. Then *Weihnachtsmann* came and presented each of us children with a gift. I received a colorful ball made from rags tightly wrapped with yarn from old sweaters.

Soon after that wonderful party, we were fleeing again, this time in an uncovered hay wagon with snow blowing in our faces. But the warm memory of that Christmas celebration shone like a candle in the darkness.

Because of You, Jesus, I need not be afraid of the dark.
— HELEN GRACE LESCHEID

MON **29** *BLESSED IS HE WHOSE TRANSGRESSIONS ARE FORGIVEN, WHOSE SINS ARE COVERED.* —*Psalm 32:1 (NIV)*

"FORGIVES NEGLECT" reads the description for the sunflower seeds in my wildflower catalog. Looking over catalogs of seeds and bulbs is one of my favorite things to do. There's something peaceful and hopeful in looking forward to a field filled with blooms.

Growing up, I spent fall and winter evenings sitting on the couch next to my mother, her nose deep in a bulb catalog and a pad resting beside her so she could jot down her order. A single mother with four children, Mom always made time for a flower garden. And when the bulbs came in the mail, together we would push them into the earth. "They'll be beautiful," Mom would say. "Just wait."

Months later, a cold winter behind us, the bulbs I had forgotten about would begin to sprout. I was too young to understand exactly why those spring blooms meant so much to my mother. She kept watch as the pale green shoots rose from the cold ground. Each bloom was too precious to cut.

Forgives neglect. I couldn't get past those words. Tiny seeds that would grow to the king of flowers, standing strong, heavy head filled with hundreds of small blooms that follow the sun—even if I neglected them.

I circled the sunflower seeds in the catalog and pictured exactly where they'd sprout and flourish in my backyard.

Lord, thank You for my mother's love for flowers and for the sunflowers that remind me of Your boundless forgiveness. —SABRA CIANCANELLI

TUE
30

GET RID OF THE OLD YEAST. . . .
—I Corinthians 5:7 (NIV)

"I MEANT TO DO my work today—"
That's the first line of a favorite poem by Richard Le Gallienne. Today I "meant to do my work," specifically, to set up my account books for the new year. But I got distracted by a plastic wastebasket I walk past several times a day. It's full of papers I've let pile up all year because I've been waiting for a spare minute to slip them through the shredder. I couldn't seem to turn my full attention to my new-year accounts until I'd properly disposed of last year's.

I rather mindlessly shredded the old accounts, until a twinge of anger welled up at the sight of an old work order. I had completed the job on time. Why had they waited three months before paying me? "Shred it," a small voice urged. As the machine slashed the paper and its print, my memory relinquished the experience. I picked up another paper—representing another grudge still intact, stashed away earlier in the year. A guest's tactless comment. A friend's neglectful slight. With each *zwip* of the blades, I let the Holy Spirit rip.

Tomorrow I'll be ready to turn to my new-year work, now that I've shredded the contents of two wastebaskets, only one of them made of plastic.

Lord, before I tackle the projects of the new year, distract me with the task of shredding last year's resentments. —EVELYN BENCE

WED
31

I WILL FORGIVE THEIR INIQUITY, AND I WILL REMEMBER THEIR SIN NO MORE.
—*Jeremiah* 31:34

WHEN MY WIFE SHIRLEY AND I are in Florida, we go out our back door every evening and watch the sun set over the Gulf of Mexico. Some of our neighbors do the same, and they know all about my sunset rating system—ten for the most colorful, on down to one. Usually, I rate them midway on the scale, depending on the intensity of the red afterglows that cascade off the clouds. Tonight's was about a six, but it was special because it was the last day of the year. When the orange orb disappeared behind the sea, it marked the end of the year of our Lord 2008.

As the shadow of years grows longer, I have a tendency to look back (sometimes perhaps too much) on my wins and losses, my successes and failures. Tonight, after the sun had set, I studied the sandy shore and the gentle waves that caressed it. As I listened, I was reminded of something the late Anne Morrow Lindbergh wrote in her classic *The Gift from the Sea* about the tide erasing everything it touches . . . all our scribbling, all our footprints. Like lost memories. Sometimes we forget things we'd like to remember, but it's also true that some baggage is best left behind.

That's why this is a good day to accept God's forgiving grace for mistakes and shortcomings of the year past, and get on with life. He is indeed a God of second chances, and if I truly seek His pardon, He will wash away my sins like waves cleansing the beach. With His help, I can turn away from old sunsets— no matter how beautiful—and look to the redeeming dawn of the new year.

In the next year, Lord, help us aim high,
To heed our best angels—and upon You rely.
—FRED BAUER

MY DIVINE SURPRISES

1 _____

2 _____

3 _____

4 _____

5 _____

6 _____

7 _____

8 _____

9 _____

10 _____

11 _____

12 _____

13 _____

14 _____

15 _____

16 _____

17 _____

18 _____

19 _____

20 _____

21 _____

22 _____

23 _____

24 _____

25 _____

26 _____

27 _____

28 _____

29 _____

30 _____

31 _____

MARCI ALBORGHETTI of New London, Connecticut, and her husband Charlie have been surprised by God in many ways over the past year. Charlie is working with Pastor Michel Belt and using his many years of government experience to help their church establish a homeless shelter. Marci and Charlie are working at a local soup kitchen and at a food pantry in Sausalito, California, where they spend half the year. They've also participated with more than a thousand other volunteers in San Francisco's Homeless Connect project in which close to two thousand poor people receive health and social services six times a year. "One of the nicest surprises from God was Guideposts published my latest book, *How to Pray When You Think You Can't*," Marci said. "It's always been a dream for me. This year a lot of dreams have come true!"

"One of the great blessings in my life has been having the grandkids close by," says *FAY ANGUS* of Sierra Madre, California. "Alas, my complacency has been shattered. 'I've taken the job offer,' my son said, his eyes glistening with excitement. 'I'm up to the challenge. Relocating to Colorado will be like living in our vacation spot [Mammoth] year 'round. Good fishing!' He grinned, knowing that would hook me. *They're moving away . . . away . . .* pounded through my heart. 'We'll get a house with a guest suite for when you come to visit.' *Away . . . away . . .* 'Granma, we're each gonna have our *own* e-mail!' I hugged them close. 'Wow! I'll write you every day.' *Be still my hurting heart . . . Dear Lord, do all things really work together for good for those who love you?* (Romans 8:28). I'm clinging to the promise."

"I guess I shouldn't be surprised at how busy our family has become as the children have grown," says *Daily Guideposts* editor ANDREW ATTAWAY of New York City, "but every once in a while I'm overcome with amazement at how they find time to do all the things they do." Last year, Elizabeth, 13, began singing in a children's choir, joined a home-school math team, helped out at a food pantry, and spent many hours studying biology and her beloved math. John, 11, and Mary, 9, continued to study ballet, while Mary and Maggie, 6, performed at the local children's theater. Stephen, 4, enjoyed music classes and playdates with neighborhood friends. "I'm sure there are new surprises ahead and that God will be faithful to see us through them. And the blessings that come to us through the prayers and kindness of our Guideposts family are an unceasing source of wonder and thanksgiving."

"Sometimes it's clear that God is calling us to something new," writes JULIA ATTAWAY of New York City, "but other times we have to be driven out of our old path before we realize that God wants us on a new one." After eight years of home-schooling, the Attaways are making a major shift. John has already started in a specialized school, Elizabeth will head off to high school in the fall, and the two little girls Mary and Maggie will be at a local church school. Stephen will be partly at home and partly in pre-K. "I can't say this is what I want," reports Julia, "but it's what I think God wants us to do. Surprises aren't always good or bad. Sometimes they're about discovering that God has different plans for you than you thought!"

"This year I was amazed by the way God sends people who help us when we face huge challenges," writes KAREN BARBER of Alpharetta, Georgia. "Our son Chris spent most of 2007 serving in the U.S. Army in Iraq, and countless people prayed for him, including strangers on prayer chains, *Daily Guideposts* readers and a rural preacher I met on a mission trip to Honduras. In the same way, God assembled an outstanding group of helpers when I undertook a video project called *Personal Prayer Power*.

Friends helped evaluate my ideas, my husband Gordon, our son John and other volunteers supervised scripts and marked the slate, and our son Jeff developed a Web site, www.personalprayerpower.com. The group of helpers grew when we ran a twelve-week prototype at our church, giving me hundreds of reasons to be thankful for God's incredible network of support."

 *ALMA BARKMAN* of Winnipeg, Manitoba, Canada, writes, "My husband Leo and I continue to be delighted by the little surprises God brings across our path—the quiet beauty of a hoar-frosted neighborhood on a winter day; a rarely seen woodpecker vigorously hammering on our phone pole in early spring; enough wild Saskatoon berries to pick for pies in summer; pink sedum plants that bloom in late fall, living up to their name 'Autumn Joy.' Hints all around me in nature should remind me that God reveals Himself in unexpected times and places, and yet in light of His majestic powers, I tend to feel like Job, who humbly said, 'If I called and He answered me, I could not believe that He was listening to my voice' (Job 9:16, NAS). Nevertheless, God *has* heard and answered many of our family's prayers over the last year, and their very timeliness is often a delightful surprise."

"Those of you who have lost a loved one know how wrenching grief can be," *FRED BAUER* of State College, Pennsylvania, and Englewood Beach, Florida, writes. "I experienced it this year with the loss of my mother, but I was also surprised by God's perfect timing. I had visited Mother in Ohio just a month before her death. I found her to be more frail, but of sound mind and strong spirit. Though physically weakened, her faith was as unwavering, certain, indomitable as ever. Then a couple of weeks later she suddenly worsened, and after a short period of suffering God called her home. Though I wasn't ready, she was; she had fought the good fight, run a magnificent race and, I'm sure, heard God's welcoming words at heaven's gate: 'Well done, thou good and faithful servant . . . enter thou into the joy of thy Lord' (Matthew 25:21)."

"When I'm at home I'm nearly always listening to classical music," says *EVELYN BENCE* of Arlington, Virginia. "This doesn't surprise me. I played Bach and Chopin on the piano as a teenager. My mother played record albums of hymn orchestrations. And then in college I chose—as a required 'overview' course—music rather than art appreciation. At the time I had no interest in deciphering meaning in someone's drawing or painting. But I am surprised that I now find great enjoyment in writing devotionals about paintings or sculptures that catch my eye when I visit museums or peruse art books. My old interest in music remains, but I'm grateful for broadened vistas. This year my world widened in another way: I offered to facilitate a Sunday morning Scripture discussion at my church. Every week we look for some special encouragement in the Word, which is always full of surprises."

 "My husband Keith and I have been surprised by everything for years," says *RHODA BLECKER*. "We were surprised that two people from such different backgrounds not only met and fell in love, but that we could still be together after thirty years. We both came from difficult childhoods and were surprised by happiness. And since one of our favorite sayings has always been, 'If you want to hear God laugh, just tell Him your plans,' we were really surprised when every facet of our move to Bellingham, Washington, came off exactly as we'd hoped more than two years before we did it. We love it here in the Pacific Northwest and with our new synagogue community, and we truly enjoy being so close to the nuns, who are like our family. We experience God best through each other and through those who offer us their prayers and their emotional support."

"We're still in the process of rebuilding since Katrina," writes MELODY BONNETTE of Mandeville, Louisiana, "whether it's our homes, our families or our communities. And along the way, I'm constantly surprised by moments of grace. A few weeks after one of our family gatherings, my daughter surprised me with a picture she'd taken. There I was, surrounded by all my precious grandchildren. Indy, 5, with his arms tightly around my neck; a precocious Sophia, 4, who was all smiles for the camera; Noah, 3, holding on to his favorite action figure; and the two newest babies nestled in my arms, Micah, a playful 7-month-old, and redheaded Thomas, only 12 weeks. Looking at the photo, I quietly said a thank-you to God for showing me such a tangible example of rebirth and renewal—and faith in our future."

AMANDA BOROZINSKI of Rindge, New Hampshire, is happy to be joining the *Daily Guideposts* family. "I'm a writer and photographer for the *Keene Sentinel*," Amanda writes. "My husband Jacob runs his own business, and in his spare time enjoys fishing and falconry. We have a 3-year-old son, Trace, one dog, one horse and a red-tail hawk. Last May, my husband and I celebrated our fifth anniversary by having dinner at our favorite Indian restaurant. In June, I received a Master of Fine Arts in Creative Nonfiction from Antioch University.

Someday I hope to teach creative writing at the college level. This past year, by sharpening my eye and my heart, I began to see God at work in the most subtle slices of my life. God surprises me every day!"

"If God surprises us in any way," says GINA BRIDGEMAN of Scottsdale, Arizona, "it's how He continually opens windows after closing doors." Gina finished her two-year term as president of the parents' organization at her children's school, ready to move on to volunteering at church and part-time work. After her husband Paul's university theater department closed, he moved on to freelance work around Phoenix, giving him the opportunity to design scenery in new theaters and learn some new technology. Maria, 12, danced her first solo performance, and added tap to her studies of jazz, ballet and hip-hop. "But the greatest opportunity—and the greatest adjustment—has been our son Ross, 18, heading off to Belmont University in Nashville, Tennessee, to study music. Our whole family is excited about where God will lead him from there. We can't wait to see what surprises are in store for him."

MARY BROWN of East Lansing, Michigan, is expecting to be surprised by God as she, her husband Alex and their son Mark, 14, head overseas for a six-month sabbatical. "We leave in three weeks," writes Mary, "and we still do not have anyone to rent our house here or a place to live in England. Yet on each previous sabbatical we were amazed at how beautifully God worked out all the details." Daughter Elizabeth, now a freshman at Michigan State University, will join the family in London for her spring break. Another delightful surprise is how Elizabeth has gone from having no idea what to study to choosing a major in chemical engineering, so she can pursue a passion for developing biodegradable substitutes for environmentally harmful plastic and petroleum products. "Instead of being so astonished at how God guides and provides for us, I'm trying to surrender my anxieties and trust in His faithful love."

 "Surprises? I love 'em!" says MARY LOU CARNEY of Chesterton, Indiana. And this year brought a surprise party for son-in-law Kirk when he turned 40. "Amy Jo held it at the bowling alley. I think I broke a record for gutter balls!" Joining in the fun were grandsons Drake, 3, and Brock, 1. Son Brett and his wife Stacy came, but Stacy (seven months pregnant) opted out of bowling. "This summer we'll have another grandchild, plus both my nieces will give birth too. Surprises aplenty!" But the best surprise of all was a divine one. "Brett took his first commercial construction job, and as he was setting roof trusses, he fell thirty-five feet!" After a frantic run to the hospital and lots of tests, Mary Lou was able to drive

him home. No broken bones, no serious injuries. "It was God's gift to our family. And we'll be forever grateful!"

 "This year has been filled with blessings and adjustments," says SABRA CIANCANELLI of Tivoli, New York. "Going from a family of three to one of four has been challenging, but I'm pleased to say that with God's grace we made it through the transition. Big brother Solomon is getting used to sharing both the spotlight and his toys with Henry, who is finally old enough to play. Solomon enters kindergarten this fall, which I'm sure will bring its own set of adjustments and challenges. Henry is finding his footing, moments away from his first steps. Renovations on our old farmhouse are still ongoing. We just had a new tin roof put on, and the only sound sweeter than rain on our new roof is the sound of Solomon and Henry giggling as they play peekaboo."

 "When I was a news reporter, we had a nickname for all the births, marriages and obituaries," says MARK COLLINS of Pittsburgh, Pennsylvania. "We called them 'hatches, matches and dispatches.' God knows I've seen my share of all three in the last few years—sometimes in the same week. I wonder if God is trying to teach me—teach all of us—some

kind of lesson, passed down from the Carter Family: 'Will the circle be unbroken, by and by, Lord, by and by? There's a better home awaiting in the sky, Lord, in the sky.'" Mark and his lifelong match Sandee have three little hatches, Faith, 16, Hope, 15, and Grace, 11, "although they're not so little anymore," he says. "At some weird point I turned around and saw these three beautiful young women in my kitchen and wondered who they were and where they came from. Then I looked at my amazing wife and realized the circle truly is unbroken."

"One of the wonderful surprises God has had for our family," says *PABLO DIAZ* of Carmel, New York, "is the longevity of our dog Bandit, the 'schnoodle' we adopted in 1999 when he was eight years old. We'd always wanted to get a dog for the kids but never got around to it. The timing was right, and so was Bandit. I didn't grow up in a household with pets, so I didn't expect a dog to fill our home with so much love. I'm amazed how our dog has enriched our family. God outwitted us when He gave us Bandit. Meanwhile, our daughter Christine is enjoying her career, traveling and life in New York City. Our son Paul graduated from college—no more tuition payments! If that's not a surprise, I don't know what is!"

 *BRIAN DOYLE* of Portland, Oregon, is the editor of *Portland* magazine at the University of Portland and the author of eight books, most recently *The Grail,* an account of a year in an Oregon vineyard. "Oh, I'm startled and stunned and teased and hammered and made to laugh fifty times a day by the Coherent Mercy," he says. "I'm the richest man who ever lived, having been surprised by three children and graced by a most mysterious and confusing spouse. I am cupped in the oceanic hand of the Maker every moment and am very aware indeed that my labors are to celebrate and sing miracles. Also I have to do the dishes and fold the laundry and pay almost all the bills and bark at the puppy to 'Stop eating that!'"

 *ERIC FELLMAN*'s biggest surprise from God last year was not being in *Daily Guideposts, 2007* because he had his hip replaced. He is thrilled to be back this year with stories from that experience. His new hip is functioning well. Eric and his wife Joy continue to live in the Washington, DC, area. Two of their sons live nearby, and their third is teaching school in New Hampshire and is married to their first daughter (-in-law), Jessica. "No grandkids yet," says Eric, "but Joy and I are hopeful!"

SHARON FOSTER of Durham, North Carolina, writes, "God continues His faithfulness to my family and me, stretching us and leading in ways that we had not planned. My son Chase will be graduating this summer and hopes to go on to graduate school or to join an opera company's young artist program, so please pray for him. My daughter Lanea will be finishing her graduate studies and is being prayerful about where to go from there. I have completed my seventh novel, *Abraham's Well*, and in the process learned a great deal about my Native American heritage. Please pray and rejoice with my family and me as we await the Lord's next wonderful adventures for our lives!" You can visit Sharon at www.sharonewellfoster.com.

"One day, my wife Nicole and I sat across the table from each other and prayed desperately," writes *DAVE FRANCO* of Encinitas, California. "That was the day when our liquid assets had reached six dollars between the two of us. And this is how I know God answered us: I don't really know how we made it, but we did. Invoices we thought were never going to be paid were paid. Money showed up in the mail from only God knows who. My daughter walked in from school one day with an envelope filled with twenty dollar bills. She said she got it from a lady in a catsuit. *A lady in a catsuit?*

Today, with my business resurrected and growing, we've bought a home where we live with our two children, Julian, 11, and Noelle, 8. Three years ago, I asked God, *Lord, are You really there?* His answer was a most definite *Yes.*"

JULIE GARMON of Monroe, Georgia, writes, "This year God surprised us with some unexpected pleasures. Jamie and Katie graduated from college, even though they had both dropped out, went part-time and threatened to quit. But hallelujah, they graduated a day apart! A year ago I'd have never predicted it. Katie got married in May. Thomas, our son, writes for his high school paper. He's our only child who enjoys writing and books. I was invited to teach at a conference in Texas. I almost said no. I hate to fly, I have no sense of direction and speaking to groups is intimidating. The first day, a teacher befriended me and drove me around. The people in my classes seemed pleased. But the biggest surprise was discovering my hotel room number: 1. No way to get lost looking for it! Thanks, God. I won't forget."

For OSCAR GREENE of Medford, Massachusetts, it's been a year of observing changes. "The grammar school across the street was converted into luxury condominiums and eight families moved in," Oscar reports. "Our beloved next-door neighbors of twenty-eight years moved away suddenly. Then two new neighbors moved in two doors down the street." As yet, Oscar hasn't seen or spoken with the new arrivals. "Volunteer activities changed also. After thirteen years of coconvening the Monday evening Bible study and forty years of ushering at Sunday services, I've had to step away. But there's been renewed activity at the monthly Coffee and Books gathering, plus the huge May and September book sales and my triweekly book-donating ministry." The most appreciated change has been Oscar's return to glowing health. God continues to use him.

Sadly, EDWARD GRINNAN of New York City had to bid farewell to his 16-year-old cocker spaniel Sally Browne this year. "Dogs are so completely present in our lives that when they go they leave a huge hole behind. I wrote a lot about Sally, both in *Daily Guideposts* and in *Guideposts* magazine. Readers got to know her and there was a lot to know. She was a very complex little dog, believe it or not, with a personality that never ceased to surprise me. She could be a little devil, but mostly she was an angel, especially in her later years. Recently one reader wrote, 'You are blessed to have such a dog.' I certainly was and I am looking forward to the next dog God brings into my life." Edward is vice president and editor-in-chief of Guideposts.

 *RICK HAMLIN* of New York City writes, "I've heard it said that we boomers are the sandwich generation—sandwiched between the needs of our parents and our children. Well, I'd say it's a nice club sandwich, full of good things. This past October my siblings and I and all our kids gathered to celebrate a significant birthday for my mom (I'm not giving any numbers because my mom is afraid her tennis pals will hit too softly if they know). Let's face it, all birthdays are significant. This year our son William turns 21 and Timothy turns 18. The former dazzles Carol and me with his math skills (he didn't get it from us), and the latter wows us with his songwriting and singing. And the biggest surprise of all: I don't feel any older than when I first recorded their birthdays in *Daily Guideposts*."

 "One of our granddaughters now plays the cello," reports *MADGE HARRAH* of Albuquerque, New Mexico, "a special joy to me since I once played the piano and accompanied a number of instrumentalists, including cellists, when I was a music student at the University of Missouri. It makes my husband Larry and me happy to watch the younger generations in our family blossom. We are active in our church, a small diverse group of believers with insights that bring us closer to God, Who continues to

surprise us every day with new blessings, new challenges. With His guidance and help, we look forward to the surprises yet to come."

"After eight years in Southern California," writes *HAROLD HOSTETLER*, "my wife Carol and I, daughter Laurel and granddaughter Kaila, 9, are happy to be in the mid-Hudson Valley, seventy miles from New York City and only a few miles from our daughter Kristal, son-in-law Derrick and grandsons Konner, 4, and Brennig, 3. Even though we miss our friends and the wonderful climate in San Diego County, the joy of being together again as an extended family makes up for those losses. Besides, the temperatures stayed so mild for months after we arrived that we all joked about bringing our California weather with us. We've enjoyed getting to know our grandsons (all our grandchildren call us "Papa" and "Mimi"), and we're only a day's drive from our other relatives in Virginia and Pennsylvania. We're looking forward to the new adventures God has in store for us."

JEFF JAPINGA of Holland, Michigan, says he continually discovered wonder and joy and gratitude, not in monumental events or significant change, but in the little things that simply kept happening this year. "A friend last seen thirty years ago rediscovered through the Internet and met at a French chateau. A South Carolina sunrise and a Lake Michigan sunset—one seen for the first time, the other for the thousandth, yet both stunning in their beauty. Talking baseball and life with your college-aged son at a Chicago Cubs game; marveling at the save your teenaged daughter, the goalkeeper, just made in soccer and then packing her off for a church group mission trip; reading a chapter of your spouse's book and thinking, *That's really good!* That made the same house and the same job and the same car with 150,000 miles—and even turning 50!—part of the surprising daily journey through God's extraordinary ordinary."

Blessings abounded this year in the form of nieces and nephews for Alabama native *ASHLEY JOHNSON*. She celebrated the birth of three nieces and enjoyed playing with her 2-year-old nephew. She writes, "The best way to be reminded of God's personal notes to us in creation is to walk through a backyard with a toddler. Amazement and wonder are everywhere." This year, Ashley welcomed a new sister-in-law, celebrated several friends' engagements and weddings, and made time to enjoy her latest endeavor: cooking. Ashley lives in Florence and works in Birmingham as a freelancer for a national magazine and a city newspaper.

"This past year, my son Harrison has been a constant reminder of the surprises that God has in store for us," says *BROCK KIDD* of Nashville, Tennessee. "Recently, we went fishing together, and being a typical 7-year-old, he was easily distracted by a turtle swimming by the dock. When he turned back toward his rod and noticed it bent over with the weight of a large crappie, he exclaimed with utter joy, 'Daddy, God just caught me a fish!' My career continues to be blessed. My company just expanded its offices to Knoxville. In looking back on my decision of faith to join the company at its inception just eight years ago, I'm more and more convinced that God will always take care of us in our major life decisions."

"There's always something new happening," says *PAM KIDD* of Nashville, Tennessee. "Recently my mother and 'near' father, Arlene and Herb Hester, gave me a trip to France for my birthday. Our entire family is deeply involved in our Zimbabwe adventure. Even my parents pitched in, helping create DVDs of the project for donors. Someday we all hope to travel to Africa together. As for our real estate venture, my daughter Keri and I recently moved to an office with a window—a real mark of success! Keri's husband Ben enjoys his dental practice in nearby Dickson, and they still live near enough to allow our granddaughter Abby to drop by daily. Our son Brock continues to shine in his investment work and as a father to Harrison. My husband David continues as senior minister at Hillsboro Presbyterian Church. Everyone in the family considers his study the place to go and talk things out—and believe me, there's always something new to talk about!"

 Thirty-nine years ago, MARILYN MORGAN KING of Green Mountain Falls, Colorado, was surprised to learn that, though her two older children were about to enter their teens, she was going to have another baby. This surprise seemed too much! Besides, wasn't she getting too old for healthy childbearing? The nurse smiled and said, "You'll count it a blessing." "I held on to those words during my pregnancy," says Marilyn, "and through all the years since, it's clear that what the nurse said is true. John has truly been one of my greatest blessings. This year God surprised me again with three new grandbabies. The first was John and Tasha's own later-life baby, Isaac, who arrived October 10. Then came two *great*-grandchildren from Paul's branch of the family: Zack and JoAnn's little Alexandrea arrived on my birthday, November 1. Finally, Josh and Brook's baby, Nolan, joined the family on December 12. I will never again question life's surprises because I have learned that God always tucks great joy into them."

"I've recognized God as 'God of my surprise' for the many surprises He's offered this past year," says CAROL KNAPP, "including a calling for elder care through fifteen months with my 101-year-old Aunt Betty Blackstone in Southern California. As her new caregiver steps in, I find myself on the verge of returning to my home in Lakeville, Minnesota . . . where there will be no more 5:30 AM swims in a heated outdoor pool! Terry and I received the surprise of two grandchildren, David and Tirza, born five days apart to daughters Brenda and Kelly. That makes ten grandcuties, which astounds me every time I add them up! I'm maturing through both welcome and less welcome surprises. And I'm learning to wait—and to work—for the 'prize' that lies within each surprise when my life belongs to Jesus Christ."

"My husband Lynn and I began last year with fears about the cancers that had just entered both our lives (his, a malignant brain tumor; mine, stage four ovarian cancer)," writes CAROL KUYKENDALL of Boulder, Colorado. "As we begin this year, we rejoice that we're both done with chemotherapy for now, and our current tests look good. We are learning to live well—with cancer.

That's God's great surprise. As difficult as cancer is, it also brings some gifts we wouldn't give back. We savor relationships and the desire to know and do what matters most each day. We're looking forward to our first-ever cruise—to Alaska—to celebrate our fortieth wedding anniversary. We cherish time with children and grandchildren. We're trusting God in deeper ways and look forward to the future with great hope."

 "This past year has been full of surprises for our family," writes HELEN GRACE LESCHEID of Abbotsford, British Columbia. "Two new granddaughters have joined our family: Evangeline in Toronto, born to son Jonathan and his wife Cheryl, and Kaari in England, born to daughter Cathy and her husband Eric. I arrived at Heathrow Airport just in time to catch a ride to the hospital as Cathy was being wheeled up to the delivery room. What a blessing to watch their first baby being born! Sadly, my younger sister Agnes died just six months before. Her sudden and unexpected passing was made easier by many kind friends. Speaking at Christian women's clubs and writing devotionals give me cause to reflect on the ways God meets our very practical needs. 'The Lord longs to be gracious to you; he rises to show you compassion' (Isaiah 30:18, NIV)."

PATRICIA LORENZ is still thrilled to be living in Largo, Florida, with its warm, sunny days. "My tolerance for the cold Midwest has decreased. I nearly froze during a snowstorm while visiting my dad and stepmom Bev in northern Illinois in December. So now I encourage all my friends and relatives to visit me in Florida during the winter months. My friend Jack and I (our condos are just fifty-seven steps from each other) see each other almost every day, swimming or exploring the beauty of Florida . . . except when I'm working at my computer or when he's settled into his big green recliner watching sports on TV. Putting Jack in my life has been one of God's most wonderful surprises, one I try to cherish and nurture every day."

"This has been a year filled with God-surprises for *DEBBIE MACOMBER* of Port Orchard, Washington, and her husband Wayne. "I was asked to throw out the first pitch when the Seattle Mariners played the Oakland A's in July," Debbie says. "Wayne is still shaking his head over that one." With the release of her first nonfiction book, *Knit Together*, based on Psalm 139:13–14 (NIV): "For you created my inmost being; you knit me together in my mother's womb. I praise you because I am fearfully and wonderfully made; your works are wonderful, I know that full well," Debbie was able to share her love of knitting and her faith in Christ with her readers. Her children and grandchildren continue to bring constant joy to her life.

 Was ROBERTA MESSNER of Huntington, West Virginia, ever surprised by God this year! When her car was totaled in an accident, she searched and searched for a car—any car—that would support her back as her prior "Old Faithful" had. But her search turned up absolutely nothing. "I was near tears when a man pulled up beside me in a charmingly nostalgic PT Cruiser with a FOR SALE sign in the window," says Roberta. "I felt God's gentle nudge to take it for a ride, and it was perfect. The price and condition were perfect too. God's surprises are truly awesome and so detailed."

 "Who would have thought twenty years with the Guideposts Outreach ministries could go so fast?" marvels TED NACE of Poughquag, New York. From director of ministries with the Foundation for Christian Living in 1988 to vice president of the Guideposts Foundation today, Ted continues to find the Guideposts family a source of inspiration. His own family has grown from children to adults, and his youngest son Kyle will enlarge the family as he

marries his beloved Alicia in July. Ted and Kathy, his bride of thirty-eight years, are acutely aware of God-moments since the births of their grandsons Austin and Conner in 2005. "As a family we are upheld by the prayer and caring of our friends and Guideposts family. Even as we carry such a difficult prognosis for Austin, who has been diagnosed with MPS–Hurler's disease, we are continually surprised by God with His incredible blessings."

 *LINDA NEUKRUG* lives in Walnut Creek, California, and works in a bookstore, helping customers find that elusive book "with a blue cover." (Linda is lobbying her manager to have the books shelved by color rather than subject, just so they'll be easier to find.) This year, after Linda was surprised by a curb (How did *that* get there?) and broke her leg, she went to return the dog she was watching for her neighbor and was surprised to find the apartment empty and the neighbor gone. Linda renamed the dog Yappy and is now its new owner. "I had always thought of God's surprises as joyful ones," Linda says, "but I was not joyful about this. After I forced myself to make a gratitude list (*Thank You, God, that it was a Chihuahua and not a Great Dane . . .*), I realized that it could be good exercise for me once my leg healed." Now Linda is actively looking forward to whatever other surprises God has in store for 2008.

"I'm loving my new life in Hamilton, Montana," explains REBECCA ONDOV. "Starting life over as a middle-aged woman in a new career and a new town makes every day an exciting adventure. I've been blessed with fabulous customers in my high-paced, challenging job of brokering lumber. Best of all, I've been able to give back to my community by teaching creative writing and prayer. And in the lumber industry, God surprised me when I was elected to the board of directors of the Fellowship of Christian Lumbermen. This summer I'm planning a horse-pack trip into the Bob Marshall Wilderness, and my horse Wind Dancer will be coming! Be blessed, my friends!"

MARY ANN O'ROARK of New York City continues to be amazed at how each phase of life brings its own special gifts and sense of renewal. Now that she no longer keeps nine-to-five hours, she remembers her dad saying, "There aren't enough hours in the day," when he retired from his job. Like her dad, Mary Ann loves to garden, travel, write letters, and hang out with family and friends. It's one of her happiest surprises, "feeling so close and delighted by nephews and nieces and cousins and their children. It's genuinely fun to be a great-aunt, emphasis on the word *great*." Now a roving editor for *Guideposts* magazine, Mary Ann has recently traveled to Scotland, Italy and France, and, best of all, to Pennsylvania, Arizona and Ohio, where her beloved Aunt Dick celebrated her 100th birthday. "And once again the rest of us could barely keep up with her!"

RUTH STAFFORD PEALE, now 102, continues to thrive in Pawling, New York. Her daughter and Guideposts chairman Elizabeth P. Allen says, "Mother is doing very well in the company of a wonderful caregiver who lives at the Hill Farm and tends lovingly to her. They are often outdoors, enjoying the sunshine! Mother is a regular at church each Sunday and joined many others at the Peale Center for the annual Good Friday Day of Prayer. She loves visits from friends at the Peale Center and our local church, and often picnics with our family on holidays. We are grateful for her each and every day."

"My childhood sweetheart Billy has been my husband for the past forty-two years," writes *PATRICIA PUSEY*. "In 1970, we moved to Halifax, Vermont, from Long Island, New York, and bought a fixer-upper farm. It was the middle of winter (twenty-one feet of snow) and with the spring thaw, we discovered that we had bought a three thousand-car junkyard! Today, our bed-and-breakfast has become a hospitality ministry for us, caring for all the guests who stay on our small working farm. We have seven children: five natural and two adopted. Our youngest daughter Brittany is severely handicapped and does not walk or talk . . . yet! Bill, Sean, Noah, Damien, Bonnie and Kiernan are married to wonderful people, and they have given us numerous scrumptious grandchildren. I try to follow the path that God puts me on. Sometimes that route is predictable, and other times it is unique, challenging and full of surprises. One thing's for sure: God always keeps me from getting lost!"

 "My husband Bill and I were *not* surprised by God when we rejoiced in a second grandson this year," writes *ROBERTA ROGERS* of New Market, Virginia. "The last Rogers-born girl arrived in 1898! But we, and mother Susan, father Tom and brother Jack, welcomed Luke Francis with great joy. God-given blessings this year included the end of our son David's army days and his acceptance by the FBI, a childhood dream. His brother Peter found himself a slot in the Federal Aviation Administration control tower in Providence, Rhode Island. John, our home-loving son, surprised us by flying to Croatia with friends. Bill celebrated seventy with a weeklong mission trip to Mississippi to work on a Katrina-destroyed house. He's been sworn in as a sheriff's deputy (auxiliary), while still making EMT runs with our volunteer rescue squad. This summer I

made quantum leaps in learning trust and fearlessness. I am so endlessly awed by God's detailed personal care!"

 DANIEL SCHANTZ teaches Christian education, literature and Bible at Central Christian College in Moberly, Missouri. He just moved into a new office and a new classroom, as the college expands to receive a growing enrollment. Both new rooms are larger and more convenient, making his fortieth year teaching there more interesting. His wife Sharon moved to a new school, Gratz Brown Elementary, where she works with third- through fifth-graders— more to her liking. She specializes in reading aloud to students, and they seem to love it. Dan is surprised at how fast God took the forty-plus saplings he planted on their new property and turned them into trees. He is also surprised at how fast little grandchildren grow up. Silas, 12, was baptized, and Hannah turned into a 14-year-old beauty. She was diagnosed with myasthenia gravis, which affects her vision, but she is handling it well.

 GAIL THORELL SCHILLING of Concord, New Hampshire, writes, "Surprised by God? All the time! So often when I think God has ignored my most earnest prayers, I find myself in the midst of unexpected answers. For example, I'm again

in heaven serving homey family Sunday dinners, no matter that I use a borrowed table with yard sale dishes because my things still languish in storage in Wyoming! After years of an empty nest, Trina moved back, Tess and Hanna visit weekly, Tom regularly pops up from Boston, and Mom, 88, can still manage the stairs. Only Greg in Los Angeles misses the gatherings. Why am I still in New England teaching reading to adults and tutoring students with disabilities? Only God knows—and that's good enough for me."

 "My retirement from Guideposts in November 2006 was not what I expected," says RICHARD SCHNEIDER of Rye, New York. "After sixty-six years of working, thirty-eight of them with Guideposts, I looked forward to unhindered writing at home. As it happened, life had its own priorities: illness in the family and unexpected demands. So my year's writing is pretty much what you see here in *Daily Guideposts*. But isn't that the way it usually is? We make plans and then something comes along to change the whole picture. Thankfully, in my case the detours were not of major consequence, so I found myself settling into the life I believe God had planned for me: taking things as they come, enjoying more time with my wife Betty, our two sons, three granddaughters and our old dog Bitsy. And, oh yes, still keeping myself open for any writing assignments He sends my way."

"My husband Don and I are entering another stage of our lives," says *PENNEY SCHWAB* of Copeland, Kansas. "I am retiring, and we look forward to surprises God has in store for us. I'm sure our schedule will include traveling to our grandchildren's sports and music activities. Ryan starts college this fall and David is a high-school junior. Mark and Caleb turn 13, and Olivia will be 11. Caden, 5, had such fun singing in a Christmas program that he wanted to do it again the next night. However, not all of our surprises have been pleasant. Don was diagnosed with heart problems and can't be as physically active as he'd like. But God's grace surrounds us as we face both routine and unexpected life circumstances."

When *ELIZABETH* (Tib) *SHERRILL* and her husband John of Chappaqua, New York, went to Venice on a recent trip, they discovered that they'd unwittingly arrived in the middle of Carnevale. "At first," Tib says, "it seemed like bad timing—jam-packed hotels and restaurants, all-night street parties." Soon, though, the contagious gaiety drew them into the celebrations. Since everyone was wearing a mask, they bought masks too. "It got me thinking about the masks we wear all the time. The courteous social mask that eases awkward situations, the harmful mask we hide behind for fear of letting our real self be known. Masks were fun for Carnevale, but I left determined to discard any disguise that gets in the way of relationships."

This was the year when *JOHN SHERRILL* of Chappaqua, New York, finally organized his office. Ten years ago, John's wife Tib agreed to give up her dining room and let John move his office there from the basement. Each year more boxes, files and equipment crowded the dining room. Then came a big family reunion when the office was again needed as an eating place. It took them days to move files to Tib's office, where they occupied every inch of floor space. "At first it seemed a sacrifice, giving up my office," John says. "But after the reunion, as I carried things back, I reviewed every single file, throwing away anything out of date." The dining room is bulging again, but now everything is current.

JOSHUA SUNDQUIST of Harrisonburg, Virginia, writes, "God surprised me in a big way when my ski coach told me that I made the U.S. Paralympic Team. I had been training toward that goal for six years, but I didn't think I had much of a chance. I got to race against top athletes from all over the world, and my parents traveled to Torino, Italy, to watch me. Happily, it was also their 25th wedding anniversary, so they took time to visit Rome and Venice too. I'm surprised by the many letters from *Daily Guideposts* readers who, among other things, write to suggest that I date their granddaughters. I've chosen to take this as a compliment to my character rather than as a suggestion that I lack the necessary skills to find a girlfriend. I will also be graduating from college this year."

"My wife Danelle and I are both turning 40 this year," says JON SWEENEY. "We married straight out of college and began having children soon after. Sarah-Maria is now 14, and Joseph, 12. We moved around a lot, from state to state because of job promotions, but we settled in White River Junction, Vermont, nearly ten years ago. So many times, I find myself easily caught up in the busyness and seriousness of life that I fail to really look around. But, when I *do* look around, pause and reflect, I am surprised by God. Not only God's presence, which is unfailing even when I can't easily feel it, but God's surprises. Finally, I think I can honestly say that I'm glad *not* to know what is coming around the corner."

"I never dreamed I'd be able to find my own book sitting in the shelves of bookstores," says KAREN VALENTIN. "Seeing my first book, *The Flavor of Our Faith* (Doubleday), in Barnes & Noble was a surreal experience." Now that her second book, *The Summer She Learned to Dance*

(Kamani Publishing), came out in September 2007, she got to experience it again! Even as a child, Karen had a passion for writing stories, but she struggled with a learning disability. She spent years in special education classes and never envisioned much for her future. "It's amazing what God has done," Karen says. "Whoever thought that insecure little girl would be a published author?" God has also blessed Karen with a passion for singing. She is now a member of the Karl Brown Band, based in New York City.

VAN VARNER of New York City writes, "Shep, my constant companion and a presence in many of the devotionals I've written over the years, died in June 2005. Having lost so many dogs over a long lifetime hasn't made it any easier to go through the process. But I knew I had to have another dog. I could have gone to the animal shelter right away, but I was afraid I wouldn't be able to choose and would be haunted by the memory of dogs I hadn't been able to rescue. In the end, I went anyway, and there I found Coke, who seemed to take to me right away. She looks a lot like Shep and is six years old, so the people at the shelter said. They had dubbed her Coco, but I prefer one-syllable names. She is well and happy to be mine, never leaving my side. She's the big news of my year. The way I see it, I rescued Coke from the shelter, and Coke renews my life."

 *SCOTT WALKER* of Waco, Texas, writes, "The past twelve months have been a time for Beth and me to adjust to the empty nest syndrome. Drew is now a law student at the University of South Carolina, Luke a senior at Samford University and Jodi a sophomore at Furman University. All three have jobs, internships or clerkships this summer, and will not be coming home. But Beth directs the international student adoption program for Baylor University, and we now have two wonderful adopted students: George from the Philippines and Lulu from Singapore. And every Wednesday night, about thirty students gather in our home for Bible study, fellowship and dessert. Last week our golden retrievers Beau and Muffy presented us with a litter of nine puppies. Talk about being grandparents! This past year we've learned that God never gives us an empty nest— there's always someone new to love. Refilling the nest is what makes life so very rich."

 *DOLPHUS WEARY* writes, "What an exciting year for us! Our grandson Little Reggie is now 3, our son Ryan is a junior at Belhaven College, our daughter Danita is enjoying her medical practice in Natchez, Mississippi, and my wife Rosie gives leadership to REAL Christian Foundation. We continue to use the sale of my book *I Ain't Comin'*

Back to support the work of the foundation in rural Richland, Mississippi, and other parts of the state." As president of Mission Mississippi, Dolphus remains quite amazed at the number of churches that still don't invite people to become members because of race. But he's also amazed at the number of doors that are opening to hear the message: "The church has the greatest opportunity to eliminate racism, not only in Mississippi but throughout this country."

"This has been a quiet year," writes *BRIGITTE WEEKS* of New York City, "something I don't say all that often. I've been reading a great deal and writing book reviews. My two grandsons, Benjamin and Hugo, are turning into toddlers with strong—and funny—personalities. Right now, I'm busy knitting a blanket for a third grandson expected shortly, and I can see my life will soon be run by small boys! On the darker side of the ledger, depression has been a recurrent problem in my life, and a particularly nasty attack recently led me to the hospital and a course of electroconvulsive therapy, known as ECT. It was a frightening prospect, but the results have been amazing. After ten treatments I'm feeling stronger and more focused than I have in a long time. And for that, I wholeheartedly thank the Lord."

"None of us who fiercely love my son Jeremy interrupted his three-month confinement caused by risky behavior from untreated bipolar disorder," writes *MARION BOND WEST* of Watkinsville, Georgia. "It felt harsh, cruel, wrong—impossible. But we were convinced that jail sometimes serves God's purposes. When Jeremy was released, he immediately sought the help of the longtime caring counselor and the same fine psychiatrist he'd previously abandoned. He attended all group meetings and even contributed in them. He resumed taking his medications *exactly* as directed. He avoided risky situations, lived by the rules, worked tirelessly, and developed a newfound attitude of gratitude and compassion. He paid his debt to society and the law eagerly, meticulously and faithfully. He even phoned me some days, often ending our conversations with 'I love you.' Watching joy and stability steadily transform his life, I marvel quietly but praise God ecstatically. *Father, You surprise my socks off sometimes. Help me trust You even when I can't understand You.*"

BRENDA WILBEE moved out to Birch Bay, Washington, last year, a mix-and-match village of overpriced condos and rusty singlewide trailers that run alongside each other in the curve of a shoreline ten minutes south of the Canadian border. Here she writes and pursues her art as a graphic designer, and it's a good place to enjoy the many unexpected gifts from God. Each morning she wakes to the call of gulls, the cry of bald eagles and the sonorous honk of Canada geese flying home in the spring. With eclectic neighbors, a supportive church, a vibrant writers group and a part-time job at the local (but famous) candy shop, she feels as if she's fallen into a storybook community of salty characters and sea air that fosters her soul. For those interested, her artwork can be viewed at BrendaWilbee.com, and if you want to chat, she invites you to "Tea Time" at BrendaWilbee.blogspot.com.

 "My wife Dianne and I raised two sons," says TIM WILLIAMS of Durango, Colorado, "so we didn't know what it would be like to have a daughter. Gladys, our daughter-in-law, spent Christmas with us this year. Most of my memories of my sons are of climbing mountains, camping, river rafting and other action-filled activities. Gladys is content just to spend time with us. Now that I've reached the age when some physical activities are a part of my past but not my future, God surprised me with someone who doesn't seem to mind. Our son Ted, who lives in Seattle, plans to be married at our home in Colorado next summer. To gain two daughters at the age of 54, I don't know if Sarah and Abraham were more richly surprised by God than I've been this year."

"God's surprises come every morning," *ISABEL WOLSELEY* writes, "but one stands out this past year. When five American missionaries were killed in Ecuador back in the 1950s, my two sons, John and Kelly Champ, then ages 9 and 6, promised to serve the Lord in whatever way He wished. John was particularly affected by the death of Nate Saint, the pilot, and vowed, 'Someday I'll become a missionary pilot to replace him!' The years since have been spent fulfilling that commitment. John was present at the opening of *End of the Spear*, a movie about the tragedy. So was Saint's son and Mincaye, the Ecuadorian man who'd killed his father fifty years before. In one of God's ever surprising evidences of love, these three men from diverse backgrounds showed lives transformed by His grace." Isabel, a newspaper columnist, and her husband Lawrence Torrey live in Syracuse, New York.

"The highlight of the past year was a family trip to the small Mediterranean island of Malta," writes *PHILIP ZALESKI* of Northampton, Massachusetts. "My mother's family emigrated from there about seventy years ago, so this was a chance for Carol and me to show our two sons some of their family roots, see distant relatives and enjoy the beautiful seascapes. It was also a welcome respite from a very busy year. John has been studying Latin and Attic

Greek in college; Andy has been playing piano, twirling yo-yos and writing stories; and Carol and I have begun work on an intellectual history of the Inklings, the Christian literary group spearheaded by C. S. Lewis and J. R. R. Tolkien. All these projects contain their share of surprises, but we know that God's love surrounds us, and so we move forward with hope and thanksgiving."

A Note from the Editors

DAILY GUIDEPOSTS is created each year by the Books and Inspirational Media Division of Guideposts, the world's leading inspirational publisher. Founded in 1945 by Dr. Norman Vincent Peale and his wife Ruth Stafford Peale, Guideposts helps people from all walks of life achieve their maximum personal and spiritual potential. Guideposts is committed to communicating positive, faith-filled principles for people everywhere to use in successful daily living.

Our publications include award-winning magazines like *Guideposts, Angels on Earth* and *Positive Thinking*, best-selling books, and outreach services that demonstrate what can happen when faith and positive thinking are applied in day-to-day life.

For more information, visit us online at www.guideposts.org, call (800) 431-2344 or write Guideposts, 39 Seminary Hill Road, Carmel, New York 10512.